£2

CAMBRIDGE
IGCSE®
GEOGRAPHY

John Belfield, Jack and Meg Gillett and John Rutter

Complete coverage of Cambridge IGCSE Geography syllabus 0460

William Collins's dream of knowledge for all began with the publication of his first book in 1819. A self-educated mill worker, he not only enriched millions of lives but also founded a flourishing publishing house. Today, staying true to this spirit, Collins books are packed with inspiration, innovation and practical expertise. They place you at the centre of a world of possibility and give you exactly what you need to explore it.

Collins. Freedom to teach.

Published by Collins Education
An imprint of HarperCollins Publishers
77–85 Fulham Palace Road
Hammersmith
London
W6 8JB

Browse the complete Collins Education catalogue at www.collinseducation.com

© HarperCollins *Publishers* Limited 2012
10 9 8 7 6 5 4 3 2 1

ISBN 978-0-00-743882-2

John Belfield, Jack and Meg Gillett and John Rutter assert their moral rights to be identified as the authors of this work.

® IGCSE is the registered trademark of University of Cambridge International Examinations.

Exam questions on pages 234–315 are reproduced by permission of University of Cambridge International Examinations. University of Cambridge International Examinations bears no responsibility for the example answers to questions taken from its past question papers which are contained in this publication.

British Library Cataloguing in Publication Data.
A Catalogue record for this publication is available from the British Library.

Commissioned by: Andrew Campbell
Project management: Barry Page
Editing: Katherine James
Picture research: Caroline Green
Design: JPD
Typesetting and artwork: Q2A Media
Cover design: Angela English

With thanks to our reviewers: Alex Cook (Sri Lanka), Annabel Hoareau (Seychelles), Pallavi Jha (India), Penelope Law (Antwerp).

Special thanks to Alan Parkinson and the Geographical Association.

Contents

Section 4: Geographical Skills

Section 5: Exam Preparation

Introduction

Welcome to your new textbook for IGCSE Geography! This book has been written to provide support for all students taking Cambridge IGCSE® Geography (0460).

'Writing the earth'

Geography literally means 'writing the earth', and this book tells the story of many fascinating places, cities, people, environments and cultures. It will open your eyes to a world that is both familiar and unfamiliar, and support you through the next stage of your educational journey. The book aims to provide you with the skills and knowledge to be able to 'write the earth' in your own words, and be confident that you can take your place as a **global citizen**, with all that involves. It will also explore some of the big decisions that you have yet to make, and the impacts they will have:

- Where will I live?
- What will I do as a job?
- How big will my family be?
- What will the world be like in ten or twenty years' time?
- Where will my food, water and energy come from?

About this book

The topics and activities in this book will take you on a journey which starts with **you**. Each topic begins by asking you to think about how geography is relevant to your life. The book introduces you to a range of information: maps, graphics, data, reportage, facts and opinions for you to use, and sets out a range of tasks which will challenge you to think like a geographer.

Cambridge IGCSE Geography is a qualification which expects quite a lot of you as a student, and also of your teachers. There is an expectation that by the end of the course you will have:

- An understanding of the **impacts** which both physical and human geography can have and the **processes** which affect their development;
- A **sense of place** and an understanding of **relative location** on a local, regional and global scale;
- A developing range of geographical skills, such as map-reading and the ability to use and understand geographical data and information;
- An understanding of how **communities** and **cultures** around the world are affected and constrained by **different environments**.

This book will guide you through all of these areas and, if you follow all the advice, will help you to succeed in your exams.

How to use this book
Sections of the book

This Student Book covers all the content necessary for the Cambridge IGCSE Geography syllabus. It is divided into five sections and a glossary.

Sections 1, 2 and 3 match the three themes of the syllabus (Section 1: Population and Settlement; Section 2: The Natural Environment; Section 3: Economic Development and the Use of Resources). Topics within each section follow the order of contents within the syllabus. These sections cover the content you need to know for Paper 1 of the IGCSE Geography exam.

Section 4 covers Geographical Skills. It looks at using maps, graphs, illustrations and numerical data. It also covers a range of fieldwork skills, including conducting questionnaires and surveys and measuring natural processes and human impacts. These sections cover the content you need to know for Paper 2 of the IGCSE Geography exam.

Section 5 will help prepare you for your exams – Paper 1, Paper 2, and either the coursework option (Paper 3) or the alternative to coursework (Paper 4). Here you will find lots of hints and tips about the exams, how to interpret the 'command words' (instruction words) used in the exam papers and how to answer different types of exam questions. You will also look at real past paper example questions and different candidate answers as well as comments on what the candidates have done well and not so well.

Investigative geography

You'll notice that most double pages start with a big question which will be explored in depth. This develops the idea of **'geographical enquiry'**: a structured way of exploring the world, using a range of resources and reaching conclusions which need to be explained and then reflected on. The activities in the book will support your thinking, and help you work through these enquiries.

Case studies

Case studies in many topics focus on particular areas of the world: sometimes a region, sometimes a city (these different locations are shown on the world map on the opposite page). Remember that no matter where you live, there are global connections that exist across the continents and the oceans to all of these places. Take the time to explore further and find out more about these places, so that you appreciate how the world fits together.

Glossary

The key terms are highlighted in the text like this, and are explained in the glossary. These are words and phrases which have specific meanings in Geography – meanings that it would be helpful for you to know.

Locations of case studies used in the book

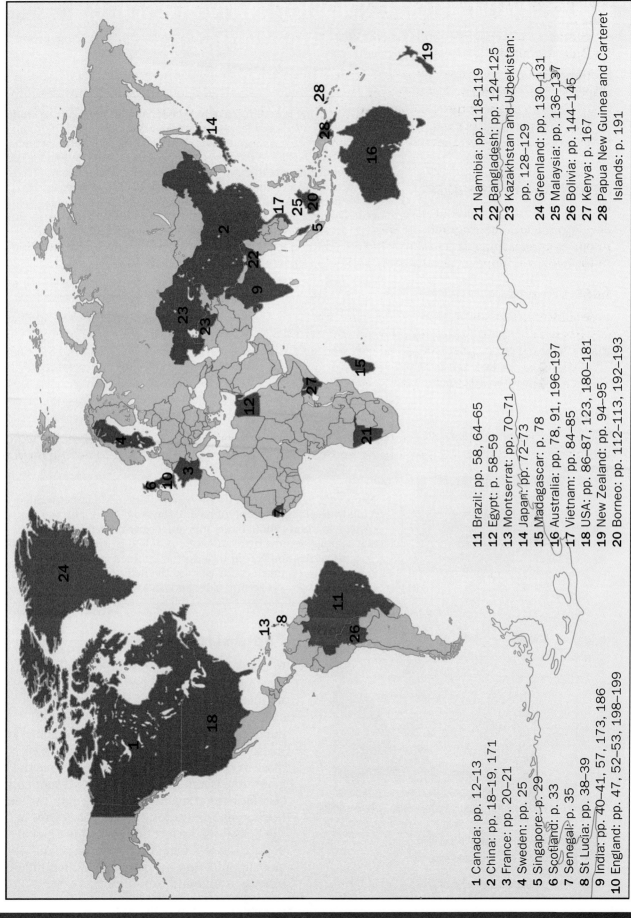

Learning objectives:

- understand how the world's population has changed over the last 2000 years
- know where, and why, the world's population has changed the most
- explain how birth and death rates can affect population change
- describe how population change can affect people.

Halbi! My name is Kadlin. I live in Svelvik, a small town not far from the capital city, Oslo. I live with my parents and my grandmother. Like many children in Scandinavia, I'm an only child. I often wonder what it would be like to have even one brother or sister. When I asked Mum about this, she told me, 'Your father and I wanted you to have the best – and a chance to go to university. That's very expensive, so we decided not to have any more children.' Mum also said she needed to get a good start to her career before she settled down – she was 31 before she and Dad got married.

B Daksh's family live in India, which has many poor people

Kadlin and her family live in **A** Norway, one of the richest countries in the world

Now Investigate ❗

What are some factors that influence family size? How many people are there in your own family?

Namaste! I'm Daksh and I live in Nindar, Jaipur. My father wanted to follow the local tradition of having sons to help him on the farm. After I was born, though, my four sisters arrived before a brother came along – so now there are six of us. I used to dream of going to university and becoming a doctor, but I left school at 14 and now do much of the work in the fields because father is getting older and isn't well.

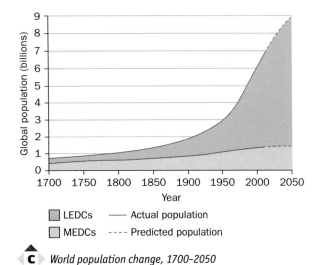

C World population change, 1700–2050

Population growth

In the last 50 years, the world's population has grown faster than ever before. This happened so quickly, it is known as the population explosion. Graph **C** shows how the world's population has changed over the last 300 years. It also shows that most of this increase took place in poorer countries. For a long time the graph line is almost level and then it suddenly becomes much steeper. This is the point when the population explosion took place. Dips in the line show the few times when the global population fell. Graph **D** shows the points when global population increased by another billion (one thousand million).

Effects of population growth on people

Population increase affects people and places in different ways. A population can grow so rapidly that there are no longer enough essential resources such as food and water. This is called over-population.

An increasing population can also have economic benefits:

- There are more customers to buy locally made goods. This creates jobs close to where people live.
- Manufacturing large quantities means goods can be made more cheaply, so more people can afford to buy them.
- Cheaper goods means they are easier to sell abroad, which earns extra money for the country.
- More jobs means less unemployment, which enables parents to provide their children with a better standard of living.

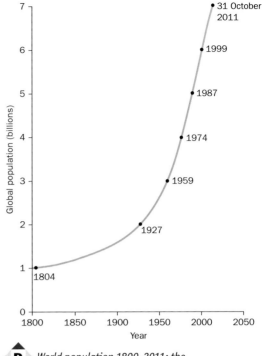

D World population 1800–2011: the 'billion-person points'

More people ⟶ more workers ⟶ increased output ⟶ more to sell ⟶ greater wealth

Now Investigate !

1 The world's population increases by 150 people every minute. Use a calculator to work out how many million extra people there are in a year.

2 a Copy and complete the following table, using information on graph **D**.

   b What does your table tell you about how quickly the world's population increased after the year 1900?

3 Referring to graph **C**, select the correct number from those shown in brackets.

   a The world's population in 1700 was about (*50/100/250/750*) million people.

   b The world's population in 2000 was about (*6/7/8/9*) billion people.

   c In 2000, most people lived in (*developed/developing*) countries.

   d The population explosion began (*before/after*) 1750.

   e The rate of world population growth is (*slowing down/speeding up/staying about the same*).

   f The global population in 2050 is predicted to be about (*7/8/9/10*) billion people.

Skills link

Graphs **C** and **D** are different types of line graph. Learn more about line graphs in Topic 4.3 page 212.

Fantastic fact

Every minute of every day, the world's population increases by about 150 people!

Topic link

You can learn more about over-population in Topic 1.2 pages 8–13.

Billion-people points		Number of years between these two points
First	Second	
Second	Third	
Third	Fourth	
Fourth	Fifth	
Fifth	Sixth	
Sixth	Seventh	

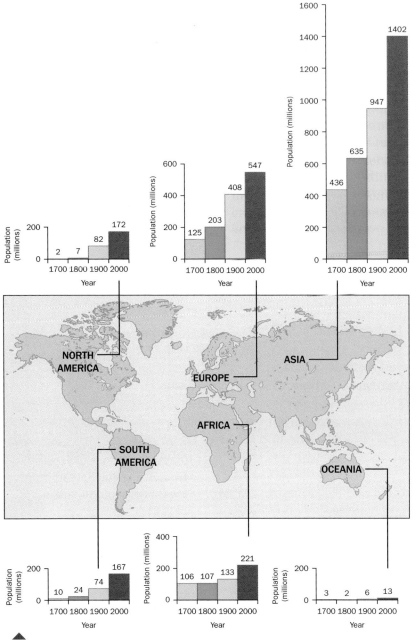

The population explosion took place in two stages. The first was in the earliest industrialised countries like the UK. The second was much later, in poorer, mainly agricultural countries (map/graphs **A**). This later stage is continuing in some parts of the world.

There were four main reasons for the population explosion:

- **Economic** Children can be an important source of income. In the poorest communities, every contribution, however small, is vital to the family budget. A child's income can mean the difference between starvation and survival for a family (photo **B**).

- **Care of the elderly** Older children can support the family by looking after elderly parents, or parents whose working lives are cut short by illness and accidents. The children may be the only support in countries that don't provide pensions or care facilities for the sick and elderly.

- **Infant mortality** Parents want to make sure that at least some of their children will survive and become adults. In poor societies, where medical facilities are limited, there is a high infant mortality rate. Having a large family provides security against the problems of old age.

- **Life expectancy** People are now living longer because of improved medical knowledge and treatment. Better farming methods have increased crop yields so there is more food and a more nutritious diet

A ▸ *The population explosion happened in different places at different times*

B ▸ *Children at work*

C ▸ *Modern machinery helped to increase global cereal production by over 250% in the late 20th century*

(photo **C**). At school, children learn how to stay healthy for longer. The average life expectancy of the world's population is now 67 years, compared with only 40 years 200 years ago.

Stages of the population explosion

Stage one

In the 18th and 19th centuries, the development of industry led to rapid population growth, especially in Europe. The new factories needed large numbers of workers. Many people moved into the towns from surrounding rural areas. More children survived infancy, so the fertility rate increased.

Stage two

In the 20th century, improved medical facilities worldwide increased the life expectancy of ordinary working people. There was now a much greater difference between the death rate and the birth rate.

Diagram **D** explains why the rate of population growth has slowed down in recent years. In fact the world's fertility rate is now 2.6 children, half what it was in 1950.

Birth control – allows people to choose how many children they will have

National population control policies – lead to a lower birth rate, e.g. in China

Lower fertility rate – parents know that most of their children will survive

Why has the population explosion slowed down?

Higher cost of living – so families in the richest countries tend to be smaller

Career decisions – more women take up a career rather than having several children

D Declining rate of population growth

Now Investigate

1 a One way of remembering facts is to use letters that stand for key words. These words can then be joined to make a simple phrase that is easier to remember. Try doing this with the four reasons for the population explosion (E C I L). You can put them in a different order, if this helps!

  b Now think of another way to remember facts, and use this to help you remember the information in diagram **D**.

2 Match each of the following key terms with the correct definition:

Key term	Definition
1 Birth rate	**a** the average number of children women have in their lifetime
2 Death rate	**b** the average number of deaths in a year (for every 1000 people)
3 Fertility rate	**c** the average number of live births in a year (for every 1000 people)
4 Growth rate	**d** the average number of years people can expect to live
5 Infant mortality rate	**e** the difference between the birth rate and the death rate
6 Life expectancy	**f** the proportion of children dying at birth or before their first birthday

3 Refer to map **A**.

  a Name the continent that was most affected by the first stage of the population explosion.

  b Name three continents that experienced the second stage of the population explosion.

  c Write a few sentences about how quickly population has increased in the countries you have named.

Population growth in the future

The global population growth rate is now thought to be slowing down. There are several possible reasons for this, for example:

- People have better knowledge of birth control methods.
- Birth rates usually fall as countries become wealthier. Parents want to maintain their higher standard of living, so they choose to have fewer children.
- People in poorer countries may also decide to have fewer children. Improved medical care enables more people to survive, so there is less need to have many children to support parents in their old age.
- Some countries with very large populations have introduced strict measures to reduce their birth rate. This is usually to reduce the risk of famine.

Topic link

You can learn more about the DTM in Topic 1.4 pages 22–25.

Diagram **A** shows what may happen to a country's population as it develops. Each stage of the Demographic Transition Model (DTM) shows the main reasons for what is happening to both the birth and death rates at any particular time. The diagram shows not only what has happened in the past, but what is taking place now and is likely to happen in the future.

The Demographic Transition Model **A** ▼

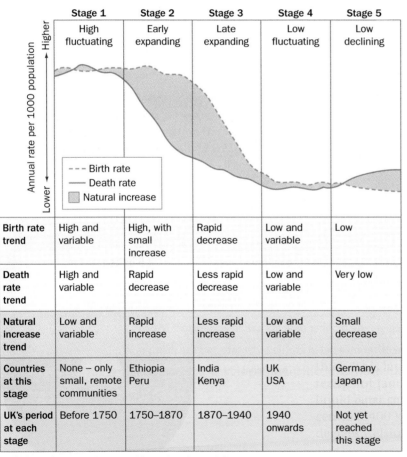

	Stage 1	Stage 2	Stage 3	Stage 4	Stage 5
	High fluctuating	Early expanding	Late expanding	Low fluctuating	Low declining
Birth rate trend	High and variable	High, with small increase	Rapid decrease	Low and variable	Low
Death rate trend	High and variable	Rapid decrease	Less rapid decrease	Low and variable	Very low
Natural increase trend	Low and variable	Rapid increase	Less rapid increase	Low and variable	Small decrease
Countries at this stage	None – only small, remote communities	Ethiopia Peru	India Kenya	UK USA	Germany Japan
UK's period at each stage	Before 1750	1750–1870	1870–1940	1940 onwards	Not yet reached this stage

- *Demographic* means it is something to do with populations.
- *Transition* means that change is taking place.
- A *model* is a way of showing what often happens in real-life situations.

Diagram **B** gives key population data for Germany, a more economically developed country (MEDC), now at Stage 5 of the model, and Kenya, a less economically developed country (LEDC), which is currently experiencing its own population explosion. In the future, Kenya too will probably pass through to the later stages in the model, but it is not yet certain when this will happen.

Diagram **B** shows that most countries are still progressing through the stages of the DTM, and that population growth rates usually become slower as a country moves through the stages. It is likely that the global population will continue to rise, but much more slowly than in the past.

Fantastic fact

The world's highest annual population increase was 87.3 million, in 1989.

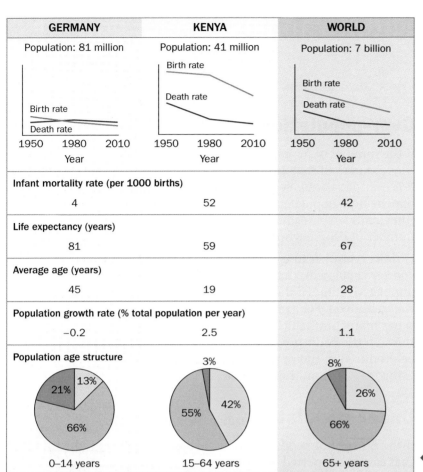

	GERMANY	KENYA	WORLD
	Population: 81 million	Population: 41 million	Population: 7 billion
Infant mortality rate (per 1000 births)	4	52	42
Life expectancy (years)	81	59	67
Average age (years)	45	19	28
Population growth rate (% total population per year)	−0.2	2.5	1.1
Population age structure	13%, 21%, 66%	3%, 42%, 55%	8%, 26%, 66%
	0–14 years	15–64 years	65+ years

B Population factfiles for Germany, Kenya and the world

Further research

Use the internet to create a factfile for your own country, like those in diagram **B**. Then compare your data with that for the world as a whole. (If you live in Germany or Kenya, choose any other neighbouring country.)

Topic link

What you have learned on these two pages will help you when you study other sections of Topic 1, and also Topics 3.2 and 3.3.

Now Investigate

1 a Copy the following table, and complete your table using information from diagram **B**.

  b Write at least two statements about what happened between 1950 and 2010 to the populations of Germany, Kenya and the world as a whole.

2 It is predicted that the world population will grow more slowly in the future. Use the data in diagram **B** to support this idea. (*Hint:* Look very carefully at the last three rows of the table.)

Type of information	Germany		Kenya		World	
	1950	**2010**	**1950**	**2010**	**1950**	**2010**
Population	68 million		6 million		2.5 billion	
Birth rate						
Death rate						
Infant mortality rate	53		150		152	
Life expectancy	65		39		46	
Average age	36		17		23	
Population growth rate	0.6		2.9		1.8	

Learning objectives:

- know what it means for a place to be over-populated or under-populated
- know what it means for a place to be densely populated or sparsely populated
- know what people need to survive, and to have an acceptable standard of living
- understand the problems caused by over-population.

Over-population

If the number of people living in an area cannot be supported by the resources in that area and enjoy a reasonable standard of living, it is over-populated. Regions like the African desert in photo **A** may be over-populated, even though very few people live there (they are sparsely populated), because the land cannot support the number of people who live there.

However, just because many people live in an area (that is, it is densely populated), that does not always mean a place is over-populated. Some of the most densely populated places on Earth are well resourced. For example, Japan is not over-populated, because it has many profitable industries which provide jobs and income through the country's exports (photo **B**). Those items that cannot be produced in their own country can be bought from abroad using money from these exports.

Under-population

If the number of people living in an area is fewer than the number that can be supported by the resources in that area, then it is under-populated. For example, Canada has many resources which are not all being used. Many more people could live there and enjoy a high standard of living.

Fantastic fact

Just 29% of the world's surface is land, but only about 40% of this is suitable for food production.

Now Investigate

Do you think your country is sparsely populated or densely populated?

Is it over-populated or under-populated?

A Oasis in the Sahara Desert

B An industrial site in Japan

Resources and population

There are two questions to ask when deciding whether a country is over-populated or under-populated:

- Do people have what they need in order to stay alive and to provide for their families? The most basic needs of all people are food, water, clothing and shelter (diagram **C**).
- Are the country's resources sufficient to support its population?

Too many people, too few resources

There are a number of reasons why a place may not be able to support a large number of people – that is, why it may be over-populated. For example:

- **A lack of clean water** may force people to use polluted sources and possibly fall ill with diseases such as bilharzia, dysentery and typhoid – all of these are life-threatening, especially for the very young and old.
- **Droughts** are becoming more frequent and severe due to climate change. They increase the risk of starvation in already over-populated countries.
- **Loss of jobs** – when valuable natural resources become exhausted, workers are no longer needed and they will no longer be able to support their families.
- **Population growth** – when there is rapid population growth, or an increase in immigrants, a country may be less able to provide for its people.
- **Clearing of forested areas** can result in families not having the fuel they need for cooking, heating and washing.
- **Natural disasters** such as earthquakes and floods often deprive local communities of the resources they need, for example water, food and shelter.

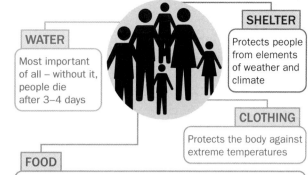

WATER
Most important of all – without it, people die after 3–4 days

SHELTER
Protects people from elements of weather and climate

CLOTHING
Protects the body against extreme temperatures

FOOD
Most people need 1500–3000 calories every day. A balanced, healthy diet includes:
- fats, e.g. from meat, cheese, milk, fish – provide energy to fuel the body's activities
- carbohydrates, e.g. from rice, potatoes – provide warmth and aid body tissue growth and repair
- protein, e.g. from meat, fish – provide immunity to disease and infection
- minerals, e.g. iron from red meat helps blood to circulate oxygen to all parts of the body
- vitamins, from fruit, vegetables, nuts, cereals, fish – keep body in good working order

 C *People's basic needs*

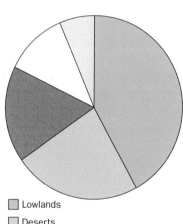

- ☐ Lowlands
- ☐ Deserts
- ■ Dense coniferous forest
- ☐ Polar regions (tundra)
- ☐ Mountains

D *Environments of the world's land areas*

Now Investigate ❗

1. Study figure **C**, then describe the main ways in which your own family's basic needs are met.

2. Use an atlas for this activity.

   Study graph **D**. For each of the five environments, name three places with that type of environment.

Quality of life

What is 'a good life'?

There is a significant link between over-population, under-population, and the quality of life or standard of living in a country. There are different views on what makes for 'a good life' (diagram **A**, photo **B**). People in over-populated countries generally have a lower standard of living, and some are so poor that they actually live below the poverty line. But people living in under-populated countries experience problems, too:

- Valuable natural resources are not fully used. Exports of these resources are limited to what can be extracted, so the opportunity to earn more from international trade is lost.
- There are few people to buy locally made goods. Making small quantities of goods is expensive, and companies are often reluctant to build factories where there are likely to be few customers. More foreign-made goods have to be imported, and possibly transported over large distances.
- There are too few people to fill key jobs in engineering, teaching and other important areas of employment.
- It is necessary to attract extra workers from other countries who may face language difficulties or have experienced a very different educational system in their own countries.

The optimum population is the number of people needed to make the best possible use of a country's resources.

The answers to the questions in diagram **A** can provide only a rough guide to the kind of life people are living. More accurate measures of quality of life and standard of living are needed. Two of these are the Human Development Index (HDI) and the Quality of Life Index.

```
         ┌─────────────┐              ┌─────────────┐
         │ Do I have    │             │ Do I have    │
         │ enough food  │             │ shelter?     │
         │ to eat?      │             └─────────────┘
         └─────────────┘
  ┌──────────────┐                         ┌─────────────┐
  │ Do I have     │      What is           │ Do I have a │
  │ enough clean  │    'a good life'?      │ job?        │
  │ water...      │                        └─────────────┘
```

- Do I have enough food to eat?
- Do I have shelter?
- Do I have enough clean water for drinking, cooking, washing?
- Do I have a job?
- **What is 'a good life'?**
- Do I have enough of the right kinds of food?
- Can I read and write?
- If I become sick, will I be able to get the medical care I need?
- Are my children likely to survive to become adults?
- Can I expect to live for many years?

A What is 'a good life'?

B A shanty town in Manaus, Brazil

Human Development Index

The Human Development Index (HDI) was devised by the United Nations. It is based on three crucial sets of population data:

- adult literacy
- life expectancy
- GDP per capita.

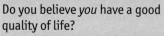

Now Investigate

Do you believe *you* have a good quality of life?
Do you think the people who live in the area shown in photo **B** consider *they* have 'a good life'?

GDP means gross domestic product and *per capita* means 'per person'. The GDP per capita is obtained by dividing the total monetary value of all goods and services produced in a country in a year by that country's total population.

Quality of Life Index

Another useful indicator is the Quality of Life Index. This also takes GDP per capita and life expectancy into account, but includes a number of other factors which, together, indicate how 'happy and secure' people feel within their family, workplace, local community and country. On a scale of 1 to 10, the most 'contented' country in the world is the Republic of Ireland, but its score is only 8.33 – which proves that there is no 'perfect' place in which to live (table **C**)!

Country	Quality of Life Index
The top five	
Republic of Ireland	8.33
Switzerland	8.07
Norway	8.05
Luxembourg	8.02
Sweden	7.94
The bottom five	
Uzbekistan	4.77
Tajikistan	4.75
Tanzania	4.49
Haiti	4.09
Zimbabwe	3.89

C *Quality of Life Index: the top five and bottom five countries*

D *A residential area in an MEDC*

Now Investigate

1 Study photos **B** and **D**.

 a Explain why the people who live in the area shown in photo **B** may be living below the poverty line.

 b Why do you think the people who live in the area in photo **D** probably have a better quality of life?

2 a In your opinion, which are the six most important questions in diagram **A**?

 b Give reasons for each of your six choices.

3 Look at the three main sets of data used to create the Human Development Index, listed above, and at the questions in diagram **A**.

 a Which of the questions in diagram **A** do you think could be answered by the data used to create the HDI?

 b Which of the questions, if any, are unlikely to be useful when calculating a country's HDI?

Fantastic fact

The USA is the richest country in the world, but 12% of its 312 million people still live in poverty.

Both large and small countries can be under-populated and over-populated. On these pages we look at one very large country in terms of area, which has a relatively small population. The task is to decide whether this country is over-populated or under-populated.

Canada – under-populated or over-populated?

Canada is a huge country – the second largest in the world after Russia. Vast stretches of the nation are almost totally uninhabited (photo **B**). Significantly, though, GDP per capita for the country is high.

Table **A** and figure **B** summarise information about Canada's resources and population. The country's greatest natural assets are its mineral resources such as oil and gas. Many of these are found in remote, wilderness areas.

Area (km²)	9 984 670 (2)
Population (millions)	34.4 (37)
Average population density (people per km²)	3.4 (229)
Annual population growth rate (%)	0.8 (136)
Annual immigration rate (per 1000 inhabitants)	5.7 (15)
Infant mortality rate (per 1000 live births)	4.9 (183)
Fertility rate (average number of children per woman)	1.6 (178)
Life expectancy (years)	81.4 (12)
Literacy (% of population)	99 (25)
GDP per capita ($)	39 057 (22)
GDP per capita annual growth rate (%)	3.0 (127)
Unemployment rate (%)	8.0 (88)
Quality of Life Index	7.6 (14)
Human Development Index	0.88 (8)
Population living in poverty (%)	9.4 (137)
Value of exports ($ billion)	407 (10)
Value of imports ($ billion)	406 (12)

A Canada factfile – the figures in brackets indicate Canada's world ranking

Natural resources
- Longest coastline in the world – so fish are plentiful
- Huge coniferous forests in the north, producing large amounts of timber
- World's largest producer of zinc and uranium
- Major producer of gold, nickel, lead, aluminium

Farm produce
- Huge country, so has a range of climate types, which allows production of many different crops
- Major global exporter of wheat

Water resources
- More lakes than any other country, holding much of the world's fresh water reserves

Main industries
- Aircraft and car manufacturing
- Timber industries
- Oil refining
- Aluminium smelting

Support services
- Healthcare is paid for by the state

Energy resources
- Huge deposits of oil and natural gas
- A net exporter of energy

International migration
- Encourages 250 000 new residents every year – to increase the workforce
- Also welcomes 10% of the world's refugees

Trade
- One of the world's top ten trading nations – most of trade is with USA, UK and Japan
- The St Lawrence Seaway is a vital inland shipping route
- Major ports on both Atlantic and Pacific Ocean coasts

B Canada's resources

 Canada occupies most of the North American continent above latitude 41°North

The figures in factfile **B** and the information in figure **C** clearly show that Canada is not over-populated:

- The infant mortality rate is very low and life expectancy is high – this suggests that there is adequate medical care.
- Literacy rates are high – this shows that education facilities are well funded and effective.
- Unemployment rates are very low – which means that most people are able to find suitable paid work.
- The Quality of Life Index rating is high by global standards, showing that most people in Canada are generally content with their standard of living.

Now Investigate

1 a What evidence in table **B** and figure **D** proves that Canada is *under*-populated?

  b Give reasons for your answers to (a).

2 Study table **D**, which is a factfile for Singapore.

  a From the figures in table **D**, would you say that Singapore is over-populated or under-populated?

  b What additional information would help you in making your decision?

Area (km²)	697
Population (millions)	4.7
Annual population growth rate (%)	0.8
Infant mortality rate (per 1000 live births)	2.32
Fertility rate (average number of children per woman)	1.1
Literacy (% of population)	94.4
GDP per capita ($)	57 200
Unemployment rate (%)	2.1
Quality of Life Index	7.7
Human Development Index	0.85

 D *Singapore factfile*

3 a List some ways in which the data for Canada (table **A**) and Singapore (table **D**) are *similar*.

  b How are the two countries *different*?

Fantastic fact

Canada has a land area 14 325 times larger than Singapore, one of the smallest countries in the world, but its population is only 7.3 times bigger!

Further research

Use the internet to find information like that in table **A** and figure **B** for your own country. (If you live in Canada, investigate another country.) Use all the information you collect to decide whether your country is over-populated or under-populated.

Topic link

This topic has links with Topics 2.3, 3.2 and 3.3.

Topic link

- Look back at Topic 1.1 pages 2–7 to remind yourself about population increase.
- You will learn more about international migration in Topic 1.6 pages 32–35.

As in any country, the rate of population growth in your country is due to changes in three variables:

- birth rate
- death rate (including the infant mortality rate)
- international migration.

The infant mortality rate is usually the most important of these. Parents may be aware that some of their children are likely to die before they reach adulthood, because of a lack of a good diet or poor healthcare, and they may have this in mind when deciding how big their family should be. This topic explains why children's survival is so important to the future of many families in LEDCs. Apart from old age, the main causes of death are:

- diseases and infections such as cholera and typhoid
- natural hazards, especially earthquakes and floods
- human conflict.

Human conflicts and natural hazards can have a serious impact on a country's population (map **A** and graph **B**). However, there can be significant differences in their long-term effects on population change.

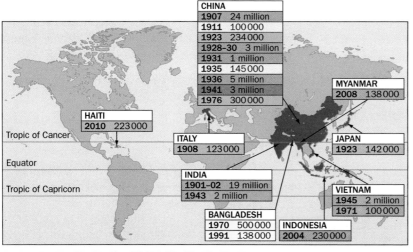

CHINA	
1907	24 million
1911	100 000
1923	234 000
1928–30	3 million
1931	1 million
1935	145 000
1936	5 million
1941	3 million
1976	300 000

MYANMAR	
2008	138 000

HAITI	
2010	223 000

ITALY	
1908	123 000

JAPAN	
1923	142 000

INDIA	
1901–02	19 million
1943	2 million

VIETNAM	
1945	2 million
1971	100 000

BANGLADESH	
1970	500 000
1991	138 000

INDONESIA	
2004	230 000

Tropic of Cancer

Equator

Tropic of Capricorn

☐ Cyclone/Hurricane	▨ Earthquake	▨ Tsunami
▨ Drought	▨ Famine	▨ Flood
		☐ River flood

Year	Fatalities
2010	223 000

 Natural hazard events since 1900 that killed over 100 000 people

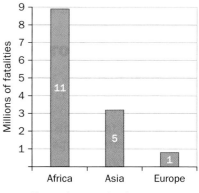

The number on each column represents the number of events involved.

 Conflict events since 1960

For example, a natural hazard such as a tsunami or powerful earthquake may sweep away almost everything and everybody in the area (photo **C**). That place may be abandoned, or be re-populated. The main impact of such events is on the *total* population – there is no selection of individual age and gender groups.

Fantastic fact 🌐

Locusts can make famines much worse. A swarm of 80 million locusts can eat 160 tonnes of cereal and fresh fruit *every day*!

 C *The Indonesian tsunami, 2004, which caused a huge loss of life on the coasts around the Indian Ocean*

Human conflict has a similar effect. It can involve the death and injury of hundreds and even thousands of people, as for example in Bosnia-Herzegovina in Europe (1992–95) and in Darfur in Sudan (2003–06).

Armed fighters in the 20–45 year age range are most likely to die in such conflicts. However, modern warfare can affect people of any age, and can have long-lasting effect on a country's total population (photo **D**).

 D *When there is conflict in a country, people often lose their homes and their land*

Now Investigate

1 a Describe the global distribution of each type of natural hazard shown on map **A**.

   b Try to identify any world regions where there appear to be 'clusters' of similar events.

2 a Draw a line graph to plot the numbers of fatalities in the six famines shown on map **A**.

   b What trend in the number of famine casualties does your line graph show?

   c Suggest possible reasons for the trend.

3 Study graph **B**.

   a Which continent has been most affected by human conflict over the last 50 years, in terms of:

   i the number of events

   ii the total number of fatalities?

   b Using your answers to question (a), suggest the long-term effects of conflict on the populations of continents.

 Topic link

You can learn more about famines – a widespread shortage of food – in Topic 3.2 pages 140–45.

 Topic link

Look at Topic 2.10 pages 120–25 to learn more about how people are affected by natural hazards.

 Further research

Find out what events may have influenced the death rate in your own country or continent in recent times.

Diseases are deadly!

Further research 🔍

Use information from the internet to create a factfile on a widespread disease like cholera or typhoid. Include details about:

- what causes it, and how its spreads
- what medicines are available to treat it
- those parts of the world where it still a common cause of death
- especially serious outbreaks: when and where they took place, and how many people died.

Death rates across the world have decreased significantly over the last 50 years, largely due to improvements in healthcare, although the cause of death is noticeably different in different parts of the world (graphs **A**). Reasons for this decline include:

- increased medical knowledge
- more effective medicines and healthcare
- education about the importance of a balanced, nutritious diet.

However, many diseases are still major killers. For example, malaria kills at least 1 million people every year. Most deaths from malaria occur in tropical countries, where breeding conditions for mosquitoes are ideal. Even now, one in every five childhood deaths in Africa is due to this disease. Diagram **B** explains how people are infected with malaria.

A **pandemic** is an outbreak of an infectious disease so widespread that it kills millions of people in a very short time. There have been several pandemics in the past, for example:

- The so-called 'Black Death' of the mid-14th century, which we now know was spread by rat-born fleas, killed over 75 million people in Europe. It had a significant impact on the global population at that time.
- The 'Spanish Flu' pandemic of 1918–20 killed a similar number of people. It was probably particularly deadly because many people had been weakened by the effects of the First World War (1914–18).

HIV/AIDS is the most recent pandemic. It is particularly widespread among people under 60 years of age. Since it was first identified in 1981 it has caused 25 million deaths – equivalent to the population of Ghana or Malaysia or Peru. HIV and AIDS are very closely linked, but are not the same. HIV (human immunodeficiency virus) is a *virus infection*, transmitted by the exchange of bodily fluids, usually through sexual activity. It reduces the body's resistance to illness and other infections and, so far, has no known cure. AIDS (acquired immune deficiency syndrome) is the *medical condition* of a person in the later stages of HIV, when victims become weak, lose weight and develop flu-like symptoms which can prove fatal.

LEDCs

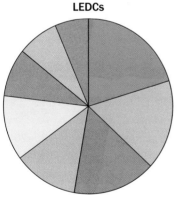

- HIV/AIDS
- Bronchitis & other breathing problems
- Heart attacks
- 'Childhood diseases', e.g. chickenpox, measles, scarlet fever, whooping cough
- Cholera and dysentery
- Strokes
- Malaria
- Tuberculosis

MEDCs

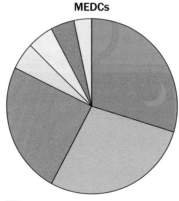

- Heart attacks, incl. stress-induced attacks
- Lung cancer, bronchitis & other breathing problems
- Strokes
- Road traffic accidents
- Stomach cancer
- Tuberculosis
- Suicide & other non-medical causes

A *The main causes of early death (that is, not due to old age) in LEDCs and MEDCs*

The number of people living with HIV continues to rise, in spite of advances in medical knowledge. Sub-Saharan Africa is the most affected region, but Botswana, in south-central Africa, has the highest percentage of sufferers nationally, with around 24% of the total population being infected (table **C**). Many African countries now use the 'ABC' slogan to advise people on how to avoid HIV/AIDS:

- **A** stands for *abstinence* (from sexual activity)
- **B** means *be monogamous* (have only one sexual partner)
- **C** stands for *contraception*.

This advice has helped African countries like Kenya and Uganda to reduce their HIV infection rates (photo **D**). Scatter graph **E** presents a possible link between population infection percentages and GDP.

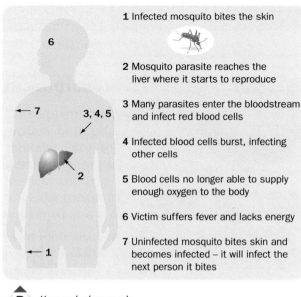

1 Infected mosquito bites the skin

2 Mosquito parasite reaches the liver where it starts to reproduce

3 Many parasites enter the bloodstream and infect red blood cells

4 Infected blood cells burst, infecting other cells

5 Blood cells no longer able to supply enough oxygen to the body

6 Victim suffers fever and lacks energy

7 Uninfected mosquito bites skin and becomes infected – it will infect the next person it bites

B How malaria spreads

	Botswana	World
Life expectancy (years)	60.1	67.1
Adults as % of total population	57.9	65.9
Average age	21.7	28.4
People living with AIDS	300 000	30.8 million
% of total population infected with AIDS	23.9	0.8
Children orphaned as a result of HIV/AIDS	Approx. 100 000	Approx. 15 million

Note: all figures are estimates

C Botswana: some of the effects of HIV/AIDS

Skills link

You can learn more about scatter graphs in Section 4 page 214.

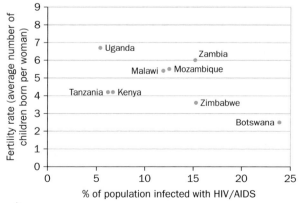

D A new AIDS hospital in Lusaka, Zambia

Now Investigate

1 a What is the most noticeable difference in the causes of early death shown for LEDCs and MEDCs in graphs **A**?

 b Suggest some reasons for these differences.

2 Look carefully at diagram **B**.

 a How can the spread of malaria be reduced?

 b Suggest how people can help to do this.

3 Study graph **E**.

 a Place a rule or the edge of a piece of paper along the position of the best-fit line.

 b According to this line, what appears to be the general link between the fertility rate and HIV/AIDS infection rates?

 c How might the fertility rates be linked with the number of 15–49 year olds who are infected by HIV/AIDS?

E Relationship between HIV/AIDS and fertility rates in eight East African countries

Anti-natalist population policies

Case study

The governments of several countries have imposed direct laws, or policies, to control their population growth rate. This includes China, which has the largest population in the world.

China's one-child policy

A country like China needs to keep its population growth under control. The policies it has put in place in order to do this are described as anti-natalist policies:

- *anti* means to be against (or in disagreement with)
- *natalist* is anything to do with childbirth.

This term describes any policy that aims to control or limit a country's birth rate rather than stimulate it. China's strategy is the 'one-child policy', which was introduced in 1979.

Before 1979

After 1949, China experienced a population explosion, or 'baby boom'. The government decided to restrict family size and recommend that people married later in life. But between 1958 and 1961, droughts and floods caused the deaths of 2 million Chinese. Then the harvests returned to normal and the Chinese leader encouraged people to have as many children as possible, creating a second 'baby boom'. China's birth rate soared to 5.8 children per couple – well above the 2.1 needed to keep the population stable. This is known as the 'replacement level'. In the 1970s, the Chinese government again wanted families to have fewer children. In 1979, it introduced its 'one-child policy' (photo **A**).

Did the policy work?

Family planning advice and contraceptives were made freely available, and a 'One-child Certificate' was awarded to families who had followed the policy. They were also entitled to extra benefits (diagram **B**), while those who had additional children were penalised (diagram **C**). Baby girls and second children were often abandoned, or secretly adopted by childless families.

The policy was generally more successful in the cities than in rural areas. In country areas farming families needed a son to help work the land, so these families were usually allowed a second child if the first was a girl.

Since 1979

In 1992, China relaxed the rules and adoption was legalised. In 2004, the city of Shanghai introduced a local law allowing divorcees who re-marry to have a second child without incurring the usual penalties. In 2008, the National Population and Family Commission stated that the one-child policy would continue for at

Fantastic fact

One in every five people in the world today lives in China!

Topic link

Look back at Topic 1.1 pages 2–7 for more on the population explosion.

A A Chinese one-child policy poster, encouraging couples to have just one child

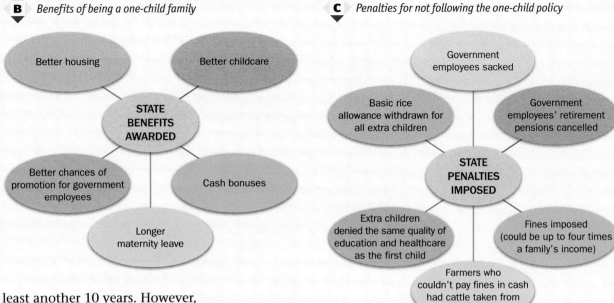

B *Benefits of being a one-child family*

- Better housing
- Better childcare
- **STATE BENEFITS AWARDED**
- Better chances of promotion for government employees
- Cash bonuses
- Longer maternity leave

C *Penalties for not following the one-child policy*

- Government employees sacked
- Basic rice allowance withdrawn for all extra children
- Government employees' retirement pensions cancelled
- **STATE PENALTIES IMPOSED**
- Extra children denied the same quality of education and healthcare as the first child
- Fines imposed (could be up to four times a family's income)
- Farmers who couldn't pay fines in cash had cattle taken from them

least another 10 years. However, in March 2011 the Chinese government announced a review – in future it may allow all parents to have a second child.

Problems of age dependency

China now has a very 'unbalanced' population structure, with more men than women – 117 men to every 100 women. Another concern is age dependency (graphs **D**), which means that the elderly population becomes dependent on the younger generations. It is described as China's '4-2-1 problem', because many single children (1) will become responsible for caring for their parents (2) *and* their four grandparents (4).

China's fertility rate is now about 1.8, which is still above its official target. However, the one-child policy does seem to have avoided the financial burden of 400 million extra births, which has enabled China's development as a global economic super-power.

D *Age dependency in China and the world*

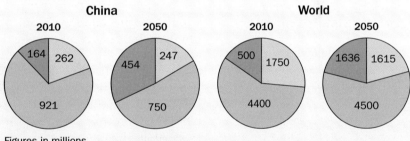

China

2010: 164, 262, 921
2050: 247, 454, 750

World

2010: 500, 1750, 4400
2050: 1636, 1615, 4500

Figures in millions

- ☐ 0–15 years
- ☐ 16–59 years
- ■ 60+ years

Now Investigate

1 a If you were a young person living in China in 1980, would you consider having a second child?

  b Give reasons for your answer to (a).

2 Draw a timeline for population events in China between 1945 and 2020. Add labels for the following years, giving details of what happened:

  1949, 1958–61, 1970, 1979, 1992, 2004, 2008, 2012.

3 Age dependency compares the total number of children and elderly people with the number of wage earners who are able to support them. The formula for calculating a community's age dependency ratio is:

$$\frac{\text{The total number of people in the 'childhood' and 'elderly' age groups}}{\text{The total number of people in the 'adult', working-age group}} \times 100$$

  a Use data in graphs **D** to calculate the dependency ratios for China and the world as a whole in 2010 and 2050.

  b What do the four ratios tell you about the scale of China's dependency situation?

Pro-natalist population policies

Skills link

See page 18 for an explanation of 'replacement level'.

Other governments have created policies to encourage people to have more children in order to boost their population growth rate. These are known as pro-natalist policies (*pro* means 'for'). In Western Europe, for example, between 1980 and 2011 only one country had a fertility rate above the critical 2.1 population replacement level (table **A**). In fact, 47% of all the world's countries now have a fertility rate below 2.1. One reason for this is that, as countries become richer, women marry later in life and delay starting a family.

Most fertility rates in Western Europe have stayed below 2.1 since 1980

Fantastic fact

The world's average fertility rate is 2.46. In Western Europe it used to be 2.7, but is now only 1.65.

Topic link

Look back at Topic 1.1 pages 2–7 for an explanation of fertility rate.

Country	Fertility rate, 1980	Change in fertility rate, 1980–2011	Fertility rate, 2011
Austria	1.62	− 0.22	1.40
Belgium	1.68	− 0.03	1.65
Denmark	1.55	+ 0.19	1.74
France	1.95	+ 0.01	1.96
Germany	1.56	− 0.15	1.41
Ireland	3.25	− 1.23	2.02
Italy	1.64	− 0.25	1.39
Luxembourg	1.49	+ 0.28	1.77
Netherlands	1.60	+ 0.06	1.66
Norway	2.10	−0.33	1.77
Portugal	2.18	− 0.68	1.50
Spain	2.20	− 0.53	1.47
Sweden	1.68	− 0.01	1.67
Switzerland	1.80	−0.34	1.46
UK	1.90	+ 0.01	1.91
Western Europe	**1.88**	**−0.23**	**1.65**

= fertility rate above 2.1 – an increase in the fertility rate

= fertility rate below 2.1 – reduction in the fertility rate

Germany has the largest population in Europe, but it is still concerned about its declining fertility rate. New measures to increase the birth rate include subsidising childcare and contributing to parents' income while they are caring for infants.

Case study

France: population strategies

France has some of the most extensive state-funded childcare facilities in Europe. Diagram **B** shows some of the ways France is encouraging people to have more children in order to maintain its fertility rate. Immigration from southern Europe and former French colonies in North Africa has contributed one quarter of all population growth in recent years, but the growth is due mainly to immigration, and not to a rise in the fertility rate.

France's pro-natalist policy has clearly been successful in stabilising its fertility rate (table **A**). One of the country's most popular strategies has been the *Carte Familles Nombreuses* ('Large Family Card'). This gives families with three or more children reductions on the national train network and half-price fares on the Paris Metro underground system. Families living in Paris, the French capital, also have a *Carte Paris-Famille* ('Paris Family Card'), which gives children free entrance to all swimming pools and subsidised entry to other sports facilities provided by the city.

Skills link

See Section 4.3 page 213 to learn more about drawing bar graphs.

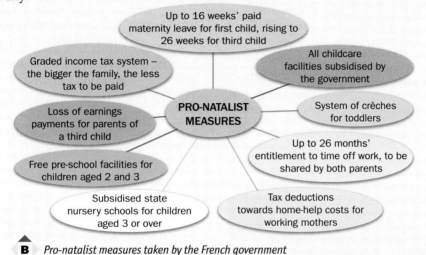

B   *Pro-natalist measures taken by the French government*

Now Investigate

1 a What do you think of the French 'Family Card' schemes?

   b Would your family, or any family that you know, qualify for this card if it was available in your country?

2 a Use the data in table **A** to create a bar graph showing the fertility rates for each country, for 1980 and 2011, and the change in fertility rate between 1980 and 2011. Shade the three bars for each country in three different colours.

   b Draw a line across your graph at 2.1; annotate this line to explain its significance.

   c Comment on the success (or failure) of these countries in maintaining their fertility rate since 1980.

3 a Make a copy of the following table. Complete your table with reference to diagram **B** and the text, putting ticks where appropriate in the last three columns.

   b From the results shown in your table, what kinds of benefit are most likely to persuade French parents to have a larger family?

Type of benefit	Economic	Educational	Recreational
Childcare facilities			
Crèches for toddlers			
Entitlement to time off work			
Graded income tax system			
Large Family Card			
Loss of earnings payments			
Maternity leave			
Nursery schools			
Paris Family Card			
Pre-school facilities			
State nursery schools			
Working mothers' tax deductions			
Total (ticks)			

1.4 Population structure: why are there more older or younger people where you live?

Learning objectives:

▸ know how to draw a population pyramid

▸ understand how a country's population structure may change as it becomes more economically developed

▸ know that the life expectancies of males and females are different

▸ explain how population pyramids are linked to the five stages of the Demographic Transition Model.

Topic link

• Look back at Topic 1.3 pages 14–21 to check on age dependency.

• See Topic 1.3 pages 14–15 to learn more about how a population pyramid is constructed.

Fantastic fact

On average, women live 3 years and 10 months longer than men.

Walk along a busy street in your local area, and guess the ages of the people you see. How many are elderly people? How many are young people and children? If you recorded what you saw, the information wouldn't be very reliable, because many people could be indoors or in other places. A lot would also depend on the day and the time.

In order to find out about a country's population accurately, a census is taken. This is an official count of all the people living in a place (usually a country) at one time. People are asked questions to do with their age and gender. The data collected from the answers helps to monitor changes in the country's population structure and in its total population. A census can also investigate issues such as ethnic background and certain measures of the quality of life. Many countries carry out a census regularly, at 10-year intervals. Some countries are unable to conduct regular censuses, because they are expensive and difficult to organise, and people need to be able to read and write in order to answer the questions.

Census data is used to plan how many facilities will be needed in the future, such as schools and hospitals. It also provides a guide as to how many people of working age will have to support the very young and the elderly in the future. Age/gender census data is usually displayed as a population pyramid (diagrams **A** and **B**).

Further research

You will find population figures and pyramids for most countries on the internet. Type in the name of the country, 'Population pyramid', and the year you are investigating.

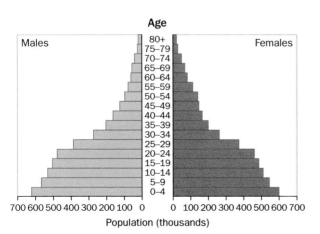

*Note the significant proportion of people under the age of 15.

A *Population pyramid for Haiti, a typical LEDC*

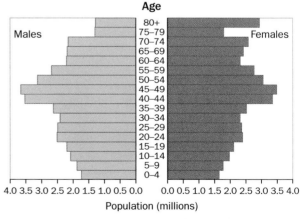

*This pyramid has a much higher proportion of people over the age of 65 than pyramid **A**.

*Note that the units of measurement (thousands/millions) are different in diagrams **A** and **B**.

B *Population pyramid for Germany, a typical MEDC*

Now Investigate

1 Carry out a class census, or one of your school year, to discover its gender structure. Then use your results to answer these questions:

   a How many boys are there in your census group?

   b How many girls are there in the group?

   c What is the total number of students in the group?

   d What is the percentage of boys in the group? Use this simple formula and a calculator to find the answer:

$$\frac{\text{Number of boys}}{\text{Total number of students}} \times 100 = ... \% \text{ of boys in the group}$$

2 a If you can, use the same formula for *all* the boys and girls in your school. Then write a statement comparing percentages in your class/year and the whole school.

   b Find out the gender structure for your own country, and then compare it with that of your whole school.

   c Suggest some reasons why the structures for your school and your country might be different.

3 List at least five ways in which census information might be useful to a country.

4 a Use the data in the table below to create a population pyramid. Refer to graphs **A** and **B** to see how the pyramid should be presented.

Male population (millions)	Age range (years)	Female population (millions)
1.5	Over 80	3.2
1.4	75–79	2.0
1.9	70–74	2.3
2.5	65–69	2.8
3.7	60–64	3.8
3.5	55–59	3.6
3.6	50–54	3.5
3.6	45–49	3.5
3.3	40–44	3.2
3.0	35–39	2.8
3.2	30–34	3.1
3.3	25–29	3.1
3.1	20–24	3.0
3.1	15–19	3.0
2.8	10–14	2.7
2.8	5–9	2.6
2.7	0–4	2.7

5 With reference to your population pyramid, which of the following statements are true?

   • There are fewer females than males over the age of 60.

   • There are fewer elderly people aged 60 or over than young people in the 0–15 age range.

   • The numbers of males and females are about the same in most 5-year age groups below 60 years.

   • This graph shows the population structure of a typical LEDC.

   Using arrows pointing to the appropriate places, add the *true* statements as labels to your pyramid. Then re-write any false statements about your pyramid to make them true, and add those as labels.

Changing stages of the DTM

Fantastic fact

There are no longer any countries at Stage 1 of the DTM.

Topic link

You first learned about the Demographic Transition Model (DTM) in Topic 1.1 (pages 6–7).

You learned (on pages 22–23) that the population pyramids for LEDCs and MEDCs generally have different shapes – especially in the 'childhood' and 'elderly' age groups. The model is a way of showing how birth and death rates change as a country develops economically and progresses through several stages.

On these two pages are several population pyramids typical of countries at each stage of the DTM. These show how population structures are affected by changing birth and death rates.

The population pyramids in diagram **A** are examples of population structures for each of the five stages of economic development. There are now only a few remote communities at Stage 1 of the DTM, such as some tribes living in the tropical rainforest of the Amazon Basin in South America (map **D**).

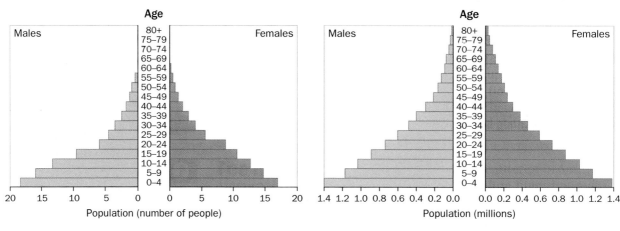

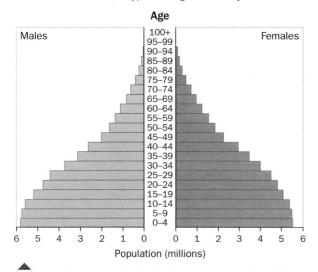

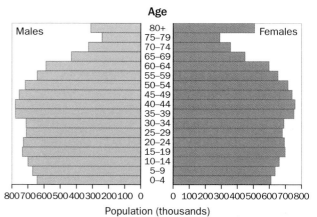

A Population pyramids for the first four stages of the DTM

Sweden's changing population

◄B *Sweden today has low birth and death rates*

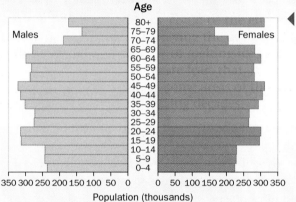

Age

Males — Females

| 80+ |
| 75–79 |
| 70–74 |
| 65–69 |
| 60–64 |
| 55–59 |
| 50–54 |
| 45–49 |
| 40–44 |
| 35–39 |
| 30–34 |
| 25–29 |
| 20–24 |
| 15–19 |
| 10–14 |
| 5–9 |
| 0–4 |

350 300 250 200 150 100 50 0   0 50 100 150 200 250 300 350

Population (thousands)

◄C *Population pyramid for Sweden, a typical Stage 5 country*

Sweden is one example of a country that has progressed through the five stages of the DTM. The shape of its population pyramid today is typical of Stage 5 (diagram **C**).

Further research

Use the internet to find and print out a population pyramid for your own (or a neighbouring) country. Describe the main features of the population structure of your chosen country.

Topic link

What you have learned about population structure will help you when you study Topics 1.1–1.3 pages 2–21.

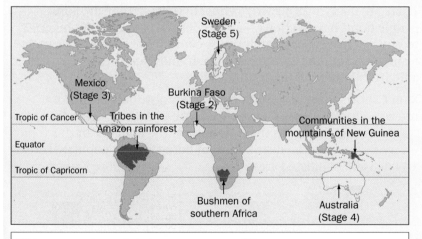

Sweden (Stage 5)

Mexico (Stage 3)

Burkina Faso (Stage 2)

Tropic of Cancer

Tribes in the Amazon rainforest

Communities in the mountains of New Guinea

Equator

Tropic of Capricorn

Bushmen of southern Africa

Australia (Stage 4)

☐ Countries at Stages 2–5 of the DTM   ■ Remote communities at Stage 1

▲D *Location of countries/places at different stages of the DTM*

Now Investigate

Study the population pyramids in diagrams **A** and **C**.

a Copy the outline of the 0–14 age groups for each pyramid, drawing your outlines side by side with Stage 1 at the left, Sweden at the right. Insert a horizontal arrow, pointing to the right, between each outline.

b Below the outlines in (a), draw similar outlines for the age groups aged over 60.

c Label each outline to show the changes, from Stage 1 at the left to Stage 5 at the right. Include at least one statistic for each outline.

Learning objectives:

▷ know how people are distributed around the Earth's surface

▷ understand why some places are more densely populated than others

▷ know about the problems of people living in very densely and sparsely populated areas.

Many people are living very close together in the place shown in photo **A**. But the place in photo **B** is very different! Here there are very few people. Take a very good look at both of these places – perhaps one of them is like the place where you live.

Now Investigate

Which of the two places shown in photos **A** and **B** would you prefer to live in? Why? (Think especially about how many people live in each place.)

Five key terms are used frequently in this topic. Some you may already know, but it is important that you understand what each one means:

- **Population distribution** – the way people are spread out over the Earth's land surfaces.
- **Population density** – how many people live in an area (usually one square kilometre, or 1 km^2).
- **Densely populated** – describes places where many people live.
- **Sparsely populated** – describes places where very few people live.
- **Uninhabited** – describes places where nobody lives.

There are many reasons why people live where they do. Some people don't have a choice – a few countries never allow anyone to enter or leave. Fortunately, most countries do not impose such restrictions and their people are free to move elsewhere in search of a higher standard of living.

Map **C** shows that the world's population distribution is very uneven. One reason is that there is twice as much land in the northern hemisphere as there is south of the Equator. In this topic we look closely at the distribution of both sparsely populated areas and densely populated areas.

A *In cities, many people live very close together*

B *In other parts of the world, people are more scattered across the landscape*

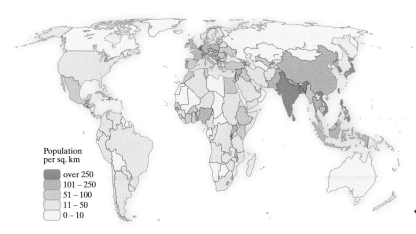

Population per sq. km

- over 250
- 101 – 250
- 51 – 100
- 11 – 50
- 0 – 10

C *World population: distribution and density*

Challenges of extreme environments

Photos **D–G** show four particularly extreme environments which are either very sparsely populated or totally uninhabited.

D *A hot desert*

E *A dense forest*

F *A mountainous region*

G *Polar region*

Topic link

See Topics 2.8–2.10 to find out more about extreme environments.

Topic link

See Topic 1.6 pages 32–35 to learn more about why people move from one place to another.

Fantastic fact

Antarctica is the only continent where *everyone* is a visitor!

Now Investigate

1 Study photos **D–G**.

   a Explain why each of these regions is a challenging place for people to live.

   b Where would *you* prefer to live? What environments would be most and least attractive to you as places to live?

2 a The following table lists the population and physical size of each continent. Calculate the population density of each continent. (To do this you need to divide the population for each continent by its area.)

   b Which are the most and least densely populated continents?

3 With the help of an atlas, add the following information to an outline world map.

   a Shade in all the most sparsely populated areas shown on map **C**.

   b Locate and name at least five hot deserts and five mountain ranges.

   c Locate five large forested areas, adding names to them where possible.

   d Locate and name: (i) Antarctic wilderness (ii) north polar wilderness.

   e Give your completed map a suitable title and a key.

Continent	Total population	Total area (km²)	Average population density (people per km²)
Africa	1 033 000 000	30 065 000	34.4
Asia	4 167 000 000	44 579 000	
Australasia	35 000 000	7 687 000	
Europe	733 000 000	9 938 000	
North America	352 000 000	24 256 000	
South America	589 000 000	17 819 000	

High-density areas of population

Topic link

- See Topic 1.6 pages 32–35 to learn more about migration.
- See Topic 1.8 pages 42–47 to learn more about the site and situation of settlements.

 Many coasts are densely populated because they offer a wide range of opportunities for work and leisure

Now Investigate

a Would you describe the place where you live as a high-density area or a low-density area?

b Which of the reasons for settlement listed above applies to the place where you live?

In some parts of the world, there are very good reasons why people live in certain places (photos **A**, **B** and **C**). For example:

- Flat or gently sloping land makes it possible to farm and build towns, roads and railways (**A**, **C**).
- Fertile soil is ideal for growing crops and rearing animals (**B**).
- When floods occur, most rivers deposit alluvium (silt), which is rich in the minerals needed by plants for growth (**B**).
- Climate – adequate, reliable rainfall and suitable temperatures are needed for crops to grow and ripen (**A**, **B**).
- Fossil fuels – resources such as coal, oil and gas can be used to generate electricity and meet transport needs (**C**).
- Mineral deposits provide essential raw materials, for example iron ore for industries such as steel-making and car manufacture (**C**).
- Fishing – coasts, rivers and lakes provide plentiful, nutritious food (**A**, **B**).
- Fresh water – rivers and lakes are a major source of fresh water, and some can be used to generate power (**B**).
- Coasts and other waterside locations can be developed into ports with trading links to other countries (**C**). Such places are also often popular with tourists and retired people (**A**).

Towns and cities grow rapidly at suitable settlement sites (photo **C**). They also provide employment opportunities for people. Migration of people from other, less favourable places also increases the size and density of the population.

B *A densely populated agricultural area along the Nile Valley, Egypt*

At present, 40% of all people on Earth live within 100 km of a coast. Photo **A** is a typical scene in many highly developed and densely populated coastal areas. The bullet points above suggest some of the reasons why this particular stretch of coastline has attracted so many people.

Singapore – a high-density country

Singapore is one of only 10 countries in the world that has all its people living in urban areas. It is a small island, but this does not explain why it is so heavily urbanised.
Its location at the most southerly tip of the Asian mainland means it is at a major shipping 'crossroads'. Ships sailing between Indian Ocean ports and the industrialised countries of China, Japan and Australia refuel and discharge or load their cargoes here, creating thousands of jobs for local people. Large, modern industrial estates employ many more, and are one of the main reasons why Singapore is so successful (photo **C**).

Only 2% of all adults of working age are unemployed in Singapore. Natural population increase and immigration bring a rise in the total population of almost 5% every year. Providing homes for so many people in such a small area has led to the building of 28 new towns – four of these have over 200 000 inhabitants each. Two-thirds of all Singaporeans now live in new towns.

 C *Singapore is a busy international port*

Now Investigate

1 The list of bullet points on page 28 explains why people live in particular areas. Use the information on page 28 to suggest five annotations that could be added to photo **C**.

   Note: Annotating is *not* the same as labelling! Labels only identify what is there; annotations explain *why* places are important.

2 a Find several photographs of densely populated areas (they should look different from photo **C**).

   b Annotate copies of these photographs to explain why the places are densely populated.

3 With the help of an atlas, add the following information to an outline world map.

   a Shade in all the most densely populated areas shown on map **C** on pages 26–27.

   b Locate and name all the main densely populated areas. Refer to the names of countries, regions and rivers, for example Japan, east coast of North America, Nile river.

   c Referring to your answers to question 2 on page 27, name the six most densely populated continents, in order of most populated first.

   d Make sure your map includes the Equator, the two Tropics, and the Arctic and Antarctic Circles. These should be named, and labelled with their latitude (in degrees).

   e Give your completed map a suitable title and a key.

Fantastic fact

The most densely populated areas of all are urban settlements such as towns and cities. At present, half of the world's people live in urban areas.

Topic link

See Topic 4.4 pages 222–25 to learn more about annotation.

Low-density areas of population

Topic link

See Topic 1.2 pages 8–13 to learn more about over-population.

Case study

North Africa is one of the most sparsely populated regions on Earth. It is also over-populated in many ways, because there are too many people for the few resources available to them. The main reason is that the Sahara, the world's largest hot desert, occupies most of the region. The area to the south of it is experiencing increasingly severe famines.

The Sahel – a low-density area

The area to the south of the Sahara is called the Sahel (map **A**). Diagram **B** highlights reasons why the Sahel today is known as Africa's 'famine belt'.

Farming is the main economic activity in the Sahel. Dry-land crops such as millet, sorghum and cowpea are the main food crops. The main cash crops are groundnuts (peanuts) and cotton. Most farmers are nomadic herders, who migrate northwards during the wet season then return when that area becomes too dry. Many farmers now use cell phones to get weather forecasts and move their animals to places

Fantastic fact 🌍

The largest desert in the world took its name from the Arabic word for desert: *sahara*. *Sahel* is another Arabic word, meaning 'on the edge' of the desert.

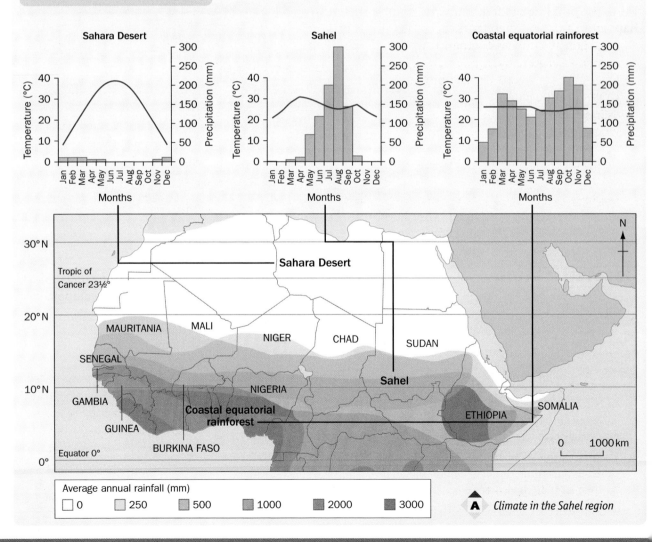

A *Climate in the Sahel region*

Sahel's population doubles every 20 years – faster than its increase in food production

Aid agencies now subsidise 30% of food in the region – many people now dependent on food aid

Region includes three of the four poorest countries on Earth

Many farmers grow cash crops on their best land instead of food

PROBLEMS FACED BY THE SAHEL

Anopheles mosquito on the increase, so more people suffering from malaria

Many farming methods unsustainable – annual crop yields continue to fall

Few natural resources to stimulate local industry and provide exports to increase wealth

B *Why the Sahel is under-populated and sparsely populated*

where rain is predicted to fall. Some water is available where there are rivers and lakes, but in many areas deep wells are the only reliable source of water. During the worst famines, many cattle die as much from starvation as from thirst, because there is not enough water to irrigate fodder crops.

Now Investigate

1 Describe how the natural environment of North Africa changes from north to south. You should include changes in climate and natural vegetation in your answer.

2 Imagine you are a farmer in the Sahel. You have received a letter from a friend who lives far away and has no idea what farming in your area is like. Your friend blames you and other farmers for all the recent problems of the Sahel region. Write a reply explaining why many of the problems in the Sahel are beyond the farmers' control.

Soil degradation

A major problem faced by farmers in many parts of the world is soil degradation. This is the process of the soil becoming less fertile. It can happen in three different ways:

- **Erosion** Soil can be eroded and carried elsewhere by strong winds. Over-grazing by cattle is a common cause of soil erosion.
- **Salinisation** In a hot, dry climate, where evaporation rates are high, the salts (minerals) in water can build up in the soil, causing it to become toxic (poisonous) to plants.
- **Leaching** Soil is leached when heavy rain dissolves valuable plant nutrients (food) in the topsoil, then washes them downwards below the depth that plant roots can reach.

NATURAL FACTORS / **HUMAN FACTORS**

- Lower total annual rainfall
- Less protective natural vegetation
- Fewer plant roots to bind the soil
- Heavy rain causes rapid erosion of exposed soil
- Greater evaporation of water from unprotected land surface

Climate change: change in environment due to human activity

- Trees cut down for fuelwood and building materials
- Over-cultivation due to economic pressure to grow more cash crops – leads to soil degradation and erosion
- More animals (cattle, sheep, goats, camels) leads to overgrazing
- Trampling by animals increases soil erosion

C *Factors in the process of desertification*

Desertification

Desertification is the process by which semi-arid environments become desert-like. It is *not* the spread of true deserts, but rather what happens to the areas next to them. In the Sahel, for example, every year 80 000 km² become too dry and infertile for farming as a result of desertification. Desertification is a global problem:

- One-third of the world's total land area is already desertified or is under serious threat. Climate change is a major natural cause of desertification because it raises global temperatures and changes seasonal rainfall patterns (diagram **C**).
- Twenty per cent of the world's population lives with the threat of desertification.
- An estimated 850 million people are directly affected by desertification, mostly in Africa.

Skills link

- See Topic 4 pages 202–03 to learn more about using and interpreting a cross-section.
- See Topic 2.11 pages 126–31 to learn more about human activity and the environment.

1.6 Migration: why, where and how do people move around?

Learning objectives:

- describe why people move from one place to another

- explain the different types of migration within and between countries

- give details of some of the major migrations taking place around the world.

People on the move

All over the world people are moving around. This is called migration. As geographers, we are concerned with how these movements take place both within a country, for example from rural areas to the city, and from one country to another. There are many different reasons why people need to move. Some of these are voluntary movements but there are also forced migrations when people have no choice but to flee their home.

The bright lights of the big city

In many parts of the world, life in rural areas can be very hard. For example, rural areas in LEDCs have very few services for local people. People in rural areas hear of the big cities where there are jobs and opportunities. Friends and family write letters telling them about freely available health services, housing and education (although this may not always be true). The factors that encourage people to move to towns and cities, in a process known as rural–urban migration, are shown in figure **A**. Things that make people want to leave are called *push* factors and those that attract them to a different area are known as *pull* factors.

PUSH FACTORS	PULL FACTORS
• Lack of running water • Lack of basic services such as electricity • Long distances to schools and hospitals • Farming is hard without machinery • Wealthy landowners buy machines and local workers are made unemployed • Population growth means food shortages and less land to farm • Natural disasters (flood, famine etc.) destroy crops	• Schools available for children's education • Lots of shops to buy food • Running water and electricity • Plenty of entertainment and things to do • A wide variety of jobs • Doctors, medicines and hospitals • The possibility of a better quality of life

A Migration push–pull factors

When my father died, our farm was divided between me and my brothers. It was impossible to grow enough rice to feed my family.

I sold my land to one of my brothers and took my family to what I thought would be a better life in Manila.

But things are much worse here in the city. Thousands of people are arriving every month and the jobs have gone. We couldn't afford the high prices for a house so had to build one ourselves in the slums.

The water is dirty and makes us sick but we can't afford a doctor. It's hard enough finding money for food. I wish we'd stayed in the country.

B The migration of Bagwis Manaloto (pictured right)

The problem is that life in the city rarely turns out as well as people from rural areas expect it to be. Read about the experiences of Bagwis Manaloto, who moved from rural Luzon to Manila in the Philippines (figure **B**).

The peace and tranquillity of the country

While cities in LEDCs are finding it hard to cope with all the extra people moving in, the opposite is happening in richer parts of the world. In many MEDCs, counter-urbanisation is taking place. People are getting fed up with crowded, polluted and congested towns and cities and are moving out into rural areas. There are a number of reasons why this type of migration is taking place:

- Many jobs are now found on the outskirts of cities. Commuting (daily travel) to these out-of-town areas is getting easier.
- As people get richer they want bigger houses with gardens – there is much more housing of this kind available in rural areas.
- Rural areas are often seen as a much safer place in which to raise a family, and they often have better schools.
- City centres may have higher crime rates, vandalism and social problems.

Counter-urbanisation in the capital of Scotland

Case study

Edinburgh, the capital of Scotland, has seen a lot of movement of wealthier families to surrounding rural areas. These families use local services and may save them from being closed down. However, migration can also cause problems for the small rural towns, such as North Berwick, that they have moved to (photo **C**).

In recent years many people have been moving into Edinburgh – it is one of the UK's most popular cities. Many young people are taking advantage of the city's increasing job opportunities and entertainment facilities.

C Problems of counter-urbanisation in North Berwick

- Higher property prices mean local people can no longer afford houses in the area
- Pressure on services such as schools and hospitals
- Many new families commute to Edinburgh, shop in the city and bring little money into local businesses
- Increased numbers of cars make roads dangerous for local children
- Building new houses destroys the countryside and habitats for wildlife
- Some recent arrivals do not mix well with the local people

Now Investigate

1 What is the difference between:
   a temporary and permanent migration
   b voluntary and forced migration?

2 Using examples, explain in detail why people would want to move from:
   a rural to urban areas
   b urban to rural areas.

3 Think about the rural–urban migration taking place in your own country.
   a Write down all the push and pull factors that might make somebody move to your country's main city.
   b Would you prefer to live in the city or in a rural area? Explain your answer.

Fantastic fact

The greatest rural–urban migration is currently in China. Many cities are expanding their population by 10 per cent a year.

Now Investigate

Have you moved around different places during your lifetime? Where did you move from? Where did you move to? What were the reasons for your migration?

Moving from one country to another

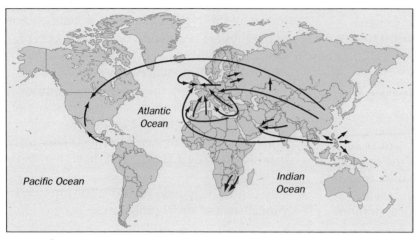

A *Major global migration routes*

Both migration within countries and migration between countries are extremely important on a global scale. Emigrants are those leaving a particular country and immigrants are those coming in. As with internal migrations, this can be either voluntary or forced migration. Some of the world's major migration routes are shown on map **A**.

Many people move to find a better life for themselves and their families. These people are known as economic migrants and they often want to return home when they have earned enough money. In the meantime many will send some of what they earn back to their families. Some may enter a country unofficially without making themselves known to the authorities – these are called illegal immigrants.

Forced migration on an international scale is much more serious and happens for a variety of reasons:

- when people are persecuted or threatened because of their religious beliefs
- as a result of war when people are forced to leave their homes
- when people are forced into slavery, again often as a result of war
- because of racial discrimination
- when famine strikes a country and the people have to move to find food
- because of natural disasters such as earthquakes, volcanic eruptions, floods or hurricanes.

People who are forced to move are called refugees. The US government estimates that there are over 60 million refugees in the world today. Many of these refugees are forced to live in poverty in camps with little food, water or access to healthcare and education (photo **B**).

Now Investigate ❗

Using an atlas and map **A**, describe some of the major global migration routes. You should refer to specific countries in your answer.

Skills link 🔗

One clear way to illustrate information about migration on a map is to use arrows like those shown on map **A**. Some maps also use flowlines where the arrows are wider or thinner depending on the information they display. For more details, see Topic 4.3 page 217.

B *A refugee camp in Dabaab, Somalia*

Now Investigate ❗

1. Why might you want to migrate to another country? What might be the advantages of leaving? What things would you miss about your home?

2. Do people migrate to your country? What are the reasons for this immigration?

3. What are the main reasons for forced migrations? Can you think of any examples in the countries near where you live?

4. List all the advantages and disadvantages of migration for Senegal. Do you think it has a positive or negative effect for the country overall? Explain your answer.

International migration: Senegal to the rest of the world

Senegal is a fairly small country (about one-third the size of France) in West Africa. It has a population of around 13 million, which is growing at a rate of just over 2 per cent each year. For many years after independence from France in 1960 it was the destination for immigrants from the rest of Africa. They were attracted by Senegal's stable government and opportunities there for jobs and setting up businesses. This has changed completely over the last decade for a number of reasons:

- An economic crisis from the 1990s onwards saw a huge drop in living standards.
- There was a big increase in unemployment and a lack of jobs even for educated people.
- Rapid population growth has meant competition for the few jobs available. It has also put pressure on resources such as food supplies.

Many young Senegalese males have decided to emigrate to find work to support their families. Many of them have gone to France because of Senegal's links with that country – the old colonial power – and because they were attracted by images of life in Europe seen on the television and in magazines (diagram **C**). A large number have also settled in Germany.

This migration has had a number of benefits for Senegal. Migrants send a huge amount of money back home to their families. They often return having learned new skills that can be put to use in developing their own country. The reduction in population also means a decrease in the demand for scarce resources. However, as diagram **D** shows, there are many disadvantages both for Senegal and for its emigrating population.

Despite the possible advantages of living abroad, many migrants are not happy. A large percentage of Senegalese migrants interviewed in Germany said they wished they had stayed at home.

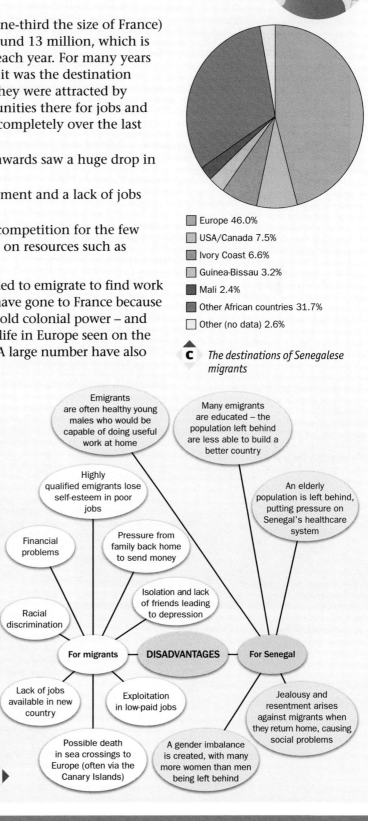

- ☐ Europe 46.0%
- ☐ USA/Canada 7.5%
- ☐ Ivory Coast 6.6%
- ☐ Guinea-Bissau 3.2%
- ☐ Mali 2.4%
- ☐ Other African countries 31.7%
- ☐ Other (no data) 2.6%

C *The destinations of Senegalese migrants*

Emigrants are often healthy young males who would be capable of doing useful work at home

Many emigrants are educated – the population left behind are less able to build a better country

Highly qualified emigrants lose self-esteem in poor jobs

An elderly population is left behind, putting pressure on Senegal's healthcare system

Financial problems

Pressure from family back home to send money

Isolation and lack of friends leading to depression

Racial discrimination

For migrants   **DISADVANTAGES**   **For Senegal**

Lack of jobs available in new country

Exploitation in low-paid jobs

Jealousy and resentment arises against migrants when they return home, causing social problems

Possible death in sea crossings to Europe (often via the Canary Islands)

A gender imbalance is created, with many more women than men being left behind

Disadvantages of Senegalese **D ▶** *migration*

Learning objectives:

▸ understand which factors are important when deciding where to site a new village

▸ know the factors that influence the growth or decline of rural settlements

▸ know that there are three types of settlement shape: dispersed, linear and nucleated

▸ explain what influences patterns of settlement in rural areas.

Do you live in the countryside (a rural area)? Or in a town or city (an urban area)? Do you know *why* you live where you do? Perhaps it is because the family members who support you have lived there for a long time, or maybe you moved there because of personal circumstances. Geographers like to ask questions, and to find out the reason for the locations of towns and villages. There are many reasons why people first create a settlement in a particular place.

Every settlement is different. Your own village, town or city will have its own unique arrangement of roads and buildings. How it looks today depends on how old it is, the shape of the land it is built on, and what has happened there in the past. In fact, history is a good place to start when investigating places, because most settlements, however large they are now, started off very small in what were then completely rural areas (photo **A**). (Just a few places don't develop in this way, because they are planned and built as complete 'new towns'.)

Deciding where to build a new settlement is very important, because it may only become successful if it is built in an appropriate location. Diagram **C** lists the main village site factors, and explains why each one is so important to the success of a new settlement. Site is the land on which the first part of a settlement is built. The more site factors a settlement has, the more likely it is to flourish, to have more functions (activities) and to grow in size.

 A small village in a rural environment

Topic link 🔗

What you learn in this topic about rural settlement will help you when you study Topic 1.8 pages 42–47, on urban settlement.

 Most towns and cities began as small villages

Accessibility, or the ability to reach places, is one of the most important of these factors, because people need to trade with other people and places. Other key factors in the early growth of settlements include the availability of water, food and basic raw materials such as wood and stone.

Topic link

You can learn more about meanders in Topic 2.3 pages 80–87.

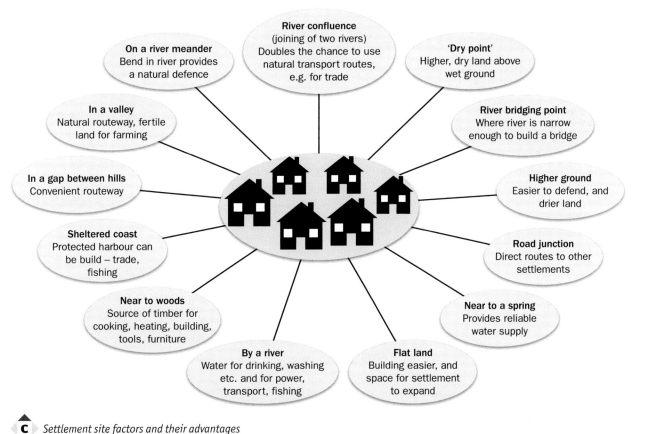

On a river meander
Bend in river provides a natural defence

River confluence
(joining of two rivers)
Doubles the chance to use natural transport routes, e.g. for trade

'Dry point'
Higher, dry land above wet ground

In a valley
Natural routeway, fertile land for farming

River bridging point
Where river is narrow enough to build a bridge

In a gap between hills
Convenient routeway

Higher ground
Easier to defend, and drier land

Sheltered coast
Protected harbour can be build – trade, fishing

Road junction
Direct routes to other settlements

Near to woods
Source of timber for cooking, heating, building, tools, furniture

Near to a spring
Provides reliable water supply

By a river
Water for drinking, washing etc. and for power, transport, fishing

Flat land
Building easier, and space for settlement to expand

C Settlement site factors and their advantages

Now Investigate

1 Investigate the location of a settlement you know well, then list all the factors in diagram **C** that help to describe its site.

2 a Re-arrange the site factors in diagram **C** into three groups according to how important you think they are:

   i must-have

   ii good to have

   iii could do without

   b Explain your selection of the 'must-have' site factors.

3 a Suggest some site factors that are likely to *hinder* the growth of settlements. Try to think of up to five factors.

   b Explain why each of these factors is a disadvantage for a settlement.

Rural settlements on Ordnance Survey maps

Topic link

See Topic 4.1 pages 200-201 to help you answer the questions on this page.

Over time, villages often develop quite distinctive shapes and patterns. The three most common types are: dispersed, linear and nucleated (table **A**). Many villages have combinations of two or more of these basic patterns.

Dispersed settlement	Linear settlement	Nucleated settlement
Individual farms and houses are widely scattered over a rural area (countryside) and are linked by a network of tracks and minor roads.	Linear settlements are long and narrow, with most of their buildings along a road, river bank or shoreline.	Buildings are tightly clustered around a road junction, church or bridge. Nucleated settlements are about the same distance across in different directions.

A Different settlement types

C Grande Rivière, a village in north-west St Lucia

Now Investigate

1 a Find the following places on map **B**. A four-figure or six-figure grid reference is given for each settlement. Note that not all settlements are named.

    i   Almondale 1249

    ii Babonneau 140480

    iii east side of 1451

    iv Grande Rivière 1351

    v La Feuillet 1453 and 1454

    vi north-east part of 1352

    vii west side of 1149

  b Which type of settlement pattern – dispersed, linear or nucleated – does each of these places have?

2 Look for the following settlements on map **B**, and list the advantages of the *site* of each settlement:

  a Babonneau 140480

  b Bois d'Orange 1153

  c Grande Rivière 1351

  d Gros Islet 1356.

Case study

Rural settlements in St Lucia

Only 28 per cent of the population of the island of St Lucia lives in an urban area. The Ordnance Survey (OS) map extract **B** shows clearly the many small settlements in this part of the island and two larger places. Port Castries is the largest settlement on the island, and the capital of St Lucia.

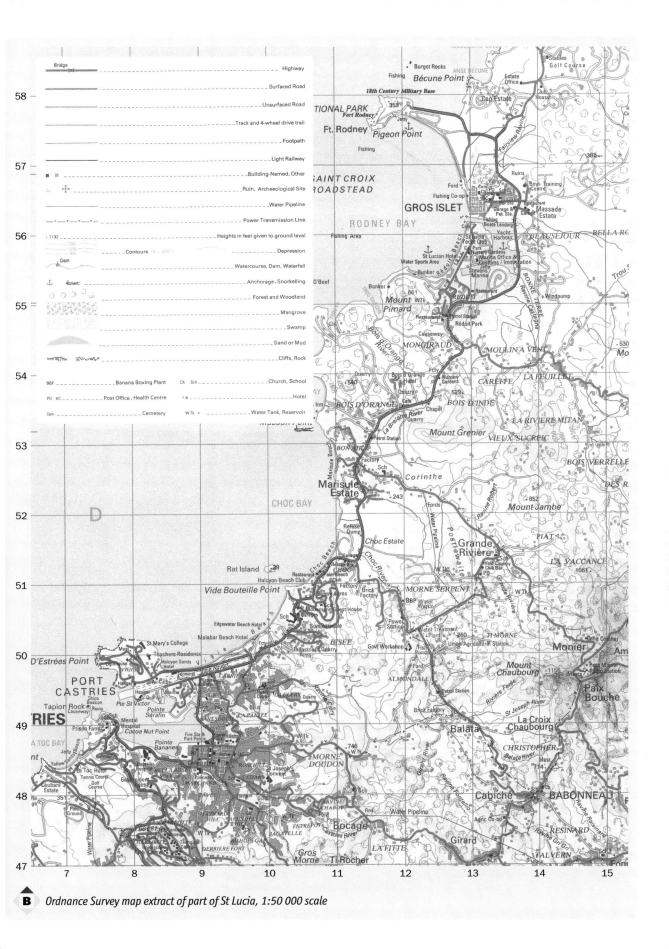

Ordnance Survey map extract of part of St Lucia, 1:50 000 scale

Legend:

Bridge	
	Highway
	Surfaced Road
	Unsurfaced Road
	Track and 4-wheel drive trail
	Footpath
	Light Railway
	Building-Named, Other
	Ruin, Archaeological Site
	Water Pipeline
	Power Transmission Line
▪ 1132	Heights in feet given to ground level
Contours (V.I. 200')	Depression
Dam	Watercourse, Dam, Waterfall
	Anchorage, Snorkelling
	Forest and Woodland
	Mangrove
	Swamp
	Sand or Mud
	Cliffs, Rock
BBP	Banana Boxing Plant
Ch Sch	Church, School
PO HC	Post Office, Health Centre
H	Hotel
Cem	Cemetery
W Tk	Water Tank, Reservoir

Life in rural areas

Worldwide, 37 per cent of all people live in villages and work on farms. In India, though, the figure is much higher – 52 per cent. Even in this rapidly industrialising country, rural areas are still very important.

Case study

Chembakolli – a village in southern India

Chembakolli is one of 200 villages in southern India inhabited by the Adivasi tribe (map **A**). *Adivasi* is a local word meaning 'the people of the forest' – a good name for them because the forest used to provide all the food they needed as well as materials for building huts. The forest still provides fuelwood for cooking and for heating water for washing, although many of the trees have already been cleared to create extra farmland. The forest also provides a habitat for deer, rabbits and wild boar which are hunted by the Adivasi.

Most of Chembakolli's 50 families are farmers. Their main crops are rice, onions, tomatoes and peppers. These are all subsistence crops (grown to feed the local people), but some farmers have started growing tea as a cash crop, which they can sell to earn money for themselves. Every member of a Chembakolli family helps to grow these crops, and the women and older children are usually also responsible for looking after the goats and chickens. Only the better-off villagers can afford to buy a cow. Most people work very hard just to survive, and rely on the summer monsoon rains for the success of their crops (graph **C**).

All the farmwork is done by hand (photo **B**), although elephants are used to help with heavy tasks such as moving logs from the forest. Some of the men add to their family's income by working on the tea and ginger estates owned by more wealthy farmers. This helps to buy materials the children need for school.

A *Location of Chembakolli in southern India*

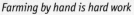

B *Farming by hand is hard work*

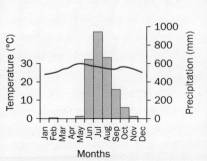

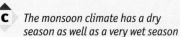

C *The monsoon climate has a dry season as well as a very wet season*

Map **D** shows that the village now has a range of basic facilities, and a school for the younger children. It does not yet have an electricity supply. The village well is used for washing cooking pans and for drinking water. Typhoid is a common, life-threatening illness because the well is also used by animals. Diarrhoea is another common symptom, which can be fatal, especially for children and old people. The village now has a small clinic, and a doctor makes regular visits.

Chembakolli is linked by bus to other villages and the nearest large town, Gudalur, which has a population of 180 000.

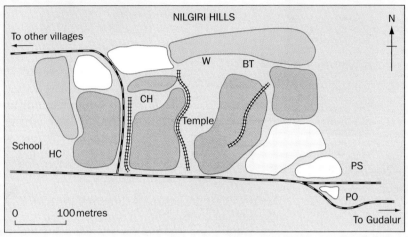

 D Chembakolli is a nucleated settlement, clustered around the temple

E A typical street scene in a rural town in the Tamil Nadu region of Southern India

Gudalur is a different world: it has supermarkets, cinemas and a hospital. Some people in Chembakolli have never travelled along the road to the town, even though it is less than 20 km away!

Now Investigate

1 How is life in Chembakolli village different from your own? Use the following headings to structure your answer:

- Food and water
- The work that people do
- Health problems and medical support

2 a Describe the monthly temperature and rainfall patterns shown in graph **C**.

b How do these patterns compare with those for your own region?

c What problems is Chembakolli's climate likely to cause for:

i farmers

ii other village people?

Topic link

To learn more about how climate graphs, see Topic 4.3 page 212.

Further research

Study maps of your local region and try to identify examples of the different types of settlement: dispersed, linear and nucleated. You might take photographs or obtain pictures of your chosen examples. You could then produce a display of all the resources you have collected, annotating them to highlight their main features.

1.8 Urban settlement: what kind of settlement do *you* live in?

Pedro lives in a large city, while Maria's home is in a small town (figures **A** and **B**).

A Pedro

B Maria

I live in a big city. It's got everything – including crime! All the big department stores are here, and the latest fashions. My Dad's mad about cars and there are showrooms here selling every make you can think of. There's a great social scene, with plenty of discos, nightclubs and cinemas. There are theatres and museums, too, as well as colleges, universities and hospitals ...

My town is quite small. Its shops sell the basics like food, of course, but not much else. You can get second-hand cars and vans here but anyone who can afford to buy a new car has to go to the city. There isn't much for young people to do in the evenings, so we find our own amusement – and that sometimes gets us into trouble! I can't wait to move to the city when I leave school.

Now Investigate ❗

Do you live in a large city, a town, or a smaller settlement? Compare your own settlement with those of Pedro and Maria. Does it have more or fewer advantages than theirs?

The previous topic introduced the idea of a settlement's site – the small area where its first buildings were built. Here we look at their situation – the position of settlements within the much larger region. Site and situation are both about places – the difference between them is scale and distance. To grow, and move up higher in the settlement hierarchy, a hamlet or village needs a site and situation with many advantages.

Case study

Paris: location and growth of a capital city

Both the site and the situation of Paris have many advantages. It has an ideal island site (map **C** and photo **D**), and a situation in the centre of the most fertile region in France, an area known as the Paris Basin (map **E**). An abundant supply of food, and being at the centre of road and later railway networks, helped Paris to grow faster than any other French city. Today it is a huge built-up area, known as a conurbation, which includes many settlements that were once separate towns.

Fantastic fact 🌍

One in every five French people lives in the Paris conurbation.

The population of Paris is now almost seven times greater than France's second biggest settlement, Lyon (graph **F**). Much of the population increase in Paris has been due to the migration of people from poorer regions of France.

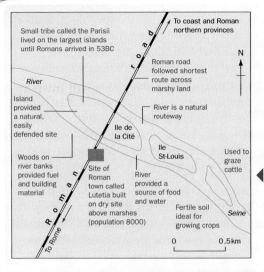

Small tribe called the Parisii lived on the largest islands until Romans arrived in 53BC

Roman road followed shortest route across marshy land

River is a natural routeway

Used to graze cattle

Ile de la Cité

Ile St-Louis

River

Island provided a natural, easily defended site

Woods on river banks provided fuel and building material

Site of Roman town called Lutetia built on dry site above marshes (population 8000)

River provided a source of food and water

Fertile soil ideal for growing crops

Seine

To coast and Roman northern provinces

Roman road

To Rome

N

0   0.5km

C The site: the oldest part of Paris is built on two islands – the Romans used the Ile de la Cité as a river crossing-point along a military road

Ile de la Cité is now dominated by important buildings such as Notre Dame Cathedral **D**

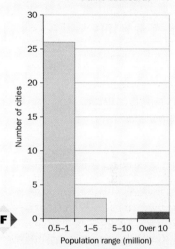

F French cities with populations greater than half a million

Number of cities / Population range (million): 0.5–1, 1–5, 5–10, Over 10

E The situation of Paris, which is an important focus of European road and rail links

Routes to Belgium

A1

A15

River transport route to English Channel

Le Bourget

Charles de Gaulle

Routes to Germany

A13

Orly

0   10 km

N

Routes to Atlantic ports and Spain

A10

A6

Seine

Routes to Italy and Switzerland

City of Paris
Motorway
Railway
Industrial areas
International airport
Paris conurbation
Fertile lowlands of Paris Basin

Skills link

See Topic 4.4 pages 222–25 to learn more about how to draw and annotate a sketch map.

Now Investigate

1 a Using information on these two pages, state whether each of the following statements is *true* or *false*. Re-write any false statements to make them true.

   • Early settlers had a plentiful supply of water and fish from the river Seine.

   • One of the islands provided an easy crossing point of the river.

   • The land on the banks of the river Seine is steep and difficult to build on.

   • The river made transportation by boat very difficult.

   • The site of Paris consists of two islands in the river Seine.

   • Two islands in the river Seine provided a safe, easily defended site for the first settlement.

2 a Describe the situation of Paris, using information in map **E**. Include details on the following:

   • distance to the coast

   • general relief (height and shape of the land) of the Paris Basin

   • rail and road links (national and regional)

   • location of international airports

   • any nearby industrial areas

   • land use in the Paris Basin

   • size of the Paris conurbation, from north to south and east to west.

   b Explain why each of these features was important to the city's growth.

3 Using the survey map on page 39 as a guide, draw a sketch map to show the situation of Castries, the largest settlement on the island of St Lucia. Annotate your map to show the advantages of its situation.

The settlement hierarchy

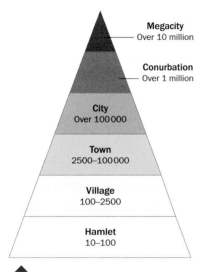

All settlements can be put in order according to their functions and size of population. This is called a hierarchy. Diagram **A** shows a settlement hierarchy based only on population size. Its levels range from isolated buildings such as farmhouses, to the world's 26 megacities, each having over 10 million inhabitants. It is impossible to give precise ranges for some of the settlement 'layers' because definitions of towns and cities vary from country to country. For example, Swedish cities must have at least 50 000 people, but Romanian cities need only 5000.

Settlement hierarchies can also be based on functions (table **B**). These are the services a settlement provides for its inhabitants and for people living within easy travelling distance. Clusters of houses called 'hamlets' are too small to support any permanent facilities such as shops and schools; their only service provision is likely to be a bus stop and perhaps a telephone kiosk!

Fantastic fact

The smallest 'city' in the world is believed to be Hum, in Croatia (in Eastern Europe) – a 900-year old hill-top community with only 23 inhabitants.

Topic link

Look back at Topic 1.7 pages 36–41 to check on what the functions of a place are, and to see a survey map showing Castries in St Lucia.

Settlements at the top and bottom of the settlement hierarchy	Educational facilities	Shopping facilities	Transport facilities
Megacity	University	Out-of-town regional shopping centre	International airport
	College	Specialist shops	Regional airport
		Department stores	Major rail and road 'hub'
		Supermarket	
	Secondary school	Local row of shops	Railway station
		Local general store	Bus station
			Taxi rank
			Bus stop
Isolated farm or house	Infant/primary school		

B   Function hierarchies based on service provision

Settlements at the top of a hierarchy fulfil a wide range of functions. Castries, the capital of St Lucia, is a good example of this. Although its population is only 15 000, it is the largest settlement and has many of the functions of megacities. Two of the main functions of Castries are as a port and as a centre for sports. Photo **C** shows the main harbour at Castries with its quays at full capacity with large visiting cruise ships.

Many countries, especially LEDCs, are dominated by one very large, densely populated city. Graph **D** shows one way of plotting the populations of the 10 largest cities of a country to show their relative sizes.

C   Harbour at Castries with a large cruise ship at every quayside

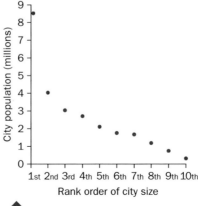

D   City size rank order

1 a What is the population of the settlement where you live?

b What level of population settlement do you live in, according to the hierarchy shown in diagram **A**?

2 Create at least one hierarchy like those in table **B**, from this list of other settlement functions: entertainment facilities, medical facilities, sports facilities. Start with the smallest and the largest, for example a village football pitch (smallest) to an international stadium in a major city (largest).

3 Using the map extract in Topic 1.7 page 39, copy and complete the following table by adding:

a the six-figure grid references for its named features

b the missing 'first' and 'second' features at the grid reference positions shown.

Function	First feature grid reference	First feature	Second feature grid reference	Second feature
Administration	082482		–	–
Culture	085475	Caribbean Museum	–	–
Education		St Mary's College	083472	
Health	077491		099496	Health Centre
Hotels		La Toc Hotel	085483	
Industry		Industrial area	106494	
Leisure	084494		106511	Halcyon Beach Club
Places of worship	091480			St Joseph's Convent
Public buildings		Police HQ	089487	
Public utilities	092488			Reservoir
Residential	082500		098486	Rose Hill residential area
Sport		Golf course	096480	Stadium
Transport	092498		*See question C*	Cruise ship quays

c Study photo **C** to locate the main quays in Castries Harbour on the map extract, then write their six-figure grid reference positions on the last line of your table.

4 a Using graph **D** as your guide, plot these urban populations onto two separate graphs.

City rank order	Urban area populations in France, an MEDC		Urban area populations in Nigeria, an LEDC	
First	Paris	11 300 000	Lagos	9 123 000
Second	Lille	1 728 000	Ibadan	3 670 000
Third	Lyon	1 666 000	Kano	3 519 000
Fourth	Marseilles	1 532 000	Kaduna	1 458 900
Fifth	Toulouse	975 000	Port Harcourt	1 191 000
Sixth	Nice	943 000	Benin	1 052 000
Seventh	Bordeaux	935 000	Maiduguri	972 000
Eighth	Nantes	719 000	Zaria	899 000
Ninth	Strasbourg	652 000	Aba	898 000
Tenth	Toulon	570 000	Ilorin	765 000

Note: These are the populations of urban conurbations, not just the cities at their centres.

b Compare your two graphs, and highlight any similarities and differences between them.

All settlements perform at least one function for the people who live there, or are within easy travelling distance. For example, an isolated house fulfills a function as a home for those who live there. Functions will only be provided if there is sufficient demand for them. For example, a cake shop can only survive if there are enough people who:

- like eating cakes
- can afford to buy that shop's cakes
- are within easy travelling distance of the cake shop.

Online shopping is increasingly important to many businesses – but probably less so for cake shops and other businesses selling perishable food.

The number of people needed to support a business or service is called its threshold population. The size of a threshold population is closely linked to the needs of the particular activity. For example, a secondary school needs a cluster of primary schools to provide enough students to make it viable (table **A**). Graph **B** presents suggestions for population threshold requirements for some non-educational services.

Facility	Threshold population
Small village primary school	500
Pre-school nursery	1000
Town primary school	3000
Secondary school	10 000
College	50 000
University	100 000

 A Population thresholds in the educational hierarchy

Care needs to be taken when using population threshold data. For example:

- Some communities are wealthier than others, and better-off people can afford to buy more goods or services, so fewer people are needed to make the same service viable.
- Not all people share the same interests or needs. For example, in a community where many retired people live, a shop selling football kit would be less likely to succeed than one specialising in aids for the elderly!
- Communities often have very different preferences and traditions. In France there is a long tradition of eating hand-crafted bread, so a baker's shop in that country can thrive in a community of only 600 people. However, in Britain, where more mass-produced bread is eaten, the population threshold of a similar shop would have to be three times greater.

B Population thresholds vary widely between different services

(Graph B: Threshold population (thousands) vs Type of service provision — Hospital, Department store, Large food store, Shoe shop, Clothes shop, Convenience store, Post Office)

Now Investigate

List 10 items owned by your family. For each one, find out how far away from your home each one was bought.

Elland – the service functions of a typical small town in England

A good way of comparing the population thresholds of different services is to carry out a land use survey. Graph **C** shows results of a survey of service provision in Elland, a town of 15 000 people in northern England. Photo **D** shows part of that survey area.

Because each type and level of service has its own population threshold, it also requires a minimum area from which enough people can be drawn. This is called its catchment area. Low order goods such as bread and newspapers, which are cheap and bought frequently, have much smaller catchment areas than high order (expensive) items like beds and cars. Another term for 'catchment area' is sphere of influence.

D *Part of Elland's main shopping street*

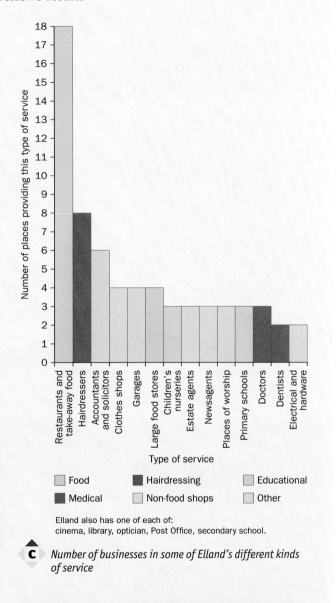

Elland also has one of each of:
cinema, library, optician, Post Office, secondary school.

C *Number of businesses in some of Elland's different kinds of service*

Now Investigate

1 Imagine that you have been given the job of planning a new leisure centre to meet the recreational needs of your local community. What criteria (for example transport and threshold population) will you need to consider to make sure that the new centre will be a success?

2 Suggest why the threshold population of a doctor's surgery might be different from that of a dentist's surgery.

3 How might population density influence the size of a shop's catchment area?

Fantastic fact

The catchment area for the highest-quality jewellery sold in central London is the whole of the British Isles!

Learning objectives:

▶ know that an increasing proportion of the world's people live in urban areas

▶ know that large urban settlements are made up of zones with different functions

▶ use land use models to understand patterns in urban areas

▶ understand the main functions and characteristics of each urban zone, and that these can change over time

▶ explain how land use zones in LEDCs and MEDCs are both similar and different.

A   *Keetan, a resident of Kolkata in India*

Topic link

See Topic 1.6 pages 32–35 to learn why some cities are growing so fast.

Fantastic fact

By 2008, more than half of the world's population was living in urban areas.

The *proportion* of the world's population living in urban areas has been growing for the last 200 years. This process is called urbanisation.

Keetan lives in Kolkata, one of the largest cities in India. Read what Keetan has to say about the place he calls home (figure **A**).

> Hi! I'm Keetan. My dad is a taxi driver. Sometimes he takes me with him so I can get to know my city.
>
> Yesterday we started off in Howrah, in the northern part of the city. There are lots of squatter settlements here – we Indians call them bustees! Dad usually has to drive around these areas, because there aren't many proper streets between the houses – just narrow dirt tracks, which become flooded in the heavy monsoon rains. We then drove south, through the textile area, where thousands of small businesses make all kinds of clothing. Then 1 km further on is the city centre, with its huge, modern office blocks and hotels and some fine old stone buildings from when India was a British colony. Nearby are the docks, on the east bank of the Hooghly river, with lots of factories nearby.
>
> We came back home through the area where the better-off people live. This is quite close to the city centre where there are big stores which have everything you could ever dream of!

Two models can help us understand how towns and cities develop. These are based on the location of land use zones, which have one or more important urban function – commercial, industrial, residential, recreational – as well as facilities such as roads and schools which form the infrastructure. These facilities make it possible for a place to function effectively.

The land use model in diagram **B** shows a series of concentric circles, all of them sharing the same centre point. This theoretical model applies to a town that has grown at exactly the same rate in every direction.

The model in diagram **C** is more realistic, because it allows for growth at different rates in all directions. It also shows that functions can extend to the edge of the built-up area. For example, industrial developments often follow canal, road and railway routes linking the city centre and the countryside. Wealthier people try to build their houses where they won't be affected by industrial pollution.

Now Investigate

Imagine that, like Keetan, you have the chance to travel around a city or large town in your own region. Write about what you might see on the way, for example where there are different kinds of buildings and what they look like. How is your town or city similar to and different from Kolkata?

It can be difficult to match these models to the towns and cities of today because:

- many old inner city areas have been redeveloped and their original functions changed, for example retail parks have replaced areas of poor-quality housing
- new by-pass roads around towns have attracted industrial and residential developments away from busy inner city areas
- both models assume that the oldest part of a town will always be in the middle, but many town and city centres are closer to one side of the urban area.

These models are based on urban areas in MEDCs, but most cities in developing countries share similar characteristics. Diagram **D** is a transect through a typical MEDC city, from its modern commercial centre to the outer edges. Cities in LEDCs have similar land use patterns, including a central business district, or CBD, at their heart, although in some cities the suburbs have developed as squatter settlements.

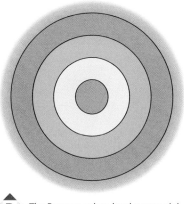

B *The Burgess urban land use model*

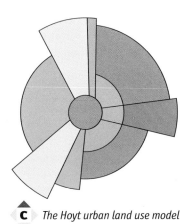

C *The Hoyt urban land use model*

 Central Business District (CBD)   Industry   Low quality housing

Middle quality housing   **a** Rural–urban fringe
b High quality housing

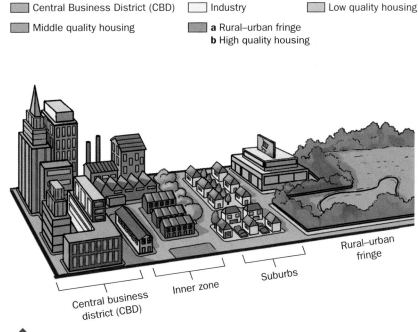

Central business district (CBD) Inner zone Suburbs Rural–urban fringe

D *Transect across a typical MEDC city*

Now Investigate ❗

These questions are based on diagrams **B**, **C** and **D**.

a Which urban zone is in the same central location in all of the diagrams?

b Which model is more likely to show how a town's growth has been influenced by natural land and water features?

c Which model recognises that people may have some choice in where they live?

d Which model recognises the role of transport in urban development?

e Explain how the zones in an MEDC city might be different from those in an LEDC city.

Skills link 🔗

See pages 56–59 to learn more about transects.

Topic link 🔗

See Topic 1.10 pages 56–57 to learn more about squatter settlements.

There are four main types of urban zone:
- the central business district, or CBD
- the inner zone
- the outer zone (suburbs)
- the rural–urban fringe.

You will need to know the main characteristics of each zone, and be able to recognise each zone on photographs, maps and street plans.

Central business district

A Part of the CBD in Shanghai, China

The central business district (CBD) is the commercial 'heart' of a settlement and is easily recognised on photographs by its impressive buildings. The first large buildings were made of stone and designed to show the wealth and importance of a city. More recent big buildings are just as impressive, but are generally made of steel and glass (photo **A**).

Although the CBD is smaller than the other zones, it is an economic centre of any major settlement. It is also the central meeting point for road and railway routes and has plenty of space for car parking. This good access makes the CBD an ideal place to locate banks, offices and large department stores and specialist shops selling comparison goods such as expensive furniture, watches and antiques. Major public buildings like cathedrals, theatres, hotels and museums often cluster around parks and gardens – the few open spaces that are not built on.

Only the rich can afford to buy spacious accommodation in the CBD, and many people rent small 'studio' apartments instead. They want to live in the centre because they like the excitement of city life and prefer to spend more money on rent instead of on high commuting costs. The street patterns in most European city centres developed in a random, irregular fashion – unlike the grid patterns of newer cities like Chicago and Detroit in the USA, and island capitals such as Castries in St Lucia and Port Louis in Mauritius.

The inner zone

B The old and the new in an inner zone

In many MEDCs this zone dates from the 19th century, during the Industrial Revolution, when factories and houses were built next to each other and when people worked long hours and walked to work. Much redevelopment has taken place in this zone to replace low-quality housing and remove old industries. They are replaced by inner ring roads, retail parks, recreational facilities such as multi-screen cinemas, and car parking areas.

In LEDCs the inner zone often includes some high-quality housing close to the cultural and social attractions of the city centre.

The outer zone (suburbs)

In LEDCs, squatter settlements are very common (photo **C**). There are many challenges for the people living there, but they are very resilient and try hard to improve their quality of life. The location of such settlements means that the inhabitants can take advantage of employment opportunities in both the inner zone and on the rural–urban fringe.

In MEDCs, many families in the outer zone live on estates of large houses with gardens and garages, and many people commute daily to work. Retired people often live in single-storey bungalows. In other MEDCs, apartments, villas and condominiums are the more usual type of housing (photo **D**). The standard of living tends to be high, but there are generally few local facilities such as schools, health centres and shops, because most people have cars and are able to travel further.

C   *Scene in an LEDC outer zone*

Rural–urban fringe

This zone is where town and country meet. Photo **E** shows that it is a very 'busy' area, in spite of its semi-rural location and appearance.

Now Investigate ❗

1. a Find at least one photograph of the CBD of a major city in your own country and annotate it to show its main land use functions.

   b Do the same for a city in another, contrasting country.

   c Compare *and* contrast the two scenes, referring to your annotations for each group of land use functions.

2. For this activity use the Ordnance Survey map on page 39. For Castries:

   a write down the grid references for the squares in which the CBD is located

   b list all the key buildings which indicate that it is a CBD.

3. a Draw a spider diagram to display land uses in inner zones of cities.

   b Use different colours or styles of writing to highlight any differences between land use in LEDC and MEDC cities.

4. a Describe the type of land use in a typical MEDC outer zone.

   b Explain how land use in city suburbs in an LEDC is different from that in (a).

5. Make a larger copy of the following table. Complete your table by writing in its correct column each rural–urban fringe activity you can see in photo **E**.

Agricultural	Commercial and industrial	Recreational	Transport	Other

D   *Suburban scene in an MEDC*

E   *A typical rural–urban fringe landscape*

Topic link 🔗

See Topic 1.10 pages 56–57 to learn more about life in a squatter settlement.

Fantastic fact 🌍

Half of all people in the UK now live in the outer zone (suburbs) of a city.

To understand what a modern city is like, you need to know how, when and where it started, and how it has developed and changed.

Case study

London – an example of urban development

The Romans first built Londinium beside the river Thames almost 2000 years ago (map **A**). This site was chosen because it was easily defended and the Romans knew that it could become an important route centre. The actual site is now occupied by London's financial district, between the areas now known as the city's 'East End' and 'West End'.

From the earliest times, the western and eastern sides of London have developed in very different ways (photos **B** and **C**). The East End has always been heavily industrialised and housed many of London's poorly paid workers. By contrast the West End is well known for its royal palaces, government buildings, large houses and expensive shops.

The East End developed first. Roman ships could not sail under London Bridge, the lowest bridging point across the Thames, so a port was established downstream of this. Industries developed behind the quays, as well as low-quality housing for the dock and factory workers, many of them refugees who migrated here from mainland Europe.

The West End developed later, around the 11th-century Westminster Abbey, and became the preferred location for royalty, the very wealthy, and the most influential people in government. One reason for choosing Westminster was that the

Fantastic fact

In 1900, London was the world's largest city, with 6.5 million people.

Map A labels:
N
Walbrook
Fleet
Bridge – where river narrows and both river banks are firm ground
To Camulodunum (Colchester)
To Eboracum (York)
Lea
To Verulamium (St Albans)
Ford – where river is shallow enough to cross without a bridge
Thames
To Noviomagus (Chichester)
To Dubris (Dover)
0   2 km
Ermine Street
Watling Street

Marsh (difficult to cross and build on)
Higher land (clay and gravel)
Londinium
Roman road

A Original site of London

B London's East End

C West End of London

prevailing winds blow from the south-west, so any air pollution from the East End's industries blows towards the North Sea, *away* from the West End. The large parks in this part of the city were originally hunting forests for the nobility, and they have been used as recreational areas ever since. It is quite unusual to find so much open space in the heart of a city, where the competition for land is intense.

By the 1980s, sea-going ships had become too big for the East End docks, and most of the industries that depended on them for imported raw materials had re-located elsewhere. The East End's economy had seriously declined and local unemployment had reached record levels. In 1981 The London Docklands Development Corporation was established to redevelop the whole area and give it a new lease of economic life. Photo **D** shows what this area looks like now.

In 2008, construction work began on the site for London's 2012 Olympic Games. This is in the valley of the river Lea, a **tributary** of the Thames, just east of London Docklands. A major aim of the project has been to transform this area of dereliction and deprivation into one where people will want to live and work long after the games have finished. Map **E** shows what has been done to transform the whole of this area.

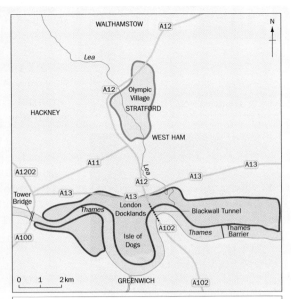

DOCKLANDS	OLYMPIC VILLAGE
22 000 new homes, many in renovated warehouses	High-speed rail link to central London
10 000 upgraded local authority houses	Park and ride car parks
New shopping centres	Wetland habitats restored
New college/university campuses	New bridges across main roads
Indoor sports centre and yacht marina	Olympic Stadium – accommodates 80 000 people
Docklands Light Railway – 10 minutes to central London	Aquatics Centre – future training and competitive events
London City Airport – 500 000 passengers a year	Velodrome – links to cycle circuit and cycle routes across London
New road link to M11 motorway	Olympic Village – will provide 3300 new homes, 30% affordable housing
43 000 new jobs	370 000 m² for future business developments
1500 new businesses	Media centre – office facilities for 8000 people

 E *Modern development of East London*

 **D** *London Docklands today*

Now Investigate ❗

1 Make a sketch of map **A** and annotate your map to show how London's original site and the East End and West End have developed over the centuries. (Do not include detailed information about the Docklands and Olympic Games redevelopment projects.)

2 a Outline the reasons why it became necessary to regenerate London Docklands and the Lea Valley area.

   b Make a well-presented list of the regeneration plans for each area.

Topic link 🔗

What you have learned about urban change will help you when you study Topic 1.11 pages 60–65.

Further research 🔍

Investigate the impact of a previous Olympic Games on its host city. For example, the 2004 Games was in Athens – you could find out how it stimulated economic growth and improved recreational facilities in that city.

Learning objectives:

▷ know that traffic congestion is now a global urban problem

▷ know what strategies are available for reducing traffic congestion

▷ understand that many cities grow so rapidly that they cannot meet people's needs

▷ understand that a lack of suitable housing is one of the main problems caused by city growth

▷ know that squatter settlements are a major feature of most large cities in LEDCs

▷ explain how housing can be upgraded by renovation and redevelopment.

Traffic congestion in urban areas

People travel for a number of reasons, as shown in diagram **A**.

Commuting and going to school or college are the most common reasons for travel. These are also the main causes of traffic congestion because they peak at certain times on work days (graph **B**). The morning and late afternoon/early evening peak travelling times are often called 'rush hours', because of the usually frantic nature of travel at those times. Congestion is worst in the CBD, where many main roads meet, and some of the oldest roads are too narrow for modern traffic.

Now Investigate !

Is there a rush hour in your neighbourhood? What times of the day are the busiest?

Rush hours are a very inefficient use of the resources both of a city and of individual families. Car ownership continues to grow in most countries (see graph **C**), and most commuters prefer to travel alone rather than car sharing. Young children are often driven the short distance to school, instead of walking to school.

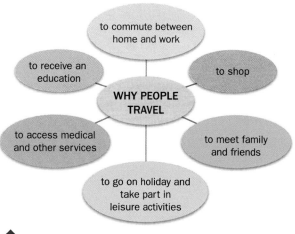

A ▶ Why people travel

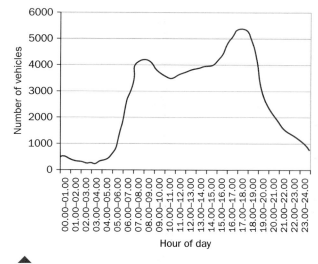

B ▶ The changing volume of road traffic on a typical work day

C ◀ Rising car ownership in India since 2000

Topic link

See Topic 1.11 pages 60–65 to learn more about the effects of pollution in cities.

Traffic congestion wastes fuel and causes air pollution along busy routeways. It is now a common feature of most large settlements, but there are several ways in which it can be reduced, for example by:

- making public transport services more frequent and more affordable
- building rapid transit systems such as underground railways and surface city links (guided buses and trams) – photo **D**
- integrating transport systems, so that train and bus timetables are linked and passengers can transfer easily between different modes of transport
- installing roundabouts and traffic lights and imposing speed restrictions to reduce road accidents
- operating bus lanes on wide roads during rush hours
- making narrow roads one-way and restricting parking along busy or narrow roads
- making busy shopping streets traffic-free and building by-passes and ring-roads to divert through traffic away from city centres
- providing park-and-ride facilities along main routes
- introducing congestion charges for vehicles entering the busiest parts of a city.

 D A section of the Metro Monorail in Sydney, Australia

Fantastic fact

Some places have created a 'reverse-flow lane' to carry in-bound traffic during the morning rush hour and out-bound traffic in the evening – overhead signs tell people which direction it is safe to drive in!

Now Investigate

1 a If your family or a friend has a car, keep a week-long tally of how often it is used for each type of journey shown in the spider diagram.

  b Display your tally-totals in the form of a bar graph, then comment on what your completed graph shows.

2 For each rush-hour period shown in graph **B**, write down its approximate:
- start time
- finish time
- peak traffic volume.

3 Quoting data from graph **C** as necessary, describe how car ownership in India has changed since 2000.

4 Using a street plan or Ordnance Survey map of an urban district you know well, annotate it to show examples of congestion reduction strategies. (Hint: Two of the more common strategies are traffic lights and roundabouts.)

Squatter settlements

Topic link

You can find out more about how people make a living from informal employment, in Topic 3.3 pages 146–53.

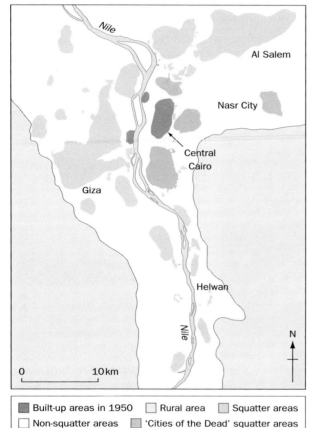

Built-up areas in 1950 | Rural area | Squatter areas
Non-squatter areas | 'Cities of the Dead' squatter areas

A *Squatter settlements occupy a huge part of Cairo – some of these areas have population densities well over 30 000 per km²*

Topic link

See Topic 1.9 pages 48–53 to learn more about land use zones in cities.

Fantastic fact

At least one in seven people on Earth now lives in slum conditions such as squatter settlements.

As a visitor to any LEDC city centre you might think that traffic and pollution were the only serious problems caused by urbanisation. Travelling beyond the centre would quickly change that first impression! This is because you would see huge areas of deprivation (see map **A**) – the squatter settlements, also known as shanty towns – where many people are unemployed and can't afford to live anywhere else. City authorities are aware of the conditions in these areas, but they can't afford to improve them all.

Two of the greatest challenges facing newcomers to LEDC cities are getting a job and finding a place to live. The two problems are connected, because those lucky enough to be in full-time employment may only earn enough to provide food and shelter for their families. Wages are low, even for the employees of transnational companies such as clothes manufacturers. They are far below those earned in the formal sector of employment, by professional people like lawyers. Textile workers receive little money even though they spend many hours each day in difficult working conditions.

Newcomers are desperate to find work, but education in rural areas is very basic, so many migrants are illiterate and lack the practical skills that employers look for. Many immigrant families are so desperate that children as young as 6 years old are sent out to earn money doing informal sector jobs like shoe-shining and peddling cheap goods on the streets.

Life in squatter settlements

In the world's fastest growing LEDC cities like Dhaka, Kolkata and Mexico City, over half of the population are squatters. Some countries have so many squatter settlements that they have their own names for them: *barriadas* in Peru, *favelas* in Brazil, *bustees* in India and *bidonvilles* in north Africa.

Photo **B** shows a typical squatter settlement in India. There are significant problems in areas like this:

- **Disease** There is no effective system of sewage disposal and the dirt tracks between the dwellings serve as open sewers, so disease is easily transmitted. Also, most household waste is dumped outside, where it rots in the open air, attracting rats and flies. Few families have their own water supply, so communal taps have to be shared by up to 50 families. Water-borne diseases such as cholera and typhoid are common, so life expectancy remains low.

- **Poor building construction** These settlements are illegal, so the city's minimum building and safety standards are not applied (photo **C**). There is little incentive to improve the shacks when they are under constant threat of being bulldozed by the city authorities.
- **Risk of fire** Fires can spread very quickly between the shacks.
- **Unsuitable location** Shortage of land means that newcomers often settle in dangerous and unsuitable places, sometimes close to docks, factories or railway lines or on steep slopes.
- **Crime and anti-social behaviour** Domestic stress levels are high, so family breakdown is common. Many children who are abandoned by their parents join street gangs.
- **Lack of education** The city authorities do not recognise illegal settlements, so do not feel the need to provide schools and health centres there.

B Shacks in squatter settlements are made of any available materials

Further research

Use online resources to investigate ways in which people in squatter settlements are positive and do much to improve their quality of life.

Case study

Focus on Dharavi

Dharavi is often called 'the largest slum' in Asia' (photo **C**). It is huge – an area of 3 km² on what used to be a mangrove swamp – right in the centre of Mumbai. It is one of many squatter settlements in this rapidly expanding city, whose population increased from 2.9 million in 1950 to 12 million in 2011. Every day, an average of 250 families migrate to Mumbai, which is partly why 54 per cent of its total population live in such settlements.

Most of the dwellings in Dharavi have no water or electricity and families have to rely on other people to provide what they need – at a high price. In some streets, every household has its own tap, and these families take great pride in hosing down the street to keep it clean. Most workers have employment in the informal sector, such as recycling plastic bottles, oil drums and cardboard boxes. Textile workers cluster together in districts called *kaarkhanas*. People in both types of employment usually work from home, not in factories, so there is serious air pollution and constant noise in many parts of the residential area.

C Dharavi in Mumbai, India – a typical squatter settlement

Now Investigate

1 a List the difficulties faced by shanty town squatters, under these three headings:

Environmental problems   Social problems
Economic problems.

  b Now consider some of the good things about living in a shanty town, again listing your ideas under suitable headings.

2 Describe and suggest reasons for the distribution of Cairo's shanty towns as shown in map **A**.

3 Some Brazilian favelas are being cleared by the authorities, in advance of the football World Cup in 2014. Imagine you are a local newspaper or TV reporter. It is your assignment to file a report on how one favela is being cleared to make way for just a few weeks of football.

How will people in the favela feel? Where will they go? Are the authorities right to do this? Will the clearance improve people's lives?

Ways of upgrading residential areas

Pages 56–57 described the challenges faced by many families living in squatter settlements in LEDC cities, and some of the ways in which they try to improve their quality of life. The following case studies provide information about two different strategies used by poorer countries to reduce the amount of low-quality housing in their cities. They are called self-help and site and service schemes.

Case study

A self-help scheme in Brazil

In this type of scheme, town and city authorities support families wishing to improve their homes. Grants, building materials and small cash loans are provided to help them to start work. Water and sanitation are vital to people's health, so self-help schemes often include standpipes which groups of households can share. People are often encouraged to buy their land, which makes them feel it is worth the effort of making improvements. Whole communities may also be assisted in building schools and health centres.

Roçinha in Rio de Janeiro is one of Brazil's largest *favelas*. It first developed on a steep hillside in the 1950s and now has over 100 000 inhabitants. Its early dwellings were small wood and canvas cabins, but most have since been enlarged and improved with bricks and tiles, and with vital help from the local authority (photo **A**). With its many shops and small businesses, most parts of Roçinha now look more like a well-ordered residential area than a poverty-stricken squatter settlement!

A *A self-help scheme in Roçinha, Rio de Janeiro*

Case study

A site and service scheme in Egypt

Site and service schemes are much more ambitious than self-help schemes. They need enough land to create a whole new development. Water, sanitation and electricity services are provided for each plot before any building starts. In small schemes, the people use the materials they can afford at that time; any improvements can made later, after the families have saved enough money.

B *High-rise flats in 10th of Ramadan City*

The 10th of Ramadan City in Cairo is a good example of such a scheme. This was Egypt's first 'new town' and many of its 500 000 inhabitants live in high-rise blocks of flats (photo **B**) and work on its large industrial estates. New whole-community facilities such as schools, shops, mosques and parks are included in all of Egypt's new towns, which were viewed as the best way of housing Egypt's rapidly expanding population.

Housing problems are not confined to LEDCs. In the 19th century, during the industrial revolution in Europe and North America, millions of migrants from rural areas were accommodated in cheap, rapidly built terrace houses. These now form the inner residential zone of some industrial cities in Europe and North America (photo **C**). By the mid-20th century, many of these needed to be renovated (upgraded) by re-wiring them and fitting new windows, indoor bathrooms and toilets. Those that had deteriorated to become slums were demolished and replaced with new buildings – a more expensive process called redevelopment.

 C Low-quality terraced housing in Harlem, New York

Many people displaced by redevelopment were re-housed in high-rise flats. These were welcomed at the time, because they offered a higher standard of accommodation – but in the process of moving many communities disappeared. These high-rise flats have since become much less popular due to the inconvenience of living in such tall buildings.

Another solution has been to build new towns. These provide all the facilities that people need – including recreational and employment opportunities. In the 1940–60s, the UK built more than 30 new towns, most of them within 50 km of large, overcrowded cities. Singapore, which was a British territory until 1963, built 22 new towns during the same period (photo **D**).

 D A 'new town' area in Singapore

Now Investigate ❗

1 Define clearly the terms 'renovation' and 'redevelopment', to show that you understand the difference between them.

2 List at least eight possible disadvantages of living in a high-rise block of flats.

3 Write a brief 'revision summary' for each of the two case studies on these pages.

4 Imagine that you are in charge of your local area's urban planning department. You have been given a grant of $100 million to improve the quality of life for people in your area. You must invest all of that grant in one of two ways:

   either redevelop just one part of your area, by building a complete new town on that site

   or

   renovate every dwelling in the whole of your local area, using both self-help and site and service schemes.

   a Decide which option *you* would take.

   b Give detailed reasons to justify your decision.

Fantastic fact 🌍

Each of Cairo's new towns houses more than 500 000 people – so they are really 'new cities'!

Further research 🔍

Identify a squatter settlement or other area of low-quality housing in your country or region. Produce a case study about that settlement, including a location map and some annotated photographs to describe it. Add as much detailed information as you can about its dwellings.

1.11 The environmental impact of urbanisation: what causes pollution where you are?

Learning objectives:

▷ know that there are different types of pollution, and how urbanisation can increase the level of each type

▷ understand that urban sprawl can change land use in rural–urban fringe areas

▷ explain how some types of land use can lead to conflict between people

▷ describe some measures that can be taken to reduce the environmental impact of urbanisation.

Our actions and behaviour can damage our local environment. The ways in which we harm our environment are known as pollution (diagram **A**).

Pollution causes some measure of harm to the environment. Wherever people live, work or travel there is some form of pollution. Spend a few minutes thinking about your area – what people do there, and how their activities might pollute it. Consider all types of pollution – some are less obvious than others (take a careful look at the items **A–D** on these pages).

Air pollution

Air pollution is one of the most serious forms of damage in the urban environment. It has many causes, including traffic exhaust fumes from air, road and rail traffic when gases such as sulphur dioxide are emitted. Air pollution is also caused by smoke from houses, factories and power stations. This type of pollution is often worst on very foggy or hot days (photo **B**), because that is when smog – a combination of **sm**oke and f**og** – is most likely to form. Smog is very dangerous to health, and can cause serious breathing problems in people, especially the young and elderly.

Water pollution, e.g. untreated sewage flowing into a river, oil tanker spilling oil into the sea

Air pollution, e.g. exhaust fumes from cars, smoke from factory chimneys, dust from quarries

THE FOUR TYPES OF POLLUTION

Visual pollution, e.g. litter blown about, a natural landscape spoiled by quarrying

Noise pollution, e.g. aircraft flying low overhead, heavy traffic on main roads

A Types of pollution

Other kinds of pollution

Other environmental problems in urban areas include:

● noise pollution – for example from passing traffic and aircraft taking off and landing (diagram **C**)

● water pollution – due to industrial and domestic waste and causing diseases such as bilharzia, cholera, and typhoid

● visual pollution – people have different reactions to new buildings or other constructions, and may consider some offensive to the eye (photo **D**).

B Smog over Tel Aviv, Israel

Fantastic fact

When the Eiffel Tower was built in 1889, many French people thought it was the ugliest thing they had ever seen. Now the French love it, and 'their tower' has become one of France's best-known global images.

Assessing how 'green' cities are

The Mercer Survey assesses how eco-friendly some of the world's largest cities are. Its rank order is used by some large international companies when they are deciding where to build new factories and where their workers might like to live. The Survey awards a score based on six environmental criteria:

- availability of water supplies
- quality of water supplied to homes, factories, offices and schools
- how efficiently domestic and industrial waste is collected and disposed of
- how effectively sewage is made environmentally safe
- how polluted the air is
- the level of traffic congestion.

The Mercer Survey is updated every year. The latest survey puts Calgary, in Canada, at the top of its eco-city list, with 145.7 points. Calgary has many urban parks and its 600 km network of paths is used for recreational activities such as walking, cycling and roller-boarding. Its reputation as a sustainable city helped it to be chosen to host the 1988 Winter Olympic Games.

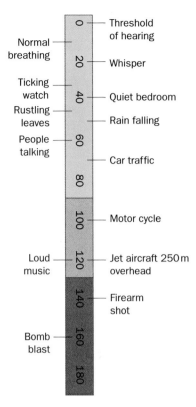

	0 — Threshold of hearing
Normal breathing —	20 — Whisper
Ticking watch —	40 — Quiet bedroom
Rustling leaves —	Rain falling
People talking —	60
	Car traffic
	80
	100 — Motor cycle
Loud music —	120 — Jet aircraft 250m overhead
	140 — Firearm shot
Bomb blast —	160
	180

☐ Safe noise level for most people

☐ Serious risk of hearing loss if noise level continues for more than 8 hours in a day

■ Risk of immediate, permanent loss of hearing

C *Levels of noise*

D *Would you like to have a working wind turbine near you?*

Now Investigate ❗

1. Write down at least five activities in your local community that might cause pollution. Suggest the kinds of pollution they are most likely to cause. You could display your ideas in several ways:

   - as a table, with activities listed in the left column, and their effects described in four other columns – one for each type of pollution
   - as a sketch map, annotated to show the location of each type of pollution
   - as a series of annotated photographs, with each annotation describing a different cause or effect of pollution

   or as a combination of these.

2. a In your opinion, would a wind turbine in your own community be a beautiful (and useful) landmark – or an example of visual pollution?

   b Give reasons for your answer.

Further research 🔍

Find the Mercer Survey online and note the Survey's top 50 ranked eco-cities. Which continent has the most eco-cities? How many are there in your own continent?

The effects of urbanisation on the rural–urban fringe

Topic link

You can learn more about counter-urbanisation in Topic 1.6 page 33.

Urbanisation doesn't just change the centres of towns and cities, it can also have major effects on nearby countryside. Urban areas expand to accommodate their increasing population – a process called urban sprawl. They can also 'urbanise' the rural areas near to them because people:

- have greater mobility, due to improved transport networks
- have more 'spare' money to spend on non-essentials such as holidays and recreational activities like camping and golf
- have longer holidays and more leisure time at weekends
- lead a hectic life working in the city and so prefer to live in a quiet, country village 'retreat'.

It is not easy to limit the impact of urbanisation on rural–urban fringe areas. These areas provide ideal locations for a wide range of land uses such as golf courses, power stations, modern industrial estates, retail parks and supermarkets (photo **A**). Fringe areas are also the kind of place where people seeking a better quality of life wish to live – even if that means having to spend more time and money commuting daily to work. This outward movement of people is called **counter-urbanisation**. It often results in small, traditional villages becoming more suburbanised in character.

In some places green belts around cities have helped to control urban sprawl, by limiting new residential and other developments in rural–urban fringe areas. Another strategy is to build new towns well away from a city's boundaries, which helps both to meet the need for more housing and reduce the rate of urban sprawl (photo **B**).

- Residential area (workforce for retail park)
- Land available for future expansion
- Main road leading to/from motorway nearby
- Retail units selling large items, e.g. furniture
- Large parking area

A Why modern retail parks are located in rural–urban fringe areas

B A new town

Conflict in the rural–urban fringe

Each land use places a different demand on rural–urban fringe areas, often causing conflict between different groups of people. For example:

- a coal-burning power station creates air pollution, and this could increase the health problems of patients in a nearby hospital
- farmers are often involved in conflict because careless visitors can damage their crops or allow valuable animals to stray onto busy roads (diagram **C**)

quarries are often sited in otherwise attractive areas of countryside, but the product (stone) has to be transported to where it is needed for building (houses and other buildings, roads), causing conflict among people living nearby (photo **D**).

- Noise pollution: machinery in quarry, lorries transporting stone from quarry

- Air pollution: dust

- Visual pollution: dust, machinery, exposed rock faces

Topic link

You can learn more about environmental issues in Topic 3.9 pages 188–93.

- Roads: congestion and vibration caused by lorries transporting stone

- Local settlements: affected by noise, air and visual pollution

D *Quarrying has many damaging effects on the local environment*

Now Investigate

1 a Refer to the map extract of Port Louis in Mauritius, on page 259. Copy the table shown right. Complete your table by identifying the various land uses on the rural–urban fringe of Port Louis or by giving a grid reference for the stated land use.

Six-figure grid references	Type of land use
971057 and 987066	
978067 and 978069	
972032 and 984053	
	Industrial estate
985069 and 997065	
	Power substation
	Race course
990038 and 984032	
990039 and 990047	
	Sports ground
964028 and 998022	

b Refer to the map extract of Port Castries in St Lucia, on page 39. Using a table with the same headings as those for (a), state the type of land use that can be found at each of the following grid references:

071479   074482   077490
081501   092499   106494
114518   120508   123503

c Use four colours to highlight the following land uses in each table:

Economic   (including power generation)
Recreation   Transport   Others.

Include a key with each table.

2 What activities take place in the rural–urban fringe of a large urban area in your own region?

3 a Suggest reasons why the rural–urban fringe is the ideal location for at least five of these land uses:

fishing   golf   hospital   modern industrial estates   power station   reservoirs   supermarkets.

b Pair-up at least eight land uses on the rural–urban fringe that are likely to be in conflict, and suggest why. You can use each type of land use more than once.

4 What kinds of pollution and other environmental problems are quarries likely to cause for people living in rural–urban fringe areas? Consider all sources and types of pollution.

Rapid urbanisation creates many problems for the world's cities and the people living in them, but much can be done to make them more sustainable, or 'green'. Some strategies that aim to do this include:

- reducing all forms of pollution – especially air pollution due to emissions from vehicles and factories
- using fewer natural resources such as fossil fuels, for example by making vehicle engines more efficient and encouraging people to use public instead of private transport
- disposing of waste materials in environmentally less damaging ways – mainly by recycling
- improving the natural environment within urban areas by creating more recreational open spaces and planting more trees and other plants.

Case study

Curitiba – Brazilian city leads the way!

Curitiba provides a good example of what can be done to control some of the worst effects of urbanisation. It was a typical Brazilian city that originally developed due to its position on the main beef-cattle route to São Paulo. In the days before motor transport, herds of cattle were driven along this route.

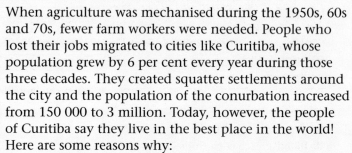

When agriculture was mechanised during the 1950s, 60s and 70s, fewer farm workers were needed. People who lost their jobs migrated to cities like Curitiba, whose population grew by 6 per cent every year during those three decades. They created squatter settlements around the city and the population of the conurbation increased from 150 000 to 3 million. Today, however, the people of Curitiba say they live in the best place in the world! Here are some reasons why:

- **In the 1960s:** Curitiba's new 'Master Plan' is approved. Its aim is to control urban sprawl, reduce city centre traffic congestion, provide affordable public transport and build more direct highways leading out of the city.
- **In the 1970s:**
  - city centre shopping streets are pedestrianised
  - bus-only lanes are introduced
  - many streets are made one-way
  - industrial areas are established on the city's outskirts, where air pollution is less likely to affect the main residential zones (photo **A**).
- **In the 1980s – Curitiba's 'Greenest Decade':**
  - urban 'green zones' are created to protect them from future unsustainable developments
  - the mayor, Jaime Lerner, allocates 1.5 million young trees to deprived neighbourhoods

A Industrial location on the rural-urban fringe of Curitiba

- 17 large urban parks are established, some of them which celebrate different ethnic groups within the city's population (photo **B**).
- **In the 1990s:**
  - botanical gardens are created
  - buses capable of carrying 270 passengers are introduced on the busiest routes – high-speed bus stops called 'tubes' mean that buses have fewer emissions because they discharge and embark passengers at the same time
  - the Bus Mass Transit system reduces car journeys by 70 per cent (a huge saving as cars emit twice as much carbon dioxide as buses do).
- **Since 2000 – the success story continues:**
  - the city introduces sight-seeing buses for tourists, so they don't have to use taxis or their own cars
  - a new technology park is built with research facilities to develop non-fossil fuels
  - Curitiba now has the highest recycling rate in the world
  - buses in the city carry 50 times more passengers than they did 20 years ago
  - 150 km of urban pathways have been created, for use by walkers, cyclists and roller-boarders
  - a city-wide waste re-cycling programme is introduced
  - all bus routes are colour-coded and provided with the size of bus best suited to the needs of passengers using that route (photo **C**).

 B *A park in the centre of Curitiba*

C *A three-section bus and 'tube' bus stop*

Now Investigate !

1 Describe how the city of Curitiba has managed to fulfil each of the four strategies listed at the top of page 64.

2 Describe the activities that take place in the rural–urban fringe of your own town or city, or one very close to where you live. You could create a display, including a sketch map and either drawings or photographs, to show how the land is used now and, if possible, how that land was used in the past.

3 Investigate the environmental problems in a city of your choice (anywhere in the world), and the measures taken to reduce these problems. Three cities to consider are Cairo, Mumbai or Rio de Janeiro.

Fantastic fact 🌍

It is cheaper and more 'green' to use sheep rather than machines to graze Curitiba's parks. Their wool is sold to raise money for local orphanages.

Topic link 🔗

You can learn more about sustainable development in Topic 3.10 pages 194–99.

Volcanoes and earthquakes: why does where you live make a difference?

Learning objectives:

▷ understand about the structure of the Earth and why its surface is always changing

▷ describe where volcanoes, earthquakes and fold mountains are found, and why

▷ explain the effects that natural hazards have on people's lives.

> This is what remains of the area that used to be our home. We have lived in Montserrat all our lives and heard tales of the volcano but we never thought it would affect us. We just carried on farming and fishing as we had always done. How could we have been so wrong? The eruptions destroyed everything and killed one of my best friends. The effects will be with us for a long time to come.

Karney Davis, farmer and fisherman, who lives in the shadow of the Soufriere Hills volcano, Montserrat **A** ▷

Karney Davis

Your constantly changing planet

How would you feel if you lived near a volcano? Perhaps you do! Or perhaps you live in an earthquake zone. If so, is it a scary experience or just something you are used to? Whether you live in such an area or not, the ground under your feet is constantly changing. It is always moving, although often no more than a few millimetres a year. This has been going on since the Earth was formed 4600 million years ago. The powerful forces that make this happen are responsible for some of the world's most dramatic scenery – fold mountains. These forces also create volcanoes and earthquakes, natural hazards that affect millions of people like Karney Davis, a farmer and fisherman who lives in the shadow of the Soufriere Hills volcano in Montserrat (photo **A**).

The structure of the Earth

When it was first formed the Earth was liquid rock but, as it cooled down, the outer surface hardened to become a thin crust. Underneath the crust is the mantle which makes up 82 per cent of the volume of the Earth and is 2900 km thick. This layer is a liquid and flows rather like really hot jam. Underneath are the extremely hot liquid **outer core** and solid **inner core** which, at its centre (6400 km from the Earth's surface), is 5500 degrees Celsius (°C) – diagram **B**.

Plate tectonics

The Earth's crust is broken up into a number of enormous pieces called tectonic plates. There

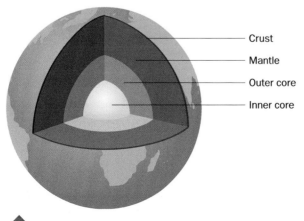

— Crust
— Mantle
— Outer core
— Inner core

B *The structure of the Earth*

are seven major plates, some of which are bigger than continents. These plates are constantly on the move, rubbing against, crashing into or moving away from each other. The edges where this happens are known as plate boundaries or **margins** (map **C**) and it is here that most of the world's volcanoes and earthquakes are found.

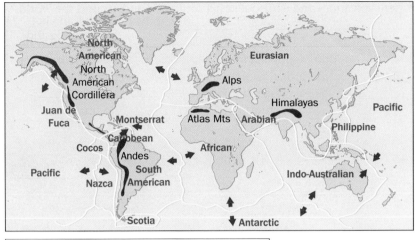

C Tectonic plates, plate boundaries and their direction of movement

Direction of plate movement ■ Fold mountains

Plates are made up of two types of crust. Continental crust is light but very strong. It cannot sink and it cannot be destroyed. Oceanic crust, on the other hand, is heavier and sinks under the continental crust. It is continually being destroyed and replaced. The plates move because they are floating on the extremely hot mantle. The mantle is made of a liquid called magma and the intense heat coming from the Earth's core gives rise to convection currents. These currents push under the plates and cause them to move (diagram **D**).

The study of plate movement and the effects it has on the formation of volcanoes and earthquakes is known as **plate tectonics**.

Fantastic fact

It took more than a billion years for the molten surface of the Earth to cool down enough to form the crust.

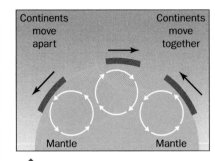

D Convection currents in the mantle

Continents move apart — Continents move together

Mantle — Mantle

Now Investigate

1 Draw an annotated diagram showing the structure of the Earth. Add labels showing the crust, mantle and outer and inner cores.

2 a Name the plate that you live on.

b Name the plates next to your own.

c Describe the direction of movement between your plate and that of its neighbouring plates.

3 Using named examples, describe the formation of fold mountains.

Further research

Search the internet for 'tectonic plates' or 'structure of the earth' to find out more.

The world's greatest mountain ranges are found at converging plate boundaries where the plates are moving together. The rocks that make up these mountains were originally laid down in layers at the bottom of lakes and oceans. As they move together, the plates squeeze these layers and force them upwards as if they are being folded. These ranges of fold mountains (shown on map **C**) can be thousands of metres high and include such giants as Mount Everest and K2 in Asia and Chimborazo and Huascaran in the South American Andes. Many are still rising at a rate of a few millimetres each year.

E Fold mountains such as the Himalayas are formed on plate boundaries

Plate boundaries

Recent earthquakes and volcanoes are found on the edges of the plates making up the Earth's crust. You may know of volcanoes in your region that are not on plate boundaries but these are probably very old and will have moved since the time they were **active**. Map **A** shows the areas where volcanoes and earthquake activity are found around the world.

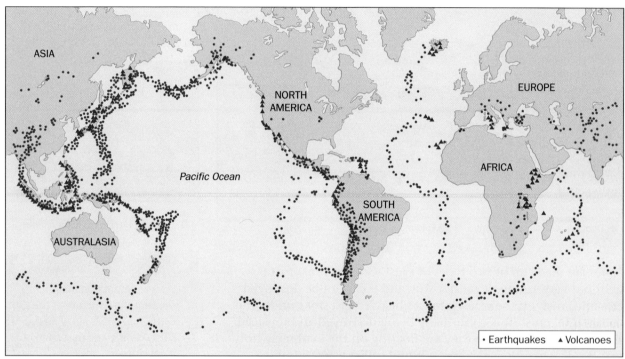

• Earthquakes ▲ Volcanoes

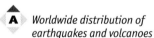
Worldwide distribution of earthquakes and volcanoes

These **zones of activity**, where the plates are in almost constant motion, are the **plate boundaries** or **margins**. These margins can be classified as either constructive, destructive or conservative. A fourth type, a collision margin, consists of two plates of continental crust moving towards each other. It is in these areas that fold mountain ranges are formed.

Now Investigate ❗

Look at map **A**. What patterns can you see in the distribution of earthquakes and volcanoes? You may want to use an atlas to find the names of some of the areas on the map.

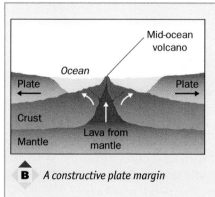

 A constructive plate margin

Constructive margins

When two plates move away from each other a constructive margin in formed. Molten rock (magma) rises from the mantle to fill the gap that is created and this forms new oceanic crust. The process is also known as sea-floor spreading because these margins are found under the ocean. The mid-Atlantic trench, for instance, is widening at a rate of around 3 cm a year, taking Europe further away from the Americas. Earthquakes and volcanoes can both occur in these areas.

Destructive margins

Where plates containing oceanic crust move towards those containing continental crust, a destructive margin is formed. The heavier oceanic crust is forced underneath the continental crust in an area called a subduction zone. Friction (and the increase in temperature as the crust moves downwards) causes the crust to melt and some of the newly formed magma may be forced to the surface to form volcanoes. The structure of a typical volcano formed in this way is shown in diagram **D**. The increase in pressure as the plate is forced downwards can also trigger severe earthquakes.

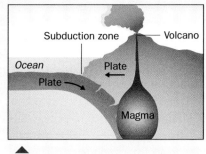

C *A destructive plate margin*

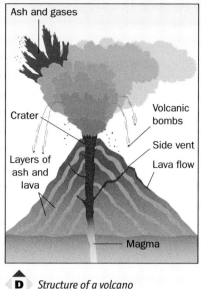

D *Structure of a volcano*

Conservative margins

Where two plates slide past each other (often at different speeds) no new landscape is formed and, therefore, there is no volcanic activity. However, earthquakes can occur at these conservative margins if the plates get stuck. Pressure will build up until it is released, causing the earth to jerk violently. The most famous example of this type of plate boundary is probably the San Andreas Fault in California.

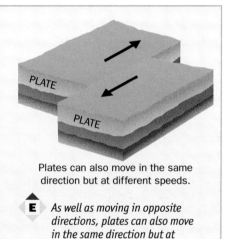

Plates can also move in the same direction but at different speeds.

E *As well as moving in opposite directions, plates can also move in the same direction but at different speeds*

Now Investigate

1 Describe the worldwide distribution of volcanoes and earthquakes. You should include some named examples either from the information on these pages or by using an atlas.

2 a What kind of a plate margin is the plate boundary nearest to you?

  b Describe and explain how the plates are moving at your nearest plate boundary.

  c How does this movement relate to tectonic activity in your part of the world?

3 What is seismic activity and how can it be measured?

Measuring seismic activity

Seismic activity is the name given to the movement of the Earth in an earthquake. Once an earthquake has taken place, it can be measured using a seismograph (or **seismometer**). This is a machine that records how much the Earth shakes and plots this on a graph. The strength of the earthquake (its magnitude) is measured using the Richter Scale. An increase of 1 on the scale means the shaking is 10 times greater, so the damage is likely to be much more severe.

Further research

Put the words 'collision, conservative, constructive margins' into a search engine to find out more about the different activity at plate boundaries.

Why live next to a volcano?

Topic link

There is more information on how people cope with natural hazards in Topic 2.10 pages 120–25.

When volcanoes erupt they can cause huge destruction and many deaths. Despite this, millions of people around the world live near to active volcanoes. This is because of both historical factors and the economic opportunities that volcanoes can bring.

- The land around a volcano is often very fertile – the ash from eruptions forms an excellent soil for growing crops and providing food for animals.
- Farming near volcanoes has been going on for centuries, so small settlements have grown over time into important regional centres.
- More recently, many volcanoes have become tourist attractions and local businesses have sprung up around them, providing much needed employment.
- Despite the economic opportunities, many volcanoes are in poor countries so the people do not have the money to move away when disaster strikes.

Living with an active volcano can bring prosperity to a region but, if it erupts, this can be wiped out in a matter of minutes.

Case study

Living with a volcano in Montserrat

Before 1995 the small Caribbean island of Montserrat was famous as a peaceful, sunshine-filled tourist destination (map **A**). Most of the 11 000 people living on the island – like Karney Davis whom we met at the beginning of this topic – depended on the tourist industry and on farming the fertile volcanic land.

Montserrat sits on the boundary between the small Caribbean plate and the Atlantic plate. These two plates are moving towards each other resulting in seismic activity as the denser oceanic crust is forced downwards under the continental crust.

 The Soufriere Hills volcano on the Caribbean island of Montserrat

The Soufriere Hills eruption

In July 1995 increased activity from the Soufriere Hills volcano (which had not erupted for 400 years) caused the authorities to order everyone to move out of the south of the island. As volcanic activity increased many went abroad to other Caribbean islands or to the UK. By April 1996, the south of the island was empty.

Eventually a huge eruption in June 1997 resulted in five million cubic metres of lava flowing from the dome on top of the volcano down its northern side. Meanwhile, scorching hot clouds of fine ash and small rocks – known as pyroclastic flows – spread out to the north and west. These combined effects killed 19 farmers who had entered the southern exclusion zone set up by the authorities. It was reported that they were gathering crops to feed the people who had moved to other parts of the island. Many towns and villages, including the former capital of Plymouth (photo **B**), were buried and over 60 per cent of the south and central areas of the island became uninhabitable. Some of the major effects of are shown on map **C**.

Further research

Use key words 'Montserrat' and 'Soufriere Hills' to find more information about Montserrat and its volcano.

The aftermath

The population of the island is now around half what it was before the eruptions began and entry to the south is still not allowed. Life has improved for those who remain, as explained by Karney (figure **D**).

The north has seen a great deal of development as housing, schools and hospitals have been built to serve the remaining population. The people who are left are beginning to make a living from tourism again and visitors are being encouraged to take 'volcano tourism' holidays to see the still smoking Soufriere Hills. They can also view the destruction it caused, by taking a boat trip along the island's south coast.

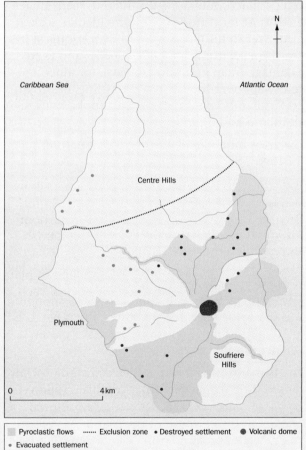

C Post-eruption Montserrat

B Plymouth after the eruption of Soufriere Hills

> Now we're getting back to normal. We have a new home in the north of the island and new jobs taking tourists to see the damage the volcano caused. One day soon we may even be able to go home to the south, rebuild our house and start farming again.

Pyroclastic flows ⋯⋯ Exclusion zone • Destroyed settlement ● Volcanic dome
• Evacuated settlement

D

Now Investigate !

1 Using a named example, outline the reasons why people might choose to live near active volcanoes.

2 Study the map of Montserrat after the eruption (**C**). Using map evidence only, describe the effects of the eruption of Soufriere Hills on both people and the landscape.

3 What will life be like for Karney Davis if he goes back to live in the south of Montserrat? Write a brief essay explaining his thoughts on what he finds.

Skills link

As geographers we tend to use maps with a grid system so that we can accurately locate and identify features. However, as shown on these two pages, maps come in many shapes and forms. More details on how to interpret different kinds of map can be found in Sections 4.1 and 4.2.

Earthquake – Japan 2011

Background

Japan is well prepared for earthquakes. It is located on the borders of the Eurasian, Pacific and Philippine plates and the country experiences about 20 per cent of the world's most serious seismic events. Schoolchildren are taught earthquake drills from a very young age, households keep earthquake survival kits in handy locations, and buildings are made 'earthquake-proof' to sway as the earth moves. Messages are sent to mobile phones within seconds of an earthquake happening, to tell people what to do and where to find help.

The country was well prepared, therefore, for the huge earthquake of Friday 11 March 2011. At magnitude 9.1 on the Richter Scale it was the most powerful ever to hit Japan and the fifth strongest in world history. The earthquake itself caused few deaths and there was relatively little damage (map **A**). It did, however, produce a deadly **tsunami** which swept over the Japanese coastline, destroying buildings, roads and farmland. The wave washed people, houses, trucks and cars both inland and out to sea.

The case study below gives more detail of the greatest natural disaster in Japan's history.

Case study

Tsunami! Japan, 11 March 2011

When earthquakes occur at sea they can jolt the seabed upwards. This creates huge waves which move away from the epicentre in all directions. In the case of the Japanese earthquake the wave quickly travelled the 80 km to the coast at Sendai, the capital city of Miyagi prefecture. As it approached the shoreline and the seabed became shallower, the wave rose to 10 metres high and swept over the coastal defences (photo **B**).

The tsunami spread across the Pacific but, luckily, caused little damage in other countries (photo **C**).

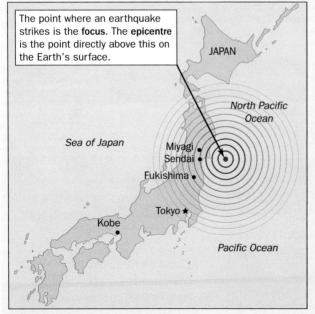

The point where an earthquake strikes is the **focus**. The **epicentre** is the point directly above this on the Earth's surface.

A *The Japanese earthquake of 11 March 2011*

 B *The tsunami hits the coast of Japan*

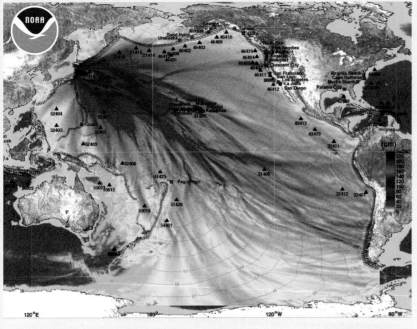

C *The tsunami spreads across the Pacific*

D *Fukushima nuclear power plant*

Within hours of the earthquake taking place, social networking sites on the internet were helping people donate to disaster relief funds and to find out about the location of loved ones. Facebook set up a donations page, Google launched Person Finder and online gaming sites allowed people to donate money to the emergency relief effort as they played.

Fatalities	15 000
Injuries	3 000
Missing	15 500
Evacuated	206 400
People without access to safe water	500 000
Economic cost	US$232 billion

 E *Effects of the Japanese earthquake and tsunami*

Now Investigate !

Use the information here, and on previous pages in this topic, to prepare an A4 page report on the Japanese earthquake. Include information on the causes (including the plates involved) and the effects on both people and the landscape.

Extension
If you want to go further, add extra detail to your report explaining how Japan prepares for earthquakes and how technology helped to deal with the disaster.

Further research 🔍

The 2011 Japanese earthquake is already the most studied in human history – search for extra information on the internet.

Learning objectives:

▷ talk about the differences between weathering and erosion

▷ describe the different types of weathering

▷ explain why some types of weathering break down rocks more quickly than others

▷ investigate the rock features and weathering processes in your local area.

 Landslide showing newly exposed rocks

Topic link

We will look in detail at two agents of erosion through river and marine processes in Topics 2.3 (pages 80–87) and 2.4 (pages 88–95).

Fantastic fact

The oldest known rocks in the world, found in the Australian outback, are minerals called zircons. They are 4.4 billion years old.

Your constantly changing world

Your local environment is in a constant state of change. The rocks underneath your feet are wearing away and will be replaced by others forming elsewhere. For most of the time, these are changes you cannot see. They are taking place in geological time – over hundreds, thousands, hundreds of thousands and millions of years. Occasionally (for instance, when landslides occur), changes may be much more rapid (photo **A**). Even though you cannot see many of the actual processes at work, evidence of them taking place can be found all around you.

Changes due to weathering

All rocks that are exposed on the Earth's surface are attacked by the weather and the atmosphere. Weathering is the wearing away (through decomposition and disintegration) of these rocks *in situ* (that means 'in the same place'). However, after rocks have been broken up, they are occasionally moved by the action of gravity, for example by sliding down a slope.

Changes due to erosion

When the Earth's surface is worn away by moving agents such as water (in the form of either rivers or the sea), ice or the wind, erosion is taking place. One of the important differences between erosion and weathering is that the agent of erosion also *removes* the eroded material (through processes known as transportation). For instance, waves attack a cliff face, break off material and then carry it away.

Weathering and erosion are not just destructive processes but are part of the cycle by which new rocks are formed. After being broken up, rock fragments and particles are transported by the agents of erosion (such as rivers and the sea) and finally deposited to form new rocks. Again, this cycle is on a geological timescale and can take millions of years to complete.

Rocks and weathering

The Earth's crust is made up of many different types of rocks. These rocks have different features that influence the speed of weathering and erosion. Resistant rocks, for instance, are very hard and will not weather easily. Because of this they often make up hills and mountains and steep valleys. On the coast, resistant rock will form steep cliffs and stand out as a headland.

The following rock features all have an influence on weathering:

- **Mineral composition:** rocks contain many different types of minerals and these undergo chemical reactions when they come into contact with water and air. One example can be seen when iron is exposed to oxygen. The normal grey or blue colour which the mineral gives to rocks changes to a reddish-brown – this process is known as rusting (photo **B1**). Other changes can be seen in rocks containing copper, mica or feldspar, for example. The chemical reactions produce stresses within the rocks and can lead to their disintegration over time.

- **Grain size:** variations in grain size (and hardness) lead to different rates of weathering. Rocks with coarse grains, including sandstone (photo **B2**), are likely to be weathered and broken down more quickly than fine-grained ones like basalt (photo **B3**).

- **Presence of lines of weakness:** some rocks are formed from layers of living things or sediments that originally built up at the bottom of lakes or the sea. Limestone, for instance (photo **B4**), is composed of the remains of shells and skeletons of small organisms that lived in the sea millions of years ago. The lines between these layers (known as bedding planes) together with vertical cracks, called joints, make rocks weaker and more likely to weather (photo **C**).

These properties are important in figuring out which rocks will be eroded quickest. They are also useful in understanding the different types of weathering described on the following pages.

Topic link

To learn more about the Earth's crust go to Topic 2.1 pages 66–73.

Further research

Type 'geology' and 'toolkit' into your search engine to find more information on rock features and rock types.

C Bedding planes and joints in rocks

Now Investigate

1. What is the difference between weathering and erosion?

2. Explain how different rock features influence weathering.

3. Have a look at some maps and photographs of your local landscape.

   a What are the main characteristics of the environment around you?

   b Can you think of ways in which the landscape may have been affected by the different rock features described on these pages?

 Some rock types

1 Rusting in iron-bearing rocks

2 Sandstone

3 Basalt

4 Limestone

Types of weathering

There are three different types of weathering:
- physical (or mechanical) weathering
- chemical weathering
- biological weathering.

The type and rate of weathering (how quickly it happens) is often dependent on the climate, particularly temperature and precipitation, as explained below.

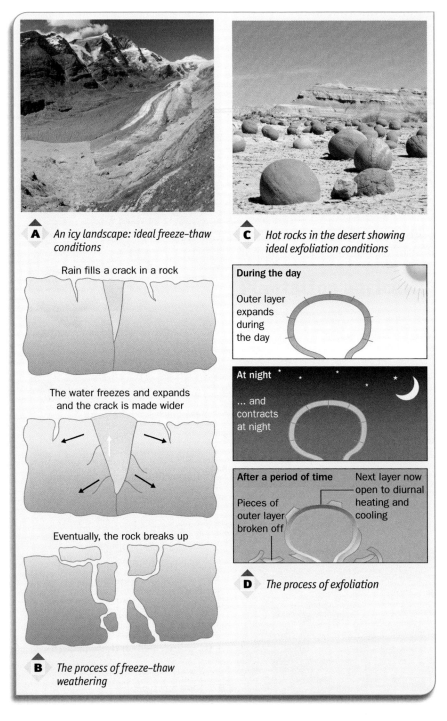

A An icy landscape: ideal freeze–thaw conditions

Rain fills a crack in a rock

The water freezes and expands and the crack is made wider

Eventually, the rock breaks up

B The process of freeze–thaw weathering

C Hot rocks in the desert showing ideal exfoliation conditions

During the day

Outer layer expands during the day

At night

... and contracts at night

After a period of time

Pieces of outer layer broken off

Next layer now open to diurnal heating and cooling

D The process of exfoliation

Physical weathering processes

Physical weathering processes involve the breakdown of rocks into smaller pieces or fragments without any change in their chemical composition. They are usually driven by the climate and take place in areas of bare rock where there is no influence from plants.

Globally, the most important and widespread physical weathering process is freeze–thaw (or frost-shattering). This occurs in areas where there are big changes in diurnal temperature (the difference between day and night), such as in high mountains and other cold climates (photo **A**). Water, from rain, dew or melting ice and snow, finds its way into cracks or pores in a rock. If the temperature then drops (usually at night) the water can freeze. As it freezes, the water expands by up to 9 per cent and exerts a great deal of pressure on the rock. Under higher daytime temperatures, the ice melts and takes up less room, only to freeze again at night. This repeated process of freeze and thaw eventually weakens the rock so much that pieces break off (diagram **B**).

In warmer climates, the physical weathering process of exfoliation or onion-skin weathering becomes more important (photo **C**). Rocks expand when they are heated during the day, and contract at night. In some areas, such as the hot deserts, extreme variations in the diurnal temperature range lead to repeated expansion and contraction and this weakens the rock so much that the outer layers break off, in much the same way that an onion is peeled. When one layer has been removed the process begins again on the layers underneath (diagram **D**).

Chemical weathering processes

Chemical weathering is when rocks are broken down by a change in their chemical composition. It is most likely to occur in warm, moist climates.

Carbonation is the most important type of chemical weathering in areas of limestone rock. Rainwater contains chemicals picked up in the atmosphere. These chemicals, including carbon dioxide, make the rainwater acidic and it reacts with the alkaline limestone. The rock dissolves into a solution rich in calcium carbonate. In tropical areas, higher temperatures and high rainfall increase the rate of carbonation.

Oxidation occurs when oxygen in the air reacts with minerals in a rock. The addition of oxygen changes the structure of the rock and can weaken it. The simplest type to see is when iron minerals, which are normally blue or grey in colour, rust into a reddish-brown colour (see photo **B1** on page 75). The rock crumbles much more easily when oxidation has taken place.

Biological weathering processes

When plants are involved in the weathering process, both physical and chemical weathering can take place, together described as biological weathering. As plant and tree roots enter cracks in rocks and begin to grow, their strength can force the rocks apart. Over time, the rock will be weakened and it disintegrates into fragments.

Plant roots also produce chemicals that can react with the rocks they are growing on and change the chemical composition. In some cases the plants also extract specific minerals. Lichens, for instance, take iron from rocks to help their growth.

Animals can contribute to biological weathering. Burrowing animals and smaller creatures including earthworms help break down weaker rocks. During their lifetime, and when they die and decompose, animals may also release chemicals that contribute to the weathering of certain types of rocks.

E

Further research 🔍

Using key words such as 'weathering processes', 'landscape' and 'rock type' will bring up plenty of further information on the different types of weathering.

Fantastic fact 🌍

Limestone is one of the world's most widespread types of rock. It is quite likely you will find some near you.

Now Investigate ❗

1 Study photos **E**.

 a Identify which weathering processes are taking place in each of the pictures.

 b Describe the processes involved. You should use diagrams to help explain the physical weathering processes.

2 a Use an atlas to research the climatic conditions for both tropical and temperate climatic zones. Use this data to complete a larger copy of the table below.

 b For each of the climatic factors you have researched, explain how it affects both the type and rate of weathering.

	Tropical climate	Temperate climate
Annual temperature range		
Diurnal temperature range		
Precipitation		

Weathering: global case studies

Case study

Madagascar: Stone Forest

Limestone landscapes provide some of the world's most dramatic examples of chemical weathering, and many limestone areas are popular tourist attractions. The Tsingy de Bemaraha National Park and reserve in Madagascar consists of rows of knife-edged towers separated by canyons with a maze of wet caves underneath.

Slightly acidic water has caused weathering by carbonation and solution. Caves and tunnels have formed underground and the roofs have collapsed, leaving the towers exposed on the surface. Less dramatic landscapes, formed in a similar way, can be found in China, Russia, Slovenia, Mexico and England.

> **Further research** 🔍
>
> Dramatic pictures and further information can be found by searching the internet using 'Madagascar' and 'Stone Forest' as key words.

A Stone Forest, Madagascar

Case study

Uluru (Ayer's Rock), Australia

Perhaps the best-known example of exfoliation is Uluru (formerly known as Ayer's Rock), the sacred site of Australia's Aboriginal peoples.

Uluru is a huge slab of sandstone rising 350 metres above the surrounding flat landscape. Located in an arid area the rock is subjected to high temperatures (often over 40°C) during the day, and cold mornings – especially in winter – when the temperature can drop below 5°C. These extremes put severe strain on the rock, through expansion and contraction, with the resulting onion-skin weathering pattern. Chemical oxidation also affects the rock, as the iron-bearing minerals on the outer surface react with oxygen and then rust to give Uluru its distinctive red-brown colour.

B Uluru, Australia

Fieldwork skills: Investigating weathering in your local area

Think about the characteristics of your local environment, the landforms and climate and some of the rock features discussed earlier in this topic. Decide on some hypotheses you can test to find out about the kinds of weathering going on where you live.

For example, if you live in a hot climate you may want to ask: is exfoliation the most important type of weathering? If you live in a cold climate you may want to ask: is freeze–thaw the most important process? Other questions could look at the relative importance of chemical or biological weathering.

To investigate these hypotheses you need to look for evidence from rock samples in the field. Note down their characteristics under the headings shown on diagram **C**.

Now look at the evidence you have gathered and use your knowledge to decide on the types of weathering occurring where you live.

Skills link

Understanding and identifying weathering processes may help with your coursework for Paper 3 if the focus is on the formation of selected landforms (for example along rivers or at the coast), or if there are questions on physical geography processes as part of the investigations on Paper 4.

C

Fresh or weathered? Rough or smooth?

Fresh rocks will not have started to weather yet. They are more likely to have rough edges. Rocks sitting out in the sun or rain will develop rounded edges from erosion and may give clues about the weathering that has affected them.

Hard or soft?

You can test a rock's hardness by trying to scratch it with a screwdriver or a coin. If it is very soft, it may even scratch easily with your fingernail. Soft rocks are often much more susceptible to chemical weathering.

Colours

Rocks will look different depending on how close you are to them, so make a note of their colour from 2 metres away and also close up. Remember that rocks change colour under chemical weathering processes, so think about the minerals that may be affected.

Layers

All sides of the rock need to be looked at before you decide if it contains layers or not. They can be extremely close together, very wide apart, straight or irregular and are often hard to see. Both physical and biological weathering rates increase if rocks have these lines of weakness.

Grain size

Look closely to see if there are any large particles such as sand and remember that coarse grains are eroded more quickly than fine ones.

Further research

If you're interested in finding out more about how to identify the most common types of rock, search for 'rock identification table' on the internet, or look for one in your local library.

Now Investigate

Describe the landscape of either Stone Forest in Madagascar (photo **A**) or Australia's Uluru (photo **B**). Explain fully the processes that formed the features.

Your constantly changing river

It is likely that you live fairly near to a river. Even if you don't, there will be at least one major river in the country where you live. You will also have heard of the world's major rivers, such as the Mississippi, the Amazon and the Nile. What you may not know is that all these rivers have similar features (although on different scales) and that these features are formed by similar processes.

River processes

Diagram **A** shows a river's long profile from its beginning (the source) to its end (the mouth). Along the profile it gets flatter and the bottom of the river (the bed) gets smoother. The volume of the river also increases as more water is added to it.

Rivers have **energy** which means they do **work** as they flow. This work is either **transportation** or **erosion**. When a river runs out of energy, deposition occurs.

Processes of transportation

Rivers carry a lot of particles of different sizes – boulders, pebbles, sand and silt. Collectively this is known as a river's **load**. A river with lots of energy will be able to carry much more load.

A ▲ *A river's long profile*

Source

Highland

Lowland

Mouth

Upper	Middle	Lower
Mainly erosional processes	Erosional and depositional processes	Mainly depositional processes

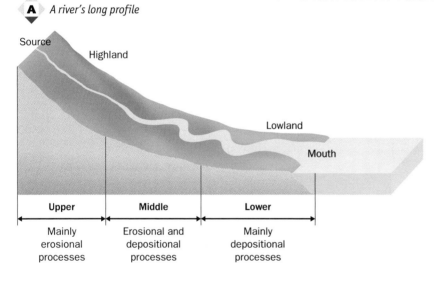

Minerals that are dissolved in the water are transported in **solution**

The lightest particles of soil and sand make the river look cloudy as they are carried along in **suspension**

Smaller particles such as stones bounce along the river bed by **saltation**

The heaviest particles – large stones and rocks – roll along the bed in a process called **traction**

River bed

Processes of transportation **B** ▶

Processes of erosion

Transported material is used by a river to erode its banks and bed. As the velocity (speed) of a river increases, so does the amount of load it can carry and the amount of erosion it can carry out. There are four ways (processes) in which a river erodes:

- hydraulic action – when the force of the water knocks particles off the sides (banks) and the bed of the river
- corrasion – when sand and stones carried by the river rub against the bank and bed and knock off other particles; this process is also known as abrasion
- attrition – when boulders and large stones carried by the river (normally along the bed) collide with each other and break up into smaller pieces
- corrosion – when acids in the river dissolve the rocks that make up the bank and bed; this process is also known as solution.

Topic link

Look back to Topic 2.2 on pages 74–79 to remind yourself of a definition of erosion.

Deposition

Along a river's long profile there will be places and conditions that cause it to slow down, for example following a spell of dry weather, when it spreads out over a wide valley or when it flows into a lake or the sea. As it slows it loses energy and can no longer carry its load. Deposition takes place with the largest stones dropped first, then pebbles, sand and smaller particles (photo **C**). Dissolved material may remain in solution and eventually be carried out to sea.

 Deposition in a river

A river's course

Along its length a river goes through three stages known as the upper, middle and lower courses. The length of each of these will depend on the particular conditions where the river flows, such as the type of rock, the landscape and the climate. In the different courses different processes of erosion, transportation and deposition are dominant. The effectiveness of these river processes will vary according to how much water is in the river and how fast it is flowing. It will also depend on the nature of the load which, in turn, is influenced by the bedrock the river is passing over.

Now Investigate !

1 Write down definitions for the following:
   a river features: *source   mouth   bed   bank   load*
   b river processes: *corrasion   attrition   hydraulic action   corrosion*

2 Find out about your nearest river. If possible, use a map to draw a rough sketch of its long profile. Include sites of interest such as major towns, cities and other landmarks.

3 a Why does deposition take place in a river?
   b Explain how this deposition takes place, referring to the different types of material carried by a river.

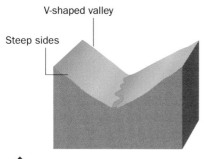

A *Cross-section of a river in the upper course*

As you have seen on the previous pages, different processes operate in each course of the river. These give rise to very different features and landforms.

Features of the upper course

Near the source the river has a steep-sided, V-shaped valley with a steep gradient, and the water in the river channel occupies most, if not all, of the valley floor (diagram **A**). The load is large because it has not had enough time to be eroded. Most of the load is found on the bottom of the river so it is known as bedload. There is plenty of friction between the water and the large bedload and this can slow down the river's velocity.

Common features of the upper course include waterfalls, rapids and potholes (**B**).

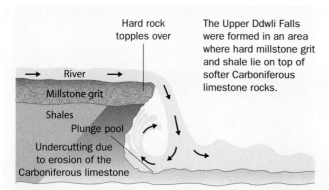

B

The Upper Ddwli Falls were formed in an area where hard millstone grit and shale lie on top of softer Carboniferous limestone rocks.

The formation of the Upper Ddwli Falls, South Wales

Rapids form in areas of differing rock type

Upper Ddwli Falls, South Wales

Potholes forming in a river

Waterfalls

Waterfalls tend to occur where the river crosses resistant rock and the softer rock downstream is eroded more rapidly. Under the waterfall a plunge pool is formed where erosion by hydraulic action and abrasion is greatest. The harder rock is undercut and collapses, causing the waterfall to retreat upstream.

Potholes

If the river bed is uneven, pebbles can become trapped. Swirling currents cause the pebbles to rotate and erode circular holes in the river bed.

Alternating bands of hard and soft rock crossing the course of a river form an uneven bed and areas of turbulent water called rapids.

Fantastic fact

At almost 1 km from top to bottom, Angel Falls in Venezuela (also known as Kerepakupai Meru) is the highest waterfall in the world.

Features of the middle course

In the middle course the river channel is wider and deeper with gentler valley sides and a wide flood plain (diagram **C**). The river has been joined by others (its tributaries) and these have added more water to the channel. Lateral erosion (from side to side) becomes more important than vertical erosion and the river begins to bend (or meander) across its flood plain. Bedload size decreases and there is more chance of deposition.

The main features of the middle course are meanders and oxbow lakes (**D**) but waterfalls are also common.

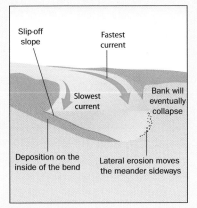

C *Cross-section of a river in the middle course*

Meanders

The velocity of a river can change across river channel. There will be more erosion on the side where velocity is greatest. On this faster-flowing side the river cuts into the bank and becomes deeper. Increasing deposition on the opposite side of the river forms a slip-off slope and the meander takes on a fairly common shape. Meanders maintain this shape as they erode sideways and move across the flood plain.

Oxbow lake

As the loop of a meander gets bigger, the outsides of the bend get closer together. It becomes known as a 'swan's neck' meander. In times of flood the river may erode a new channel to straighten its course and completely cut off the meander neck. The old channel becomes an oxbow lake as its ends are sealed by deposition. Eventually the oxbow lake may dry out completely and become filled by vegetation.

Formation of a meander

1 Swan's neck meander

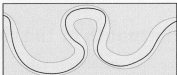

2 River takes shorter route in times of flood

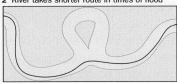

3 Oxbow lake is cut off as river starts new route

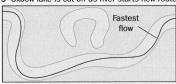

Deposition occurs at the ends of the oxbow lake

D *Formation of an oxbow lake*

Skills link

Make sure you are able to identify specific river features so that you can sketch them accurately when doing fieldwork. Go to Topic 4.4 pages 222–25 for more information on how to draw field sketches.

Remember: You should learn how to draw diagrams and label them to explain the formation of various river features. But don't forget you also need to know the processes behind their formation.

Now Investigate

1 Describe the differences in channel cross-section between the upper and middle courses of a river.

2 Draw diagrams with detailed labels to explain how **a** waterfalls and **b** meanders are formed.

3 Explain how changes in rock type in the upper course can lead to different river features.

River features (2)

Features of the lower course

In the lower course near to the mouth the river is broad and deep (diagram **A**). The bedload is transported in either suspension or solution and deposition becomes the most important process. The river is fast-flowing because there is very little friction with the bed, banks and load.

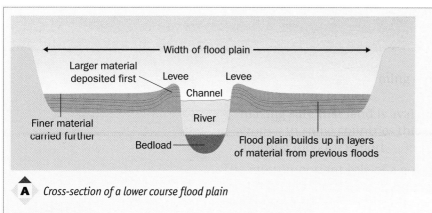

A *Cross-section of a lower course flood plain*

The river meanders across its flood plain – the area either side of the channel which floods if the river bursts its banks. The wide flood plain in the lower course is covered in clay, silt and sand from flooding events (known as alluvium). The river channel's edges have natural ridges called **levees**. When the river floods, the largest particles are deposited first, building the levees up higher with each successive flood. Finer material is spread out in layers over the rest of the flood plain.

Now Investigate

Is your nearest river in its upper, middle or lower course? Can you identify any of the common river features in your local river? If possible, go and make field sketches to show what they are like.

The mouth of the river

The river channel can take on a number of different forms when it reaches the sea (or a major lake). These forms will depend on the rock type, the strength of the waves and tides and the amount of load being carried by the river. The river may end in a wide, deep estuary, which is especially useful for shipping, or it could finish as a narrow mouth. In many cases a delta may mark the end of a river's long profile.

Case study

The Mekong delta, Vietnam

Deltas form when rivers carry lots of sediment. As it reaches the sea, a river's velocity slows down dramatically and massive deposition occurs. As sediment is dropped and blocks the water flow, the river divides up into separate channels called distributaries. Deposition continues, the delta forms and it builds upwards and outwards. Photo **B** shows this happening at the end of Vietnam's Mekong river.

The travel guide company Lonely Planet describes the Mekong delta as 'a watery landscape of green fields and sleepy villages, everywhere crisscrossed by the brown canals fed by the mighty Mekong River'. The delta is formed of silt deposits dropped as the river enters the sea. These deposits continue to extend the shoreline by as much as 80 metres a year. The river is so large it has two tides every day.

The sediment that forms the Mekong delta is very good for farming and provides the soil that produces enough rice in the area to supply the whole of Vietnam and have some left over for export (photo **C**). The delta is also home to many fish farms as well as the growing of sugar cane, fruit, coconut and shrimp. The good farming has led to the delta becoming one of the most densely populated regions in the country.

Although it is currently very productive, there are fears for the future of the Mekong. China has so far built (or planned) eight dams in the upper reaches of the river (photo **D**). The effects of this downstream could include increased salt in the soil and a loss of fertility that could lead to a drop in rice production. There is also evidence that rainfall patterns are changing and there are more drought years which is leading to reduced flow in the river channel.

Most importantly, perhaps, could be the effect of climate change on the delta. As it is so low-lying the delta could easily flood if the sea level rises because of melting ice caps and higher ocean temperatures. There are fears that, if current predictions about flooding are correct, some areas of the delta will become uninhabitable over the coming decades.

 Satellite image of the Mekong delta

Fantastic fact 🌐

More than 60 million people depend on the Mekong river and delta for their livelihood.

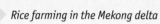 *Rice farming in the Mekong delta*

 Hydro-electric power on the Nam Tha river, Laos

Further research 🔍

Using 'Mekong delta' as a search term will help you access plenty of information to develop this case study.

Topic link 🔗

For another river case study, go to Topic 2.10 on pages 120–25 for information on flooding in Bangladesh.

Now Investigate ❗

1 Describe the formation of a flood plain and explain the processes that are involved.

2 Describe the layout and features of the Mekong delta as shown on photo **B**.

3 a Using a named example, describe how a river delta is formed.

   b Explain some of the economic opportunities that the delta may present.

   c Outline some of the threats that may face people living in the delta in the future.

The world's great rivers

The world's greatest rivers often play a very important part in the history and development of the countries where they are found. They have a huge impact on the people, the economy and the landscape, which continues to the present day. Many of these rivers provide excellent case study material, and they still have the standard features of the upper, lower and middle courses.

Case study

The mighty Mississippi, USA

The Mississippi is North America's longest river. At its source, at a height of 446 metres above sea level at Lake Itasca in Minnesota (map **B**), it is just over a metre wide and half a metre deep. If flows through a series of lakes, and passes over a number of important rapids, before dropping 20 metres at the Falls of St Anthony in Minneapolis. The falls were originally a large waterfall, but they have now been straightened and smoothed by engineers, and a channel with locks has been added to help boats continue up the river (photos **C**).

Many tributaries, such as the Missouri, Illinois, Wisconsin and Rock, add water to the river, vastly increasing the amount of load it can carry. Different types of rock mean that in some sections the river is channelled through 60-metre deep gorges while in others it meanders out over a wide flood plain (photo **D**).

Flooding on the Mississippi

At various points along its course the Mississippi has built up its bed so that it flows above the level of its flood plain. Huge deposits have created natural levees and these have been artificially strengthened to stop the river overflowing its banks. Other flood prevention measures have also been put into place, such as the building of dams and channels to take water out of the main course. Despite these efforts there have been several major floods over the last fifty years. Following particularly severe floods in 1993, many scientists and engineers argued that floods were a natural part of the river's life and that prevention measures should be abandoned. However, it is difficult to do this when so many people live along the river's flood plain.

One of the worst areas for flooding is the point where the river finally enters its delta at the Gulf of Mexico and spreads out through a number of distributaries. Very careful management is needed here in order to stop the build-up of sediment causing even more floods.

- The total area covered by the river and its tributaries (called the **river basin**) is the fifth largest in the world (map **B**).
- At 3800 km it is the second longest river in the USA (after the Missouri).
- The river releases almost 600 million tonnes of load each year – along its course and into the sea.
- The flood plain is 200 km wide at its widest point.
- The Mississippi flows through 10 states.
- The river carries 13 per cent of all freight traffic in the USA.

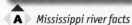

A Mississippi river facts

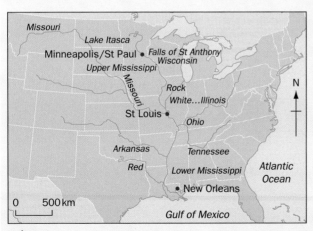

B The course of the Mississippi river

C ▲ *The Falls of St Anthony 150 years ago (left) and today (right)*

◀ **D** *The meandering Mississippi*

Topic link 🔗

There is more information on the impact of the Mississippi on people and the landscape in the Case Study on Hurricane Katrina in Topic 2.10, pages 120–25.

Skills link 🔗

It is important that you can identify river features on maps as the basis for answering questions on how these features are formed. For more information on how to do this check out Topic 4.1 pages 204–05.

Fantastic fact 🌍

In 2002, the Slovenian endurance swimmer Martin Strel swam the whole length of the Mississippi in 68 days.

Learning objectives:

▶ describe and explain the processes of coastal erosion, transportation and deposition

▶ draw annotated diagrams to illustrate each process and its associated landforms

▶ use case studies to provide examples of each coastal process and landform.

Specialised ecosystems develop along coastlines, with plants and animals adapting to extreme – and constantly changing – habitats.

Coastal processes

Coasts around the world **A** ▶

Now Investigate (!)

If you are familiar with a coastline in your region, try to answer these questions as fully as you can. Otherwise use some of the photos **A** to help you.

- What are the main landscape features, such as cliffs, that can be seen on your chosen coastline?
- How is the coast likely to be affected by high tides and strong winds?
- How is it used?
- Is it a safe place to visit / live and work ... or is it sometimes dangerous?

Topic link

Look back at Topic 2.1 pages 66–73 for more on earthquakes and tsunamis.

Photos **A** shows a variety of coastal environments around the world. Coasts may be on high or low land, in wet or arid (very dry) locations, and be densely vegetated or with little plant life.

Coasts are constantly changing. Every high tide brings some minor change; every storm brings much greater changes. The main agent of change is the sea itself – the power and effects of its waves. But coasts are also affected by earthquakes and tsunamis, weathering, and changing sea levels.

Waves are created by the wind blowing across the sea's surface. In mid-ocean, waves appear to rise up and down but in fact what we see is the effect of a circular motion *within* the water. As each wave approaches the shore, the gradient of the sea bed becomes steeper and the sea shallower. Contact with the beach slows down the wave, causing it to rise higher and eventually to 'break'. Breaking waves cause water to rush up the beach (swash) then draw the water back down the beach (backwash).

High, powerful waves are the result of windy conditions. The distance the wind blows over the sea (fetch) and the length of time it blows, also contribute to the height and strength of waves (map **B**).

Two very different types of wave affect coastlines: constructive waves build up beaches and destructive waves remove material from them (diagram **C**).

In a similar way to rivers, waves erode, transport and deposit materials. Coastal erosion involves the same four processes – attrition, abrasion, solution and hydraulic action. Weathering processes also break up exposed rock surfaces above the high-tide line. Much of the sea's load is made up of sediment which is transported and then deposited in the sea by rivers. Material is also weathered and eroded at the coast itself. When waves become less powerful, the water cannot transport as much sediment, so deposition occurs (see pages 92–95).

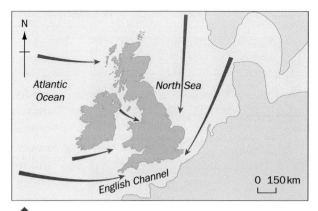

 B *The directions of maximum fetch affecting the coastlines of the British Isles*

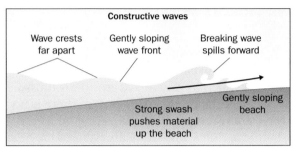

Swash is stronger than backwash, so waves run gently up the beach – material is carried onto the beach and deposited there.

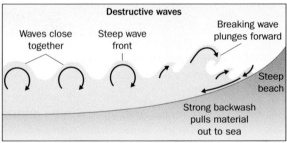

Backwash is stronger than swash, so waves crash onto the beach – material is eroded from the coastline.

 C *The features of constructive and destructive waves*

Fantastic fact

The biggest wave ever recorded was caused by an earthquake off the coast of Alaska on 9 July 1958; its height was an incredible 530.5 metres.

Topic link

Look back at Topic 2.3 pages 80–87 to check the main processes of erosion.

Skills link

Check out Topic 4.4 pages 224–25 to see how to draw, annotate and label a sketch.

Now Investigate

1 Briefly describe *either* the most interesting memories you have of a visit to the coast *or* what you might see and do during a visit to the coast.

2 In what ways are constructive and destructive waves different?

3 Draw a series of annotated sketches to tell the story of how the processes of weathering, erosion and deposition take place.

3 Describe and explain the factors that affect the power of a wave. Illustrate your answer with fully annotated diagrams.

4 Choose two of the photographs included on these pages. Practise your field-sketching skills as if you were actually at the coast. When you have completed this topic, add annotations to demonstrate your understanding of the processes at work at each location.

Coastal erosion

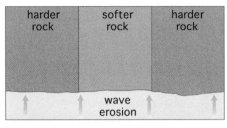

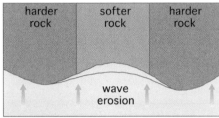

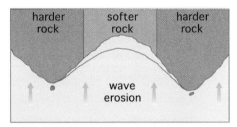

 A *Development of headlands and bays*

Now Investigate ❗

1 Describe the main differences between a bay and a headland.

2 Draw a labelled diagram to illustrate the formation of each of these landscape features:

   a bay and headland coast

   b notch

   c wave-cut platform.

The rate of coastal erosion depends on a number of factors, for example the:

- geology of the area – softer rock such as clay is easily eroded, whilst harder rock, for example granite or chalk, is more resistant
- type of wave – destructive or constructive
- shape of the coastline – bays are often sheltered from the full force of the sea while headlands are exposed (diagram **A**)
- width of the beach – beaches absorb wave energy and protect the coastline from the power of the waves, so a wider beach gives more protection.

Cliffs and wave-cut platforms

Cliffs are steep, sometimes vertical, rock outcrops along a coast (see photo **A**, top right on page 88). You might think that all cliffs are made of hard, resistant rock, but they can also be formed of softer rocks such as clay. Wave erosion is most intense at the base of a cliff face – especially where there is no beach to absorb wave energy. Large waves breaking on a cliff face combine hydraulic action with strong abrasion to erode a wave-cut notch (diagram **B**). As the notch develops, it gradually undercuts the cliff above, eventually leading to cliff collapse and inland retreat and creating a wave-cut platform.

Cliffs formed of resistant rock usually retreat at a steady rate. However, where the rock is weaker, the process of undercutting can suddenly accelerate the slipping and slumping of cliff materials.

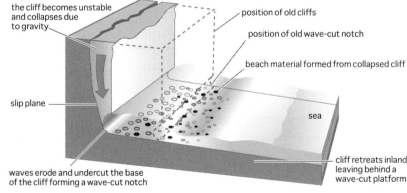

the cliff becomes unstable and collapses due to gravity

position of old cliffs

position of old wave-cut notch

beach material formed from collapsed cliff

slip plane

sea

waves erode and undercut the base of the cliff forming a wave-cut notch

cliff retreats inland leaving behind a wave-cut platform

 B *Development of a wave-cut platform*

Caves, stacks and stumps

Even the most resistant rocks contain some weak points which are eroded more easily than the surrounding rock. Even a small crack or fault can start the erosion sequence shown in diagram **C**.

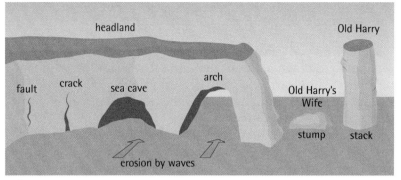

C Erosion from cave to stack to stump, demonstrated by the Old Harry Rocks, Dorset, southern England

Coastal erosion on the Australian coast

Port Campbell National Park, in Victoria, south-east Australia, has a range of coastal features including arches, caves, dunes, islands, beaches, stacks, stumps and cliffs. The cliffs are made of soft limestone, which are weathered and eroded by storms from the wild Southern Ocean. The exposed rock faces are chemically weathered by high levels of salt spray, and pounding waves undercut the cliffs at sea level.

This 'heritage' coast is so rich in spectacular features that it is now protected by National Park status. Its world-famous landforms include 'The Twelve Apostles' and 'London Bridge' (photo **D(i)**) – which is now known as 'London Arch' (photo **D(ii)**). The 45 metre high stacks on this stretch of coast were called 'The Twelve Apostles' to attract tourists, and they became so popular that helicopter tours of the area have become an additional tourist attraction. Over 2 million people now visit the area every year.

(i)

(ii)

D Until 5 January 1990, this feature was known as 'London Bridge' (i) – and then the sea broke through and it became 'London Arch' (ii)

Fantastic fact

Holderness, in eastern England, is Europe's fastest eroding coastline. Parts of it retreats 2 metres every year!

Topic link

See Topic 2.2 pages 74–79 to learn more about weathering of eroded material.

Case study

Great Barrier Reef

Further research

Investigate the development of other erosional features within the Port Campbell National Park, such as the stack system known as the Twelve Apostles.

Now Investigate

Using diagram **C** to help you, describe and explain the sequence of events that occurred to produce the feature in photo **D** (ii). (Hint: Begin with the headland being attacked by wave action.) Include an annotated diagram – or a series of diagrams – to illustrate your answer.

Coastal transportation and deposition

On pages 88–89 you learned how the sea is able to transport material up and down a beach. Here we see how sediment moves along a beach and learn about the features that can form when it is re-deposited. Diagram **A** explains the process known as longshore drift, which is so powerful that it can remove all the beach material from a stretch of coast. On many beaches that experience longshore drift, long wooden fences, called groynes, are built down the beach to reduce the movement of material (photo **B**).

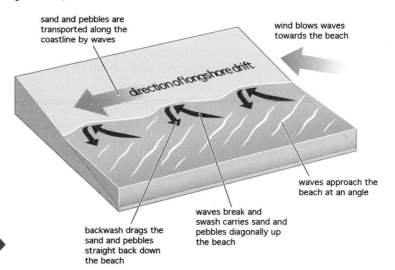

sand and pebbles are transported along the coastline by waves

wind blows waves towards the beach

direction of longshore drift

waves approach the beach at an angle

waves break and swash carries sand and pebbles diagonally up the beach

backwash drags the sand and pebbles straight back down the beach

The process of longshore drift ◀ **A** ▶

Material transported by the sea is later deposited, often in sheltered bays or where the coastline changes direction. Beaches are the result of deposited sand, shingle or pebbles. These materials are often well sorted by size. Usually, the larger the sediment, the steeper the beach is likely to be.

Sand dunes are often found at the top of a wide beach, but they are not really coastal features, because they are formed by wind, not by the sea. Sand that is blown inland from a beach is deposited when the wind speed drops, forming a series of ever-shifting dunes. If they are not held in place by special vegetation such as marram grass, dunes can extend far inland (photo **C**).

Photo **D** shows how a typical spit, with its long, narrow ridge of sand and shingle, grows outwards from the coast. Spits develop where longshore drift is strong and the coastline suddenly changes direction.

Spits that continue to grow across a river estuary, or a bay, are known as bars, and a lagoon often forms behind the bar (diagram **E**). Like all coastal landforms, bars are temporary features in the landscape. Eventually, either sea currents change direction and break through, or the lagoon fills with sediment deposited by a river flowing into it.

Where a spit begins to grow across a river mouth, a salt marsh often develops on the sheltered (inland) side of the spit. Fine sediment builds up in this shallow water and is eventually

▲ **B** *Where there are groynes, there must be longshore drift!*

Further research 🔍

Find out why marram grass is particularly suited to helping to establish vegetation cover in a dune system.

colonised by halophytes (salt-tolerant plants). Further sedimentation increases the height of the salt marsh so that it is submerged less often. Most salt marshes form a network of tidal creeks – shallow inlets which fill with sea water at high tide. These fragile environments provide an ideal habitat for waders and other migrant birds.

C *A sand dune system in Natal, Brazil*

D *Development of a spit: Farewell Spit, South Island, New Zealand*

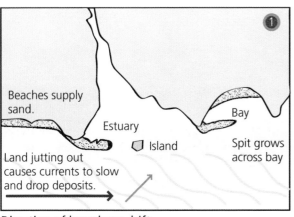

1

Beaches supply sand.

Estuary

Island

Bay

Spit grows across bay

Land jutting out causes currents to slow and drop deposits.

Direction of longshore drift

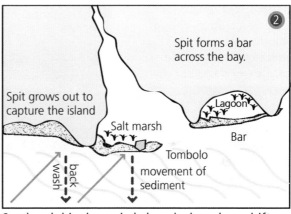

2

Spit forms a bar across the bay.

Spit grows out to capture the island

Salt marsh

back wash

movement of sediment

Tombolo

Lagoon

Bar

Sand and shingle carried along by longshore drift

Prevailing

Wind

Waves

E *Like spits and bars, tombolos are low-lying ridges of deposited material, but they link offshore islands to the mainland. A tombolo forms a causeway which can give access to the island at low tide but is submerged at high tide.*

Now Investigate

1 Describe how sediment is transported along a beach. Illustrate your answer with an annotated diagram.

2 Explain what you understand by the terms spit, bar and tombolo. Your answer should include diagrams with labels that highlight both the similarities and the differences between these three depositional features.

3 Lagoons and salt marshes are indirectly the result of coastal deposition. Explain why they are both only short-term landscape features.

4 Use any two of the illustrations on these pages to practise your field sketch drawing and annotating skills.

F *Features of a typical salt marsh*

A coastline of deposition

Just as in many parts of the world coastlines are constantly being eroded, in many other areas the sea continually creates new features.

Case study

Coastal deposition in New Zealand

Omara Spit is located on the north-eastern coast of North Island, New Zealand. It is a stable area of land that has developed as a result of marine deposition. Its gentle, low relief has made it an ideal location for the development of a major golf resort and it provides shelter for the harbour of Whangapoua.

Omara Spit, North Island, *New Zealand*

Further research 🔍

The Ordnance Survey map shows some ways in which this part of North Island, New Zealand is used. Use Google Street View to discover more about people's activities along this coastline.

Topic link 🔗

See pages 201 and 224–25 to help you answer these questions.

Now Investigate ❗

1 Match each of these grid references to one of the coastal features:

340326   355322   378321

beach   island   spit

2 List as many pieces of map evidence as you can which prove that the feature between 350320 and 390313 has existed for many years.

3 Locate grid references 331343 and 358315.

  a For each of these sites, state whether it is likely to be a zone of erosion or deposition.

  b Give reasons to support your answers.

4 Suggest reasons why there is a headland at Te Rehutae Point.

5 a Draw a sketch map of the depositional feature between grid references 350320 and 390314.

  b Annotate your sketch to show the most likely direction of the prevailing wind and the movement of beach materials due to longshore drift.

  c Add key information about natural vegetation and human activity in the area.

  d Use your sketch to help you describe how depositional features such as this are formed.

  e Give reasons why the sheltered area behind the feature is 'swamp' land.

6 Produce a short case study of a bar or a tombolo. Include an annotated sketch of its location and its main depositional features.

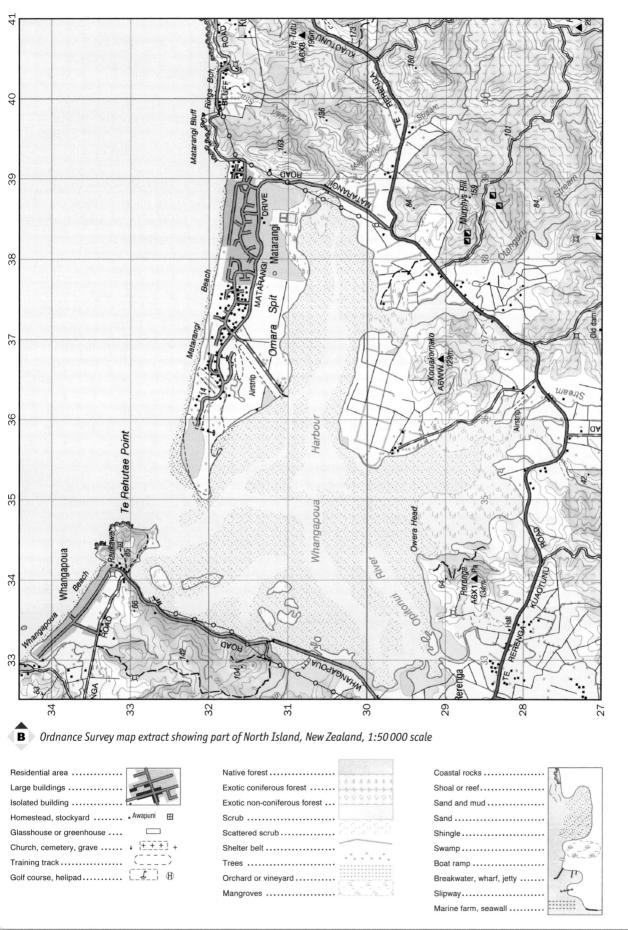

Residential area		
Large buildings		
Isolated building		
Homestead, stockyard	▪ Awapuni	⊞
Glasshouse or greenhouse		
Church, cemetery, grave	⊹	+
Training track		
Golf course, helipad..........		Ⓗ

Native forest	
Exotic coniferous forest	
Exotic non-coniferous forest ...	
Scrub	
Scattered scrub	
Shelter belt	
Trees	
Orchard or vineyard	
Mangroves	

Coastal rocks	
Shoal or reef....................	
Sand and mud	
Sand	
Shingle	
Swamp	
Boat ramp	
Breakwater, wharf, jetty	
Slipway......................	
Marine farm, seawall	

2.5 Coral reefs: are coral reefs doomed?

Learning objectives:

- describe the conditions required for the development of coral reefs

- describe the formation of the three main types of reef

- use a case study to illustrate your understanding of coral reef ecosystems.

Topic link

See Topic 3.5 pages 162–67 to learn more about tourism in coastal regions.

You may live in a part of the world where you are able to visit a coral reef, or you may never have seen one – but there is a chance that they affect your life in some way! They protect coastlines around the world from the effects of erosion, allowing coastal communities to live and work in safety. They are also a major source of income from fishing and tourism, provide must-see tourist destinations – and are home to over a quarter of all marine species.

The term 'coral' has two meanings. It is both the community of tiny marine organisms called polyps that live in and build reefs, and the reef itself (photos **A**). Reefs are made of limestone or calcium carbonate ($CaCO_3$), which is produced by the polyps. It is the algae which live alongside the polyps that give a healthy tropical reef its bright colours – coral itself is white.

Most reefs grow in warm seas, ideally with a temperature of 26–27°C and are found in moving, shallow clear water. The salinity (salt content) and temperature of the water need to remain the same throughout the year, as coral is very sensitive to any change in its environment. Ideal conditions occur in tropical seas between the latitudes of 30°N and 30°S, near to land. Map **B** shows the worldwide distribution of coral reefs.

Photos **C** illustrate the three basic reef types:

- **Fringing reefs** are found near the shorelines of islands or landmasses. They grow in coastal zones that are already protected by a larger barrier reef.
- **Barrier reefs** develop further from the shoreline, often separated from the land by a lagoon.
- **Atoll reefs** are associated with volcanic islands. They look similar to barrier reefs, but are found only around submerged oceanic islands.

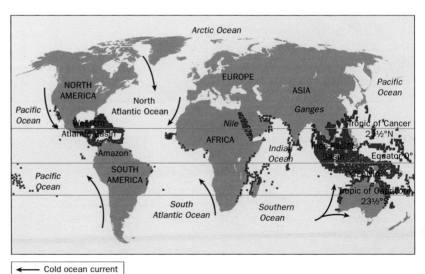

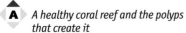
← Cold ocean current

 A A healthy coral reef and the polyps that create it

B World map to show the distribution of coral reefs

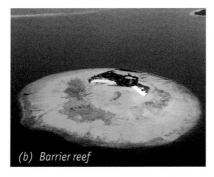
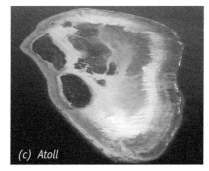

(a) Fringing reef   (b) Barrier reef   (c) Atoll

 C The three main types of coral reef

Coral reefs have a major role in both the tourist and fishing industries within the tropics. They protect coastlines by absorbing wave energy, and so act as a defence against the sea. However, reefs are dying at an alarming rate – a process called coral bleaching. The polyps within coral die when the environmental conditions change, for example the sea temperature rises or the water becomes polluted. About 10 per cent of the world's reefs are already dead, and a further 60 per cent are endangered.

Marine Protection Areas (MPAs) are increasingly important for reef conservation. These MPAs restrict damaging activities whilst promoting reef restoration, biodiversity and protection. Traditional, sustainable fishing practices are also being re-introduced to reduce damage to reefs.

The main threats to coral reefs are from various forms of human activity and from global climate change. Tourism, fishing and coral mining all affect reef systems. Pollution creates many issues, including turn-off from agriculture (pesticides and fertilisers) and from tour activities, as well as marine pollution (such as rubbish and oil spillage from ships). Climate change affects coral reefs in many ways, with rising sea levels, increasing sea temperature, the effect of greenhouse gases, acid rain and air pollution.

Fantastic fact

The annual global value of coral reefs is estimated at $375 billion.

Now Investigate

1 List the ideal environmental conditions for coral reef development.

2 Make a display of annotated images to show the three different types of coral reef, and some different varieties of coral.

3 a Why is it important to protect coral reefs?

   b Suggest how coral reefs can be protected in the future.

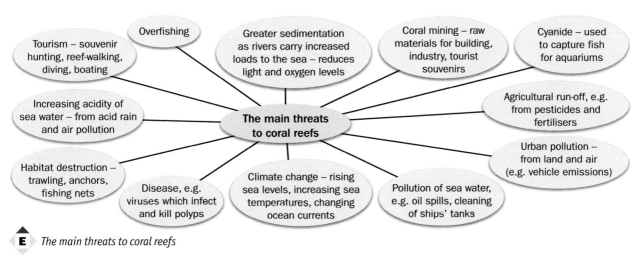

E The main threats to coral reefs

While there are coral reefs in many parts of the world, the most extensive of all is the Great Barrier Reef off the north-east coast of Australia.

Case study

The Great Barrier Reef, Australia

Australia's Great Barrier Reef (map **A**) is so large it can be seen from outer space! It is not a single structure but is made up of thousands of individual reefs and 900 islands. The Great Barrier Reef is home to a huge diversity of species, many of which are vulnerable or endangered. The reef alone comprises over 400 species of coral.

However, like reef systems around the world, the Great Barrier Reef is now endangered as never before, primarily because of threats from human activities.

Threats to the reef

- **Climate change** – possibly the greatest threat of all, because coral cannot tolerate environmental change. Major coral bleaching events occurred in 1996, 2002 and 2006, and scientists believe that by 2030 such events will occur every year. Rising sea temperatures also cause some species of fish to migrate to cooler waters, which in turn affects food chains across the reef (diagram **B**).
- **Pollution and declining water quality** – these are also major issues (diagram **C**). Agricultural activities in Queensland are the main source of pollutants in the Coral Sea.
- **Overfishing** disrupts food chains and can have a very dramatic effect on reef systems. One such effect, due to overfishing of the giant triton, is

Map labels:
N

Warrior Reefs

Great Barrier Reef

Coral Sea

Osprey Reef

Pacific Ocean

Cairns Reef
Arlington Reef
Holmes Reef
Douglas Shoals
Cairns
Flinders Reef
Lihou Reef

Marion reef

Slashers Reefs

Townsville
Whitsunday Is
Swain Reefs

Hook Reef

AUSTRALIA

Saumarez Reef
Queensland

Brisbane

0   500km

—— Boundary of the Great Barrier Reef Marine Park
—— Boundary of World Heritage Site

A *The Great Barrier Reef*

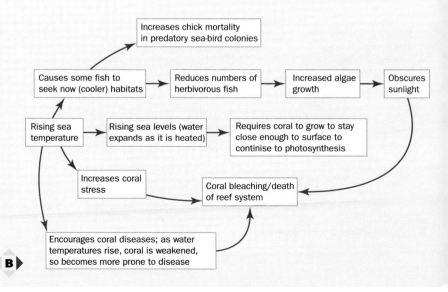

Increases chick mortality in predatory sea-bird colonies

Causes some fish to seek now (cooler) habitats → Reduces numbers of herbivorous fish → Increased algae growth → Obscures sunlight

Rising sea temperature → Rising sea levels (water expands as it is heated) → Requires coral to grow to stay close enough to surface to continise to photosynthesis

Increases coral stress

Coral bleaching/death of reef system

Encourages coral diseases; as water temperatures rise, coral is weakened, so becomes more prone to disease

Effects of a rising sea temperature **B**

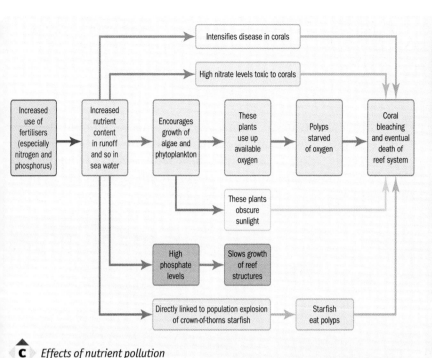

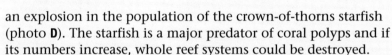

C *Effects of nutrient pollution*

(a) Giant triton

(b) Crown-of-thorns starfish

D *Two species key to the reef's survival – or destruction*

an explosion in the population of the crown-of-thorns starfish (photo **D**). The starfish is a major predator of coral polyps and if its numbers increase, whole reef systems could be destroyed.

- **Shipping** can also damage coral. In April 2010, a bulk coal-carrier ran aground on a reef, spilling over 4 tonnes of its fuel.
- **Tourism** – visitors are the greatest human threat to the reef system but they are one of Australia's main sources of income. Tourism is therefore increasingly being 'managed' to promote ecological sustainability.

Much of the reef is protected by the Great Barrier Reef Marine Park Authority (GBRMPA). It is also a World Heritage Site. Sustainability is the aim of the management strategies. However, the main environmental threat is climate change – which is a global rather than a purely national issue.

Fantastic fact

A single crown-of-thorns starfish can consume 6 square metres of living reef in a year!

Now Investigate

1   Create a display of images showing healthy and bleached coral. Annotate your work to show the causes and effects of coral bleaching, and highlight the conditions necessary for healthy coral growth.

2   Write a short brochure for tourists visiting a coral reef, explaining what they should and should not do when visiting such areas, and why this is important. This could take the form of a Code of Good Practice which includes five things that visitors should do and five things they should *not* do. Illustrations could show the effects of breaking the Code.

3   How can tropical storms and changing sea levels affect coral reefs? Think about environmental changes caused by these events. You could use online or library resources to help you with this activity.

Further research

Create a case study similar to the one on these pages for a coral reef system of your choosing. If you live in a tropical area, you may like to investigate a reef in your own region.

Topic link

You may find the information in Topic 2.11 pages 126–31 helpful in learning more about the impact of human activity on the environment.

Learning objectives:

▷ define the terms *weather* and *climate*

▷ describe the distribution of the world's main climate zones

▷ use climate graphs to describe annual rainfall and temperature patterns.

Fantastic facts

Earth's extremes of weather include:

• highest annual rainfall is in Mawsynram (north-east India): 11 872 mm/year

• lowest annual rainfall (and longest drought) is in Arica (Chile): 0.76 mm/year and a drought lasting 173 months

• hottest inhabited place is Dallol (Ethiopia): daily maximum temperature averages 41.1°C

• sunniest place is Yuma, Arizona: 4050 hours of sunshine each year.

The weather affects us all. Take a few moments to look out of the window and observe what the weather is like now. Then, before you answer question 1, think back to what it was like when you came to school this morning – and how it might affect the things you do today.

A *Weather around the world*

Weather is the state of the atmosphere at a given time. It can change very rapidly – even in quite small areas. Our weather is due to several elements within the atmosphere affecting each other. Photos **A** show you a variety of weather events in locations around the world.

Now Investigate

1 a What is the weather like as you look through your window?

   b Is the weather always like it is today where you live? Hint: Is it usually stable and predictable, or very changeable?

   c If it is changeable throughout the year, are there recognisable seasons where you live?

2 For each of the photos **A**, identify the elements of the weather that you can see *and also* those that you have to imagine by observing their effects.

3 Describe how the weather event in each image may affect the lives and economy of the people who live in that place.

4 Using your own knowledge, suggest a country or even a city where each photograph might have been taken – and at what time of the year.

As geographers, we are interested not only in day-to-day weather events but also in finding out what the weather is usually like around the world. This idea of 'typical' weather is known as climate. It is defined as average (mean) weather over several decades, or at least 30 years. By 'averaging out' elements of the weather such as temperature, precipitation and sunshine hours, we are able to disregard extreme and/or unusual weather events and identify what the weather is usually like in different places. This helps us to understand how weather actually 'works'. It also shows us that, for most of the time, the processes at work in the air behave in predictable ways. Map **B** is a simplified map of global climate distributions. Each climate type can be represented by a climate graph – just four are included on this map.

Topic link

See Topic 4.3 page 220 to learn how climate graphs are constructed.

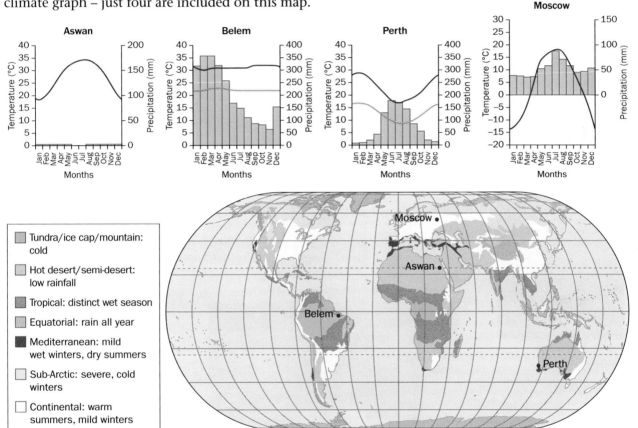

B Distribution of the world's main climates

Now Investigate

1 Describe the global distribution of climate types shown in map **B**. Make sure you include tropical rainforests and tropical deserts when you do this. Hint: Start close to the Equator and use compass directions and the named lines of latitude to locate places.

2 Choose two of the four climate types shown on map **B**.

  a State where in the world each climate type occurs.

  b Describe each of your chosen climates, using data from the map to help you. (Refer to page 220 for help if necessary).

Topic link

Refer to Topic 2.8 pages 108–13 and Topic 2.9 pages 114–19 for help with these questions.

Further research

Investigate recent extreme weather events in your own country or region.

2.7 Measuring the weather: how can you investigate the weather

Learning objectives:

▷ name and recognise the equipment used in a weather station

▷ describe the appropriate method of measuring each element of the weather

▷ record and display weather data appropriately

▷ explain how clouds form and recognise the main cloud types.

Can you tell how hot – or cold – it is where you are today? By looking around, you should be able to spot clues about the temperature. Is the sun shining? What sorts of clothes are people wearing? Is any method of heating or cooling turned on? This gives an idea of what the temperature is – but can you measure and record it precisely? Is there a thermometer in your classroom?

Measuring and recording the weather

Weather is observed, measured and recorded at a weather station. Ideally this should be located on open ground to minimise the effects of local relief and any built-up areas. The basic equipment required for a weather station is shown in figure **A**. Thermometers are always kept inside a Stevenson Screen, and other equipment is sited close by.

Maximum-minimum thermometer

Rain gauge

Shields instruments from rain, wind, sun

Cabinet may house: dry-bulb thermometer, barometer, hygrometer, maximum-minimum thermometer

Located in open area, away from buildings and tall vegetation

Painted white to reflect sunlight

Cabinet at least 1.5 metres above the ground, and slatted, to allow free flow of air

Door faces away from direct sunlight

Hygrometer

Anemometer

Barometer

Wind vane

 A The Stevenson Screen and equipment for a weather station.

Measuring temperature

Temperature is measured using a special type of thermometer. This is a maximum-minimum thermometer, designed to record both the highest and lowest temperatures in a 24-hour period (figure **A**). Diagram **B** shows how to read data from this type of thermometer and how to re-set it after the information has been recorded. Like all other weather data, temperature must be logged daily and at the same time each day. Thermometers used for weather recording have to be kept in the shade. This is why a Stevenson Screen is so important, because we measure the *air* temperature – not the temperature in direct sunlight, which can be several degrees higher.

Fantastic fact

The Stevenson Screen is named after a 19th-century Scottish engineer called Thomas Stevenson. As well as being a pioneering meteorologist, he was also famous for designing lighthouses.

Skills link

See Section 4.3 pages 212–16 to learn more about how a climate graph is constructed.

Now Investigate

1 Write a step-by-step guide to instruct another student how to measure and record air temperature accurately.

2 a What is a Stevenson Screen used for?

  b Where would you locate a Stevenson Screen within your school's grounds?

  c Justify your decision to locate it at this site.

3 Draw an annotated sketch to show where, why and how you would set up a rain gauge.

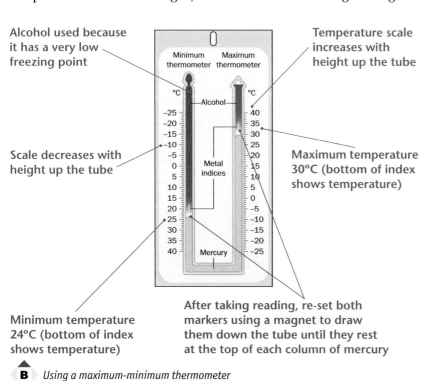

Alcohol used because it has a very low freezing point

Temperature scale increases with height up the tube

Scale decreases with height up the tube

Maximum temperature 30°C (bottom of index shows temperature)

Minimum temperature 24°C (bottom of index shows temperature)

After taking reading, re-set both markers using a magnet to draw them down the tube until they rest at the top of each column of mercury

B *Using a maximum-minimum thermometer*

Measuring rainfall

Rainfall is measured using a rain gauge, which must be located well away from trees and buildings so that water dropping from them does not distort the data. Information is usually recorded every day in a simple table and then used to plot a graph. Bar graphs are usually used but, if the data is to be displayed alongside temperature in a climate graph, a histogram is appropriate.

More complex weather measurements

Measuring relative humidity

Relative humidity describes the amount of water vapour in the air. Air contains water vapour due to evaporation and transpiration. How much it holds depends upon its temperature, because warm air can hold more vapour than colder air. Diagram **A** shows you how a wet and dry bulb thermometer (a hygrometer) is used to calculate the humidity of the air. The greater the difference between readings on the two thermometers, the drier the air and the lower the relative humidity. Relative humidity is always stated as a percentage: 50% is considered to be 'dry' air, while 100% is as wet as air can be and is described as being saturated. The humidity of the air is important because it tells us whether or not it is likely to rain – the closer the humidity is to 100%, the more likely it is to rain.

Measuring relative humidity.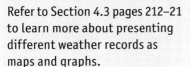
After taking these measurements you would need to use a table for calculating the difference between the two thermometer readings in percentage terms.

Two standard mercury thermometers

Read current air temperature from 'dry' thermometer

Keep bulb of thermometer in saturated sock

Dry bulb   Wet bulb
Temperature °C

Read temperature from 'wet' thermometer (usually lower because of effect of evaporation from sock: this uses heat)

Sock – must be kept saturated with end in bowl of water

Skills link

Refer to Section 4.3 pages 212–21 to learn more about presenting different weather records as maps and graphs.

Measuring air pressure

Air pressure, or atmospheric pressure, is the force put on the Earth's surface by the weight of air above it. Pressure varies from place to place around the world because of the Earth's rotation and differences in temperature and altitude (diagram **B**). However, temperature is the most important factor because when air is warmed, it rises. As it rises, areas of low pressure form at the Earth's surface. Rising air cools, becomes denser and eventually sinks back down to Earth. This causes high pressure conditions. A barometer is used to measure air pressure, which is then mapped, using isobars.

Observing and measuring wind

Differences in pressure on the Earth's surface cause air to move from areas of high pressure to areas of low pressure. This air movement is known as wind. Meteorologists record two

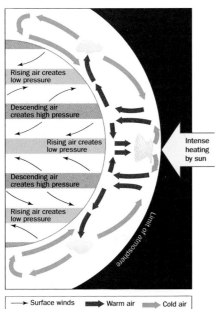

Rising air creates low pressure

Descending air creates high pressure

Rising air creates low pressure

Descending air creates high pressure

Rising air creates low pressure

Intense heating by sun

Limit of atmosphere

→ Surface winds   ➡ Warm air   ➡ Cold air
Cloud   High pressure   Low pressure

B *Global pressure belts*

different sets of information about the wind: its direction and its speed. As when measuring rainfall, we also note when wind is absent.

- **Wind direction** is recorded using a wind vane (see figure **A** on page 102). It is usual to do this at least once every hour, as wind direction can change frequently. The arrow points in the direction from which the wind is blowing.
- **Wind speed** is measured using an anemometer (see figure **A** on page 102). This instrument is rotated by the movement of the air. The number of revolutions is recorded on a meter and automatically converted into kilometres per hour (km/hr). Alternatively, wind strength can be estimated using the Beaufort Scale (diagram **C**).

Fantastic fact

The strongest gust of wind ever recorded was 408 km/hr. It hit Barrow Island, Australia, in 1996.

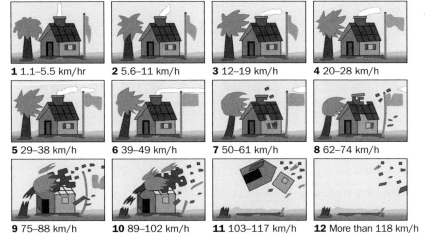

1 1.1–5.5 km/hr **2** 5.6–11 km/h **3** 12–19 km/h **4** 20–28 km/h

5 29–38 km/h **6** 39–49 km/h **7** 50–61 km/h **8** 62–74 km/h

9 75–88 km/h **10** 89–102 km/h **11** 103–117 km/h **12** More than 118 km/h

◀ **C** ▶ The Beaufort Scale

Digital equipment

Professional meteorologists often use digital measuring and recording equipment (photo **D**). They also use a range of aerial and satellite images to help them track cloud movements and record changes in the upper layers of the atmosphere. Electronic weather stations have one great advantage: they are able to monitor and measure the weather all the time, observing, recording and transmitting information instantly.

▲ **D** ▶ A digital weather station

Now Investigate ⓘ

1 Write a sentence for each of these pieces of equipment, stating what it records, and the unit of measurement used:

- anemometer
- barometer
- hygrometer

2 Write a step-by-step guide to instruct a younger student how to measure and record relative humidity.

3 Keep a diary of wind strength in your local area for the next seven days, using the Beaufort Scale as your guide. Record your data at least three times every day. Then write an account of how you undertook your work and the problems you might have encountered.

4 Draw a wind rose graph to illustrate the data in the table below:

	Monday	Tuesday	Wednesday	Thursday	Friday	Saturday	Sunday
Direction of prevailing wind	SE	E	SE	SE	S	E	Calm

Clouds

A cloud is a visible mass of water droplets or ice crystals suspended in the atmosphere. Clouds form when air is unable to absorb any more water – it becomes saturated. This usually happens when air cools, because cooler air cannot hold as much water vapour as warm air. Therefore condensation occurs and clouds form. Clouds are classified into three main types:

- **cirrus clouds** – high-altitude clouds, often described as being 'wispy'
- **stratus clouds** – sheet-like in appearance
- **cumulus clouds** – often described as being 'bubbly', with huge rounded tops, but also described as being rolled or 'rippled' clouds.

As stratus and cumulus clouds can occur at high, middle or low altitudes, these three categories are subdivided to include information about the altitude of the cloud (diagram **A**).

When meteorologists record cloud type, they also assess how much cloud there is in the sky – the more cloud there is, the greater the chance of rain. Unlike all other weather measurements, calculating cloud cover lacks precision. It is done by estimating how many eighths (oktas) of the sky are obscured by cloud. This information is recorded by shading-in segments of a small circle (diagram **B**).

When you have collected all your weather observations, your data should be recorded on a single weather log sheet. If you have access to a computer, you could set up a spreadsheet on which to record your data.

Fantastic fact

The tallest cloud ever recorded, on 28 August 1990, reached a staggering 19.8 km measured from top to base.

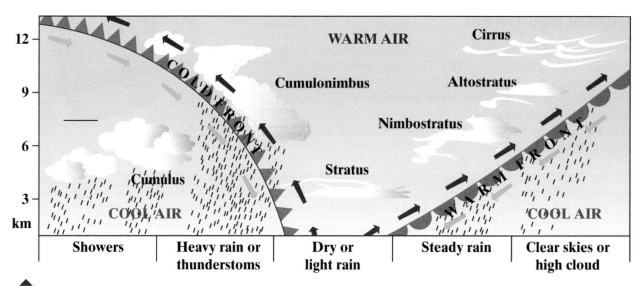

A *Different cloud types and their characteristics*

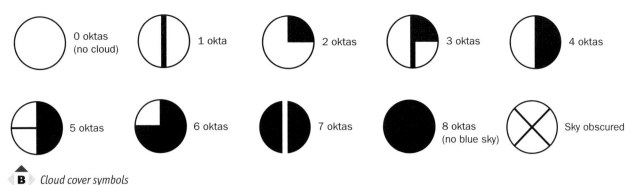

0 oktas (no cloud)	1 okta	2 oktas	3 oktas	4 oktas
5 oktas	6 oktas	7 oktas	8 oktas (no blue sky)	Sky obscured

B *Cloud cover symbols*

Now Investigate

1 Investigate what types of cloud are most common where you live. For example, do they vary from season to season?

2 Explain how clouds form and why some of them produce rain.

3 Identify the three types of cloud shown in photos **C** and write a description of each type.

4 a From the list below, select the correct cloud types i, ii and iii.

altocumulus   altostratus   cirrocumulus   cirrostratus   cirrus
cumulus   nimbostratus   stratocumulus   stratus

	Height above the ground
i	Less than 2000 metres
ii	2000–6000 metres
ii	More than 6000 metres

b Which of these cloud types can extend through all three levels of the atmosphere?

Further research 🔍

Carry out an online investigation into the activities of the Cloud Appreciation Society.

Topic link 🔗

What you have learned about weather and climate will help you when you study Topic 2.8 pages 108–13, Topic 2.9 pages 114–19 and Topic 2.11 pages 126–31.

C *Some cloud types*

Learning objectives:

▶ describe and explain the main climate characteristics of the tropical rainfall areas

▶ describe and give reasons for the global distribution of tropical rainforests

▶ describe how rainforest vegetation has adapted to local conditions

▶ describe and explain the characteristic features of Borneo's rainforest ecosystem.

Now Investigate ❗

Do you know any ways in which your local vegetation has adapted to the climate?

Topic link 🔗

Look back at Topic 2.7 pages 102–07 for more information on humidity.

Take a moment to think about the climate where you live.
- What are the mean (average) temperatures during the year?
- Does the temperature vary, or is it relatively constant?
- Is it mild, tropical or cold for most of the year?
- Does rain fall throughout the year or is it seasonal?
- Is it reliable?

Wherever you are, these aspects of the climate affect the natural vegetation growing locally. This is because plants need heat, light and water – as well as nutrients from the soil – in order to grow well. Where the climate provides all of these, the vegetation is rich and dense. Where one or more key factors are limited or absent, plants adapt to survive.

The climate in equatorial regions

Map **A** shows an almost continuous climate zone along the Equator, extending about 5 degrees north and south of it. It is interrupted only by two areas of high land. Graph **B** illustrates this climate type, which characteristically has:
- high annual temperatures, averaging 27°–28°C
- a very low annual temperature range (the difference between the highest and the lowest average monthly temperature) – usually less than 3°C
- frequent, heavy rainfall – often more than 2000 mm per year
- rain – usually convectional rainfall all year (there is no dry season), with over 60 mm falling every month
- a diurnal temperature range greater than the annual temperature range
- no obvious seasons
- high humidity levels
- light winds.

 A Parts of the world with an equatorial climate

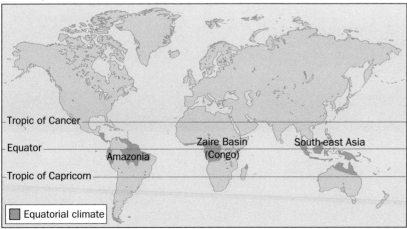

Tropic of Cancer
Equator
Amazonia
Zaire Basin (Congo)
South-east Asia
Tropic of Capricorn

 Equatorial climate

 B Climate graph for Manaus, in the Amazon rainforest

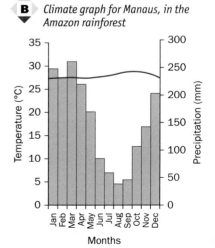

Temperature (°C) / Precipitation (mm) / Months (Jan–Dec)

There are a number of reasons for the climate along the Equator being like this:

- **Latitude** Along the Equator, the sun is high in the sky all year round. This means that this region receives high-intensity insolation, so temperatures are high throughout the year.
- **Altitude** Generally, air temperature decreases with increased altitude. The main areas of equatorial climate are also lowland areas. In such regions, the air at ground level is under greater pressure (because of the increased weight of air above it) than the air in mountain regions. It is therefore denser and can become much warmer than the less dense air at higher altitudes.

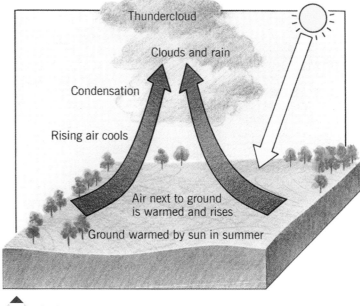

 C *The formation of convectional rainfall*

- **Atmospheric pressure** Intense heating of the Earth's surface at the Equator means that air which is in contact with the ground is heated, becomes lighter and rises. This reduces the air pressure at the surface, giving rise to extensive areas of low pressure along the Equator. This low pressure is associated with heavy convectional rainfall (diagram **C**).
- **Diurnal temperature range** This is the difference between the maximum and minimum temperatures within a 24-hour period. During daylight, temperatures rise quickly as a result of intense heating from the sun. However, after dark the heat absorbed by the Earth's surface during the day is quickly lost, causing temperatures to fall rapidly. At the Equator, after afternoon rain, there is less cloud cover. After dark, without heat input from the sun, the remaining cloud cover breaks up. Because of reduced cloud cover, heat is lost into space through the process of radiation and temperatures fall, to around 23° or 24°C from an afternoon maximum of 33° or 34°C.

Now Investigate

1. Use map **A** to describe the distribution of equatorial climates. (Hint: Look at Section 4.2 pages 208–11 to help you do this.)

2. Give reasons why temperatures in equatorial regions vary so little throughout the year.

3. Using the text and diagram **C**, explain why rainfall is so high in equatorial regions.

4. What do you understand by the terms:
   a annual temperature range
   b diurnal temperature range?

Fantastic fact

On average, temperatures fall by as much as 10°C for every kilometre above sea level, which is why mountaineers wear so many extra layers of clothing.

Tropical rainforest vegetation

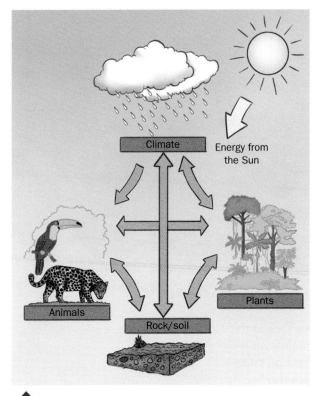

The plants and animals that live in an area together are called an ecosystem. However, they do not exist in isolation; they interact with each other and their non-living environment – the climate, geology and soils that make up their habitats. Diagram **A** shows that some interactions are two-way (the two components interact with each other and affect each other) whilst others are one-way (one component affects the other, but is not affected by it).

The natural vegetation that has adapted to equatorial climates is known as tropical rainforest. Plants need warmth, light and moisture in order to thrive, together with nutrients from the soil. Growing conditions within the equatorial lowlands are ideal, with growth possible throughout the year. Rainforests, which cover just 6 per cent of the world's land surface, are known for their biodiversity – the wide range of vegetation and wildlife that they support. Tropical rainforests are home to over 10 million different species of plants, animals and insects – in other words, over 50 per cent of all species on Earth live on just 6 per cent of its land surface.

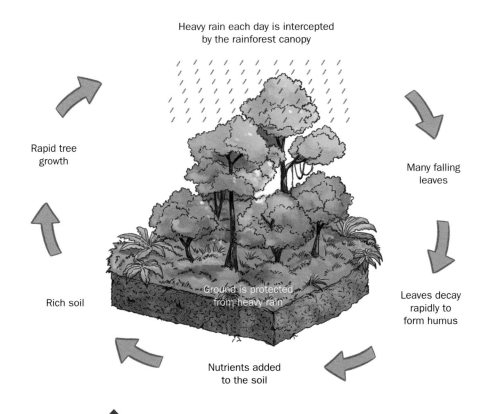

Heavy rain each day is intercepted by the rainforest canopy

Rapid tree growth

Many falling leaves

Rich soil

Ground is protected from heavy rain

Leaves decay rapidly to form humus

Nutrients added to the soil

B *Nutrient recycling in the tropical rainforest*

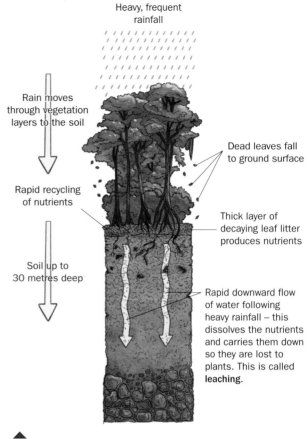

Heavy, frequent rainfall

Rain moves through vegetation layers to the soil

Rapid recycling of nutrients

Soil up to 30 metres deep

Dead leaves fall to ground surface

Thick layer of decaying leaf litter produces nutrients

Rapid downward flow of water following heavy rainfall – this dissolves the nutrients and carries them down so they are lost to plants. This is called **leaching**.

 C *View of the tropical rainforest in the Loboc River, Bohol, Philippines*

Although the tropical rainforests are majestic, they are in fact very fragile ecosystems, dependent for their survival on the continuous recycling of nutrients. This is because of the poor fertility of the soils which support them. Hot, wet conditions have weathered the surface rocks intensively and so forest soils tend to be deep. However, their depth does not make them fertile. Heavy rainfall leaches nutrients from the soil. Without a constant input of leaf litter from the forest above, nutrients are easily and quickly removed. This produces infertile soils which are quickly eroded – see diagrams **B** and **D**.

 D *A typical rainforest soil*

Now Investigate

1   Describe the global distribution of tropical rainforests as shown on map **A** on page 108.

2   Plants need warmth, heat and light to grow. Use the information on pages 108–09 to help you explain how these needs are met in equatorial lowland areas.

3   a   How are nutrients recycled in tropical rainforests?

　　b   Why is this nutrient recycling so important?

　　c   Create a diagram similar to diagram **B**, to show the effects of deforestation on soil fertility.

Fantastic fact

The Brazil nut tree of South America has a seedcase so hard that only one animal, the agouti, can open it, allowing the tree's seeds to germinate.

Topic link

See Topic 2.11 pages 126–31 to learn more about the natural environment.

A tropical rainforest environment

Regions of equatorial rainforest around the world are decreasing rapidly, for a number of reasons. One place that was originally covered almost entirely by rainforest is the island of Borneo in south-east Asia.

Case study

Borneo's tropical rainforest

Borneo is the world's third largest island, and its position on the Equator means that most of its natural vegetation is tropical rainforest (map **A**). It still has a low population density – even though its valuable natural resources include oil, coal, gold, timber and very fertile soil. It is now the world's biggest producer of oil palm, which is used to manufacture biodiesel fuel, cooking oils, cosmetics and soap.

Borneo's climate (graph **B**) is ideal for tropical rainforest because:

- it has high temperatures throughout the year, with a maximum annual temperature range of only 3°C
- there is heavy rainfall every month – up to 4000 mm in places
- its high temperatures and heavy rainfall make the air very humid.

Borneo's monthly rainfall totals vary throughout the year due to the changing direction of the wind belts (map **A**). Most rain falls during the north-east monsoon (November–January), when moist air blows in from the Pacific Ocean. March, April and May are much drier, because the south-east winds have blown over Australia's deserts.

Borneo's rainforests are very special – and not just because its 45 metre trees are the tallest in the world. What is really special is what lives in the forest. Its fauna (animal life), some of which is found only on this island, ranges from the cute to the extraordinary! It includes the world's largest range of 'gliding animals',

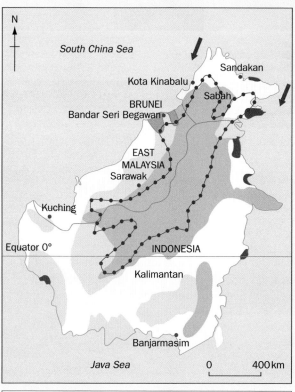

Legend:
- Mountain rainforest
- Coastal mangrove swamp
- Lowland dipterocarp rainforest
- Mainly farmland
- •–•–• Three-nation Heart of Borneo Conservation Plan area
- ➡ Wet north-east monsoon winds (Nov–Jan)

A The island of Borneo

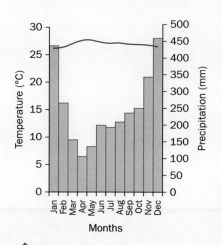

B Climate graph for Borneo

which can move between trees at great height, for example flying lizards, flying frogs and even flying snakes. Borneo is also home to the world's largest moth, flower and carnivorous plant. By far the most popular animal with tourists is the orangutan. Its population on Borneo has halved in the last 50 years – because their natural forest habitat is now much smaller, because farmers kill these animals to protect their crops, and because they fetch a high price on the international pet market (photo **C**).

Unfortunately, Borneo's forests have been in decline since large-scale logging first began in the 1970s (table **D**), and the future of the specialised dipterocarp (lowland) forests now seems bleak. The reasons for the reduction of the rainforest include:

- demand from Malaysia's plywood and paper pulp industries
- increasing global demand for valuable hardwoods for use as building materials
- the race to discover and exploit new reserves of oil and coal
- the increasing rate of oil palm production
- devastating forest fires which are started by local farmers to clear the forest – extra farmland is need to feed the growing population.

National Parks now protect pockets of the remaining forest, and the three-nation Heart of Borneo Conservation Plan, organised jointly between Malaysia, Brunei and Indonesia, aims to protect 250 000 km² of prime forest habitat (map **A**).

Fantastic fact

Borneo's rainforest is 130 million years old, making it the oldest rainforest on Earth. It beats Amazonia by 70 million years!

C *A baby orang utan*

Now Investigate

1 a Use graph **B** and the information on these pages to help you describe the monthly temperature and rainfall patterns of Borneo's climate.

   b With the help of an atlas, discover why any winds from the south-east are likely to produce drier weather for Borneo.

   c Suggest the possible effects of temperature, rainfall and winds on Borneo.

2 Suggest some ways in which the world could reduce its demand for Borneo's exports.

3 a Using the data in table **D**, plot a line graph. Make sure that you use numbers at equal intervals on the *x* axis.

   b Describe how the rate of deforestation in Borneo has changed since 1985.

   c How does the predicted rate of future deforestation compare with that of the past?

Further research

Ecotourism is tourism that stimulates the local economy but doesn't harm the natural environment or undermine the traditional culture of the local people. Use online research to help you design a poster or brochure which advises visitors on how to respect the natural environment and the local people. Try to add some information about the advantages of conserving tropical rainforests.

Topic link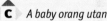

See Topic 3.9 pages 188–93 for more on environmental issues in different parts of the world.

Skills link

Refer to Section 4.3 pages 212–21 to learn how to draw a line graph.

Year	% of forest cover in Borneo
1985	73.7
2000	57.5
2005	50.4
2010	44.4
2020	32.6 (estimate)

 D

2.9 Tropical deserts: how do living things survive in tropical deserts?

Learning objectives:

▷ describe and give reasons for the main climate characteristics of tropical desert areas

▷ describe and give reasons for the global distribution of tropical deserts

▷ explain how hot desert vegetation has adapted to local conditions

▷ describe and explain the main features of the Namib Desert's ecosystem.

Fantastic fact

The longest desert drought lasted 400 years, from 1571 to 1971, in the Atacama Desert in Chile.

Perhaps you live in or near to a tropical desert area, and are used to coping with the conditions. For most of us, though, desert survival can be very hazardous. Tropical deserts are hot – often above 30°C. They are also arid (extremely dry), so every drop of water is precious. How do you minimise your usage, making every drop count, without dehydrating (losing water)? Meeting such challenges is difficult even with technology to help us. Plants and animals, however, have been adapting successfully to such conditions for thousands of years. How could you adapt your normal clothing and activities to cope with extreme temperatures?

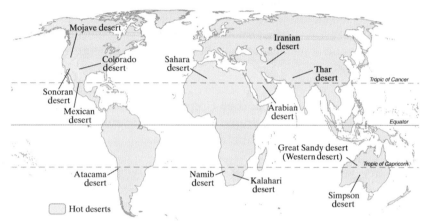

 A Global distribution of hot tropical deserts

The climate in hot tropical desert areas

Not all deserts are hot. They can also be temperate or cold. It is the lack of rainfall that determines if a region is classified as a desert. Any region with a mean annual rainfall of less than 250 mm is a 'desert'. Tropical (hot) desert climates are mainly found between 5° and 20° north and south of the Equator (map **A**). Except in North Africa and Arabia, where the desert extends from the Atlantic Ocean to the Arabian Sea, all are in the western regions of continents. This is because they receive dry prevailing winds – that is, winds that have blown over land for most of the year. Tropical deserts often experience higher daytime temperatures than equatorial regions, at least during the season when the sun is directly overhead.

Although temperatures are high all year, there is a seasonal pattern with one cooler, wetter season and a much hotter, arid one. These seasons are due to various factors:

● High atmospheric pressure: where there is high pressure, air sinks and warms, so any moisture is evaporated. The rising and cooling process needed to form clouds is prevented by the column of sinking air.

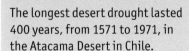 **B** The Atacama Desert, Chile

- There is an absence of cloud cover, so:
  - no rain can fall
  - the sun's heating is intense throughout daylight hours
  - night-time temperatures fall rapidly (diagram **C**).
- Diurnal temperature ranges in hot deserts are greater than those in equatorial regions – the arid air accelerates temperature loss through radiation and so night-time temperatures below freezing are common.
- In desert areas such as the Sahara, the prevailing winds blow outward from the continental interior, they cannot pick up water vapour and so clouds do not form.
- In other desert regions such as the Namib and Kalahari, although the prevailing wind blows from the ocean, it has to cross a mountain barrier. This creates a rainshadow effect (diagram **D**).

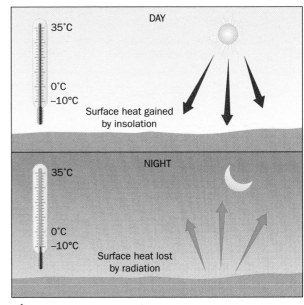

C Why daytime temperatures are high and night-time temperatures are low

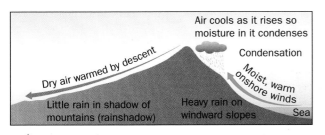

D The rainshadow effect of mountain ranges

- In South America and southern Africa, cold offshore ocean currents chill the prevailing winds and so these are unable to evaporate much water vapour. Any moisture they hold falls as showers (or precipitates out as fog) along the coastal zone before reaching inland desert regions.

However, most hot deserts do receive some rain, often during the 'cooler' season, as a result of the north–south movement of pressure systems and their associated wind belts (see diagram **B** on page 104). Changes in atmospheric pressure draw moist winds into desert areas. These winds are heated by contact with the hot desert surface and, as they rise and cool, clouds form, bringing rain.

Now Investigate

1. Think about how you would need to adapt your clothes and activities to cope with a tropical desert climate. You could make notes under headings, or draw labelled diagrams.

2. With the help of map **A**, describe the global distribution of tropical desert climates.

3. Suggest reasons why tropical desert temperatures remain high all year.

4. Explain why rainfall totals are usually very low in hot desert regions.

5. a Use the illustrations on these pages, and an atlas, to name one desert that is influenced by each of the following:
   - a rainshadow effect in southern Africa
   - cold ocean currents
   - a subtropical high pressure area.

   b For each of these, draw an annotated diagram to explain how it has contributed to the development of your chosen desert.

Tropical desert vegetation

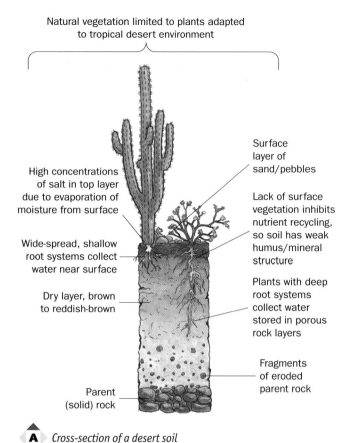

Natural vegetation limited to plants adapted to tropical desert environment

High concentrations of salt in top layer due to evaporation of moisture from surface

Wide-spread, shallow root systems collect water near surface

Dry layer, brown to reddish-brown

Parent (solid) rock

Surface layer of sand/pebbles

Lack of surface vegetation inhibits nutrient recycling, so soil has weak humus/mineral structure

Plants with deep root systems collect water stored in porous rock layers

Fragments of eroded parent rock

A Cross-section of a desert soil

In some ways, tropical desert environments are good for plant growth because they provide:

- high temperatures all year
- long hours of daylight
- unbroken sunshine.

However, not only is the rainfall light, it is often unreliable and unpredictable. Also:

- When rain does fall, little infiltration is possible as soils are baked hard, so surface runoff is high. This means that very little of the water that falls is available to plants.
- Hot, dry air means that evapotranspiration rates are high, increasing the amount of water that plants need to survive.
- Desert soils are thin and so cannot support dense vegetation cover (diagram **A**). The lack of moisture means that soil development is restricted. As vegetation is so sparse, there is little organic material to form humus in the topsoil.
- Soil erosion is a problem because of strong winds.
- Large diurnal temperature ranges, with overnight temperatures as low as –4°C, are difficult for plants to adapt to.

Together, these conditions make hot deserts hazardous to both plant and animal life. Indeed, there is very little life in some deserts, especially in those with bare rock surfaces (for example the Arizona Desert), in stony deserts (the Kalahari) and in dune deserts (the mid-Sahara). In other places, a desert may be able to support plant growth, depending on:

- the total annual rainfall
- the frequency of rainfall
- the depth of the water table (photo **B**)
- the salinity of the soil.

B Oases are found in deserts where the water table is at or near the surface

Photos **D** and **E** show two plants that have adapted to survive in harsh desert conditions. The following are particular ways in which plants adapt to local conditions:

- **Dormancy:** during drought periods, perennial plants like grasses, which can survive for more than one year, die back. Others, called annuals – which means they only last for a year – produce drought-resistant seeds which lie dormant until the next rain falls. These plants can complete their life cycle within just a few weeks (photo **D**).

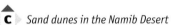
C Sand dunes in the Namib Desert

- **Water retention:** some plants can store water in their stems, trunks or leaves during wet weather.
- **Leaf adaptation:** most desert plants have adapted to reduce water loss, store water and increase protection from the sun.
- **Increasing water collection**: plants have developed various methods of acquiring the moisture they need.
- **Tolerance of saline (salty) soils:** salt is toxic to most plants but some have developed salt tolerance. Desert soils are salty because heat and aridity cause a high level of evaporation. This draws salts upwards towards the soil surface (diagram **A**).

D The Rose of Jericho survives long droughts by lying dormant

E The creosote bush protects its own water collection area of soil with chemicals that slow the growth of nearby plants

Fantastic fact

The tumbleweed plant gets its name because it rolls down hillsides to disperse its seeds!

Now Investigate

1 Draw a spider diagram to show the main reasons why plant growth is very restricted in tropical deserts.

2 How do plants increase their ability to collect and store water?

3 How do plants reduce water loss?

4 Explain how each of the following are linked:

  a drought *and* the rate of plant growth

  b oases *and* water tables

  c soil salinity *and* water evaporation.

Each desert is different, supporting different plants and animals, depending on where it is in the world. People live in these deserts, too – and they all have different ways of making a living there. Here we look in more detail at just one desert, on the south-west coast of the African continent.

Case study

The Namib Desert

The Namib Desert occupies the coastal edge of Namibia (map **A** and photo **B**).

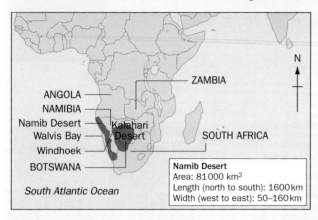

Namib Desert
Area: 81000 km²
Length (north to south): 1600 km
Width (west to east): 50–160 km

Climate in Namibia

	Walvis Bay	Windhoek
Total annual rainfall (mm)	23	362
Average rainfall in wettest month (mm)	8	81
No. of days/year rainfall is more than 0.1mm	16	41
Average temperature (°C)	16	19
Average relative humidity (%)	29	42

  A *Namib Desert location and facts*

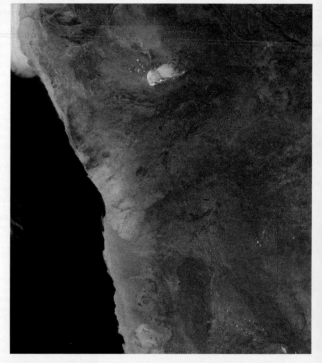

 B *Satellite image of the Namib Desert*

Fantastic fact 🌍

Dune 7, in the Namib Desert, is the highest dune on Earth (383 metres from base to summit).

Within the desert are several distinctive landscapes. The south is dominated by the tallest dunes in the world, while further north sand gives way to a rocky desert of gravel plains and bare, rugged hills. Here there is no surface water, except after rain, when for a short time streams flow into inland basins, never reaching the sea.

The climate is arid with sparse, unpredictable rainfall. Temperatures vary from west to east – cooler along the coast but hotter inland. The most important climate feature is the coastal fog, which is the only source of reliable moisture in the region. Rainfall is very low because of the combined effect of the rainshadow effect of the Drakensberg Mountains (see diagram **D** on page 115) and the cold, offshore Benguela Current. The coastal fogs and variations in temperature are the result of the interaction between two prevailing winds. Cold air from the Atlantic Ocean reduces the effects of latitude at the coast but, inland, sinking air from the Drakensberg Mountains raises summer temperatures to highs of 50°C.

C *Plant adaptations in the Namib Desert: (from left to right) the pencil bush, quiver tree and Welwitschia plant*

How plant and animals have adapted to desert conditions

As in all deserts, both plants and animals have adapted to the climate. For example, Gha grass is valuable because it helps to stabilise the southern dunes. Photos **C** show a variety of other plants that are adapted to the Namib's harsh environment.

Human activity in the desert

Human activity in the desert is restricted by the arid conditions (table **D**). However, the area produces many of the world's finest diamonds, together with uranium, tin, tungsten, zinc and salt. Mining is crucial to Namibia's economy, but it is a major threat to local ecosystems as it destroys habitats and requires the development of complex infrastructure. Decades of hunting and poaching have devastated big game populations in the country, but Namibia has become the first country in the world to incorporate environmental protection in its national constitution. Today, almost all of the Namib Desert is protected, except for areas where mining is in progress.

Economic activity	What is involved	Effects on the ecosystem
Diamond mining	Alluvial diamonds are found in gravel beds (alluvial means they have been carried there by water). Enormous quantities of sand have to be removed to expose the diamonds. Sand is dumped elsewhere.	Recovering diamonds destroys fragile habitats by removing vegetation and soil. Sand-dumping buries other habitats.
Nomadic herding	Pastoral farmers graze herds of donkeys and goats in the eastern regions where there is more rainfall and therefore more vegetation.	Animals overgraze the area, exposing it to wind and water erosion. Fragile soils are removed and the barren desert spreads further eastwards.
'Activity' tourism	Off-road driving, poaching, sand-boarding, go-carting.	'Big game' are eradicated. Desert surfaces and vegetation destroyed.

D *How human activities affect the Namib Desert*

Topic link 🔗

What you have learned in this topic will help you when you study Topic 2.11 pages 126–31 and Topic 3.9 pages 188–93.

Further research 🔍

Investigate the climate, vegetation and human economic activities in one of the following tropical desert regions: Great Sandy Desert (Australia), Sonoran Desert (USA/Mexico), Thar Desert.

Now Investigate ❗

1 With the help of information in this topic, explain the development of the desert climate in south-west Africa.

2 Select a plant that is adapted to life in the Namib Desert. Describe and give reasons for the plant's adaptations. You could present your answer as an annotated sketch.

3 Suggest how tropical deserts be used for economic benefit without causing environmental damage.

Learning objectives:

- know some of the main hazards presented by the natural environment
- understand the links between the natural environment and human activities
- describe the effects of at least two natural hazards on people's lives, including possible benefits.

I've lost everything and everyone. It was 17 March – just an ordinary day. Father had gone to work as usual. Mother was nursing my baby brother. OK – it had rained hard since December. But nothing told us this day was different. I was outside talking with friends and could only watch helplessly as our family home was taken in a flood. I've never seen water so high. It could have swallowed me – but I caught hold of a metal post and hung on tight. I survived. My family – all of them – haven't been seen since. I cry every day.

A *Fermin, aged 13. Survivor of flooding in Leyte Province in the Philippines in March 2011. Human cost: 75 dead. Economic cost: US$43 million.*

B *The damage caused by some recent disasters*

We live on an active planet. Heat trapped inside the Earth causes earthquakes and volcanoes. Heat in the atmosphere causes extreme weather events. Secondary effects of such events include tsunami, flooding, storms, and lahars. Scientists believe, though, that the last 10 000 years have been the quietest ever known on the planet! Natural hazards are a fact of life. What turns them into disasters is their scale and the impact they have on people's lives.

Natural hazard events affect people through loss of life, damage to homes and belongings, environmental damage and people's ability to earn a living. Generally, the larger the scale of the event, the greater we see the disaster to be. But the effect of a natural hazard event is not only the result of its strength and scale. The strongest of earthquakes occurring in an uninhabited area will not have an effect on people's lives. A significantly weaker earthquake affecting a densely populated region or city, particularly in one of the world's poorest countries, may be a serious disaster.

Geographically, natural hazards can be classified into three groups:

- geological events, e.g. earthquakes, lahars, volcanic eruptions
- hydrological events, e.g. floods, tsunamis
- climatic and weather events, e.g. droughts (which can lead to wildfires), tropical revolving storms, tornadoes.

Note that earthquakes are rarely the primary cause of a disaster. It is their secondary effects – such as the collapse of buildings, fires and tsunami – that can be catastrophic. Similarly, although volcanic eruptions can be disastrous, pyroclastic flows and lahars often cause far greater devastation.

Other points to note about particular events include:

- Unlike most other natural hazards, avalanches are neither rare nor random events. They are common in mountainous areas where deep snow accumulates.
- Tsunamis are always the secondary effect of an earthquake. Recent tsunamis affecting the Pacific Basin have been disastrous, for example the Japanese tsunami of March 2011.
- Climatic events appear to be intensified by human activity. Scientists are now concerned that increasing heat in the atmosphere increases its energy – which in turn causes more intense weather-related features, for example tropical revolving storms (see pages 122–23).
- Wildfires are also increasingly common – again perhaps because of climate change.

The impact of natural hazards on a population appears to be directly linked to its level of wealth. In MEDCs, more money and expertise is available for 'the three Ps' – prediction, protection and preparation (diagram **C**). For example, wealthier countries such as the USA can afford to construct more effective flood defences than an LEDC like Bangladesh, which means that their inhabitants are much better protected. For the same reason, there have been many more earthquake victims in Turkey than in the USA.

Topic link

- See Topic 2.1 pages 66–73 for more on earthquake events.
- See pages 120–21 to learn more about climate change.

Topic link

See Topic 3.9 pages 188–93 for more about how different environmental conditions affect people.

Prediction involves working out where and when a hazard might occur. *Where* is often easy – most hazards happen in identifiable zones. *When* is less easy. Storms can be forecast using satellite data. In China, scientists believe that animals act oddly before earthquakes happen. But for most hazardous events, predicting when they will happen is still a major problem.

Protection is mainly about building to high standards, using designs that can withstand shock waves, high winds or rising water levels. Providing shelters and flood defences are also protective measures. But all are very costly. Hurricane Katrina (pages 122–23) and the 2011 Japanese tsunami (pages 72–73) showed that even the richest nations cannot protect against every event.

HAZARD PREDICTION, PROTECTION AND PREPARATION

Preparation is mostly about educating local people and practising for hazard events. Then people know what to do and where to go to reduce the effects of a hazard. In the case of drought, for example, preparation is about educating people to use local aquifers, to dig wells, to reduce water loss through leakage, and to re-use water for different purposes.

 C Predicting, protecting and preparing for natural disasters

Now Investigate

1 Explain the difference between:

  a a natural hazard and a natural disaster event

  b the primary (immediate) and secondary (longer-term) effects of disaster events.

2 Use annotated images to create a mind map showing the three types of natural disaster.

3 Prepare an information leaflet for residents of a vulnerable city, telling them how best to prepare for and protect against a disaster event. Your pamphlet should cover two sides of an A4 sheet, and include illustrations such as photographs. It should provide advice for families as well as for the community as a whole.

Tropical storms

Topic link

See Topic 2.6 pages 100–01 and Topic 2.7 pages 102–04 for more on atmospheric pressure and its effects.

Now Investigate

1 Study map **A**.

  a Describe the direction in which all tropical storms move.

  b Describe the distribution of tropical storms as shown on the map.

2 Draw a series of simple illustrations, with labels, to show the conditions necessary for the development of a tropical cyclone.

Fantastic fact

At first, hurricanes were always given girls' names but, in 1979, boys' names were added, so now they are both used.

A hurricane is a tropical storm – an area of very low atmospheric pressure that can develop on either side of the Equator, between 5° and 20° north and south. Such storms are known locally by different names (map **A**) but all are characterised by very strong winds and torrential rain. Typically, they form:

- over extensive tropical oceans, where water temperature exceeds 27°C
- where the sea is warmed to a great depth at the time of year when sea temperatures are highest
- as a result of strong upward movements of very moist air – as the air rises, it cools and condenses, releasing huge amounts of heat which powers the storm (diagram **B**).

Hurricanes frequently cause extensive destruction along their path. The main reasons for this are:

- **Strong winds** (with gusts of more 200 km/hr) cause structural damage. In MEDCs, power cables are torn down, and roofing, signs and wooden buildings are often damaged – although advance warnings mean that buildings can be boarded-up for safety. In poorer regions, fragile buildings are destroyed and vegetation and crops are damaged, causing economic hardship.
- **Heavy rainfall** – often over 200 mm in a single day – leads to river flooding and landslides.
- **Storm surges:** intense low pressure raises sea levels. Strong winds drive high seas inland with waves up to 5 metres high. This causes flooding in low-lying coastal areas, and settlements can be washed away. Crops are destroyed and huge areas flooded by salt water – which leaves the land unsuitable for plant growth for years to come.

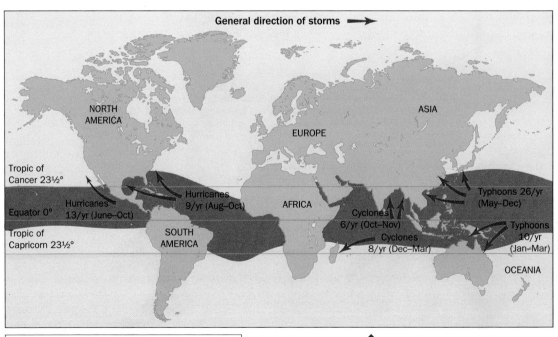

10/yr Average number per year
■ Warm sea areas (over 27°C) □ Cooler sea areas

A Global distribution of tropical storms

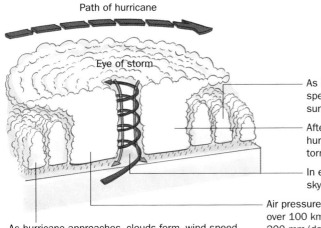

Path of hurricane

Eye of storm

As hurricane passes, wind speeds and rainfall decrease, sunny intervals

After eye of storm has passed, hurricane-force winds and more torrential rain

In eye of storm, winds are light, sky clear, little rain

Air pressure falls, wind speeds increase to over 100 km/hr, torrential rain (more than 200 mm/day)

As hurricane approaches, clouds form, wind speed increases, rain showers with sunny intervals

 B *Weather associated with tropical storms*

Hurricane Katrina

Case study

In August, 2005 a tropical depression formed over the Bahamas. It tracked westward towards Florida, gaining strength, and was then classified as a hurricane (named Katrina) as it neared the coast. As it moved inland, it caused structural damage, death and flooding, but lost energy – as all hurricanes do after they reach land. When it reached the Gulf of Mexico, the storm passed over unusually warm water which re-energised it so much that it developed into a Level 5 hurricane (photo **C** and map **D**). As it followed the Gulf coastline, Katrina became the most costly disaster ever to hit the USA and one of the strongest storms of the last century.

C *Satellite image of Katrina*

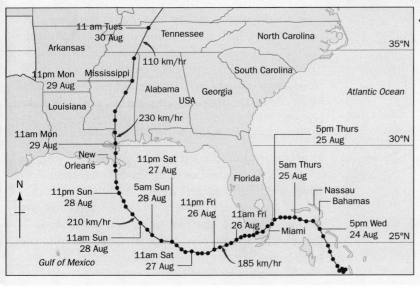

 D *Track of Katrina*

Now Investigate !

1 Use the information in the case study, and from your own research, to identify five key effects of Hurricane Katrina when it hit New Orleans.

2 Katrina was a natural disaster in an MEDC. Investigate a storm of similar strength in an LEDC (such as Cyclone Nargis). Compare and contrast its effects with those of Hurricane Katrina.

Flooding in Bangladesh

Fantastic fact

Eighty per cent of Bangladesh lies on a huge flood plain and delta, which are only 1 metre above sea level.

Bangladesh is one of the world's most densely populated countries, with 1127 people/km². It is also one of the most likely to be flooded, for a variety of reasons:

- Flash floods (particularly in the east and north of the country), resulting from heavy rain or snowmelt in the Himalayan mountains to the north, cause river levels to rise sharply and the speed of river flow to increase. Crops and settlements on the flood plains are often destroyed.
- Monsoon rains cause rivers to rise and flood every year. Large volumes of water exceed the local drainage capacity. The areas most affected are the distributaries in the delta region, especially when all three major rivers flood at the same time.
- Storm surges (linked to cyclones) affect the low-lying coastal delta area.
- Flooding in Bangladesh has a big impact, mainly because of the way local people live and because Bangladesh is one of the poorest nations on Earth.

Case study

Cyclone Aila

On 25 May 2009, Bangladesh and north-eastern India were hit by Cyclone Aila. Damage was extensive and affected between 2.5 and 3 million people. Although more than half a million people from Bangladesh's low-lying coastal areas were evacuated, at least 179 people lost their lives, 800 were injured and more than 400 000 were cut off by flood waters. A storm surge devastated western Bangladesh, submerging or destroying many rural villages. The pressure of flood water broke through river embankments, causing extensive inland flooding, and more than half a million people were left homeless. Drinking water was contaminated with sea water and sewage, as toilets were washed away and many dead animals were washed into water sources. Within four days, 7000 people were suffering from various water-borne diseases, including cholera. Over 100 relief camps were created to shelter refugees. These were funded by overseas aid organisations and by the Bangladeshi government. The final estimate put the cost of the disaster at over US$40.7 million.

However, living in such a flood-prone area does actually have some benefits. The annual river floods cover the land with fertile silt, or alluvium. This means that poorer farmers do not need to buy costly fertilisers to grow their crops. It also means that some areas do not need to be irrigated, despite the high temperatures in this region. People choose to live here because they believe that the benefits can outweigh some of the disadvantages.

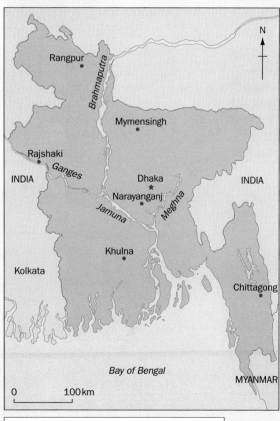

★ Capital city   • Other cities over 200 000 people

A Bangladesh

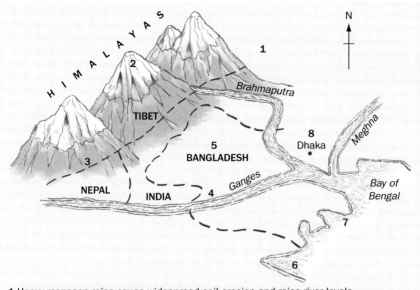

1 Heavy monsoon rains cause widespread soil erosion and raise river levels.
2 Melting snow on mountains in summer increases soil erosion and raises river levels.
3 Removal of trees on lower slopes of Himalayas adds to soil erosion and rate of surface runoff.
4 Silt from eroded soil builds up in rivers which can then hold less water and so they flood more easily.
5 Most of Bangladesh is less than 1 metre above sea level so it is easily flooded by rivers and the sea.
6 Cyclones, which are common in this region, create storm surges along the coast.
7 Ganges delta has many islands made of soft silt which is easily eroded.
8 Dhaka, the capital city (population 7 million) is only 4 metres above sea level, so is vulnerable to river flooding.

 B *The main causes of flooding in Bangladesh*

 C *The effects of Cyclone Aila*

Further research 🔍

Investigate a recent case of prolonged drought which has had a major impact on the quality of life of people living in that area. (You may find it helpful to refer to the drought in the Horn of Africa described in Topic 3.2 on page 141.) It will help you to structure your information under headings, for example:

- Location – possibly including a regional map
- Timing and duration – when did it happen, and how long did it last?
- Main causes of the drought – were they all 'natural'?
- Impact of the drought – what were its immediate and long-term effects on both rich and poor?

Topic link 🔗

- See Topic 3.2 page 141 for more about food shortages due to drought conditions.
- See Topic 2.11 pages 126–31 for more about how people use opportunities presented by the natural environment.

Now Investigate ❗

1 Draw a sketch map of Bangladesh to show the areas that are flooded regularly, and annotate your map to show the main causes of the flooding. Some of your annotations should highlight differences in the effects of flooding on the richer and poorer people of Bangladesh.

2 Summarise the effects of Cyclone Aila in a series of bullet points or a spider diagram.

3 Explain the link between:
- the removal of trees in the Himalayas and increased river levels in Bangladesh
- cyclones and coastal flooding
- snowmelt and flash flooding.

4 Suggest how Bangladesh might predict, prepare and protect against natural disasters. (Hint: look back at pages 122–23.)

 A *A farming landscape in New Zealand*

Topic link

You can learn more about the problems and opportunities presented by tropical rainforests in Topic 2.8 pages 108–13, and by hot deserts in Topic 2.9 pages 114–19.

Topic link

You can learn more about floods in Bangladesh in Topic 2.10 pages 120–25.

The human race against the natural world

Many of us live in environments where it is fairly easy to survive. If you live in New Zealand, for example, the climate is mild and there is good farmland (photo **A**), so people can grow plenty of food to eat. Not everyone is so lucky. In Topic 2.9, for example, you learned that life in the hot deserts is far more difficult, with a constant struggle to find water and food.

But humans are very adaptable. Even in places that would seem to provide little opportunity, people have settled, found food and been able to make a living for themselves. Tropical rainforests, polar areas and the high mountains are just a few of the places where people have settled despite the problems posed by the natural environment.

Now Investigate

Think about the area where you live. What are the problems and opportunities presented by the natural environment? For instance, is it really hot? If so, does this attract tourists or provide the ideal location for a solar power plant? Make a list of the problems and opportunities presented by the natural environment in your area, and compare it with a partner's list.

Finding a good place to live

Most of the densely populated areas of the world have natural environments that provide the basic needs of life – fresh water, food, fuel and shelter. If people have easy access to these then they carry out other activities to make a living and help a country develop. These needs can usually be met in natural environments that provide:

● low, flat land with deep, fertile soils
● a reliable source of fresh water such as a spring or river
● no extremes of climate and a long growing season
● natural vegetation of temperate forest or grassland
● natural resources, especially energy supplies but also mineral resources
● natural beauty that is attractive to tourists.

Those parts of the world where commercial agriculture has developed and where people have plenty to eat have most, if not all, of the above features. In places where there are mineral resources, these may have provided the raw materials for industry to develop. Tourists will want to visit some places as those areas become wealthier and more developed and can offer facilities such as top-quality hotels and restaurants.

Problems posed by harsh environments

There are other areas of the world where life is more difficult because of challenges presented by the natural environment. Some of these challenges are shown in diagram **B**.

Even in these areas there are often economic opportunities. Tropical rainforests are increasingly attractive to tourists who travel to see the amazing plants and animals there. Ski industries occupy high, steep land in winter and become popular with mountain bikers in summer (photo **C**). Desert areas are attracting more and more visitors who are looking for a different kind of holiday.

Tourism can be the main way of making money in many difficult natural environments, but there are other opportunities too. Areas of high rainfall can provide electricity through hydro-electric power, for example, and tropical rainforest can be a source of valuable timber.

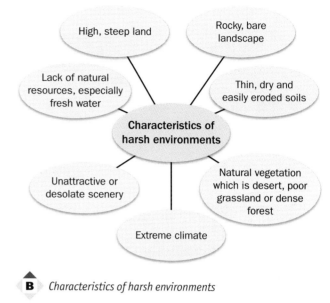

High, steep land

Rocky, bare landscape

Lack of natural resources, especially fresh water

Thin, dry and easily eroded soils

Characteristics of harsh environments

Unattractive or desolate scenery

Natural vegetation which is desert, poor grassland or dense forest

Extreme climate

B *Characteristics of harsh environments*

A balancing act

In many parts of the world the natural environment provides both problems and opportunities. In Bangladesh, for instance, the advantages of the annual river flood are balanced by the devastation that such floods can cause.

In some areas, people have also tried to change the environment in order to exploit it. This has both positive and negative consequences, as can be seen in the case studies on pages 128–31.

C *Mountain biking in the French Alps*

Now Investigate

1. Which areas of your country have few people living in them because of the natural environment? Make a list of the possible opportunities that could exist in these areas.

2. Look at the list of basic necessities to be found in the natural environment (water, fuel, food and shelter). Which of these do you think is most important and why? Which is least important?

3. Choose an economic activity – either (a) agriculture or (b) tourism. What features of the natural environment are most useful for your choice of economic activity?

Topic link

Some of the human activities featured here can also bring widespread environmental damage – see Topic 3.9 pages 188–93.

Fantastic fact

One of the most popular countries for desert tourism is Dubai. There you can stay in the world's only seven-star hotel and go skiing at the country's own winter wonderland resort.

Topic link

The theme of natural environments has links to a number of topics in Sections 1 and 3, including population distribution, agriculture, industry and tourism. Bear this in mind when you work through those sections.

Exploiting the natural environment: disaster!

Case study

Some natural environments are harsh and present many challenges to the people living there, but people still try to make a living there, through agriculture and other activities. Sometimes these attempts can have disastrous effects for the environment and the people involved.

The Aral Sea disaster

Before 1965, the Aral Sea occupied a huge area of 67 300 km² (a little larger than the island of Sri Lanka), in Kazakhstan and Uzbekistan (map **A**). It was the world's fourth largest lake and was fed by two major rivers. Into the southern end flowed Central Asia's largest river – the Amu Darya – bringing water 1500 km from its source in the Hindu Kush mountains between Afghanistan and Pakistan. The smaller Syr Darya brought water into the northern end of the lake.

The climate of the region around the Aral Sea is arid with high summer temperatures sometimes reaching 50°C. Winters can be very cold and there is low rainfall throughout the year (graph **B**). Because of this, agriculture is difficult and people traditionally made a living by fishing in the sea. In the 1960s thousands of fishermen landed 40 000 tonnes of fish a year from the Aral Sea. Many more people were employed in industries that supported the fishing. They lived in the towns and two cities on the lake shore.

A   The Aral Sea

The sea dries up

In the 1960s Kazakhstan and Uzbekistan were part of the Soviet Union. The government made a decision to use the water in the Amu Darya to grow wheat and cotton. Huge canals were built to divert water through irrigation channels to the 3 million hectares of land dedicated to the two crops. This proved disastrous for the Aral Sea. With less water reaching the lake, it began to dry up and shrink dramatically. By 1989 it was already half its original size, and it continued to shrink for many years after that (photos **C**).

The effects on people and the environment

As the Aral Sea dried up, fishing became more and more difficult. The water was further and further away from the towns where people lived. At first, canals were built to allow ships to get to the lake but, eventually, the ships had to be abandoned. As the water level dropped, the amount of salt it contained (known as its salinity) increased until it became almost as salty as the ocean (graph **D**). Most of the remaining fish died and the fishermen had to move away to find jobs elsewhere.

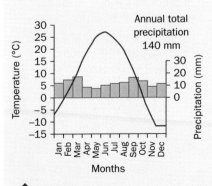

B   Climate graph for the Aral Sea

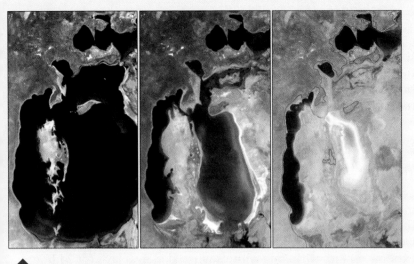

Skills link

Interpreting satellite images is a very useful skill. Used in combination with maps, comparisons can show clear patterns of change in the environment. See Section 4.4 pages 222–25 for more information.

Topic link

See Topic 3.8 page 185 for a photograph showing a ship abandoned in the Aral Sea.

C *The declining area of the Aral Sea : satellite images from (left to right) 1989, 2003 and 2009*

Worse was to follow. Summers got hotter and winters colder as the decrease in water affected the climate. Violent dust storms blew salt, sand and chemicals into the air and people developed throat cancers and breathing diseases, including tuberculosis. With no protein from fish, people suffered from malnutrition and the number of children dying increased rapidly to become the highest rate in the Soviet Union.

Signs of recovery

This situation was described by UN Secretary-General Ban Ki-moon as one of the planet's most shocking environmental disasters, but there are now some signs of recovery. The World Bank and the Kazakh government paid for a 13 km long dam to be built to raise the level of the lake. The northern part has grown by 20 per cent and salinity levels have dropped to what they were in the 1960s. Freshwater fish have returned and local fishermen have begun catching them in large numbers again. There are also plans to develop the tourist industry in the area.

Despite these encouraging signs, large parts of the Aral Sea have vanished for ever. It remains a lesson that there are often unexpected consequences when people try to exploit their natural environment.

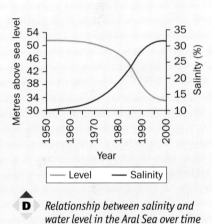

D *Relationship between salinity and water level in the Aral Sea over time*

Skills link

Relationships between different factors can be seen quickly and easily using multiple line graphs like graph **D**. For more details on how to interpret them, see Section 4.3 pages 220–21.

Now Investigate

1 Describe the environment of the Aral Sea area using the information in this case study.

2 Referring to photos **C**, draw a sketch map to show how the area has changed over the last 60 years.

3 Describe the relationship between salinity and water level as shown in graph **D**.

4 Write a few paragraphs to explain why the Aral Sea is 'one of the planet's most shocking environmental disasters'.

It is clear that extreme damage can occur when the use of the natural environment is not well managed. However, in some parts of the world careful management is allowing people to exploit the natural environment in a sustainable manner.

Polar regions

The polar regions of the planet lie inside the Arctic and Antarctic Circles, north of 66°N and south of 66°S. These areas are extremely cold, mainly covered in ice and have low levels of precipitation. Technically they are referred to as 'cold deserts' because deserts are defined by a lack of rainfall. Life for the people who live in these regions can be extremely hard, with long winters when darkness lasts for 24 hours and temperatures are very low, and with almost no opportunity for agriculture. Remarkably, there are people who make these areas their home and who manage to survive and do well economically.

Case study

Greenland – the biggest island in the world

Greenland, in the North Atlantic, lies mainly within the Arctic Circle (map **A**) and is the world's largest island (not including those that are classified as continents). It is 95 per cent covered in ice, with one-twentieth of the world's total. Its 55 000 inhabitants live in coastal areas.

Traditionally the main way for the islanders to make money has been through fishing, fish processing, seal hunting and fur trapping. Only 1 per cent of the land is suitable for agriculture but, here, farmers raise cattle, sheep and goats and grow a few vegetables.

The last ten years or so has seen some big changes to this traditional pattern. Greenland has been advertising itself as a major ecotourist destination, giving adventurous visitors the chance to see one of the world's last true wildernesses (figure **B**).

Many people come to cruise around the dramatic coastline, to go fishing or hiking, or to view some of the wildlife. There are also many opportunities for specialist tourist holidays. Adventure tourists can go dog-sledding, kayaking or heli-skiing, while other holidays cater for people who want to eat the local food or see unique sights such as the Northern Lights (photo **C**).

Map A

Arctic Ocean
N

CANADA

Thule

Baffin Bay

Greenland Sea

GREENLAND

Ilulissat

Sisimiut

Arctic circle

ICELAND

Nuuk

Denmark Strait

Qaqortoq

Davis Strait

Atlantic Ocean

0   200 km

Ice free land   Inland ice/glacier

A *Greenland*

Digging for wealth

Perhaps the most important recent development for the wealth of Greenland has come partly because of environmental problems elsewhere. A steady rise in local temperatures, perhaps brought about as part of global climate change, means that the vast ice sheet is beginning to melt, making it easier to access the huge mineral deposits on the island (map **D**). Increases in the global price of various metals have also made it attractive for companies to open up mines here.

Angel Mining is currently re-opening the Black Angel Mine to extract lead and zinc. It is also looking at taking gold from another site, and wants to look for other metals and coal. Other companies in Greenland are searching for diamonds, copper, silver and many other valuable minerals.

These developments bring employment to the people of Greenland and money for the government of the country. The exploitation of the environment is being strictly controlled to make sure there is minimal damage to the beauty of the natural landscape.

B *Tatra Mountains in Greenland*

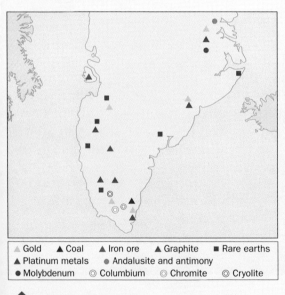

Gold ▲ Coal ▲ Iron ore ▲ Graphite ■ Rare earths
▲ Platinum metals ● Andalusite and antimony
● Molybdenum ◎ Columbium ◎ Chromite ◎ Cryolite

D *Mineral deposits around the Greenland coast*

C *The Northern Lights*

Topic link

There is more about the general rise in tourism around the world in Topic 3.5 pages 162–67.

Skills link

Map D is one way of showing information on a map, using symbols. For more information on interpreting different kinds of maps see Sections 4.1 and 4.2.

Now Investigate

1 Where are the world's polar regions? What are the main features that make it difficult for humans to live in these areas?

2 a Describe how people living in Greenland are able to make a living from their natural environment.

 b What kinds of problems could be caused by what they are doing?

3 This case study of Greenland suggests many opportunities for tourism in the Arctic. What about on the other side of the world? Using the internet, investigate tourist activities in Antarctica and write a few paragraphs explaining what they are.

3.1 Agricultural systems: what do farmers grow in your local area?

- describe what farming is all about
- explain how people, money and the natural world affect farms and farmers
- relate what you know to different types of farming around the world.

Now Investigate

What type of farming do you have in your local area? List all the types you can think of and then compare your answer with those of others in your class.

Your farming industry

Take a look at the farmer in photo **A**. He is one of millions of people around the world trying to grow crops to feed his family or to sell to make a living. In this case he is growing rice – as do many people living in east and southeast Asia. But why has he chosen this particular crop? Is it because of the landscape or the soil? Perhaps the climate is just right, with lots of sun and lots of rain. Or it may just be because this is what his father and grandfather grew and so it has been a tradition for hundreds of years. There are many different types of farming in the world. The type that takes place in a certain area will depend on a combination of natural and human factors.

A *A rice farmer in China*

Types of farming

The many different types of farming can be classified according to the definitions shown in diagram **B**.

Putting these together can help us describe different types of farming. For example, an extensive commercial pastoral farm will use a large area of land to rear animals in order to make a profit.

By what we get out of them
Commercial farming produces food for sale
Subsistence farming produces only enough food for the farmer and his family (with perhaps a little left over to sell)

CLASSIFYING FARM TYPES

By what we put into them
Intensive farms use large amounts of money, machines and technology or workers
Extensive farms have smaller inputs but usually use more land

By what is grown
Arable farms grow crops
Pastoral farms rear animals
Mixed farms grow crops and rear animals

B *Classification of farming types*

Farming is not always easy to classify. Subsistence farmers may have a small surplus to sell at a market. Some extensive farms may have periods in the year, such as harvest time, when there is intensive activity involving lots of workers.

Nomads are farmers who move around from one area to another. There used to be many nomads taking herds of animals across Africa in search of grassland to feed them on. Recently, however, many have been forced to settle down into sedentary farming with permanent farms and settlements.

The farming system

Another way to describe farming is to use a **systems diagram**. This has three main parts:

- **inputs** – the things that go into the system
- **outputs** – the things that come out of the system
- **processes** – the things that happen to the inputs to turn them into outputs.

A range of inputs, processes and outputs is shown in the systems diagram **C**. The diagram shows there may be some **feedback** in the system so that if the outputs include a profit it may be reinvested as an input of capital.

The decision-making farmer

The rice farmer in photo **A** has chosen this particular crop for a number of reasons. It grows well in the hot, wet climate where he lives. It can be grown in small fields with fertile soil. It does not need expensive machinery or fertiliser. It has been grown in his country for many centuries, so everyone understands how the system works. Most importantly, it gives a high yield (the amount of crop from a given area) so it can feed his large family using only the small plot of land that he owns.

Now Investigate

1 Write down definitions for each of the following types of farming:

commercial   pastoral
nomadic   intensive.

2 What are the characteristics of:

a intensive subsistence farming

b extensive arable farming

c intensive commercial mixed farming?

3 Choose a type of farming found in your own region. Draw a systems diagram to show its main inputs, processes and outputs.

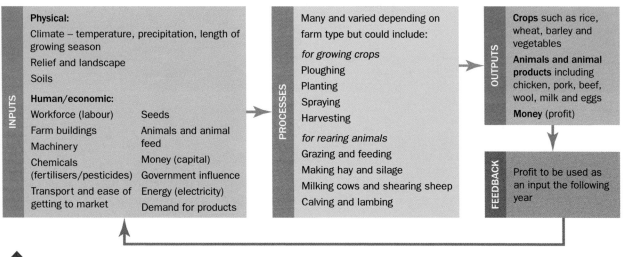

INPUTS	PROCESSES	OUTPUTS
Physical: Climate – temperature, precipitation, length of growing season Relief and landscape Soils **Human/economic:** Workforce (labour) Seeds Farm buildings Animals and animal feed Machinery Money (capital) Chemicals (fertilisers/pesticides) Government influence Transport and ease of getting to market Energy (electricity) Demand for products	Many and varied depending on farm type but could include: *for growing crops* Ploughing Planting Spraying Harvesting *for rearing animals* Grazing and feeding Making hay and silage Milking cows and shearing sheep Calving and lambing	**Crops** such as rice, wheat, barley and vegetables **Animals and animal products** including chicken, pork, beef, wool, milk and eggs **Money** (profit) FEEDBACK: Profit to be used as an input the following year

C A farming systems diagram

Inputs to the farming system

Inputs can be classified as either natural (physical) or human (and economic).

Natural inputs

Climate is one of the main things influencing what type of farming takes place:

- All plants need a minimum temperature in order to grow. When the temperature is above this minimum the plant will be in its growing season. The length of the growing season must be enough to allow the plant to develop. Low temperatures may cause frosts that kill crops or even freeze the ground so that nothing can grow.
- Mean annual rainfall (or precipitation) determines how much water is available for plants. In very dry areas, such as deserts, few plants can be grown. The type of rainfall is also important as heavy thunderstorms can cause soil erosion and destroy crops. If the rain falls when the temperature is high, the water will evaporate so little will be available for plants to use.

In some areas of low rainfall, water can be taken to fields by irrigation from rivers, lakes and underground water stores. It often requires large amounts of money to set up an irrigation system.

Relief refers to the hills, valleys and mountains found in an area:

- Height influences the type of farming because the temperature drops the higher up you are.
- Aspect (the direction the land faces) is important. In the northern hemisphere, south-facing slopes receive more sunlight and are warmer (north-facing slopes in the southern hemisphere).
- Steep slopes often mean that soils are thinner. They also make it harder to use machinery. In south-east Asia, hillsides have been terraced to take account of this (photo **A**). Some of these terraces are hundreds and even thousands of years old.

Soil type and factors such as stoniness and how deep the soil is influence what crops can be grown. **Fertile** soils like those found in river deltas like the Mekong have lots of nutrients that plants need to grow. The quality of a soil can be improved by adding fertilisers but not all farmers can afford them.

A Terraced hillsides in China

B Picking olives from trees in Palestine

Human inputs

Farms need enough workers (labour) to do all the jobs necessary to grow crops or look after animals. In some countries this work, such as olive picking (photo **B**), may be seasonal (for part of the year only).

Many of the other human inputs are **economic** and depend on how much money is available to buy, or do, certain things:

- Farm buildings – they are needed for storage of crops and equipment.

- Machinery – it can make farming much easier and means that farmers do not have to pay workers, but it can be very expensive to buy (photo **C**).
- Chemicals – fertilisers can help crops to grow, while pesticides and herbicides will stop them being attacked by insects and diseases. However, chemicals are also expensive and can be damaging to the environment.
- Transport and markets – some crops need to be taken to market quickly before they deteriorate but transport can cost a lot of money and in some countries (for example mountainous regions) transport can be difficult.
- Seeds, animals and animal feed and energy – all cost the farmer money.
- Government influence – in some countries, such as the USA and France, the government gives subsidies (payments) to farmers to grow certain types of crops.
- Demand – if there is a shortage of a certain crop, for example because of drought, then demand increases and the price the farmer gets for the crop can rise quickly.

Farmers with lots of money (capital), or agribusinesses that run big farms, can keep up with the latest technology, are much more efficient and make much bigger profits.

World farming types

The different natural and human inputs combine so that different farming types occur in different parts of the world – some of these are shown in map **D**.

The distribution shown on the map is very general. In some areas specialised crops may be grown. In others, several types of farming may take place. Often, one type of farming gradually merges with another, rather than there being a fixed boundary.

C *Machinery can be very expensive for farmers*

Topic link

You can find out more about the environmental risks and benefits of agriculture in Topic 3.9 on pages 188–93.

Fantastic fact

Strange but true – in some countries, governments pay farmers to do no farming at all on parts of their land in order to help keep the environment looking natural.

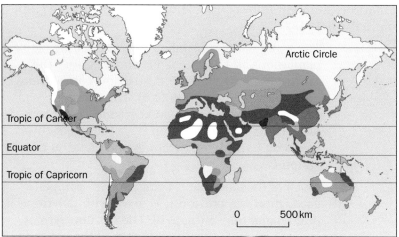

D *World farming types*

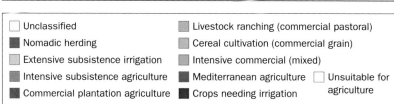

☐ Unclassified	▨ Livestock ranching (commercial pastoral)
▨ Nomadic herding	▨ Cereal cultivation (commercial grain)
▨ Extensive subsistence irrigation	▨ Intensive commercial (mixed)
▨ Intensive subsistence agriculture	▨ Mediterranean agriculture ☐ Unsuitable for agriculture
▨ Commercial plantation agriculture	▨ Crops needing irrigation

Now Investigate

1. Look at the list of natural and human factors affecting farming. Try to rank a top five in order of importance and write reasons justifying your answer.

2. Describe the global distribution of different farming types shown in map **D**.

3. According to map **D**, what type of farming takes place in the region where you live? How does this compare with the types of farming you identified on pages 132–33?

Commercial farming systems

The main feature of commercial farming is that it is carried out to make a profit. In richer countries this is often done by individual farmers. On the grassland prairies of the USA and Canada, for example, farmers own huge areas of land and grow wheat or have cattle ranches with thousands of animals. The land use is extensive, because it takes place over a large area, and the farm needs big inputs of money, machinery and fertilisers and pesticides. Workers are often employed only for brief periods of the year when harvesting or planting needs to be carried out quickly.

Topic link

There is more on the environmental effects of commercial agriculture in Topic 3.9 on pages 188–93.

In poorer countries, most farmers do not have enough money to farm on a large scale, so agribusinesses are often in control of the agriculture. Agribusinesses are huge companies that own land in many different countries. Del Monte, for instance, is the world's third largest producer of bananas. It has farms in Costa Rica, Guatemala, Ecuador, Colombia and the Philippines but, like many multinational companies, its headquarters are in the USA.

Much of the commercial agriculture in tropical areas is carried out on plantations. These are vast areas of land which have been deforested and the trees replaced with a single type of crop. This is known as monoculture and produces crops which are mainly sold for export to other countries. Examples of these crops, known as cash crops, include rubber, coffee, tea, cocoa, palm oil, sugar cane and tobacco.

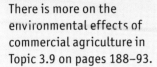

Case study

Plantation agriculture in Sarawak, Malaysia

Commercial plantation agriculture has long been a feature of the landscape in Malaysia (map **A**). The first British-owned plantations were based on coffee and then later on rubber. The British government provided the money to set up the original plantations and built railway lines and ports to export the crop around the world.

The Malaysian government now runs all the major plantations and has made big changes since the time of the British. The industry now concentrates on growing palm oil (photo **B**). The region of Sarawak, for example, exports around 10 per cent of Malaysia's total. The crop is well suited to this area with its high temperatures and plentiful rainfall (graph **C**).

Much of the land that is being used for palm oil production was previously covered with rare tropical peat swamp forests (maps **D**). There is now serious concern by environmentalists that all these forests will have been destroyed by 2020.

The palm oil is bringing in lots of money, however, for Malaysia's economy. Most of it is exported to other countries (graph **E**) through the main ports of Kuching, Sibu, Bintulu and Miri.

A *Malaysia, south-east Asia*

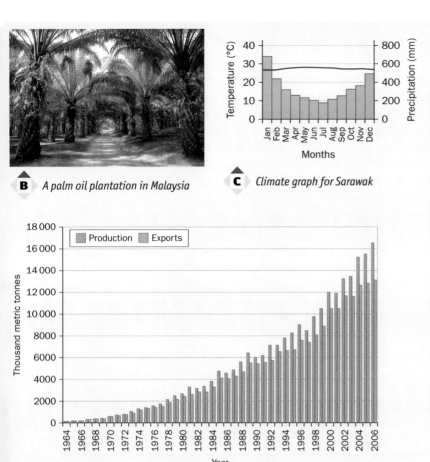

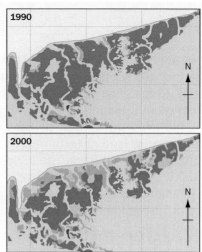

B   A palm oil plantation in Malaysia

C   Climate graph for Sarawak

E   Palm oil production and exports in Malaysia, 1964–2006

Peat swamp forest   Urban areas

Plantations   Open land

D   Destruction of peat swamp forest for palm oil production in Sarawak

Inputs to the palm oil production system are shown in diagram **F**.

The production of palm oil now accounts for 6 per cent of the economy of Malaysia.

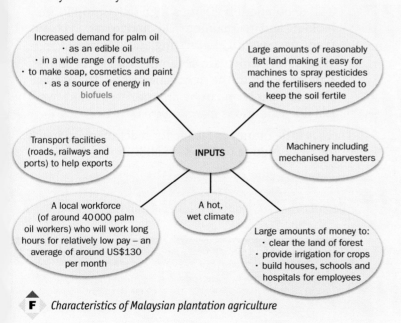

F   Characteristics of Malaysian plantation agriculture

Now Investigate

1 Find out about any commercial farming that takes place in the region where you live. Describe the characteristics of this local agricultural system.

2 Using graph **E** and the text, describe and explain the growth of palm oil production in Malaysia.

3 What are some of the problems associated with palm oil production in Sarawak?

Subsistence farming systems

Subsistence farming is carried out to feed the farmer and his family. If there is any surplus it will normally be sold in the local community. It is often the dominant form of agriculture in poor countries where people do not have the money, land or technology to increase the amount they produce. The main aim is survival and subsistence farmers are very vulnerable to conditions that cause food shortages.

Shifting cultivation

In the Amazon and Congo rainforests some tribes carry out shifting cultivation. They build a small central village and farm crops in gardens nearby.

When the soil quality starts to decrease they move their garden to a neighbouring area. Food crops (including plantain, cassava, sweet potato, yam, banana and other fruits) grow easily so very few inputs are needed apart from the natural environment and large areas of land.

The most widespread form of subsistence farming is intensive rice cultivation. Land is all-important (see photo **A** on page 132). Rice is very high-yielding and grows so fast that up to three crops can be harvested each year. Despite this, there is little surplus because of the large number of people the rice has to support (almost 3 billion people in China and India).

Case study

Rice farming in Bangladesh

Bangladesh has one of the highest population densities in the world. Almost half its 158 million people work in agriculture, with rice being by far the most important crop (map **A**). Some of the features of the rice farming landscape are shown in photo **B**.

The major inputs to the rice farming system are:
- a climate with plenty of rain and high temperatures providing ideal conditions for plants to grow all year round (graph **C**)
- fertile soils from the silt deposited by the flooding river Ganges
- a large population giving a high labour input for building and maintaining fields and irrigation channels, planting, weeding, harvesting and other tasks
- small farms which are becoming smaller as land is handed down to the next generation – the average farm size has been cut by around 50 per cent over the last 50 years and is now around 0.61 hectares.

There is little money available for machinery, so much of the work is done by hand. In addition to the major

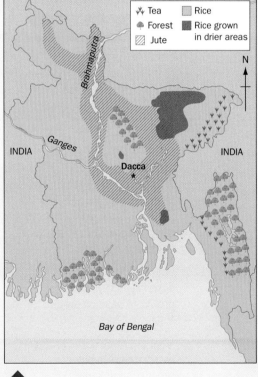

A *Land use in Bangladesh*

Now Investigate !

Describe the main land use features of Bangladesh using map **A**.

Fantastic fact 🌍

The average person in Bangladesh eats more than 200 kg of rice every year.

Fruit trees to add to diet

Small fields (called padis) which may get smaller when passed on to the next generation

Animals may be used for ploughing instead of expensive machines

Small rice plants may be grown in nursery beds before being moved to bigger fields

Low walls (called bunds) built to keep water in the padi fields

Fish may be added to padi fields to add protein to diet

Rice planted under water from heavy rainfall, flooding or irrigation

B *Features of the rice farming landscape*

output (rice), farmers may grow vegetables on small plots of land and pick fruit from trees surrounding their villages. Farmers have also been encouraged to farm fish in the flooded padi fields.

The farmers of Bangladesh have faced tough times recently with world rice prices increasing and natural disasters, including floods, wiping out crops. Despite this, production has continued to rise (graph **D**) because of hard work by rural people. There has also been considerable government investment in new irrigation schemes to allow year-round rice-growing in drier areas of the country. Over 80 per cent of this irrigation is by pumping from sources found under the ground (known as groundwater stores).

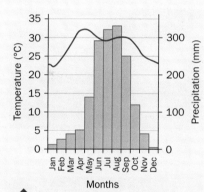
C *Climate graph for Bangladesh*

Now Investigate

1 What are the main characteristics of subsistence farming?

2 Describe and explain the main features of an intensive rice farming landscape.

3 With reference to a country you have studied:

   a Explain why it is particularly suited to rice farming.

   b Describe some of the problems faced by its subsistence farmers.

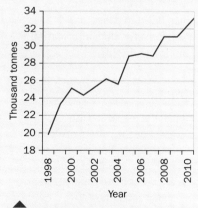
D *Rice production in Bangladesh, 1998–2010*

Skills link

You have to be able to interpret a wide range of maps for the IGCSE Geography exams, including land use maps like the one shown here. Refer to pages 200–07 in Section 4 to learn how to do this.

Further research

For more facts and figures about rice farming in Bangladesh, put 'Rice Country Profile Bangladesh' into your internet search engine.

Learning objectives:

> know why some people have lots of food and others very little

> explain how food shortages affect people

> describe how we can try to make sure everyone has enough to eat

> relate what you have learned to a global case study.

Your daily food supply

If you are lucky you will have woken up this morning and gone through the day with enough food to eat. This will have provided you with the calories your body needs. These calories give you the energy to work properly, to grow and develop into a healthy adult. Unfortunately, this will not have been the case for everyone in your country or in the wider world. As population grows, food is in ever shorter supply. Poor people such as Christian Medina, a miner in Bolivia, are the ones who suffer most (photo **A**).

Hola. My name is Christian Medina. I've always been poor but I've done my best to provide food and shelter for my family.

We can no longer afford the food we need. My children are hungry and are getting sick. Sometimes I give them all my food but then I'm too weak to work. How are we meant to survive?

A Christian Medina, miner, Bolivia, protesting against food shortages

Skills link

You need to be able to describe world distribution maps like map B. Go to pages 200–11 in Section 4 for more information on how to do this.

Now Investigate

1 Look at map **B** and use it to describe the pattern of global food supply. Remember to name individual countries in your answer and explain what the map shows about them.

2 Try to find out how many calories you eat in a day. You could try searching the internet using 'Calorie Counter' to help.

The right food in the wrong places

It would seem there is a direct connection between an increasing population and there not being enough food to eat. But the story is not that simple. Global grain production – the rice, wheat and maize that is the basic diet for most people – has increased so much over the last 40 years that the amount available per person has stayed fairly constant.

It is estimated that there is enough food in the world for everybody to get 3000 calories a day. The minimum needed to survive is around 2500 calories but, in many countries, there are large numbers of people eating much less than this. Map **B** shows where

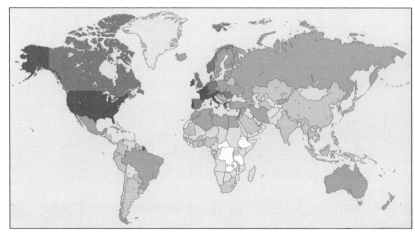

Kcal/person/day per country in 2001–03 (world average 2800 kcal/person/day)

- [ ] 1600–2000
- 2000–2400
- 2400–2800
- 2800–3200
- 3200–3600
- More than 3600

B World food supply

these people live by displaying the average number of calories eaten per person in each country. It also shows the countries where people eat far more than the amount they need to survive. The problem is not the lack of food in the world but the fact that much of it is not distributed equally.

Causes of food shortages

Demand for food from wealthier countries, including India and China, has caused the price of food to increase rapidly. Many poor countries do not grow enough food and can no longer afford to import enough for their people. Recent increases in transport and fuel costs have caused food prices to rise further. Other factors play a part:

- Drought, floods, tropical cyclones and other extreme weather events have caused crops to fail.
- Natural disasters (especially earthquakes) affect food distribution by destroying or damaging roads and other transport links.
- Outbreaks of disease including cholera, malaria and HIV/AIDS mean people are not able to work on their farms and grow food.
- In some years, pests, including locusts, destroy vast amounts of cropland.
- Civil wars, like those in Darfur (Sudan) and in Sierra Leone, disrupt food supplies as farmers are afraid to go out to their fields, transport routes are destroyed and soldiers demand food from local people.
- As population has increased, people have had to farm less suitable land. This has led to erosion of the soil so that it becomes unable to support plant life – this is known as soil exhaustion.

Some of these reasons could be due to the world's changing climate. The United Nations has estimated that three-quarters of the world's poorest people live in areas that will be affected by crop failures due to global warming.

Drought 2011 – The Horn of Africa

Months of no rain in countries including Ethiopia and Djibouti resulted, by mid 2011, in drought and crop failure affecting more than 10 million people.

Rising crop prices led to widespread malnutrition and starvation. There was a refugee crisis as starving people tried to move to areas where food was available.

The situation was most severe in Somalia. People already weakened by years of war and civil unrest fled to Kenya and Ethiopia at a rate of more than 1300 people each day. This added to the problems of food supply in the receiving countries.

Even when the crisis is over, there are fears it will take many years for the region to recover. Many of the people affected are nomads who rely on their animals to survive. The drought killed their camels and cattle, so they have lost their livelihood and long-term source of food.

Topic link

More on the environmental effects of agriculture can be found in Topic 3.9 on pages 188–93.

Fantastic fact

The largest recorded locust swarm covered 1036 km² and was estimated to comprise 40 billion insects.

Now Investigate

1 What recent natural disasters can you think of that may have affected food shortages? Name the countries where these disasters have taken place.

2 Describe and explain any factors that could cause food shortages in your own country.

3 Do you think reducing population growth would end food shortages? Explain your answer.

C *Drought can cause huge loss of livestock*

Problems

- **Protein-energy malnutrition** is caused by a lack of protein (from meat, eggs and other sources) and food that provides energy (e.g. rice, wheat and potatoes) – it is the major cause of world hunger.

- **Micronutrient malnutrition** is when the body lacks certain vitamins and minerals.

Diseases caused

- **Marasmus** causes sufferers to become very thin and stop growing.

- **Kwashiorkor** is caused by eating too many cereals and not enough protein – the stomach swells, skin peels and the hair turns orange.

- **Anaemia** is caused by a lack of iron.

- **Vitamin A deficiency** causes blindness and death.

- **Iodine deficiency** affects the brain and can be fatal.

A *Malnutrition and disease*

When something is missing from the daily diet, this causes malnutrition. This can be a lack of enough food or of certain minerals or vitamins (panel **A**). Around 900 million people (13 per cent of the world's population) do not have enough food. They are almost all found in LEDCs and many of them are children.

Those who suffer from malnutrition are not able to work because of a lack of energy, mental problems and general poor health. Family incomes fall and people continue to become ill through lack of food.

B *Distribution of food aid*

Tackling the food supply problem

When poor countries have a problem with food shortages, especially when it is the result of a natural disaster such as a drought, cyclone or earthquake, richer countries often help out with food aid (photo **B**).

Africa is particularly in need of food aid. Problems for specific countries include:
- conflict, drought and piracy in Somalia
- drought, AIDS and high population density causing a shortage of land in Malawi
- the long-term effects of civil war in Sudan
- locust attack in Niger
- increasing numbers of refugees in Liberia.

There are concerns that handing out food does little to solve long-term problems and many countries become too dependent on hand-outs. Increasingly, governments are trying to help countries improve their agriculture in order to maintain their food security. This means they would have enough food to feed their own people without relying on imports or help from overseas.

The Green Revolution

Since the 1960s scientists across the world have been helping to improve agriculture for subsistence farmers in different regions of the world. They have developed new types of rice, maize and wheat that produce more (give higher yields).

The Green Revolution has brought problems as well as benefits. Overall, however, it has helped crop production to keep up with population growth.

Now Investigate

1 a List some of the diseases caused by a lack of food.

  b What effects do these diseases have on the countries where people are suffering?

The Green Revolution

Aims: to scientifically develop new types of rice that give higher yields; to introduce new irrigation schemes; to use new fertilisers to help crops grow and new pesticides to protect them from disease.

Benefits

- Food production has increased, so more people can be fed.

- Higher yields means lower prices, so poor people can afford more food.

- Crops are more resistant to disease, so harvests are more reliable.

- Crops grow faster, so more harvests can be gathered each year.

- The better-off farmers who can afford chemicals and machinery have become richer and employ more local people.

- More jobs are available in businesses supporting farming.

Problems

- Not all farmers have felt the benefits of the Green Revolution.

- The less well-off who could not compete have sold their land and moved to the city.

- Some farmers have borrowed money to pay for crops and are now in debt.

- Machinery has caused rural unemployment.

- Chemicals have polluted local water supplies.

- Irrigation has increased the demand on drinking water stores.

- Some of the new varieties of rice are not as pleasant to eat.

A more recent development has been the Blue Revolution. Communities have been encouraged to breed fish – in mangrove swamps, padi fields, lakes and near the coast – to provide more protein.

Genetically modified (GM) crops

The latest technological advances have been in GM crops. The idea is to alter crops scientifically to enable them to withstand pests and diseases and to help them survive droughts or the very salty conditions found in some LEDCs.

These crops have the potential to increase the amount of food that can be grown by enabling farmers to plant in areas that were thought to be unsuitable. However, some countries have banned GM crops until they are proved to be safe for both people and the environment.

Intermediate and appropriate technology

Many of the methods used to increase food production need new technology. Others depend on simpler solutions that are more affordable for poor countries and use existing local skills and technology, for example:

- educating farmers to save water by building dams on seasonal rivers
- saving land from erosion by building small terraces on gently sloping land
- using solar energy (the power of the sun) to pump water for irrigation.

Closely linked to this is the development of permaculture. People living in cities are encouraged to grow their own food in urban gardens. The Caribbean island of Cuba is one of many countries where people in cities have set up local markets to sell food on at reasonable prices (photo **C**).

C Urban gardening in Hong Kong

Now Investigate

2 Describe some of the methods used to increase food production and reduce food shortages.

3 Have a look at the food you eat at home. Was it produced locally? What could be done to increase the amount of locally produced food in the area where you live?

Governments have an important role to play in both causing and dealing with food shortages. Some of the factors affecting food supply can be dealt with through government investment in the following:

- providing an efficient infrastructure for distribution – this includes well maintained roads and port facilities so that food can be taken quickly to those areas that need it
- building up reserves of food when it is available, to be handed out when drought or natural disaster happens
- avoiding wars and conflicts that can lead to people being deprived of food
- investing money in farming – perhaps by providing loans or equipment to farmers
- making sure that land is available to grow locally eaten food crops – in some countries there has been a concentration on growing food for export.

The most important role of a government should be in caring for its citizens. But not all governments can afford to take action. People feel let down when there is not enough food for them to eat. Recently, as food shortages have increased, people's anger has turned to riots in several LEDCs.

Case study

Food shortages in Bolivia

Bolivia is a country without a coastline in the interior of South America. It has a very varied landscape including high mountains and lowland rainforests (map **A**) but much of the land is very limited in its use for agriculture. Only about 2 per cent is considered good arable land (graph **B**). Producing food is difficult and distributing it across the mountainous landscape to a scattered population is expensive. Drought, frosts, hail and soil erosion add to the food supply problems.

Agriculture is the major employer. Around 40 per cent of the population make a living either from subsistence farming on the high plains or export crops (soybeans, coffee and sugar cane) in the tropical areas. There has been much criticism of foreign-owned agribusinesses in the country. They take up much of the best land which could be used to grow food for local people.

Around 60 per cent of the people are poor and unable to buy enough food. They have been badly affected by recent price rises. In a 12-month period between 2010 and 2011 the price of bread rose between 65 and 100 per cent across the country. Recent fuel price rises also increased transport costs. At the start of 2011, many towns and cities began to run out of sugar and other basic foodstuffs. The

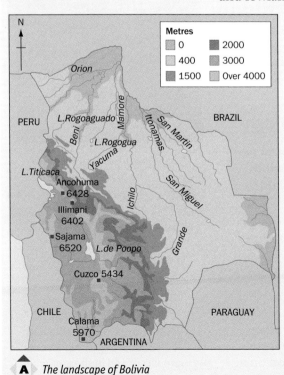

Metres	
0	2000
400	3000
1500	Over 4000

A *The landscape of Bolivia*

people, including miners like Christian Medina (see page 140), became very angry indeed and took to the streets to protest (photo **C**). Bolivian unions said a family's basic monthly needs had risen to US$1100 a month, far in excess of the average monthly wage of $96.

The Bolivian president has blamed the shortages on increased demand from China and India putting up food prices (graph **D**). Others say the government has encouraged agribusinesses to grow soybeans and other crops for export rather than growing food for people to eat.

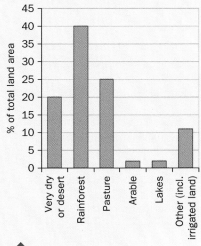

B Bolivian land use

> What can I do but take to the streets? We need action from our government. They can't leave us to starve like this.

C Miner protesting in Uyuni, Bolivia

When the Bolivians protest, they do so in a very distinctive way by blocking roads and causing general disruption. Many of the country's workers are miners and can easily get hold of explosive dynamite.

In a recent demonstration against rising food prices in the town of Uyuni, marching miners threw dynamite towards the country's president to express their anger. Luckily, as they are experienced users, people rarely get hurt by the flying explosive.

Further research 🔍

Find out more about the case study by searching for 'Bolivia Food Shortages' or 'Bolivia Food Protest' on the internet.

Now Investigate ❗

1 How can a government influence a country's food supply?

2 Describe the landscape of Bolivia and explain how it affects the country's ability to feed its population.

3 Imagine you are Christian Medina and your family is suffering from a lack of food. Write a brief essay explaining what you would do to get the government to help.

FAO Food Price Index: 2002–04 = 100

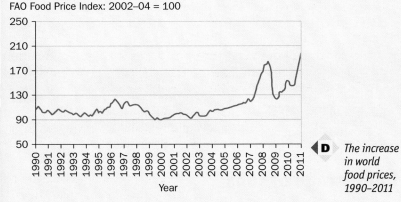

D The increase in world food prices, 1990–2011

The steady rise in the price of food has had a serious impact on the poor of Bolivia. With no extra money to spend when prices rise, the only option for them and their families is to eat less food. Long-term solutions are needed if the people of Bolivia are to have enough food to survive.

Learning objectives:

- talk about the wide range of jobs available around the world
- explain how industry finds, makes and sells things
- describe how people's jobs change as a country gets richer
- relate what you know to global case studies.

Your future employment

What kind of job would you like to do? There are a huge number of options available. If you like working with your hands, farming or factory work may appeal to you. If you want to use your brain you could be inventing the next generation of 3D televisions. Or you may want to look after others as a nurse or doctor. Some people try several different jobs before settling on a career. It may even be that the job you will do hasn't been invented yet – 20 years ago, for example, there was no such thing as a mobile phone apps designer.

A world of jobs

Now Investigate

Look at the pictures of different jobs in figure **A**. Can you identify what kinds of jobs are shown? Write down a list of the good and bad points of each job.

A huge range of jobs

Even at a very young age some people know what work they want to do. This may be because they are born into a family where they are expected to do a certain job. Farmers, for instance, often pass their land on to their children. In other cases, people may be limited by the jobs available in their local area, and some may choose to move away from home to find work.

People living in areas where there is a greater variety of work may have more choice. Those with good standards of education or specialist skills may be able to choose from a number of employment opportunities. Figure **B** gives examples of young people from around the world and their ideas on what they will be doing in the future.

My father is a miner and my grandfather was before him. There's no doubt I will be too when I am old enough. The work is hard but the pay is good, especially compared to working on a farm which is about the only other thing to do around here.

I don't really think about how dangerous it is. I know people die every now and then but I just have to hope I'm not one of the unlucky ones.

Peter Malema: Messina, South Africa

The only place to work around here is the drinks factory. Before it was built there was nobody here but the factory came and the people followed. My dad was one of the first to work, putting the liquid into the bottles.

He's gone now and left me to help mum bring up my brothers and sisters. In a year I'll be old enough to go and ask for a job. I'm sure they'll give me one – there are always people moving on and new workers needed.

Jesus do Silva: São Paolo, Brazil

Lots of tourists are coming to our island nowadays and it's been great for jobs. All my parents knew before was how to catch and sell fish but now there are many different ways we can make money. There's work in the hotels as receptionists, waiters, looking after the grounds and all sorts.

If I can get a decent education I could even become a tour guide. This is where the big money is. Good wages and loads of tips. I'd love to tell the visitors all about our history so it would be just great for me.

Evon Dunn: Kingston, Jamaica

Zhijia Jingzhou: Shanghai, China

We live in a high-tech society. Mobile phones, computers, music players are all part of our everyday life and, living here, we're right in the heart of where it all comes from.

At my school we're big on science and technology. Things are moving really fast and we're all trying to be prepared for the jobs of the future. When I start work I want to be involved in making stuff the whole world wants to buy.

Now Investigate !

1. Read through the different jobs described by the people on this page. Pick two you would like to do and write down why you would like to do them.

2. What kind of skills and qualifications might you need to be able to do these jobs?

3. What do you think is meant by 'the job you will do hasn't been invented yet'?

4. What would be your ideal job? Where would that kind of job be available? What kind of skills will you need to be able to do it?

There are many ways in which people can earn a living and help their country's economy. This economic activity involves different types of industry – the ways in which products and services are made. The car industry, for instance, includes all the businesses and people involved in making cars, from the designers to the people putting the parts together in factories and those selling the finished models in large showrooms.

All economic activities can be classified into three different types of industry, known as **sectors**:

- the primary (or extractive) sector
- the secondary (or manufacturing) sector
- the tertiary (or service) sector.

Primary industry

Primary industries are those that work by taking something out of the earth. For this reason they are also known as **extractive** industries. Examples include fishing, farming, mining (photo **A**), quarrying and forestry.

Some primary industries produce goods that are sold to the public exactly as they are when taken out of the ground. Farmers, for instance, harvest their crops and sell them directly at markets. Other industries, such as logging, sell raw materials that are used to make different products. Trees are cut down and the wood is sent to companies that make furniture, paper or other timber goods.

A Coal miners take their products directly from the ground

 B Computers are put together in factories

Secondary industry

Secondary industries take raw materials and make new products from them. This is called **processing** or **manufacturing** and includes industries making everything from clothes and computers to cars and tinned food.

In many cases the raw materials are the products of a country's primary industries, for example oil is processed to make gasoline or petroleum. Raw materials can also be bought from other countries as imports. Some secondary industries use the products from other secondary industries to make the things they sell. For instance, in computer manufacture all the components such as circuit boards (photo **B**), cases and cables have already been made by other secondary industries before being put together in the factory. The finished goods can also be sold abroad as exports.

Secondary industries are good for a country because they 'add value' to the raw materials. There is much more money to be gained from selling clothes, for instance, than from selling the cotton that is used to make them.

Tertiary industry

Tertiary industries are those that provide a service so they are also known as **service industries**. This sector includes anything from hospitals with doctors and nurses to schools with teachers and other staff, or fire brigades and the police. Other examples are financial services such as banks, everything involved with tourism, and selling in shops (retailing).

One part of the tertiary industrial sector – which some people call quaternary industry – is made up of companies that provide knowledge and information. This includes research and development for high-technology companies such as mobile phone manufacturers and those involved with the internet. Call centres (photo **C**) have recently become a very large employer in this sector.

C Call centres are a growing industry

Now Investigate

1 Write definitions of:

   primary industry   secondary industry   tertiary industry.

2 Look at the list of jobs shown in figure **D**.

   a In a table, classify each job under the heading of the industry to which it belongs – primary, secondary or tertiary.

   b Which industrial sector has the most varied range of jobs?

3 Think about the area where you live. Give an example of an industry from each type of industrial sector that takes place:

   a in your local area

   b in another part of your country.

D Examples of different job types

- Teacher
- Writer
- Lawyer
- Oil worker
- Hairdresser
- Computer maker
- Fisherman
- Tea picker
- Diamond miner
- Waiter
- Sugar cane worker
- Steel worker
- Car factory worker
- Fashion designer
- Doctor
- Banker
- Mobile phone designer
- Shopworker
- Magician
- Crane operator
- Builder
- IT expert
- Farmer
- Food canning factory worker
- Carpenter
- Baby-sitter
- Mechanic
- Secretary
- Farmhand

Fantastic fact

For (almost) guaranteed employment, become a biomedical engineer, working on the application of technology to healthcare – it's the fastest-growing job category in the USA.

Changing countries, changing work

Agricultural employment decreases as technology means less workers are needed on the land

↓

Ex-farmworkers get jobs in factories and secondary industry increases

↓

Factories become more efficient and need fewer workers → Remaining workers become more highly skilled and better paid

↓

Exports increase as countries overseas demand products made by the factories

↓

Factories employ bigger management, sales and research teams to help increase exports further

A A process of industrial development

LEDCs, especially the poorest ones, tend to have a very high proportion of people working in agriculture as subsistence farmers. As countries develop, this proportion changes. One way in which this process of industrial development takes place is shown in diagram **A**.

B 20th-century employment in the USA, 1900–2000

	Agriculture	Manufacturing and mining	Services
Afghanistan	78.6	5.7	15.7
Bangladesh	45.0	30.0	25.0
Brazil	20.0	14.0	66.0
China	38.1	27.8	34.1
India	52.0	14.0	34.0
Nigeria	70.0	10.0	20.0
South Africa	9.0	26.0	65.0
United Kingdom	1.4	18.2	80.4
USA	0.7	20.3	79.0

Source: CIA World Factbook

C Percentage of people employed in different industries in selected countries

Graph **B** shows the effects of such development on the employment structure of the USA during the 20th century. There are many countries where this change is happening now. Table **C** shows that countries such as Nigeria and Afghanistan still have a high number of agricultural workers but the percentages are falling in China, India, Bangladesh and Brazil. South Africa has low numbers while in the United Kingdom and the USA the service sector is by far the biggest employer.

The informal sector

Unfortunately, many LEDCs are not developing quickly enough. This means that, despite the loss of farming jobs, there is not enough industrial employment for all those who need it. Unemployment rates can be very high. Underemployment (where people have some, but not enough work) is also a problem. This has led to the growth of the informal sector.

People with informal jobs do not get a regular wage but work when they need to, perhaps by selling goods on street corners or beaches, washing cars or shining shoes (photo **D**).

D Working in the informal sector

Presenting and interpreting data

The study of employment figures gives you a great opportunity to practise a number of skills for presenting and interpreting data, such as drawing pie charts, divided bar graphs and triangular graphs. This section shows how this can be done using the information in table **C**.

Pie charts are a very good way of quickly comparing this information and visually checking for major differences.

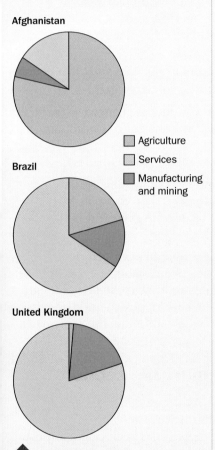

E Pie charts showing industrial employment in Afghanistan, Brazil and the United Kingdom

Divided bar graphs can be used to present this information in a different format – some people find them easier to draw.

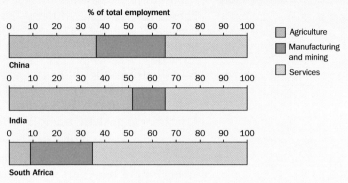

F Divided bar graphs showing industrial employment in China, India and South Africa

Triangular graphs can be used to show the information for several different countries at the same time. Although they are more difficult to draw this is probably the best technique for a good visual comparison.

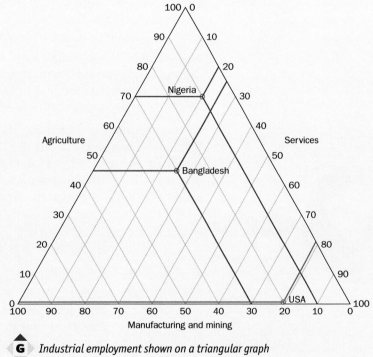

G Industrial employment shown on a triangular graph

Now Investigate

1 a Draw pie charts like those in diagram **E** for two of the other countries listed in table **C**. Describe the differences shown across all five charts.

 b Now try producing the same pie charts using the appropriate software on a computer.

2 Draw divided bar graphs like those in diagram **F** for two of the other countries listed in table **C**.

3 Make a copy of the triangular graph **G** and add the information for all the other countries in table **C**.

4 Describe the advantages and disadvantages of each of the presentation methods shown.

5 Using the information shown on these pages, rank all the countries in table **C** according to their level of development. Explain your answer.

Changes over time – Newly Industrialised Countries

Fantastic fact

Some experts think that, by 2050, the world's biggest economies will be China, USA, India, Brazil and Mexico.

Some LEDCs have economies that are expanding very quickly. They are becoming wealthier by developing their secondary industries. These LEDCs are called Newly Industrialised Countries (NICs).

The original NICs developed in south-east Asia in the 1970s. Also known as the **tiger economies**, they included South Korea, Singapore, Taiwan and Hong Kong. These countries are now regarded as MEDCs and have very advanced economies. Their place has been taken by the new NICs – China, India, Mexico, Brazil and South Africa – which share the following characteristics:

- strong government
- an economy moving away from primary industries and becoming based on manufacturing – often using raw materials produced by the primary industries
- free trade with other countries
- lots of foreign investment because of low tax rates and other benefits
- big, successful home-grown multinational companies.

The employment structure of these countries has changed so that there are fewer people employed in primary industries and the proportion in secondary industries has increased. Over time, as these industries need more services, tertiary sector employment also starts to go up.

NICs may have less strict health and safety laws and workers' organisations (unions) with less influence than those in MEDCs. This makes it easier for companies to operate there but may not be so good for the workers themselves.

As their economies expanded, the number of poor people in the original NICs quickly decreased. The governments encouraged their wealthier workers to invest in businesses to help the economy grow and made huge improvements in education, health and the general quality of life. It is hoped the new NICs will follow the same path.

Case study

Brazil – an emerging economy

Brazil is the biggest economy in South America and also the fastest growing. Over the past 20 years its economic growth has been on an almost continual upward climb (graph **A**). In 2010 it grew by 7.5 per cent while much of the world was suffering from recession.

There are a number of reasons for this success. The country has:

- a very varied (diversified) economy with money earned across many industrial sectors
- government investment in local industry and infrastructure
- encouragement of foreign investment (especially from China) through low taxes, cheap land, grants and loans

A *Brazil's economic growth, 1990–2009*

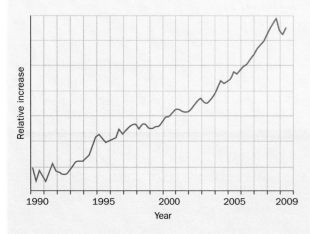

- relatively low wages, especially compared with MEDCs
- a large and increasingly wealthy population (who want to buy things) and access to markets throughout South and Central America.

China has a huge presence in Brazil. It is the country's biggest trading partner and spent US$140 billion on everything from oil exploration to building aircraft in 2008 alone. In particular, Brazil provides China with a great deal of food, especially chicken, beef and soybeans. Agricultural land is on the increase in Brazil, not just for food but also for ethanol to power motor vehicles. Around 52 per cent of Brazil's cars run on alcohol made from local sugar cane. There are concerns, however, that the increase in land for farming is leading to deforestation in the Amazonian rainforest (extract **C**).

B Unequal housing in Parasaipolis, Brazil

Cows for Trees in the Amazon

Much has been made of China's demand for soybeans from Brazil but the impact this is having on the rainforest appears to have been overestimated. Soybean farming is mainly taking place outside the Amazon region.

The biggest threat to the trees are cows. Between 65 and 70 per cent of all the deforestation taking place in Brazil is for cattle ranching. The country has the biggest cattle herd in the world, it is the world's biggest beef exporter, and it is planning to double production by 2018.

◀ **C**

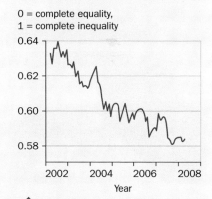

0 = complete equality,
1 = complete inequality

D Brazil's changing inequality, 2002–08

Many Brazilians are becoming much better off and there has been a big increase in the relatively wealthy middle classes. The country's index of inequality (graph **D**) has dropped sharply over the past few years. In spite of this, many Brazilians are still living in poverty in ramshackle houses with no running water or electricity (photo **B**). As the county's economy continues to improve, the challenge will be to make sure all sectors of society get an improved quality of life.

Now Investigate ❗

1 What are the main characteristics of a Newly Industrialised Country?

2 Using the information on these pages, describe economic activity in Brazil. Make sure you refer to primary, secondary and tertiary industries in your answer.

3 What problems could Brazil face as its economy keeps growing?

Learning objectives:

- list some of the things made by secondary industries

- explain how the manufacturing industry system works

- explain why high-technology industries are found in some places and other kinds of manufacturing are found somewhere else

- relate what you know to local and global examples.

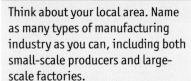

A *Manufacturing takes place at a variety of different scales*

Now Investigate ⓘ

Think about your local area. Name as many types of manufacturing industry as you can, including both small-scale producers and large-scale factories.

Topic link 🔗

See page 133 which shows how systems diagrams can also be used to explain how agriculture works.

Your local manufacturing industry

Somewhere near you somebody will be making things. This may be done in a huge factory with hundreds of workers assembling anything from saucepans to motor vehicles. Or it could be a person in their front room making jewellery from beads and bits of coloured glass. These people are all involved in some kind of manufacturing industry although, obviously, at very different scales (photos **A**). As we have seen, as a country develops, its secondary industry becomes more important than its primary industry because it brings in more money. This is a very important part of economic development for many countries around the world.

The secondary industrial system

As we have seen, systems diagrams are a useful way of showing how inputs, outputs and processes all fit together to explain how something works. Diagram **B** shows a systems diagram for secondary industry.

As with an agricultural system there are feedbacks. Profit can be reinvested as an input of capital. With an increasing demand for sustainability, waste is often recycled. In food processing, for instance, waste products from plants can sometimes be used as a source of energy to power factories (photo **C**).

Industrial location

The following inputs to the industrial system influence industrial location, or where an industry is located:

- **Raw materials** – these can be bulky and cost a lot to transport. Some industries, for example shipbuilding, may need to locate close to their raw materials because of this.

- **Energy supply** – in countries with a national electricity supply this will not be a problem. In others, factories may need to locate close to a power station.

- **Natural transport routes** – mountains will make transport difficult, while valleys are much easier.

- **Site and land** – many factories need large areas of relatively cheap, flat land to build on.

- **Capital (money)** – start-up costs can be very high for big factories. Rich investors may be needed.

- **Labour supply** – factories need skilled or unskilled workers or a mixture of both.

- **Transport** – ports, railways and good roads will make transport of raw materials and finished goods faster and easier.

- **Markets** – large numbers of people living close enough to buy products will help businesses thrive.

- **Government policies** – government can encourage industry by offering grants and tax breaks.
- **Technology** – email and other forms of global communication mean that factories can now be built a long way away from company headquarters.
- **Environment** – in some cases, a pleasant landscape and good local facilities attract the best workers.
- **Entrepreneurship** – businessmen may want to set up new companies near where they live or where they were born.
- **Research and development (R&D)** – industries that rely on advanced technology need to locate in countries where there are top scientists conducting research.

Before deciding where to build a factory, businesses will consider these location factors. It is unlikely that any one site will meet all of these requirements, so a decision may be made based on the most important ones. Political factors may also play a part. For instance, an Indian company may make a decision to locate in India rather than in Japan because that is better for its public image.

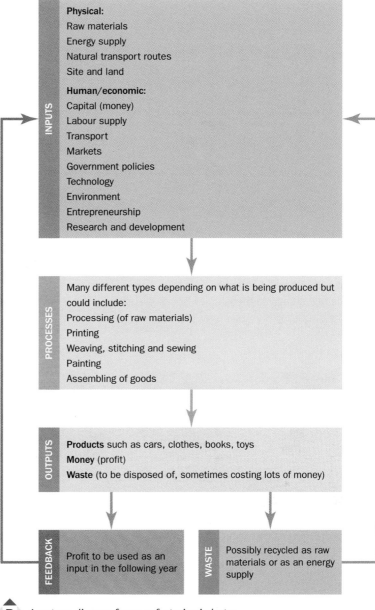

INPUTS

Physical:
Raw materials
Energy supply
Natural transport routes
Site and land

Human/economic:
Capital (money)
Labour supply
Transport
Markets
Government policies
Technology
Environment
Entrepreneurship
Research and development

PROCESSES

Many different types depending on what is being produced but could include:
Processing (of raw materials)
Printing
Weaving, stitching and sewing
Painting
Assembling of goods

OUTPUTS

Products such as cars, clothes, books, toys
Money (profit)
Waste (to be disposed of, sometimes costing lots of money)

FEEDBACK

Profit to be used as an input in the following year

WASTE

Possibly recycled as raw materials or as an energy supply

B *A systems diagram for manufacturing industry*

C *Biomass (waste plant products) being used to power a factory*

There are many reasons why companies locate their factories in a particular area. Some of the locations of the world's biggest export industries are shown on maps **B–E**. On all these maps the countries have been re-sized according to how important that particular industry is for each country. Map **A** is a world map showing actual land area for comparison.

The countries of the world by area of land

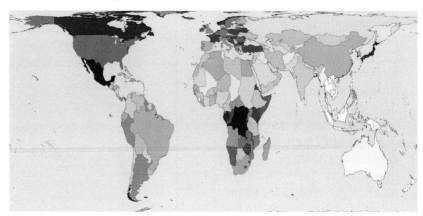

Now Investigate ❗

Look at maps **B** and **C** before you read the text alongside them. Describe the patterns you can see.

World car exports

Map **B** shows that world car exports are dominated by western Europe and eastern Asia. Germany and Japan account for 61 per cent of the total between them. One location factor for car factories is the need for skilled workers. Raw materials also need to be brought in and finished products sent to markets. The countries of western Europe are big car buyers and, both here and in Japan, it is easy to transport raw materials from coastal ports along good road networks. In Africa, South Africa is the major car maker for sales to the rest of the continent.

B *World car exports*

World clothing exports

Most of the world's clothes come from eastern Asia – over five times as many as from any other region. China and Hong Kong sell more clothes than anyone else but major producers include Mauritius and Taiwan. In Africa, both the Central African Republic and Malawi are countries without access to the sea, and they find it difficult and expensive to export around the world. Despite this, they both sell a lot to their neighbours. In many of these countries wages are low. People can easily pick up the skills to work in the clothing factories without a high level of education. In some countries, governments have encouraged businesses to set up with less strict health and safety laws and with a lack of workers' organisations.

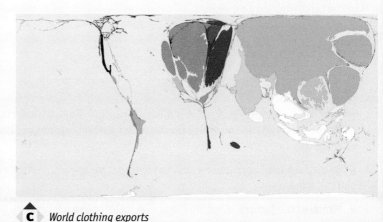

C *World clothing exports*

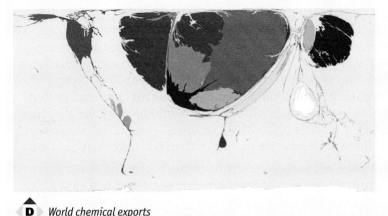

World chemical exports

Chemical production needs a great deal of research and development. A highly educated workforce, such as that found in western Europe (for example Ireland) and in Singapore, is a significant location factor. In countries such as Trinidad and Tobago, the availability of raw materials (in this case, oil) is an additional location factor that has led to the growth of a chemical manufacturing industry. Global companies may also set up in countries where they are helped by the government and where they can export their goods to local markets – for example, Swaziland serves as a centre of the chemical industry in Africa.

D *World chemical exports*

World electronics exports

The production of electronics – including television and radio receivers, photographic equipment and high-tech medical equipment – is again dominated by eastern Asia. The original Newly Industrialised Countries of Taiwan, Hong Kong and Singapore have been joined by newer ones, including Malaysia. Government influence in these countries has led to very highly organised manufacturing. Their location in the centre of world shipping lanes, surrounded by countries with huge populations, has given them excellent access to large markets.

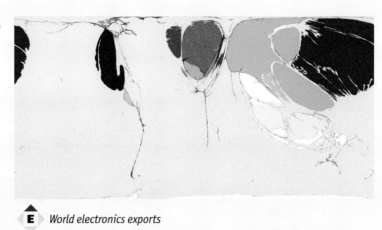

E *World electronics exports*

The maps shown here are further examples of presenting geographical information in different ways. They may appear a little difficult to interpret at first. Once you are familiar with them, however, you should be able very quickly to understand the patterns they show.

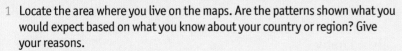

Now Investigate

1 Locate the area where you live on the maps. Are the patterns shown what you would expect based on what you know about your country or region? Give your reasons.

2 Using the maps:

 a Describe the range of export goods manufactured in either western Europe or eastern Asia.

 b Explain the distribution in terms of industrial location factors.

3 Which areas of the world appear to have very little manufacturing industry? Write down some reasons why this might be so.

Further research

There are many more examples of these types of maps at www.worldmapper.org. It's well worth taking a look.

Manufacturing industries

A *Making steel in India*

Traditionally, the most important inputs to the manufacturing industry system were raw materials and a power supply. Transport was difficult, so factories would have to locate near to bulky raw materials. In steel making, for instance, this included heavy iron ore and limestone. Meanwhile power would be made locally using water, wood or, later on, coal. As factories were set up, workers would move to be near them, rather than the other way around.

As time went on, and especially from the beginning of the 20th century, transport of raw materials became much easier, with ships sailing quickly all around the world. Availability of raw materials was no longer an important location factor. Neither was power, as this was now provided by power stations connected to a network able to provide electricity where it was needed. One of the main inputs in modern industry is the cost of employing workers. This is why the world's steel making industry has moved from places with expensive labour like the UK to cheaper countries including China and India (photo **A**).

A similar situation has been the case for many other manufacturing industries.

Case study

The textile and clothing industry

Originally starting in the UK as part of the industrial revolution of the 18th and 19th centuries, the textile industry soon spread to the rest of Europe and the USA. In the second half of the 20th century, however, a big change in the location of the industry took place. LEDCs became the world leaders in textile production. There were several reasons for this:

- Many LEDCs with a warm climate changed their agriculture and began to grow cotton – one of the most important raw materials in making clothes.
- The growth of cheaper global shipping routes meant that other raw materials could be transported easily and finished products could be taken to markets in MEDCs.
- Many LEDCs saw making clothes as an excellent 'start-up' industry – one that would let them set up a manufacturing industry and get money from exports very quickly.
- The equipment required little technology – cheap sewing machines were available almost anywhere.
- The industry needed lots of labour, especially women, many of whom may have already had experience of making clothes for their family.
- There was an increasing demand for clothes (which could be sold at much higher prices than it cost to make them) from MEDCs.

The main input has been the availability of a large, cheap workforce in many LEDCs. Caribbean and Central American countries, including the Dominican Republic, Mexico, Honduras and Haiti – all close to cotton-growing areas – were some of the first countries to use their workforce well and set up large factories. Recently, however, there has been a huge growth in production in eastern Asia (figure **B**).

Fantastic fact

In the UK, only one quarter of all clothes are recycled – the rest are thrown away, when they could be used again.

Textile production in India

The textile industry in India employs 12 million people and contributes 16 per cent of the total value of the country's exports. The Indian government has sent officials to Germany, France, Switzerland, Italy and the USA to encourage foreign investment. It has promised incentives to investors, including a workforce that is paid low wages.

While many countries are expanding their textile industry in big factories, Bangladesh is encouraging the growth of small-scale production in towns and villages (photo **D**). Over 50 per cent of all businesses operate in this way. Across the country, textiles account for 45 per cent of all jobs in industry – employing nearly 4 million people, mostly women. This brings in a major proportion of the country's export earnings, including nearly US$5 billion from the USA, Canada and the European Union.

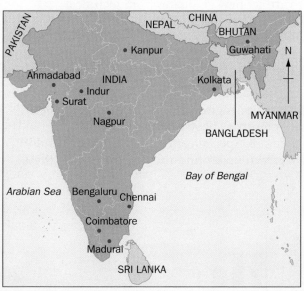

C　Textile industries in India

China's gross output of textiles rose 10.3 per cent last year – it now has more than 50 000 companies earning more than US$733 000 a year.

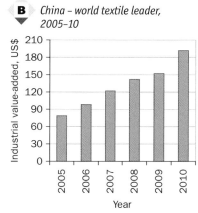
B　China – world textile leader, 2005–10

Companies are relocating from the coast to central areas where wages are lower. Growing domestic demand also means 80 per cent of all production is now sold in-country. Exports continue to soar.

China's domination of the world market has proved bad news for some countries. In South Africa, where over 80 per cent of clothing came from China, local producers closed down as they were unable to compete on price.

D　Small-scale textile industry in Bangladesh

Now Investigate

1　Look at the labels in some of the clothes you are wearing and/or in your cupboard at home. Where do the clothes come from? Does this fit with the information on these pages?

2　What are the main inputs to the textile industry system?

3　Using specific country examples, explain why the global textile industry has moved from MEDCs to LEDCs.

Topic link

Some of the environmental impacts, problems and benefits of manufacturing industry are outlined in Section 3.9 on pages 188–93.

High-tech industries are mainly concerned with the application of technology in many different forms. This includes computers, telecommunications (including mobile phones), robotics and computer gaming systems (photos **A**). Raw materials are usually very small and light so they are no longer a major factor in location. The products made are high value, small and easy to transport so the factories can be built almost anywhere in the world. Industries like this are known as 'footloose' industries.

Inputs other than raw materials have become much more important factors in determining where these industries are located (diagram **B**).

Global distribution of high-tech industries

The research and development involved in high-tech industries means they need to attract new graduates from technical universities and colleges. They often locate in attractive environments where these graduates will want to work – Silicon Valley in the USA, for instance, or the skibelt near the French Alps where employees have plenty of leisure opportunities.

However, outside of the USA and the European Union, most of the countries with major high-tech industries are in eastern Asia (graph **C**). These countries have many of the location factors listed in diagram **B**. Special centres called science and research parks have grown up around the world to house these new industries.

A High-tech products are small and easy to transport

Topic link

More information on the way all kinds of manufacturing industries have environmental risks and benefits can be found later on in Section 3, pages 188–93.

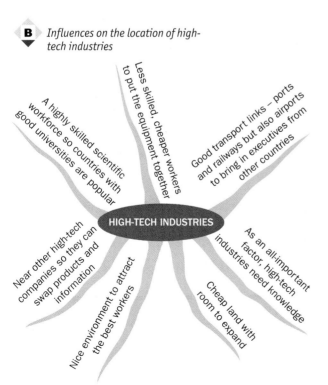

B Influences on the location of high-tech industries

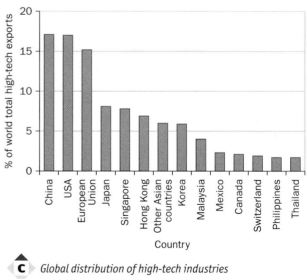

C Global distribution of high-tech industries

Science parks

Centres where many high-tech companies are found together are often called science parks. Location factors for science parks include:

- close links with universities because of the need to employ technical graduates and scientists
- large amounts of capital to buy land and build specialist laboratories and offices – often this comes from multinational companies and governments
- excellent global connections through international airports
- super-fast internet connections and reliable infrastructure
- low-density building with tree-lined streets and landscaped gardens to create a pleasant working environment.

Businesses found on these sites include those specialising in biotechnology, medical research and telecommunications.

Science parks were originally created in the USA, and most are still located in MEDCs and NICs. The UK, Canada and Singapore all have large numbers, and they are increasing in China, Brazil and India. More wealthy LEDCs are also starting to build science parks. They cost a lot of money to start up but are bringing in huge amounts of money as the quaternary industries located in them start to take off.

Biopolis, Singapore

Biopolis is an international research and development centre in Singapore (photo **D**). It is close to the National University of Singapore, Singapore Polytechnic, the Institute of Technical Education, the National University Hospital, and to other major scientific organisations.

There are continuing developments to bring new industries to Biopolis. To attract qualified professionals, facilities include tree-lined streets and parks, shops, cafés, restaurants and a childcare centre. Nearby is luxurious accommodation with serviced apartments, hotels and private houses.

Hsinchu science park, Taiwan

More than 400 high-tech companies have found a home at Hsinchu in Taiwan, including the world's top two manufacturers of semiconductors (a vital part of any computer). National Chiao Tung University and National Tsing Hua University are found next door and there is even a science-themed amusement park to bring in the visitors.

The park has strictly monitored air quality, following earlier complaints from the public and the workers, and it now prides itself on being very environmentally friendly.

 D Biopolis in Singapore

Fantastic fact

Sub-Saharan Africa's first science park – The Innovation Hub – has been built in Pretoria, South Africa.

 E Hsinchu Science and Industrial Park, Taiwan

Now Investigate !

1 Why are some industries known as 'footloose'? Give some examples of footloose industries.

2 Using graph **C**, describe the global distribution of science parks.

3 Answer *either* (a) *or* (b):

a If you live near to a science park or have one in your country, what do you think were the location factors behind it being built?

b If you live in a country without a science park, what could the government do to enable one to be built?

Your local leisure industry

A growing number of people around the world, like Jean-Claude (photos **A**), are lucky enough to have the time and money to go on holiday. Where would you like to go? Are there lots of wonderful places waiting to be explored in your own country? Or would you prefer to travel greater distances and visit other nations? Many countries, especially those where there is no important manufacturing industry, are keen to develop tourism as a way of bringing in money. There are both advantages and disadvantages to this – for local people and for their environment.

Bonjour mes amis. My name is Jean-Claude Benoix. I'm very lucky to live in France. My parents both have good jobs and they are given lots of time off to spend with me and my sister.

We love to go on holiday – usually at least twice a year. We like to spend one of the holidays taking a camper van and exploring France. It's such a great country to visit and my parents think it's important we learn a bit about its history and culture.

For our other holiday we get on a plane and head somewhere more exotic. My sister always wants to find a beach she can lie around on and I'm keen on finding out about local wildlife. Sometimes we go to French-speaking countries but we're all working to improve our English so that we have more choice.

Jean-Claude Benoix **A**

Fantastic fact

The world's most visited tourist attraction is New York's Times Square – 44 million people come to see it every year.

Now Investigate

Jean-Claude and his family would like to take a holiday in your country. Plan a week's visit for them, taking in the major sites they may want to visit. Don't just include the well-travelled routes and most popular attractions – find them something different to do as well. Explain why you have chosen these different places.

The growth of global tourism

During the last 50 years foreign travel has become available to a lot more people. In that time the numbers of tourists travelling around the world has increased rapidly. Different parts of the world have seen this growth take place at different rates (graph **B**).

This relatively recent growth in tourism has taken place for a number of reasons:

- Rapid air travel has taken over from slow sea journeys.
- The development of more efficient planes means that air travel is cheaper.
- Transport facilities have improved – cars work better and run on much better roads, motorways and express routes, so journey times have been cut dramatically.
- In many countries wealth has increased so people have more money to spend on luxuries (this is known as disposable income).
- As people have become richer and enjoy a better quality of life, they have demanded more paid holiday-time.
- The internet, advertising, and television holiday programmes have brought wider knowledge of (and a desire to visit) other countries.
- People cope with the stresses of modern life by going on holiday.

The global tourism industry has grown to take advantage of these opportunities. It is now possible to take a holiday for any kind of interest, from sports vacations to health tourism (figure **C**).

The changing tourist

For many years, almost all the world's tourists came from Europe and the USA. This situation is now changing. As NICs and LEDCs get richer, more people from these countries can afford to go on holiday. China could even take over from Germany as the world's number one 'travelling country' by 2020. This is a huge potential market to be developed.

While many Chinese tourists visit nearby countries such as Thailand and South Korea, some are travelling much further afield to major world cities including Paris, Rome and London.

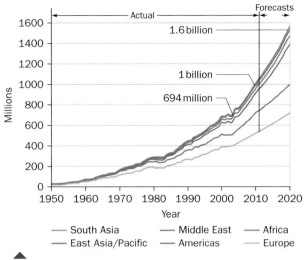

B The growth of global tourism, 1950–2020

Examples of speciality tours include:

- Culture tourism to historic Inca sites in the Andes
- Ecotourism, experiencing the natural environment in Belize and Costa Rica
- Volcano watching tours in Montserrat
- Sports tourism to South Africa for the FIFA World Cup and to Rio de Janeiro and London for the Olympic Games
- Wilderness tours to Antarctica
- Mountain climbing tours in the Himalayas
- Active adventure tourism, including bungee jumping and rafting, in New Zealand
- Bird-watching tours to the Amazon rainforest in Brazil

C Speciality tourism

Now Investigate

1 Study graph **B**.

  a Describe the general growth of global tourism shown in the graph.

  b Which regions have shown the most and the least growth over the last 50 years?

  c Which regions are predicted to have the most growth in the future?

2 What are the main reasons for the growth in global tourism over the last 50 years?

3 Using an atlas, find a country you would like to visit. Prepare a factfile giving details such as how to get there, the currency you will need, and what you plan to do when you arrive. You may need to use the internet to help find the information.

The importance of global tourism

Most countries want to develop their tourist industry. Visitors can bring huge amounts of money into the economy. Worldwide, tourism as an industry was worth US$852 billion in 2009. In LEDCs, there is the added benefit that the money coming in may be American dollars. This currency keeps its value better than those used in only one or two countries.

Tourism also brings local employment opportunities. Some jobs may be seasonal, for example available only in the summer, but many are all year round. The workers earn money and spend it in their local community, so there are knock-on benefits for shopkeepers and other local business people. This is known as the multiplier effect.

For a tourist industry, and the country where it is operating, to be a success, it also needs good infrastructure. Governments improve roads, for instance, to allow tourists to travel around easily.

Facilities such as swimming pools or ski centres may be built and these can be used by local people as well as visitors. There are other cultural and environmental benefits to come from tourism:

- Many tourists visit cultural attractions such as castles and palaces – without these visitors there may not be the money available to keep them in good condition.
- Some visitors want to enjoy beautiful scenery. This means the environment has to be protected from development.
- Tourists from different countries brings increased contact between different cultures. This helps global understanding between people.

The world's top tourist destinations are almost all MEDCs. Table **A** shows that France leads the way with almost 80 million visitors a year. The table also shows that, despite this, the USA earns almost twice as much as France in tourist revenue.

The world's top tourist destinations **A**

Country	International tourist arrivals (millions)	International tourism receipts (US$ billion)
France	74.2	49.4
USA	54.9	93.9
Spain	52.2	53.2
China	50.9	39.7
Italy	43.2	40.2
UK	28.0	30.0
Turkey	25.5	21.3
Germany	24.2	34.7
Malaysia	23.6	15.8
Mexico	21.5	11.3

Source: United Nations World Tourism Organisation

Now Investigate

There will probably be some kind of tourist industry in your local area. Make a list of all the jobs you can think of that may be associated with tourism where you live.

Draw a bar graph showing the information in table **A**. Describe the relationship between visitor numbers and tourist revenues.

Case study

Tourism in an MEDC: France

People visit France to enjoy the many famous historic attractions and the natural landscape:

- Beach holidays in Normandy and on the French Riviera
- Famous castles such as those at Mont St Michel and Vincennes
- Almost 40 000 historic monuments including the Arc de Triomphe
- Dramatic scenery of the Loire and Ardeche Valleys
- The 3900 museums, such as the Louvre and Cité de l'Automobile, that attract tens of millions of visitors each year
- Skiing in the Alps in winter, mountain biking and walking in the summer

- World-famous French vineyards in regions like Champagne and Bordeaux
- Food with a great worldwide reputation

France has a very positive image worldwide. Over 5.6 million people visit the Eiffel Tower in Paris alone every year (photo **B**). Almost 200 000 people are employed in the French tourist industry and it contributes over 6 per cent to the national economy. However, not everyone is happy with the development of the tourist industry in France, as shown in figure **C**.

There is increasing competition from other countries – especially from other European nations like Croatia, Slovenia and Estonia. The challenge for the French tourism industry now is to come up with new ideas to make sure the visitors keep coming.

'Once a year, sometimes more, we like to take the caravan and explore our own country. There is so much to see. It's easy to see why we are the world's top spot for visitors.'

Jean-Claude Benoix

B *The Eiffel Tower*

It's great in the summer when the tourists are here but everything shuts down in the winter – there's nothing for young people to do.

The people around Paris get lots of money from tourism but here in the countryside we get no visitors at all. We're poor and there's no development unless it's in the areas people want to visit.

All these people coming by air – it's ridiculous. What on earth is it doing to climate change?

These tourists really annoy me. They drive along so slowly I'm always late getting to and from work.

The visitors are so rude. They don't speak French and then get angry with us when we don't understand them – how can that be right?

C *French views on tourism*

Fantastic fact

France has 365 different types of cheese!

Now Investigate

1 Use the resources on these pages to briefly explain the benefits the tourist industry brings to France.

2 What are the main problems of tourism outlined by the people in figure **C**? Can you think of any other problems the industry may cause?

3 Imagine you represent the French Tourist Board. What can you do to keep visitors coming to France? Think of a memorable slogan to launch a new campaign to advertise the country to overseas visitors.

Tourism in LEDCs

Country	Percentage
Macau	39
Maldives	31
Aruba	24
Seychelles	23
Anguilla	23
Bahamas	22
British Virgin Islands	21
Vanuatu	19
Antigua and Barbuda	18
Cape Verde	16

A *Income from tourism as a percentage of the national economy*

While many MEDCs gain a lot of money from tourism, they are not dependent on the industry. The same may not be the case for a number of LEDCs. Table **A** shows that the national economies of some countries rely strongly on tourism.

LEDCs are often seen as exotic tourist destinations. Peru and Bolivia have mystical Inca ruins which many people are very keen to see. Southern and eastern Africa have rare and dangerous animals. The Pacific islands have miles of beautiful sunny beaches. All these places can use their attractions to bring in money from visitors – but there is a lot of competition. A country can spend a huge amount of money developing tourist facilities, only to find that somewhere else has become more popular. Popular destinations, such as Kenya, can go out of (and come back into) fashion very quickly indeed.

Diagram **B** shows some of the benefits and disadvantages that LEDCs get from tourism. Many of these also apply to MEDCs.

Topic link

There are also environmental risks and benefits associated with tourism. These are discussed later on in Topic 3.10 pages 194–99.

B *The advantages and disadvantages of tourism for LEDCs*

Better quality of life for local people

Pollution and waste may increase from tourist developments

Incomes are low, jobs may be seasonal and working conditions poor

Tourist developments may be owned by foreign companies so profits are taken overseas

Encourages people to get an education and set up their own businesses

A positive international image may lead to investment from foreign companies

Local people may take more care in protecting the environment that tourists come to see

Tourist developments use land that could be used for building homes or producing food

Advantages

TOURISM IN LEDCs

Disadvantages

The culture of a country may become increasingly 'westernised'

Improvements in local services and infrastructure paid for by tourism

Lots of different types of employment

Increased crime rates (theft and even murder) as people become jealous of richer tourists

More tax money for governments to spend on developing health and education

The multiplier effects means benefits for the local economy

Tourists may not respect local customs, dress inappropriately and take insensitive photographs

Roads, ports and other facilities may be damaged by increased tourist use

Tourist developments (hotels etc.) may use scarce resources, e.g. electricity, water

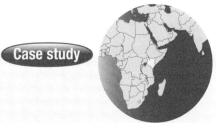

Case study

Kenya

Kenya was one of the first African countries to develop its tourist industry. From the 1930s onwards people came for big game hunting and on safari holidays. After independence from the United Kingdom in 1963, tourism was seen as one of the main ways to improve Kenya's economy. The coast was developed around resorts like Mombasa, and National Parks established to protect animals for tourists. Kenya became Africa's number one tourist destination.

Terrorist attacks in the capital Nairobi in 1998 changed that. Western tourists now felt that Tanzania, Namibia and South Africa were safer places to visit. Riots followed elections in Kenya in 2007. This led to a 36 per cent drop in tourist numbers and £500 million of lost revenue.

With more stability in the past few years, visitors have started to return to Kenya. There was a 25 per cent increase in visitor numbers in 2009 – good news for the quarter of a million people employed in the industry. Some of the reasons for Kenya's success as a tourist destination are shown below.

'For our big holiday last year we went on safari to Kenya. It was amazing seeing all the animals you normally only see on the television. At the end we spent a few days relaxing and snorkelling on the beach. It was one of the best holidays ever.'

Jean-Claude Benoix

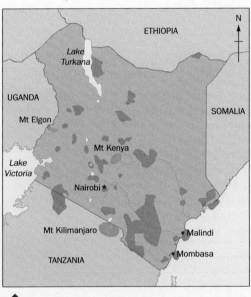

C *National Parks of Kenya (dark green)*

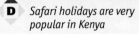

D *Safari holidays are very popular in Kenya*

E *The coastal resort of Mombasa*

Now Investigate

1 Describe the climate of Nairobi referring to graph **F**.

2 Outline the advantages and disadvantages to an LEDC of developing a tourist industry. Explain why it still makes a lot of sense for such development to take place.

3 Explain why Kenya has become so popular with tourists, especially those from MEDCs like Jean-Claude and his family from France.

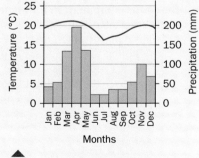

F *Climate graph for Nairobi*

Learning objectives:

- explain where the energy that powers our world comes from

- describe who uses a lot and who uses very little

- explain the differences between renewable and non-renewable types of energy

- relate what you have learned to problems in the global energy supply.

Your local energy sources

Energy sources are what give you the power for most of the things you use on a daily basis. Without these sources of energy you would not have television, cell phones, computers, hot water, electricity or gas to cook with. Most energy sources originally come from the sun. Coal, oil and natural gas (which give us 88 per cent of the total energy used worldwide) come from solar energy which has been captured and stored over a very long time. They are being used up very quickly. The amount of energy people use around the world is not the same (figure **A**). In your country the levels of consumption (how much energy you use) may be pretty low. In other places power is being used up at an incredibly high rate – for many different purposes.

Energy use around the world

A

We use a lot of energy but then oil is very cheap here. Today we went to the indoor ski centre – it's a strange sight to see in the desert but we're very proud of it.

It's hot so the air conditioning is on and the sprinklers are working to keep the flowers growing in the garden. I can get cold drinks from the chiller in the fridge or turn on the fans if it gets too uncomfortable.

Ali, Dubai

We live in a fairly poor part of a rich country. We don't have a lot of money and our energy supply is really expensive. We have a gas stove for cooking and everything else runs on electricity. My father has a small moped to get around on and, apart from that, the television is the only other major user of energy that we have.

Birgit, Germany

Mum says we need the big car to get all the sports equipment in for my tennis and my brother's football. At home we've got it all – music players, PCs, tea makers and rice boilers and all sorts. I know it's bad it uses so much electricity but I don't know what I'd do without it all.

Mei Lin, China

We've been very lucky that my father's business has done well. We can afford loads of things he couldn't when he was a boy. Now we have a car, television and computer games and music players and a really nicely equipped kitchen. My mother loves the dishwasher – she says it has made things so much easier.

Imran, Pakistan

Now Investigate ⚠

1 Read through the quotes from the different young people around the world.

a Who do you think uses the most energy?

b Draw a table with two columns marked NECESSARY and UNNECESSARY. Read through all the items used by the young people quoted and write them down under the column you think is correct.

2 Take a look at your own life.

a Complete an energy audit, listing all the things you use on a daily basis that require some kind of energy source.

b How many of them would you be able to live without?

Global energy consumption

Over the last couple of hundred years, the amount of energy used around the world has increased massively (graph **B**). This is partly to do with the increase in global population but it is not the full story. The amount of energy we use per person has also increased greatly as we buy and use more gadgets such as mobile phones and music devices.

Most of this power comes from fossil fuels which cannot be replaced (figure **C**). They are said to be non-renewable. However, the use of renewable power is on the increase as well. This includes types of energy such as wind, water and tidal power that can be used over and over again without running out.

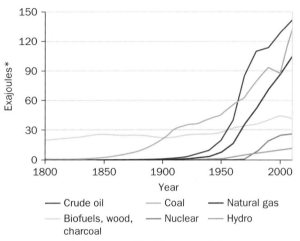

*1 exajoule = approx. 25 million tonnes of oil

B Global energy consumption, 1800–2008

Energy source	Percentage
Oil	36
Natural gas	24
Coal	28
Nuclear	6
Hydro	6

Source: www.cngalaska.com/

Note: small amounts of energy are also generated from wind, wave, solar and other sources

C Energy sources as a percentage of the global total

Now Investigate ⚠

1 Refer to graph **B**.

a Which fuels have seen the greatest increase in consumption?

b In which decades have the biggest changes taken place?

c Are there any fuels whose use has remained fairly constant over the last 200 years?

2 Using the information in table **C**, construct a pie graph showing the different energy sources as a percentage of the global total.

Topic link 🔗

The reasons for the increase in global population, and some of the effects this is having on our world, are covered in Section 1.

Skills link 🔗

Ways of presenting geographical data include line graphs and data tables like the ones shown here. You need to know how to interpret line graphs and use the information in tables to produce your own graphs. Go to pages 212–15 in Section 4 to find out more about drawing and interpreting line graphs and pie graphs. You may want to check this information before you answer the questions below.

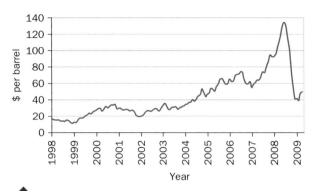

A The increase in world crude oil prices, 1998–2009

An estimated 88 per cent of the total global energy used in 2007 came from fossil fuels – oil, coal and natural gas. These resources take many millions of years to form but are being used up at an incredibly fast rate. Already it seems we may be halfway through the available resources of fossil fuels and we have only been using them in any significant quantities for about the last two hundred years.

New coal and oil fields are being discovered all the time but they are getting harder and more expensive to find. There are barely enough to keep up with the huge and growing demands from MEDCs. More recently, the growing populations and industry in China and India are leading to an even greater demand for power.

China produces more coal than any other country – 41 per cent of the global total in 2007. It uses almost all of this in its power stations and factories. In other countries, such as Saudi Arabia, huge amounts of oil are mined (12.7 per cent of the global total) but the vast majority is sold for export. In the end, the different ways the fuel is used has benefits for both of the countries involved:

- If a country can produce its own fuel it will improve its energy security. This means it does not have to depend on expensive imports, or face the threat that supplies from other countries could be cut off.

- If a country can export fuel it will bring in a lot of money for the economy. Oil gains the most money, and its price is increasing almost all the time (graph **A**). Coal and natural gas, while more readily available, still bring in lots of export money. The location and movement of fossil fuels around the globe are shown in map **B**.

Despite the big drop in prices with the world recession in 2009, the cost of oil almost constantly grows upwards, but there is little drop in demand.

As nearly everything in the world is transported using oil, the price of goods rises as well.

With growing demand from Brazil, Russia, India and China as they develop their manufacturing industry, there is little sign of significant drops in the price of oil in the future.

Now Investigate ❗

Use map **B** to:

a describe where the world's fossil fuels are found

b describe how they are transported around the planet.

Skills link 🔗

Map **B** is another kind of a world distribution map that you may be asked to interpret. More details can be found on pages 208–11.

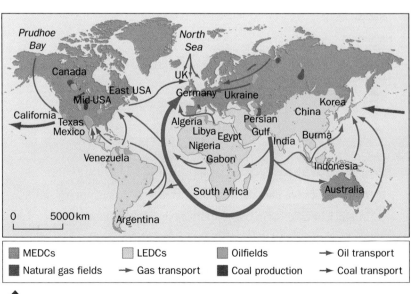

| MEDCs | LEDCs | Oilfields | → Oil transport |
| Natural gas fields | → Gas transport | Coal production | → Coal transport |

B Global movements and locations of fossil fuels

Coal in China

China's huge economic growth over the past few years has been built on coal. It provides around 80 per cent of all the electricity in the country – twice the global average. It is often said that China builds one new coal-fired power station each week, but nobody knows the real number.

Coal provides power to the factories producing all the goods China sells overseas. It also powers the energy-hungry electrical goods that people in the country are buying as they become more wealthy. Televisions, PCs, music players, cookers, dishwashers and washing machines are all becoming more popular in Chinese homes.

As the headlines in texts **C** show, these advances may not be coming without some cost to China.

PUTTING OUT THE FIRE

China's Inner Mongolia region today announced plans to put out some of the long-burning coal seam fires that are destroying large reserves underground. Some of the fires, which start all of a sudden when gas or coal dust gets too hot, have been burning for almost 50 years.

The economic effect of the coal seam fires is not well understood but it is thought that millions of tonnes of coal are burning needlessly every year. They can cause mines to collapse and destroy infrastructure above ground. Being underground, the fires are very difficult and expensive to put out.

More Miner Deaths Underground

Rescuers are battling against time to rescue 26 miners trapped by a deadly underground explosion in China's main mining area. Gas exploded causing the release of tonnes of coal dust and the collapse of the some of the mine's walls. Relatives are gathering for news as the clock ticks by.

China's mining industry is the deadliest in the world with 2600 deaths in 2009 alone. Thousands of illegal pits have been closed down but, while demand is high, miners will always work to make some money despite the dangers.

A LOCAL AND GLOBAL PROBLEM

Concerns have been expressed that China's concentration on burning fossil fuels is adding to the global problem of climate change. The carbon dioxide produced could be having a huge effect in changing the global temperature.

There are other concerns for people in China. Acid rain, caused by the pollutants from coal-fired power stations, is falling on agricultural land, killing crops and leaving the ground unsuitable for farming. This is a growing problem in a country that needs to feed an increasing population.

 C *The human and environmental cost of coal in China*

Now Investigate

1 Why is it important for governments to ensure that their countries have an adequate supply of energy? What kinds of problems do you think countries will face if they do not have an adequate supply?

2 a 'China's economic growth has been built on coal.' Do you agree with this statement? Give reasons for your answer.

 b What are some of the problems associated with China's coal industry?

 c Do the benefits of the use of coal outweigh the disadvantages for the country?

3 Think about your own country:

 a What kind of fossil fuels are used nationwide?

 b Why do some people have concerns about the environmental effects of using these fuels?

The fuelwood crisis

A Deforestation for fuelwood use

B Collecting fuelwood in Africa

Now Investigate ❗

Using diagrams **C** and **D**, and referring to specific countries, describe:

a the pattern of global consumption of fuelwood

b the distribution of the use of fuelwood in Africa.

Photo **A** shows a typical scene in some areas of the world – it is especially common in the parts of Africa south of the Sahara Desert. What do you think is happening here? Why have the trees been cut down?

Part of the answer is shown in photo **B**. In many parts of the world, people who have little money do not use fossil fuels. They are not connected to a national electricity grid and, even if there are supplies available, many cannot afford to use electricity. However, they still need fuel for cooking and have to rely on what they can find to burn to make a fire. This is usually either precious fuelwood or animal dung.

An estimated 2.4 billion people use fuelwood for cooking and heating. Much of this is from scrub land and dead wood lying on the ground. As populations have increased there has been more deforestation as living trees are cut down and burnt. This has a number of serious side-effects:

● Removing trees leaves soils open to erosion by wind and water – the soil may be removed over a large area with knock-on effects as farmers can no longer grow crops.

● As trees are removed, desertification is the result and desert areas start to grow – this is a particular problem on the edges of the Sahara Desert.

● As wood becomes more scarce, people have to travel further to find it. In some areas it is not unusual for people to take a whole day to find fuelwood and carry it home.

● There are personal safety issues in this activity for women, who are usually the ones who collect the firewood.

● In urban areas people may have to buy fuelwood for cooking. As supplies get harder to find the price rises, taking more out of already small family incomes.

Added to these problems is the fact that cooking with fuelwood on open fires in enclosed spaces causes breathing difficulties and respiratory disease, especially for the millions of women who do

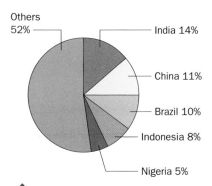

C Global consumption of fuelwood

Others 52%
India 14%
China 11%
Brazil 10%
Indonesia 8%
Nigeria 5%

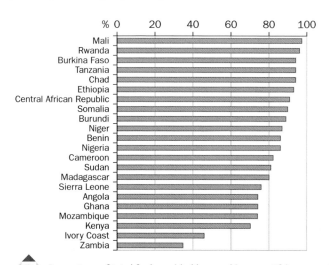

D Percentage of total fuel provided by wood in some African countries

the work in LEDCs. Despite all of this, the use of fuelwood remains high, especially in countries with large populations (diagram **C**). Graph **D** shows that, in many African countries, almost all the power a family uses comes from burning wood.

Now Investigate !

a Do you, or people you know, use fuelwood for cooking?

b If so, try to find out where it comes from and plot the information on a map of your local area.

   If not, plot the forested areas closest to you which could most easily be used as a source of fuelwood.

Case study

Forest destruction for fuelwood in West Bengal, India

Deforestation in the northern part of West Bengal state has, over the past few years, become a very serious problem. The area has attracted immigrants for a number of different reasons. Many have come to work on the tea plantations of Jalpaiguri. Others have been forced from surrounding countries – Bangladesh, Nepal and Bhutan – because of conflict, forced migration and natural disasters.

Cutting down the forests and selling the wood is an easy way for the migrants to make money. They also need it for their own cooking. Many local people, both men and women, are finding much of their time taken up collecting wood when that time would be better used in making money for their families.

More than 70 per cent of the wood taken is from state-owned forests. Armed security guards have had little effect in cutting down the amount taken – estimated to be 72 000 tonnes a week. The fuelwood business is the main source of income in 10 per cent of households in the region (figure **F**).

E West Bengal, India

We came here from Bangladesh after we lost our rice farm in the flood. Picking up and selling the wood was an easy way to make money.

I know it's illegal but I have no choice – we have a lot of mouths to feed. Things are more difficult now. I have to travel further and chop down the trees far away from home. Sometimes there are guards. If they catch me I'll be fined – or worse.

I've also noticed other things. The weather is changing and the soils are bare. There's less farming as the soil is not so fertile. Surely this can't be because of what we're doing to the forests?

F Rashid – a fuelwood collector

Now Investigate

1 a What are the main reasons for deforestation in state forests in north-west Bengal?

   b Describe some of the effects that may result from the trees being cut down.

2 Read through Rashid's story (figure **F**).

   a Explain why he feels forced into selling fuelwood when he knows it is wrong.

   b What do you think will happen if he stops?

   c What would you do in his situation?

Renewable energies

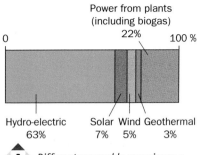

Power from plants
(including biogas)
22%

0   100 %

Hydro-electric   Solar Wind Geothermal
63%   7%   5%   3%

A *Different renewable energies as a percentage of the global total*

B *Advantages and disadvantages of renewable energy sources*

Time is running out for fossil fuels. Despite our dependence on them they will not last for ever (although some of them may last hundreds more years). A more important concern may be whether we can continue to use them knowing the damage they may be doing to the planet by causing climate change.

To solve these problems, many countries are turning to renewable energies. These are sustainable and can be used continuously without running out. Less than 10 per cent of global power is currently provided by renewable energy but this is increasing all the time. Some countries want to develop their use of renewable energy because it will:

- help reduce their reliance on expensive fossil fuels
- provide energy security
- ease the world's energy crisis brought on by increasing demand for resources that are running out.

Many countries are already improving their technology so that they can develop alternative energy sources.

The main types of renewable energy currently available are shown in graph **A**. The advantages of each are shown in table **B**.

Advantages	Disadvantages
Use almost limitless natural resources, e.g. wind, water, sun	Often require large-scale power stations that are expensive to build, e.g. wind farms, geothermal plants, solar power stations
Can use waste products, e.g. biogas	May need to be set up in difficult environments, e.g. solar in the desert
Cheap to run after initial set-up costs	Need major infrastructural development, e.g. dams for hydro-electric power
Can sometimes be set up on a small scale, e.g. solar panels or small wind turbines on individual houses	Natural resources (e.g. solar power or wind) may not always be available depending on weather conditions
Mainly produce little or no pollution after initial set-up	Can have negative environmental consequences, e.g. silting of rivers dammed for HEP
Help to fight global climate change by reducing dependence on fossil fuels	Can have negative effects on people, e.g. flooding of villages to create reservoirs for HEP

Now Investigate

Describe the worldwide use of renewable energy as shown in graph **A**.

Geothermal

Countries with active volcanoes can use energy from the heated rocks and molten magma under the earth's surface. Hot springs and naturally hot sources of water below ground can also be used to provide power. In Iceland geothermal power stations produce around a quarter of the country's electricity and almost 90 per cent of heating and hot water in buildings.

Skills link

Graph **A** is a type of graph called a divided bar graph. It is very good for showing percentages in a clear format. More information on how to draw a divided bar graph can be found in Section 4 on page 213.

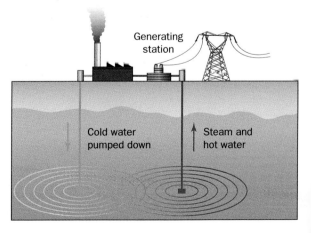

Generating station

Cold water pumped down

Steam and hot water

How geothermal power works ◄ **C** ►

Wind

Lines of wind turbines (photo **D**), known as 'wind farms', are becoming increasingly popular as an alternative source of power. These can be on land or offshore (in the sea, where turbines can be 50 metres high) but need a good supply of wind and flat areas to build on. Wind farms are expensive to build but cheap and safe to operate and almost completely pollution-free.

D An offshore wind farm

Running water

Water, either as waves, tides or in rivers, is a very successful form of renewable energy. The UK is one country currently experimenting with different forms of wave power. France has tidal barrages (dams) across the mouths of some of its big rivers (including the world's biggest across the Rance estuary). The most widely used form of water power, however, is in hydro-electric plants across large or fast-flowing rivers (photo **E**).

E A hydro-electric power plant

Solar

As much of the power we use has the sun as its original source it makes sense to harness the energy directly. Solar panels convert the heat into electricity. In many countries this is done on a small scale on individual houses. In some, such as Spain, huge lines of solar panels (photo **F**) have been set up and, given perfect conditions of cloudless skies, provide good quantities of electricity.

Topic link

A detailed case study on the global use of hydro-electric power can be found in Topic 3.7 on pages 180–81.

Biogas

Rotting fruit, vegetables, food and animal waste give off methane which can be burnt as biogas. There have been many successful initiatives to introduce this kind of power on a small scale in homes in LEDCs (photo **G**). However, many European countries are also investigating ways of using the technology on a larger scale by connecting biogas plants into natural gas pipelines.

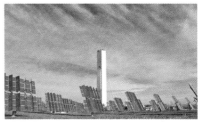

F A solar farm in Spain

G A home-based biogas plant in India

Fantastic fact

One UK farmer said about biogas: 'The dung from four cows can produce enough energy to heat and light a house for a year.'

Now Investigate

1 What are the advantages of using renewable energy?

2 Which of the forms of renewable energy described here do you think seems to be most environmentally friendly? Explain your answer.

3 Which forms of renewable energy would be suitable in your local area and in your country as a whole? Explain why they would be suitable.

Learning objectives:

- explain how electricity is made

- describe the different amounts of electricity used around the world

- explain why nuclear and hydro-electric power plants are found where they are.

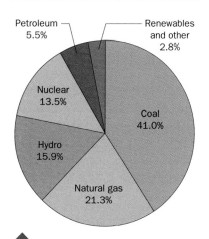

Petroleum
5.5%

Renewables and other
2.8%

Nuclear
13.5%

Coal
41.0%

Hydro
15.9%

Natural gas
21.3%

A *Worldwide generation of electricity by type of fuel, 2008*

Skills link

Map **B** is an example of another type of distribution map that you may need to analyse. You should know where some of the key countries are located so that you can refer to them if you are asked to do so. Turn to Section 4 pages 210–11 to find out what you need to know when describing this type of map, and then answer the questions below.

Fantastic fact

Iceland uses more electricity per person than any other country in the world – but most of it comes from renewable energy produced by geothermal and water sources.

Your power from a plug

Many of the energy sources described in Topic 3.6 are used to make electricity. Much of the energy you use every day will have been produced in this way. Every time you plug something into a socket or turn on the light, they work because there is a power station somewhere turning energy sources into electricity. A lot of this will be from coal, oil or gas – the fossil fuels – but, increasingly, other energy sources are being used. Nuclear and hydro-electric power are two of the biggest generators of electricity in the world (diagram **A**).

Who uses the most electricity?

Map **B** shows the biggest global consumers of electricity. The USA, with large amounts of industry and a population that likes to buy the most up-to-date electrical equipment, uses more than anybody else. The biggest consumers are almost all MEDCs but an increasing number of the richer and more industrial LEDCs are now using a lot of electricity.

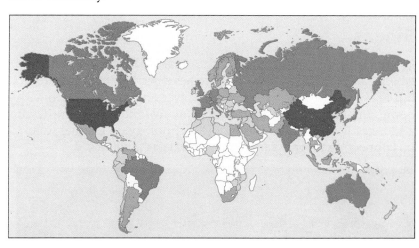

Kilowatt hours per year

☐ Under 10 000   10 000–50 000   50 000–200 000

☐ 200 000–1 million   Over 1 million

B *Worldwide electricity consumption*

Now Investigate

1 Describe the worldwide consumption of electricity as shown on map **B**.

2 Can you find your own country on the map? How does its consumption of electricity compare with that in the rest of the world?

How is electricity produced?

Most power stations convert energy sources into electricity using turbines. These turbines usually have blades which are forced to turn very fast and this produces the electricity. Making the blades turn can be done in a number of ways:

- Nuclear reactions, burning fossil fuels and geothermal power all produce steam which is used to turn the turbines.
- Hydro-electric and tidal power use running water to turn the blades.
- Large wind-powered turbines are also used in many windy parts of the world.

Since the late 19th century, most energy has come from fossil fuel power stations. These are also known as thermal power stations because they use the heat from burning the oil, gas or coal to produce steam. The three different types of power stations are found in quite different areas.

Coal-fired power stations

Coal is a heavy, bulky raw material, so it is expensive to transport. Power stations (photo **C**) are often found close to the mines and coalfields where the coal comes from. They are also often near the major towns, cities and industrial areas that use the power. When the coalfields start to run out, railways may be built to transport coal from coastal ports to keep the power stations running.

Oil-fired power stations

Oil-fired power stations (photo **D**) are often built on the coast where oil pipelines bring the liquid ashore or where tankers can bring it from other countries. The coastal estuaries where they are built need to be deep enough to allow the huge oil tankers to come in to port. Regulations in some countries mean that oil-fired power stations have to be built away from population centres, because of the pollution risk and other safety issues.

Gas-fired power stations

Natural gas is often found under the sea in the same place as oil and is piped ashore in a similar way. Some countries, such as Russia, also have large amounts of onshore gas. This still has to be transported in huge networks of pipes (photo **E**) to the power stations where it is turned into electricity.

C A coal-fired power station

D A coastal oil-fired power station

E A natural gas pipeline

Now Investigate ❗

1 Describe, in basic terms, how electricity is produced.

2 Are there any thermal power stations in your country? Find out where they are and write down the important factors influencing their location.

Where to put a nuclear power station?

Most power stations (or plants) producing electricity are very big. One of their requirements is a large area of flat land to build on. As we have seen in the previous section, other factors such as nearness to towns and cities and access to transport links are also important. The location factors for the production of electricity using nuclear power are even more important.

France	76.8
Lithuania	64.4
Slovakia	54.3
Belgium	54.0
Ukraine	48.1
Sweden	46.1
Armenia	43.5
Slovenia	41.6
Switzerland	40.0
Hungary	36.8
South Korea	35.3
Bulgaria	32.1

 Nuclear power as a percentage of a country's total energy production

Power from the atom

Nuclear power uses uranium as its raw material. Although this is not a renewable source, much less fuel is needed compared to fossil fuels such as coal or oil. Countries including the USA, France, Japan, Russia and Germany use uranium to produce a lot of their power. However, the waste material from this process is very dangerous and has to be disposed of as safely as possible. This often means burying it deep inside the earth or under the ocean, or re-processing it from fuel that has already been used. Despite this problem, some countries rely heavily on uranium to meet their demand for electricity (table **A**).

Choosing a location for a nuclear power station

What are the factors that influence the location of a nuclear power station? Most are found in MEDCs because the technology needed to develop them is expensive. The main users have been countries that do not have their own supply of fossil fuels (like Japan) or those where energy needs are far greater than other resources can meet (such as the UK and France). Nuclear power plants also need:

- a nearby water supply for cooling the nuclear reactor – most are located either next to the coast or beside large lakes
- flat, cheap land – nuclear power stations are quite large and need the space for building. In the UK, for example, most are found on land reclaimed from the sea.

Nuclear power stations are almost always found well away from large towns and cities. Since the 1950s there have been major concerns over the safety of nuclear power and the damage that potential leaks could cause. There have, however, been relatively few incidents of this kind around the world. The melt-down of the reactor at Chernobyl in Ukraine in 1986 caused widespread panic in many affected countries (figure **B**). More recently, in March 2011, there were concerns about the effects the earthquake and tsunami would have on the Fukushima power plant in Japan.

Skills link

Data tables like the one in table **A** can be easily converted into a more visual presentation, such as a graph or chart. To find out more about how to do this go to Section 4 pages 212–15.

Topic link

For more on the problems caused by earthquakes at the Fukushima nuclear plant, look at Topic 2.1 on pages 74–75.

Now Investigate

1 Construct a bar chart using the information in table **A**.

2 Using an atlas, describe the distribution of the countries that rely most on nuclear power.

B *Disaster at Chernobyl, 1986*

Early morning on 26 April 1986: one of the world's worst nuclear disasters took place when a reactor exploded at the Chernobyl nuclear power plant.

Details were slow to emerge from communist Russia but increased radiation levels were found in nearly every other country in the northern hemisphere. Europe was particularly badly affected (see map).

Around 350 000 people were evacuated from the surrounding area.

Contamination is still a problem. Scientists are also unsure about the final number of people who will have died as a result of the accident – the figure is probably around 9000.

Increased radiation across Europe, 3 May 1986

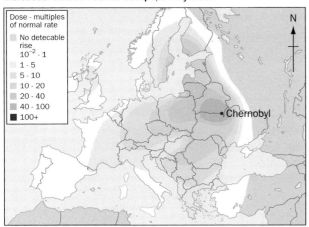

Dose - multiples of normal rate
- No detecable rise
- 10^{-2} - 1
- 1 - 5
- 5 - 10
- 10 - 20
- 20 - 40
- 40 - 100
- 100+

Chernobyl

Despite the concerns over nuclear power, it has been put forward as a relatively clean, safe technology and much better for the environment than polluting fossil fuels. The advantages and disadvantages of nuclear power are shown in table **C**.

Advantages	Disadvantages
• The amount of raw material needed is very small compared with other fuels such as coal or oil.	• Many people still have serious concerns over the safety of nuclear technology.
• It contributes relatively little to acid rain, global warming and climate change.	• There is the potential for disastrous accidents to take place.
• There is a lot of research being carried out to address fears over safety.	• People living near to nuclear power plants may suffer from poor health.
• It receives support from many governments around the world.	• Nuclear waste is difficult and expensive to dispose of and can be dangerous for many years.
• Many measures are taken to make sure it is as safe as possible.	• Nuclear power plants are very expensive to build.
• It allows countries to reduce their dependence on fossil fuels and to cut imports of these resources.	• Nuclear power plants are very expensive to close down when they are no longer used.

C *Some advantages and disadvantages of nuclear power*

D *A nuclear power plant*

Now Investigate

1 What are the main location factors for a nuclear power station?

2 Where are (or where would be) the best places to locate nuclear power plants in your country? Use maps (if possible) to find at least three suitable locations and give reasons why they are suitable.

3 After reading the information on these pages, do you think nuclear power is a safe and reasonable option for producing electricity? Explain your answer.

Power from water

A An HEP station

Hydro-electric power (HEP) is by far the most important way in which electricity is produced from renewable sources. Electricity from HEP is relatively cheap but as for other forms of power, there are advantages and disadvantages (table **B**).

Advantages	Disadvantages
● Power is cheap to produce and generally reliable. ● HEP creates very little pollution or waste. ● Dams reduce the risk of flooding. ● Dams are often built in highland areas away from major population centres. ● Reservoirs behind dams can be important sources of water. ● Reservoirs are often used for leisure and tourism. ● HEP stations can very quickly increase the amount of power they produce when required.	● Finding suitable sites can be difficult. ● Dams and HEP stations are expensive to build. ● Valuable areas of land may be flooded when dams are built. ● Dam collapse can cause widespread damage. ● There may be visual pollution and environmental damage to wildlife habitats. ● Water quality and quantity may be reduced downstream, causing water shortages. ● Large rivers can deposit a lot of very fine material which clogs up the turbines.

Advantages and disadvantages of **B** ▶
HEP stations

Now Investigate ❗

Are there any HEP stations in your country? If so, what are the reasons for their location? If not, are there any areas that would be suitable? You should use an atlas to help you answer.

Flowing water is needed to turn the turbines that produce electricity. HEP stations therefore tend to be found at waterfalls, across large valleys or where water flows down a steep hillside. Other favourable landscape features include:

- areas with heavy rainfall such as high mountains
- rivers with a large drainage basin which allows more water to be trapped in reservoirs
- steep-sided valleys so reservoirs can be deep and hold lots of water
- narrow valleys to help keep down construction costs
- valley sides and bottom made from **impervious** rock that will not let water drain through and will provide a stable base for a dam.

Major users of HEP include Iceland, Norway, Paraguay, China, Brazil and the Democratic Republic of the Congo.

Case study

HEP and the Colorado river, USA

The USA's Colorado river has long been used as a source of HEP. Its source is in the wet Rocky Mountains (graph **C**). The flow of the river is increased by water from melting snow in April and May. It has helped the USA to become wealthy, by providing the power to develop industry and create jobs.

The first dams built on the Colorado are now almost 100 years old. Some were originally built for flood control but many, including the Hoover Dam (photo **D**), have always been used to produce electricity. There are 10 other major dams in the Colorado river basin and many smaller ones. Deep canyons and gorges make ideal sites for storing water. Some, like Lake Mead, have become important tourist sites.

A huge amount of energy is produced from the Colorado river – a renewable source. However, people do have concerns:

- Environmentalists are worried about the negative effects on wildlife downstream – reduced flow means there are now few animals in the Colorado delta, where there were once jaguars, porpoises and notable bird species.
- Farmers complain about the effect that irrigation water, which is now full of dissolved salts, is having on their land.
- Native Americans are concerned that flooding has destroyed their sacred sites.

C *Climate graph for the Rocky Mountains*

Skills link

Geographers use graphs like graph **C** to describe the climate of a particular place. Climate graphs show temperature and precipitation (rainfall) for each month of the year. Go to Section 4 to find out how to draw and interpret climate graphs.

D *The Hoover Dam*

Pico Hydro plants in Vietnam

Case study

HEP schemes are often very big – but many people are starting to use the same kind of technology on a much smaller scale.

Pico Hydro units need a constant supply of water and a slope with a 1 metre drop. They can be used in almost any small stream in a mountainous area. For US$20 a family can buy a small Pico unit and produce enough electricity for their own home. Farmers such as Ho Phi Giang (photo **E**) who lives in Da Bac in Vietnam says the technology has revolutionised his family's life.

Pico Hydro power is becoming more and more common in Asia and Africa. Vietnam currently leads the way with more than 120 000 units in use.

E *Ho Phi Giang*

The Pico Hydro system is really easy to use – far easier than the electricity provided by the government on the national grid system. It is also much cheaper and we have more control over the supply.

Our home now has working lights. My children can do their homework and are getting on well at school, and my wife finds it much easier doing her work around the house.

Now Investigate

1 Using graph **C**, describe the climate of the USA's Rocky Mountains. Why does the climate make the area suitable for HEP?

2 Describe the advantages of HEP. You should refer to both large-scale and small-scale schemes in your answer.

3.8 Water: how can water supplies be managed?

Learning objectives:

- describe the ways we use water

- understand how people get the water they need

- explain what causes water shortages, and know where these are often experienced

- describe how water shortages can affect people and how they can lead to competition and conflict between people

- identify how water supplies can be managed more sustainably.

A Mary-Lou

Hi! I'm Mary-Lou. I live in the mid-west of the USA and I've just finished washing my parents' car. Do you know that, on average, every American uses 600 litres of water every day, and that most of that is for industry and farming? At home, 75 litres is used by each member of the family – for showering, bathing, washing clothes, cleaning teeth and flushing the toilet. The rest is 'lost', due to dripping taps and leaking pipes. Many of my friends have swimming pools in their gardens. These take thousands of litres of water to fill. Dad uses a sprinkler on the lawn, though Mom thinks that watering the grass every summer evening is a dreadful waste.

B Yawo

Sannu! My name is Yawo and I live in a small village in northern Ghana. Every drop of water is precious to us here because people can die of thirst if they don't get water. My family always struggled to get enough, until the WaterAid charity helped us to dig a new well. Two-thirds of all our village's water is used for irrigating the crops. Some of this is called grey water, because it has been used before, in the house. On average, Ghanaians use 5 litres of water daily in factories and workshops, but people in my village don't use any for this because we don't manufacture goods, and electricity supplies never reach this far out in the countryside! The rest of our water is used at home. I'm told this is only 15 per cent of what most Americans use every day at home, but at least we don't waste water through burst pipes and leaking taps!

The families of Mary-Lou and Yawo use very different amounts of water. They also use their water in different ways. This is because the communities they live in are not at the same level of economic development. Like most Americans, Mary-Lou's house is fitted with a washing machine and a dish washer. The family also own two large cars and have a big garden. Few families in the Ghanaian countryside can afford such luxuries, and Ghana certainly does not have the wealth to provide a large amount of drinking water for all of its villages.

Now Investigate

Keep your own personal water-use diary for a whole week, then use it to estimate the total amount of water you have used. If your home has a water meter, use its readings to add some accurate water-use figures for your household.

Using water sustainably

Unfortunately, not all families have enough water to meet all of their needs. Where there is a shortage of water, or water deficit, it is essential to use all available sources as carefully as possible. Photos **C** show some ways that people can use water sparingly, in more sustainable ways. Countries too can use their available water in different ways (table **D**). Agriculture and industry both use huge amounts of water. For example, it has taken 10 litres of water just to produce the paper for this page! Some other surprising facts about water use are:

- A slice of bread takes 40 litres to make.
- A pair of jeans takes almost 11 000 litres.
- It takes 1300 litres to grow 1 kg of wheat, but *twelve times as much* to produce 1 kg of beef.

 C How can we use water more sustainably?

Taking a shower

Car-washing by hand

Drip-feed irrigation

Washing dishes by hand

D Water use in ten countries

Country	GDP per capita (US$)	National water use (av. litres per person per day)	National % water for agriculture	National % water for domestic activities	National % water for industrial activities and electricity generation
Canada	38 000	483	12	68	20
China	7200	86	67	7	26
Egypt	6100	252	78	8	14
France	34 000	287	10	16	74
Ghana	2100	36	48	37	15
India	3300	135	86	8	6
Mexico	14 300	366	78	17	5
Russia	17 500	125	18	19	63
UK	35 000	149	3	22	75
USA	46 000	575	41	13	46

Now Investigate

1 Suggest some ways in which water can be used more sustainably – in addition to those shown in photos **C**.

2 Study table **D**.

  a Use data in the table to identify how fresh water use can vary between countries at different levels of economic development.

  b Suggest reasons for the patterns of use you have identified in (a). (Hint: Some crops, for example rice and cotton, use much more water than others.)

3 a Draw two spider diagrams, to show the most likely water uses of a family in an LEDC and in an MEDC.

  b List ways in which the information in your diagrams is similar and different.

  c Suggest some reasons for any differences you have identified in (b).

Meeting the demand for water

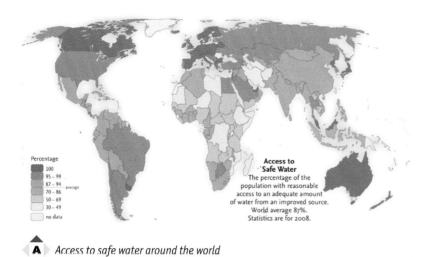

 A Access to safe water around the world

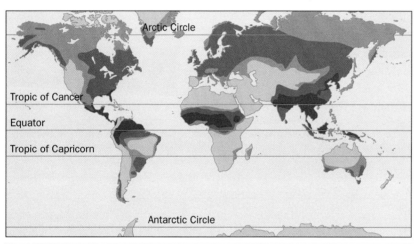

Precipitation in July (mm)
☐ Over 25 ▨ 25–50 ▧ 50–150 ■ More than 150

B Rainfall around the world

Many people have unlimited access to clean drinking water. However, 1 billion people (that is one in every seven people on Earth) struggle to get enough water to meet their basic needs (map **A**).

The number of people who are permanently short of clean drinking water seems likely to rise to at least 4 billion by 2050. The main problem facing these people is not the lack of water, but actually accessing the water. This is because often rain doesn't always fall where it is most needed (map **B**), and 99 per cent of all fresh water on Earth is stored in rocks deep underground.

Over the years, people have developed ways of storing water for future use, and moving it to water-deficit areas. Water transfer using pipes and aqueducts has been practised for centuries – cities like Los Angeles now transfer water over 300 km in order to meet their needs. Many places that already experience a deficit are likely to face even greater water supply problems in the future. This is due mainly to population increase (see graph **D** in Topic 1.1 on page **3**), but also because people use more water as their standard of living rises.

Fantastic fact 🌍

The world's demand for water is rising by 175 *billion* litres every day.

Accessing water sources

Clean water is available from several sources:
- **Lakes and rivers** are the main sources of easily accessible water. However, many of these have been heavily polluted by waste from homes, farms and industries, or are over-used (photo **C**).
- Aquifers are underground sources of water. They don't lose water through evaporation, and deep aquifers aren't polluted by towns, farms and factories on the surface. However, care must be taken not to extract more from these sources than can be replaced naturally by rainwater and water seeping downwards from lakes and reservoirs.

- **Desalination plants** distil sea water and make it safe to use by removing the salt. This is a very expensive process, and can only be afforded by wealthy countries such as the oil-rich desert states in the Middle East.
- **Large-scale rainwater harvesting** is the collection and storing of rainwater in reservoirs. 'Mega-dams' are now are now seen as the best way of storing huge quantities of water for the future, even though reservoirs in warmer regions can lose much of their water due to evaporation. The dams are often fitted with turbines for generating electricity, which is sold at a profit. This income helps to pay the building costs and reimburse people whose lives have been disrupted by the new reservoirs.
- **Small-scale rainwater harvesting** can also be very effective. Some cities in Germany and India have laws that require all new properties to have their own rainwater collection and storage systems.

 C This is what happened when too much water was taken out of the Aral Sea to irrigate farmland

Topic link 🔗

For more about the Aral Sea go to Topic 2.11 on pages 128–29.

Reducing the demand for water

Many countries are now trying hard to reduce their total use of water and yet still meet their people's increasing needs. The benefits of such measures as those shown in photos **C** on page 183 can be significant. For example, reducing the world's use of irrigation water by only 10 per cent could double the amount available for the domestic supply of everyone on the planet.

Now Investigate ❗

1 a Make a drawing of your own home.

 b Annotate your drawing to show how your home could be adapted to harvest and store rainwater.

 c Add further information about how water reaches your home, and about any treatment the water receives to make it safe to use.

2 Make a large copy of the table below. Your task is to complete your table by adding the possible advantages (benefits) and disadvantages of each source of clean water. It is a good idea to discuss your ideas with other students in your class before you start to do this.

3 For this activity you will need to refer to map **C** in Topic 1.5 page 26 and maps A and B on page 184.

 a Briefly describe the main distribution patterns shown in each of these three maps.

 b Using your answer to (a), suggest reasons for the global distribution of areas where access to water is difficult.

Water source	Benefits of this type of water source	Disadvantages of this type of water source
Aquifers		
Desalination plants		
Lakes and rivers		
Large-scale rainwater harvesting		
Small-scale rainwater harvesting		

Water supply issues

Topic link

- Look back at Topic 1.5 pages 30–31 for more information on the Sahel region.
- Look back at Topic 1.3 pages 14–21 for more information on population growth.

Now Investigate

Do you have access to a regular supply of clean water? Keep a record of how many times in one day you use water. State what you use it for, and approximately how much you use (in litres) each time. How much have you used by the end of the day?

Further research

Look for information about some agencies that help to give people a supply of clean water (for example WaterAid or Oxfam). Find out how they do this.

> Bonjour! I'm Sawadogo and I live in Burkina Faso, in the Sahel region. It doesn't rain here often and when I was younger we were always short of water. I was often ill because the water we drank wasn't clean. Then they dug a well in the village, with a pump and tap. Now we have a good supply of clean water which is safe to drink. We use some of the water to grow food. We can sell some of the food and earn money.

A Sawadogo

Sawadogo's story shows how some people in LEDCs are being given access to clean water. Another way is by water-harvesting. This is a way of saving small amounts of water for future use. Local people build small earth or stone dams across a river or stream to hold back any rainwater. This stored water allows farmers to irrigate their crops and so increase crop yields. If the water is treated to make it safe to drink, it also means women and children do not have to spend so much time collecting water from further away.

Case study

Aquifer depletion in northern India

An aquifer becomes depleted (gets smaller) when more water is extracted from it than can be replaced naturally. The aquifer beneath the Indian states of Rajasthan, Punjab and Haryana (map **A**) is becoming seriously depleted, at a rate of 1 metre every three years, because so many people are using the water in the aquifer. This region has a population of 20 million, and includes the cities of Jaipur and Delhi. The water is also needed for irrigating the crops that are vital to Rajasthan's economy – this region supplies much of India's wheat, barley and cotton. Rajasthan's industries are also expanding rapidly, and many of these use large quantities of water.

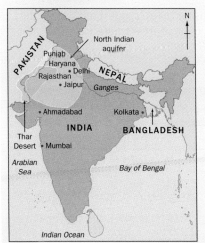

B Location of the aquifer in northern India

- Competition for water in the Nile basin
- Egyptian farmers have used irrigation water from the river Nile for thousands of years. Together the White Nile and the Blue Nile and their tributaries pass through ten countries. The Blue Nile brings floodwater and fertile sediment from the Ethiopian Highlands after snowmelt and heavy rainfall there in summer (graph **E**). Graph **D** shows that, without this river water, much more of Egypt and Sudan would be an infertile, hot desert. Egypt was the first country to build dams across the river, such as the Aswan High Dam (photo **C**). Storing the Nile's floodwater is the key to growing more than one crop of rice and cotton each year.
- In 1999 the Nile basin countries signed an agreement to promote the sustainable use of the river water in ways that would benefit them all. However, the basin's population of 160 million people is expected to double in the next 25 years, and every country is demanding more water to grow more food and generate more power. The resulting tension has split the countries into two opposing groups: Egypt, North Sudan and South Sudan in one group, and remaining countries in the other. Serious conflict could develop if the demand for more water grows.

C Aswan High Dam and Lake Nasser, the reservoir created by the dam

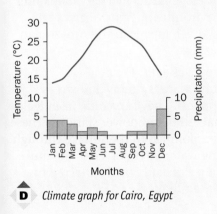

D Climate graph for Cairo, Egypt

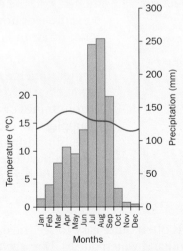

E Climate graph for Addis Ababa, Ethiopia

> ### Fantastic fact
>
> Lake Nasser is the world's largest artificial lake. It extends 100 km south of Egypt into another country, North Sudan.

Now Investigate

1 a Describe in detail the contrasts between the climates of Cairo (graph **D**) and Addis Ababa (graph **E**).

   b What is the significance of these contrasts in terms of a supply of water in Ethiopia and Egypt?

2 Imagine that you are a farmer living beside the Blue Nile in Ethiopia.

   a What are your priorities for using water from the river?

   b How are those priorities different from those of an Egyptian farmer? Explain your answer to this question.

Learning objectives:

- talk about how our use of natural resources damages the environment

- describe the effects of pollution on our air and water supplies

- understand how the greenhouse effect works and describe the effects of global warming

- explain the causes and effects of deforestation and soil erosion.

Your damaged environment

The economic activities described so far in Section 3 – agriculture, industry, tourism and electricity generation – all have huge benefits for the countries where they take place. But they can cause a number of problems for people, including food shortages, health issues and loss of culture. Most economic activities can also cause great harm to the natural environment. Think, for instance, about agriculture in your local area. What kind of damage does it do to rivers and lakes, soils, the atmosphere and the natural vegetation? Some ideas are shown in diagram **A**.

Damage to watercourses

Lakes, rivers and the sea can all be damaged by industrial activities. Many factories are located by rivers and use the water for cooling and other purposes. This water may be returned to the river containing toxic (poisonous) chemicals. This is called contamination and means people downstream cannot use the water for drinking supplies or irrigation as it may cause diseases or ruin crops. It may also affect the fish supplies that provide protein for their diet. Smaller-scale industrial activities can also have very damaging effects on the environment. Figure **C** gives an example of how this happens in the Amazonian rainforest in Brazil.

Pollutants and toxic chemicals can also enter underground water systems (known as groundwater supplies). They can come from leaks from mines or factories and power stations. These supplies are often pumped to the surface through wells for drinking water. Areas of Vietnam and Korea have been particularly badly affected by groundwater contamination.

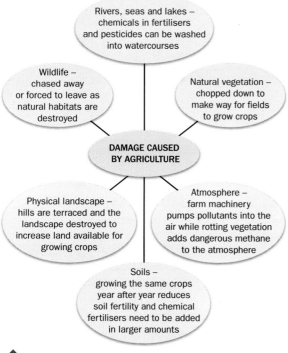

A The environmental impacts of agriculture

Damage to the air

It is often quite easy to see the damage that pollution causes to land and watercourses. Damage to the air can be much more difficult to spot. Smoke pouring out of large factories (photo **B**) is quite obvious and can cause breathing difficulties for those who live nearby. Coal dust produced by mining has a similar effect.

B Factories can cause severe air pollution

Now Investigate

Look at diagram **A**. Choose an example of either tourism or manufacturing industry from your own local area. Draw a similar diagram showing the environmental damage these activities could cause.

> We are the garimpeiros, looking for gold in the Amazon rainforest.
>
> We have to strip the land to get at the gold. We know we're causing damage. We cut down the trees to get at the earth and then we wash it into the river. Sometimes the river silts up and can't flow any more.
>
> The worst thing we do is washing the gold with mercury. It's a dangerous chemical and kills the fish. Sometimes the local people eat the fish or drink the contaminated water. It damages their bodies and sends them mad.
>
> What can we do, though? There are no jobs anywhere else and here, we may get rich!

In many countries, factories are now forced by law to keep their pollutants to a minimum. This is easier to keep under control in MEDCs. In LEDCs, where laws are less strictly enforced, the environmental damage can go unchallenged.

Other effects are much harder to detect. Some chemicals react with the water in the atmosphere and fall to the ground as acid rain. This can kill crops and, again, contaminate watercourses. In China, there are fears that an estimated 30 per cent of the country's agricultural land is affected by acid rain. This is a serious problem in a country with an expanding population that already has problems producing enough food for its people.

Perhaps the biggest impact of pollutants in the atmosphere is the change in the world's climate brought about by global warming.

How transport affects the environment

Industry can cause less direct effects on the environment. Most factories, mines and tourist developments rely on some kind of transport. This may be to bring in raw materials, move finished products or to carry people around. The transport used will add further pollutants to the atmosphere. Aircraft are particularly damaging because they release pollutants high up in the atmosphere where there are even greater effects on the environment causing global warming.

The effects of chemicals produced by motor vehicles have been shown to be very dangerous. Leaded gasoline (fuel oil) has now been banned in many countries because of health risks. Studies have shown it can be linked to brain damage and other mental health problems. Fuel with a low sulphur content is also becoming more widely available. Kenya and Tanzania, for instance, have introduced it to help reduce the diseases, such as lung cancer, that high sulphur gasoline can cause.

Topic link

- There's more information on groundwater contamination in Topic 3.8 on pages 182–87.
- Global warming is discussed in more detail later in this topic and in Topic 3.6 (pages 168–75) and 3.10 (pages 194–99)

Now Investigate

1 Using the images on these pages, describe some types of pollution that can result from industrial activity.

2 Think of examples of economic activities where you live. What types of transport do these industries use? Make a list of the possible sources of pollution from industry in your local area.

3 There are many types of pollution affecting people and countries on a global scale. Which do you think are the most dangerous? Give reasons for your answer.

The world gets warmer

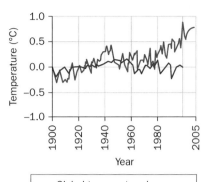

A *The effects of human activity on global temperatures*

Legend:
— Global temperature increase
— Change without the effects of human activity

Over the last 150 years there has been a gradual increase in the average global temperature. Although this increase has only been around 1°C, it has had some very big effects – especially when compared with changes over a much longer period of time. Most scientists now agree that this global warming has been caused by human activities (graph **A**). They also predict that average temperatures will continue to increase – perhaps by more than 5°C by 2100. These changes could have the potential to completely change our world.

The enhanced greenhouse effect

Greenhouse gases are produced by human activities. They are concentrated in the atmosphere and act like a blanket, keeping heat in (diagram **B**). The concentration of these gases is increasing all the time and they come from a number of different sources:

- Burning fossil fuels – coal, oil and gas – in factories, power stations and motor vehicles releases carbon dioxide, sulphur dioxide and other gases.
- Cutting down and burning trees also adds carbon dioxide to the atmosphere.
- Very damaging methane comes from decaying vegetation in padi fields, from cattle and from rubbish tips.
- Nitrous oxides are given off by agricultural fertilisers.
- Halocarbons and chlorofluorocarbons (also known as CFCs) come from fridges and aerosols – although banned worldwide they can remain in the atmosphere for 400 years.

Growing populations mean that the amount of these gases being released into the atmosphere is constantly increasing. This leads to more heat being trapped and higher global temperatures. There are fears that it may already be too late to stop concentrations growing beyond levels that would have disastrous effects for some parts of the world.

Topic link

There is more about the effects of deforestation, including the greenhouse effect, in Topic 3.6 and other topics in Section 3.

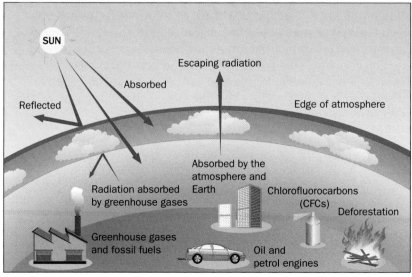

The greenhouse effect **B** ▶

The effects of climate change

It is very difficult to predict what could happen as the world gets warmer. Computer models have been used to give us some idea of what might happen in the future, and these predict some of the events set out in diagram **C**.

Although many of these changes are only predictions at the moment, some countries are already coming to terms with the effects of climate change.

Future events as a result of climate change? **C ▶**

Melting polar ice caps, ice sheets (in countries like Greenland) and glaciers could cause a sea-level rise of up to 5 metres – a severe problem for the 40 per cent of the world's population who live close to the coast.

Rising sea temperatures will mean the oceans expand, leading to an average worldwide sea-level rise of 40 cm by 2100 – this would mean widespread flooding of low-lying areas.

There could be changes in extreme weather events – e.g. temperatures over 40°C causing wildfires in Australia, more hurricanes in the Caribbean, deadly heatwaves in Europe and floods in Egypt.

THE EFFECTS OF CLIMATE CHANGE

Wars may be fought as the global population grows and precious resources such as food and water become scarce in some countries.

Changes to farming as equatorial areas become too hot and tropical crops are grown further north.

The coral reefs that provide many countries (including Belize, Australia and the Maldives) with a big tourist attraction could die.

Extinction of wildlife that is unable to adapt to the changing climate – some scientists estimate up to one third of all species could become extinct over the next 100 years.

Tropical diseases become more widespread – malaria, for instance, could become common in Europe.

Abandoning the Carteret Islands

Case study

CARTERET ISLANDS

Papua New Guinea

Australia

Pacific Ocean

In 2009 the world's first large-scale evacuation due to climate change took place from the Carteret Islands in the South Pacific. The coral islands, around 80 football pitches in size and home to 2600 people, are gradually being submerged by rising sea levels.

The islands have a maximum height above the sea of 170 centimetres so any sea level rise will have a serious effect (photo **D**). Violent storms across the islands have been increasing, perhaps as a result of climate change, and have brought widespread flooding.

D *Sea-level rise has destroyed the coastline*

Salt water has poisoned the land where islanders used to grow crops and food has become very scarce. The inhabitants have made the decision to relocate to a nearby island called Bougainville, off the coast of Papua New Guinea.

The evacuation was the first time that large numbers of people have been forced to leave their homes, apparently as a result of climate change. It is unlikely to be the last.

'Their numbers might be small, but this is the event that could show the likely mass migration of people from coastal cities and low-lying regions as a result of rising sea levels. The disaster has begun, but so far hardly anyone has noticed.'

George Monbiot, environmental author and campaigner

Now Investigate

1 a Draw a labelled diagram to show how the greenhouse effect occurs.

  b Explain how human activities have led to an increase in the greenhouse effect.

2 Using specific examples, describe some of the global impacts of climate change.

3 Think about your local area. Find out what impacts climate change might have on the place where you live.

Destruction of the forests

Skills link

Graph A shows a lot of information – different time periods and positive and negative scales. Look up the section on graph interpretation on pages 212–15 before trying to work out what exactly it shows.

Fantastic fact

More than 50 countries around the world have already lost over 90 per cent of their natural forests.

Now Investigate

1 Describe the trends shown on graph **A**. Refer to specific regions in your answer.

2 Think about your own country. Where are the woodlands nearest to where you live? Find out if they have any sort of protection.

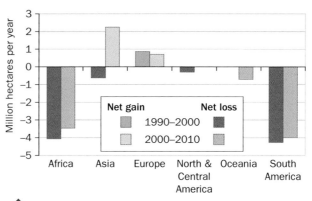

A *Changing global forest cover, 1990–2010*

As we saw in the previous section, cutting down and burning trees can have an influence on global warming. This process is called deforestation. Trees take carbon dioxide from the air and turn it into oxygen by photosynthesis. Not only does burning the trees add carbon dioxide to the atmosphere, it also means less gas can be removed in this way.

With the increased use of natural resources there are concerns about the effects on the world's natural ecosystems, including the tropical rainforests. Graph **A** shows global changes in forest cover over the last 20 years. Some countries, including China, have started planting more trees to increase the size of their forests and help combat the negative effects that deforestation is having on the environment. Many others, however, have come to rely on the money that can be made by cutting down trees. The Brazilian government has opened up the Amazonian rainforest to mining, huge cattle ranches and other forms of agriculture. Deforestation in other countries has also had severe environmental effects.

Deforestation in Borneo

Maps **B** shows that, until 1950, Borneo was covered in dense tropical forest. In the 1980s and 1990s, however, the island suffered a higher rate of deforestation than any other part of the world. Much of the wood was sent to the USA and Japan for chopsticks, furniture and paper. More recently oil palm plantations have been responsible for the destruction of the rainforest.

Deforestation in Borneo has had a number of environmental effects:

- The habitats of many animals have been destroyed or reduced – including endangered species such as the clouded leopard, pygmy elephant and orang utan.
- Forest fires have increased – these cause 'haze' pollution across Borneo and in neighbouring islands (in Indonesia, Malaysia and Singapore).

- Smoke from fires causes environmental health problems, especially breathing difficulties for local people.
- The removal of the forest cover is increasing the amount of soil erosion.

Deforestation has other effects on the economy and on people. It can, for instance, mean fewer tourists coming to visit a country. Soil erosion resulting from deforestation also reduces the amount of land available for agriculture and is an increasing problem around the world.

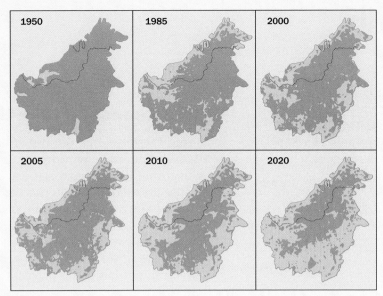

B The decline of Borneo's forests

Environmental effects of soil erosion

In regions such as Borneo, once forest cover is removed from the land, there is nothing left to protect the fertile soil. It is left exposed to heavy tropical rains which wash it away. This can cause huge gullies to form (photo **C**). The soil becomes impossible to farm and local people are forced to migrate to other areas which may be even less suitable for farming.

In drier areas, such as the countries that border the southern Sahara Desert and in the mid-west states of the USA, soil erosion by the wind is more common. Once the vegetation cover is removed, the soil quickly dries out and can be easily blown away. The soil again becomes infertile. Farming may still be possible with the use of fertilisers but these can contaminate water supplies.

Soil removed by wind and water can be transported over huge distances. When washed into rivers, the soil can kill animal life, alter the river's flow, lower the water quality and may even increase the risk of flooding. Soil in the air can travel even further. It is not unknown for soil carried on the wind to be blown from the Sahara to southern England where it collects on cars (image **D**).

C Gully formation due to soil erosion

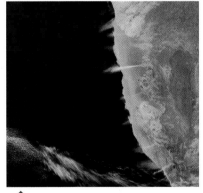

D Satellite image showing sand being blown from the Sahara towards Europe

Now Investigate

1 a Using maps **B**, describe the extent of the deforestation that has taken place in Borneo.

   b Explain some of the causes and effects of the destruction of Borneo's rainforests.

2 a What are the two main processes by which soil erosion takes place?

   b Which do you think has the worst environmental effects? Explain your answer.

3 Are there any areas of your country where severe soil erosion could take place? Use a map or atlas to identify them and outline the reasons that could be behind the erosion.

Topic link

The effects of deforestation and soil erosion on agriculture are causes of migration described in Topic 1.6 on pages 32–33.

3.10 Sustainable development: how can we conserve the environment?

Learning objectives:

> understand why we need to protect the environment

> talk about the ways in which you can live in a more sustainable way

> describe how governments and other organisations help protect the natural environment

> relate what you have learned to case studies from around the world.

Your chance to save the planet

Topic 3.9 shows that our use of natural resources can be very damaging to the environment. But it does not have to be this way. Governments and organisations across the world are starting to realise there could be alternative ways to live our lives. Many are now looking to become more **sustainable** – using resources in a way that won't leave permanent damage for future generations. Some countries have been forced into action by their own people. Across the world, ordinary citizens are demanding that the natural environment has better protection. Many people are making an effort to use less of the planet's resources (figure **A**).

 A How to be low carbon

Ben Formby has set himself a challenge to use as few resources as possible. Giving up his house, he has moved into a tent pitched in his office car park (so he can walk to work). The PC and radio in his tent are powered by hand-winding.

He cycles to local markets to buy food (without packaging) that has been transported over very short distances. For a complete lifestyle change he has also given up meat and become a vegetarian because of the damage to the environment brought about by the intensive farming of animals.

Now Investigate ❶

How much of the Earth's resources do *you* consume (use up) every day? *Either* keep a diary for the next 24 hours *or* review what you have done in the last 24 hours. Write down all the activities you can think of that use resources. Try to think of what resources you have used in each activity.

'Think global, act local'

This commonly used phrase helps us remember that we can help look after the Earth by taking action in our own community. We are all consumers, daily using up the planet's resources. When we drive anywhere we use petroleum; when we turn on the television we mainly use electricity generated in a power station; and the food we eat may have been produced using chemicals and then transported over long distances. There are ways, though, in which we can cut down on the damage that our consumption causes.

● How can you cut down the resources you use? Perhaps you could walk or cycle instead of asking for a lift in the car (figure **B**)? Maybe you could buy pizza from a local street seller instead of food from a global hamburger chain? Think about how these actions would save resources.

 B Can you cut down on the resources you use?

 ?  ?  ?

There are three helpful principles you can use:

- **Reduce** – stop using so much stuff. Take your own bag to the shops instead of using a new one. Or either turn off the heating and put on a sweater, or turn off the air-conditioning and allow a free flow of fresh air.
- **Re-use** – use the stuff you have more often, for example wash plastic cups and plates and then use them again, or fill up plastic water bottles at home instead of buying new ones.
- Recycle – over 80 per cent of household waste can be used again. This doesn't just mean paper, glass and tin cans but also computers, batteries and video games.

More and more countries are investing in recycling facilities, especially across Europe (graph **C**). This cuts down the amount of waste that has to be buried or burnt or dumped in the sea. It also saves on the energy and resources needed to make new things and used in transporting waste material around the world to be processed. Many developing countries are also heavily involved in recycling (photo **D**).

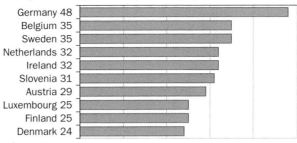

Average percentage of municipal waste recycled

Country	%
Germany	48
Belgium	35
Sweden	35
Netherlands	32
Ireland	32
Slovenia	31
Austria	29
Luxembourg	25
Finland	25
Denmark	24

C Europe's biggest recyclers

Fantastic fact

Recycling one tin can saves enough energy to power a television for three hours.

  D Recycling in Senegal

For many of the people of Senegal, small-scale recycling is a daily activity.

Local people recycle everything, including many items thrown away by richer countries. School books, glass bottles and plastic bags are all used again and again. Even fruit peel is collected and used in cheap perfume.

In villages across the country people drink water from cleaned tomato tins. Official papers thrown out by government departments are used to wrap the bread, fruit and vegetables bought from traders on the street.

Crafts people are also involved in this widespread recycling. Chairs, kitchen utensils and toys are made from metals. Even plastic bags have taken the place of worn tyres in making shoes.

Interest in recycling is spreading and people are becoming ever more resourceful. Some are now collecting waste metal in ever larger quantities and sending it back to the factories in Europe where it originally came from.

Now Investigate

1 Have a look again at the list you made of your activities over 24 hours that used resources. Decide how many and how much of these resources could be reduced, re-used or recycled. Make a table like the one below to illustrate this and compare it with those of other members of your class.

Activity	Reduce	Re-use	Recycle

2 Graph **C** shows recycling rates in Europe.

a How do you think your country compares? Carry out some research on the internet to try and find out what percentage of waste your country recycles.

b Do you have any local recycling centres? What can they recycle? Find them and mark them on a map of your local area.

3 Read the text in figure **D**. Do you know of any similar recycling measures carried out by people in your local area? Write them down, and try to add some ideas of your own.

Case study

We can all do something to cut down on the resources we use, but there is a limit to how much individuals can achieve. Governments and organisations also need to play a part in looking after the environment. Take the Great Barrier Reef in Australia, for example.

The Great Barrier Reef Marine Park

The Great Barrier Reef, located off Australia's eastern coast, is the largest coral reef system on the planet – it measures over 2500 km in length (map **A**). More than 2 million people visit the reef every year. The majority (up to 90 per cent) are domestic tourists from within Australia. Large numbers of people also come from New Zealand, Japan, the UK, Germany and other European countries. These tourists stay at hotels on individual islands, go diving, arrive by cruise ship or fly in for the day by helicopter. Many come to see the great range of wildlife (figure **B**) – some species are not found anywhere else in the world.

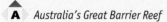
A *Australia's Great Barrier Reef*

Tourists spend around US$5 billion a year, contributing money to the local economy and creating jobs. However, the large number of people can cause considerable damage to the environment. This can be by using polluting vehicles or damaging the coral when snorkelling and diving.

There are other pressures on the environment. Large towns along the coast have factories and power stations. There is large-scale coastal agriculture using fertilisers and other chemicals. These industries can pollute the sea and destroy the fragile coral. People from the towns located near the reef use the surrounding waters for commercial fishing, and the local Torres Strait islanders have depended on the sea for food for centuries. Overfishing is a potential risk. Meeting the needs of all these users makes conservation of the reef very difficult.

- 30 species of whales, dolphins, and porpoises recorded
- 6 species of sea turtles come to the reef to breed
- 215 species of birds (including 22 species of seabirds and 32 species of shorebirds) visit the reef or nest or roost on the islands
- 17 species of sea snake
- More than 1500 fish species
- At least 330 species of ascidians (sea squirts)

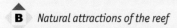
B *Natural attractions of the reef*

Topic link

For more general information about coral reefs see Topic 2.5 pages 96–99.

The Great Barrier Reef Marine Park Authority (GBRMPA)

The Australian government has made the Great Barrier Reef into a protected area by declaring it a 'marine park'. The GBRMPA is the organisation responsible for looking after the reef (figure **C**).

One of the most important developments by the Marine Park Authority has been to divide the whole reef into zones, creating areas where people are allowed to use the reef in different ways. There are areas for local people to fish, other areas for tourists to dive, and so on.

The GBRMPA has been praised for the way it has communicated with all the people who want to use the park – from tourist companies to local fishermen. It has won many international awards for helping to protect the environment while allowing sustainable development to take place.

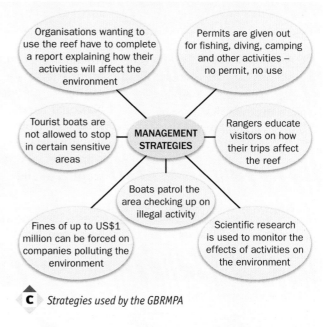

C Strategies used by the GBRMPA

- Organisations wanting to use the reef have to complete a report explaining how their activities will affect the environment
- Permits are given out for fishing, diving, camping and other activities – no permit, no use
- Tourist boats are not allowed to stop in certain sensitive areas
- **MANAGEMENT STRATEGIES**
- Rangers educate visitors on how their trips affect the reef
- Boats patrol the area checking up on illegal activity
- Fines of up to US$1 million can be forced on companies polluting the environment
- Scientific research is used to monitor the effects of activities on the environment

The problem of climate change

One of the biggest threats to the Great Barrier Reef comes from climate change. Rising sea temperatures can kill the coral and have a damaging effect on fish and other marine life. Extreme weather events can also affect the area. In 2011, huge floods caused by Cyclone Yasi washed damaging sediments and pollutants over large parts of the reef (photo **D**).

There is little the GBRMPA can do to stop climate change but it is helping local people prepare for the possible negative effects on the environment and their lifestyles and jobs.

D Damage to the Great Barrier Reef

Now Investigate

1 Assuming there are 200 000 overseas visitors to the Great Barrier Reef every year, complete a copy of the following table to show the number of visitors from selected countries.

Country	Percentage of total visitors	Number of visitors (total 200 000)
United Kingdom	30	60 000
Germany	10	
Other European countries	21	
Japan	15	
USA	11	
Other countries	13	

2 Display the information shown in your table as (a) a correctly labelled pie chart and (b) a bar graph. Think of the effects all these visitors could have on the sustainable development and conservation of the reef.

3 a Explain why Australia's Great Barrier Reef needs to be protected.

  b Explain how this protection is being carried out.

Further research 🔍

Search for 'Great Barrier Reef Marine Park Authority' to find much more official information on the work of the GBRMPA. Create a factfile displaying the information you find.

Conservation management and National Parks

Topic link

Topic 1.11 (pages 60–65) has more on problems caused by tourists in rural areas.

Australia's Great Barrier Reef Marine Park is just one example of the worldwide network of National Parks. These are areas protected from development, usually because they contain some special environmental feature, fragile environment or wildlife that may be in danger of extinction. There are many different categories of National Park including marine reserves, forest reserves and forest parks, biological reserves and wildlife refuges (figure A).

National Park	Country	Special feature
Jaldapara Wildlife Sanctuary	West Bengal, India	Indian elephants
Kruger National Park	South Africa	Wildlife
Bwindi Impenetrable National Park	Uganda	Mountain gorillas
Poas Volcano National Park	Costa Rica	Active volcano
Quttinirpaaq National Park	Canada	Tidewater glaciers
Triglav National Park	Slovenia	Limestone scenery and caves
Whanganui National Park	New Zealand	Lowland forest and birdlife
Madidi National Park	Bolivia	Tropical rainforest

 Examples of National Parks from around the world

Fantastic fact

The world's first ever National Park was Yellowstone in the USA.

Now Investigate

Find out about National Parks in your own country. They are often marked on maps. Investigate why they were set up and what they are protecting.

National Parks in the UK

The UK's National Parks were originally set up by the government in 1949. They have three main aims:
- to maintain and improve natural beauty, wildlife and culture
- to help the public understand and enjoy their special qualities
- to make sure local communities can survive economically and socially.

In most parts of the world, National Parks are wilderness areas but this is not the case in the UK. The country's high population density means National Parks are areas of the countryside where people live and work. These areas have different kinds of industry and farming that would not be allowed in National Parks in many other countries. For this reason their conservation is affected by many different pressures.

The Yorkshire Dales National Park, England

The Yorkshire Dales National Park is an area of beautiful rural landscapes in the north of England (map **A**). It is famous for its limestone scenery and wildlife. Unlike many National Parks, it is renowned as a farming landscape with unique features such as 'drystone walls'. For centuries it has also been an industrial area with quarries mining limestone and lead (photos **B**). It is close to major population centres including the cities of Leeds, Manchester and Liverpool and receives almost 9 million visitors each year.

The military also use part of the National Park for war games practice. The variety of uses puts a lot of pressure on those trying to conserve the environment of the Park.

Problems and solutions

Some of the problems caused by the different land uses in the National Park are listed below:

- **Tourism** – causing traffic congestion; leaving farm gates open; parking on narrow roads.
- **Quarrying** – causes noise and visual pollution; lorries cause congestion and pollution; disused quarries are dangerous.
- **Military** – loud noises disturb wildlife and scare tourists.
- **Local residents** – lack of affordable housing for local people; residents treat tourists as a nuisance.

A number of different organisations are trying to find solutions to these problems. Some, like the Yorkshire Dales National Park Authority, are official government bodies. Others, like the Friends of the Yorkshire Dales, are voluntary and rely on donations from the public. Solutions to the problems in the Dales include:

- stopping new quarries being set up
- 'screening' the quarries with trees to reduce pollution
- using self-closing gates in farmers' fields
- allowing 'live' firing by the army only on certain days
- increasing public transport and providing car parks on the edges of popular towns and villages
- forcing quarry companies to return the landscape to its natural state when digging is finished
- helping build rail links to quarries and limiting blasting to certain days of the week
- providing houses at lower prices for local residents
- making tourists feel more welcome.

The organisations involved work to manage the National Park carefully, and there is a lot of communication between all the parties involved. It is only by doing this that the environment will be conserved, and development within the Park will be sustainable.

Remember that some of the details you need to know are covered in previous sections of Section 3.

A The location of the Yorkshire Dales National Park

Now Investigate

1 What are the aims of the UK's National Parks? Which do you think is most important? Give at least one reason for your answer.

2 Using photos **B**, describe the varied human and natural landscapes and environments of the Yorkshire Dales National Park. Explain why these landscapes are important.

3 Construct a mind map, using different colours, to show the problems caused by the different land uses in the YDNP and some of the proposed solutions.

B Landscapes of the Yorkshire Dales National Park

Learning objectives:

- use a key to locate and identify symbols on a map

- use an 8-point compass and/ or bearings to give and follow directions

- measure distances using map scales

- use four-figure and six-figure grid references

- recognise and describe the patterns made by physical features in the landscape

- annotate and interpret relief cross-sections

- recognise and describe the patterns made by human features and activities within the landscape.

Now Investigate

1   Look at the map on page 39. Sketch four symbols shown on the map and explain what each one represents.

2   Find an open space outside. Establish which direction is north, and then describe what you can see as you turn to the south, east and west.

About maps

A number of standard mapping conventions are used worldwide, for example blue is used to show water features and brown for the height of the land. However, there are also many variations in map symbols, so all maps include a key displaying any symbols on the map, with their meanings. When 'reading' a map you must always take time to refer to its key.

Giving directions

Diagram **A** shows an eight-point compass. Using a compass is the most common way to give directions. A more accurate way to give directions is to use bearings. These provide the exact angle between two places, measured from due north. In order to calculate bearings, you need a protractor (diagram **B**).However, you do need to learn the compass points! On most – but not all – maps, north is at the top. Any map that you draw must include a north point. When using a map in an examination, be very careful to check where north is before you write any answers that include directions. Most questions can be answered by making simple statements such as 'The mountains are in the north', 'Most rain occurs in eastern areas' or 'The river flows in a south-westerly direction'. In examinations many candidates confuse west and east. They also often write directions the wrong way round, for example 'east-south' instead of 'south-east'. So do learn the names and directions well.

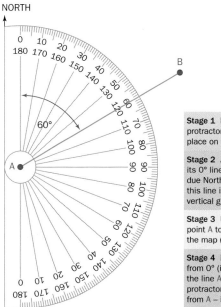

Stage 1 Place the centre point of the protractor over the 'direction from' place on the map (A).

Stage 2 Adjust the protractor so that its 0° line from the centre dot points due North. Do this by making sure that this line is parallel to the nearest vertical grid line on the map.

Stage 3 Use a pencil and ruler to join point A to the 'direction to' place on the map (B).

Stage 4 Read the number of degrees from 0° (i.e. North) to the point where the line AB crosses the edge of the protractor. This is the bearing of B from A – in this example 60°.

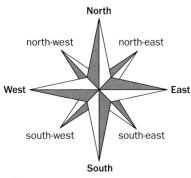

A *Eight-point compass*

B *How to find bearings using a map and protractor*

Scale and distance

Topographical maps like the ones you will see in examinations are drawn to a scale of 1:25 000 or 1:50 000. On the 1:25 000 map this means that 4 cm on the map represents 1 km on the ground. Similarly, on 1:50 000 maps, 2 cm on the map represents 1 km on the ground.

On the topographical maps you will work with in your examination, the easiest way to work out distances is to use the scale line. You may be asked to calculate a distance in a straight line – the direct distance from one point on the map to another – or you may have to measure a curved distance, for example along a river or winding road. To do this, place the straight edge of a clean piece of paper between the two points you are measuring. Mark these points on your paper, then move the paper to the scale line. The first point on your paper should be aligned with zero on the scale line. Then check where the second point is on the scale-line and note the distance. If the distance you are measuring on the map is not straight, you will need to do this several times to find the total distance. Always give your answer in metres or kilometres.

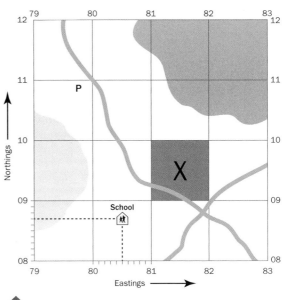

C Grid system on a topographical map

Locating places using grid references

The grid lines that run from north to south are called eastings. They are numbered along the top and the bottom of the map, and the numbers always increase in value from west to east (map **C**). The grid lines that run from west to east are called northings. They are numbered up the sides of the map, and their values increase from south to north.

In the examination, the map extract is part of a much larger map – so the grid numbers are very unlikely to start at 00 in the south-west corner!

The grid and grid lines on a map are used to give grid references. These are unique locations on that map where a feature or a place is located. Four-figure grid references identify the grid square in which a large feature such as a village, a lake or a forest can be found. For example, in map **C** the square marked X is shaded in orange:

- the line along the left of the square is numbered 81
- the line along the bottom of the square is numbered 09.

So the four-figure grid reference for that square is 8109. Notice that the easting comes first, followed by the northing.

However, to pinpoint an exact location we use a more precise six-figure grid reference. In map **C**, the six-figure grid reference for the school building (Sch) is 805087.

- The grid line to the left is 80, and the school is *five*-tenths (5/10) of the square to the *right* of that line.
- The grid line to the bottom is 08, and the school is *seven*-tenths (7/10) of the square *above* that line.

Now Investigate !

Refer to map **C**.

1 Give the four-figure grid references for:

  a the square entirely filled with woodland

  b the square that is mostly filled with water.

2 Give the six-figure grid references for:

  a the post office P

  b the crossroads.

The shape of the land

Topic link

See Topic 4.3 pages 212–21 to learn more about isolines.

Contour lines

Topographical maps like the one you will see on Paper 2 show the relief of a landscape. They do this by using contour lines – a type of isoline that joins points with the same altitude (height) above sea level. Many maps also include spot heights, which show the exact height of the land, marked as a dot and a number stating the height (diagram **A**).

In many countries, relief is shown by colour-shading of the area between the contour lines. See for example the maps on pages 39 and 259.

Contour lines tell us much more than just the height of the land. The patterns they make show us the shape of the land surface and how steeply it slopes. They also give us the information we need to calculate the gradient (steepness) of the land.

Cross-sections

A cross-section shows changes in relief between two points on a map. It is a kind of line graph, with horizontal distance plotted along the *x*-axis, and the height of the land on the *y*-axis. You do not need to learn how to draw a cross-section for Paper 2 – but you may wish to include one in your Paper 3 assessment, so it will help you to understand how cross-sections are constructed and so be able to link them to a map and annotate their features.

Annotating a cross-section

The main aim of any cross-section is to show the shape of the land – so any labels or annotations generally refer to its relief features. However, such profiles can also be used to show other physical features, for example those in river valleys. Aspects of the human landscape may also be shown, for example:

- the sites of settlements
- the locations of routeways
- land uses at different altitudes.

Cross-sections are an ideal way of highlighting relationships between relief features and human activities, for example where routeways follow valley bottoms.

Interpreting cross-sections

Although you do not have to draw a cross-section, you are expected to be able to interpret them in the examination. This involves describing and possibly explaining the relief features shown. Where land is steep, contours are close together, and the cross-section profiles will reflect this (diagram **A**). More gently

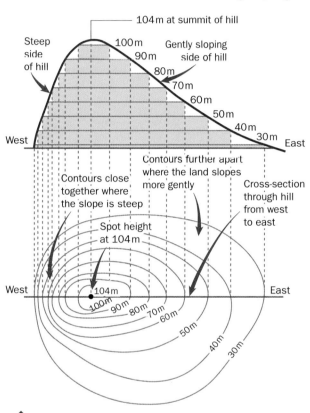

  Contours representing relief

Topic link

See Topic 4.3 pages 212–21 to learn more about line graphs.

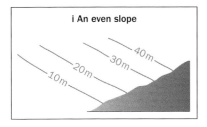

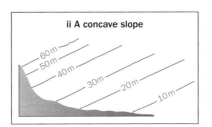

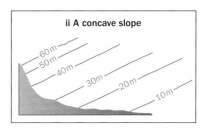

B Cross-sections of three different types of slope

sloping land is shown by contours that are further apart. Land that rises and falls gently is said to be 'rolling' or 'undulating'. Cross-sections can also indicate where land slopes very evenly (diagram **Bi**), is concave (diagram **Bii**) or is convex (diagram **Biii**).

If you are asked to describe or explain features using a cross-section, you could also comment on:

- the highest and lowest points (and their grid references)
- the difference in height between these points
- how the land slopes in each direction from the highest point, for example steeply or gently, and referring to compass directions as necessary
- the relationship between physical features and any human activities.

Gradient

Gradient is the mathematical term used to describe the steepness of a slope. It is the change in vertical height between two points compared with the horizontal distance between them. It can be given either as a ratio (e.g. 1:10) or a percentage (10%). Diagram **C** explains how a gradient between two points on a map is calculated.

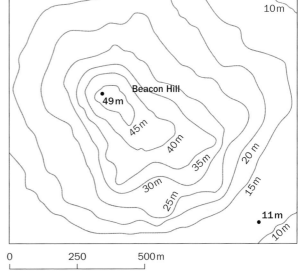

To find the gradient between the spot heights at **49 m** and **11 m**

Stage 1 Calculate the difference in height between the two places: 49 m – 11 m = 38 m

Stage 2 Calculate the distance between the two places. Using the line scale on the map shows that this is 750 m.

Stage 3 To find the gradient, divide the distance by the height difference: $\frac{750 \text{ m}}{38 \text{ m}} = 19.7$

Gradient is 1:19.7

C How to calculate gradient

Now Investigate

Draw the contours that would represent a long, isolated hill that has a steep slope on one side, a flat top, and a more gentle slope on the other side.

Landforms and drainage

You are now aware that knowing about contours, slopes and gradients helps us to understand what the relief of an area is like. They can also be used to identify landscape features such as river valleys (figure **A**).

Figure **A** shows typical contour patterns for some of the most common types of relief feature, as you will see on a large-scale map, with photographs of some of these features. Table **B** describes each of these features. You need to be able to recognise all of them on both 1:25 000 and 1:50 000 scale maps, and be able to name and describe each one.

When you describe the relief of an area, remember to:

- make a few general statements such as:

  'This is mainly a highland/lowland area'
  'Most of its slopes are steep/gentle'
  'The land is undulating'

- quote actual heights from the map (including the highest and lowest)
- calculate the height range between these two points
- identify and name key features such as mountain peaks and river valleys

 Some landscape features and their contour patterns

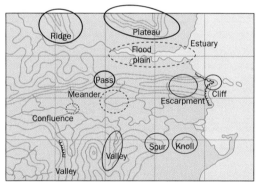

 Descriptions of landscape features

Type of landscape feature	Description
Cliff	very steep (vertical) slope
Escarpment	a ridge with one side that is much steeper (scarp slope) than the other (dip slope)
Knoll	small, isolated hill
Pass (gap)	long valley providing a natural routeway through an upland area
Plateau	flat-topped area of high land
Ridge	long, narrow area of higher land
Spur	finger of high land that juts out into an area of lower land
Valley	narrow area of low land that has higher land on both sides; valleys widen as they approach the sea

- give grid references to locate features
- use compass directions, for example 'The area of highest land is in the south-east'
- mention any coastal features such as cliffs.

Look at figure **A** again, and note how similar the contour patterns for ridges and river valleys can seem on a map – you need to look carefully at the contour values to see whether the land is rising or falling. It is important to identify these features correctly in an exam – table **C** will help you to do this.

Describing rivers and river valleys

When you are asked to describe the **drainage** of an area, you should be aware that the question is asking you about both rivers *and* their valleys. You should, therefore, try to comment on all of the following:

- The presence or absence of any surface drainage such as rivers and lakes.
- The names of the main river, any important tributaries and large lakes.
- The density of drainage – estimate the number of rivers and streams and how close they are to each other. Make statements such as: 'There are many rivers and streams in the north and west of the map area, but far fewer in the south.'
- Any major confluence points, giving grid reference locations.
- Any general drainage patterns that the rivers and streams make (diagram **D**).
- The long profile of the main river. Do this by observing how close the contour lines are where the river crosses them – the closer the contours, the steeper the profile will be.
- The features of the main river, by quoting:
  - its width at the widest and narrowest places – give a grid reference for each place
  - its general direction of flow
  - evidence of any river features such as meanders, oxbow lakes and waterfalls – give their grid references
  - any evidence of flooding, for example levees or marshy land, and locate these, e.g. 'The river appears to flood in the north-west area of the map [quote the grid reference]; the evidence for this is the levees along its banks in grid square ... .'
- The shape of the main river valley (e.g. is it V-shaped?) and its width – is there evidence of any interlocking spurs?
- Evidence of a flood plain – where is it and how wide is it?
- Evidence of any human activity, such as:
  - dams/reservoirs
  - flood control measures, e.g. river straightening or embankments.
- Again, locate these activities using grid squares/references.

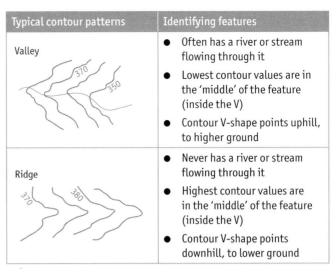

Typical contour patterns	Identifying features
Valley	• Often has a river or stream flowing through it • Lowest contour values are in the 'middle' of the feature (inside the V) • Contour V-shape points uphill, to higher ground
Ridge	• Never has a river or stream flowing through it • Highest contour values are in the 'middle' of the feature (inside the V) • Contour V-shape points downhill, to lower ground

C *Differences between ridges and valleys*

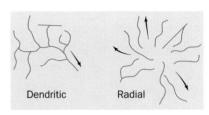

Dendritic   Radial

D *Two types of drainage pattern*

Now Investigate

Look at the map on page 259. Describe the drainage pattern of the river/stream on this map.

The human landscape

Topic link

Look back at Topics 1.7 and 1.8 to remind yourself about your work on settlement.

There are several human landscape features you could be asked about in an examination. Probably the most common of these is settlement. Settlements may be rural or urban – and you may be asked about either of these, so you need to revise this subject thoroughly for both Papers 1 and 2.

A *A village site at the base of a hill slope is easy to build on, and provides shelter*

Topic link

See pages 202–05 for more on the shape of the land and how it is represented on maps.

Describing settlement patterns

To provide a good description of a settlement pattern, follow this system:

- **Stage 1** – write some general statements about where settlements are, for example: 'Most settlements are in the north and north-west.' If there is a large settlement, name it and state how much of the map area it covers.
- **Stage 2** – provide some detailed information, for example: 'Some settlements follow the course of the river *x*' or 'Most villages avoid steep slopes' (photo **A**).
- **Stage 3** – make one or two specific points by naming features, giving grid references and referring to the height of the land, for example: 'Settlements appear to be on land below 150 metres' or 'Many are on south-facing slopes'.

Questions may also ask you about the site, situation and shape of settlements.

Site is the area of land on which a settlement is built. You should provide information about its physical and human features. The letters of the word **SHAWL** may help you here:

- **S**helter – from winds and storms (photo **A**)
- **H**eight – above sea level
- **A**spect – the direction in which sloping land faces
- **W**ater supply – from springs, rivers etc.
- **L**and – is it flat or gently sloping, on or above a river flood plain (photo **B**)?

Situation refers to a settlement's location within the larger area around it. Here, the letters **PARC** can be used:

- **P**laces – for example other settlements, National Parks
- **A**ccessibility – how easy it is for people to get to a settlement
- **R**elief – the height and shape of the land
- **C**ommunications – for example road and rail links.

Shape can take one of three basic forms: nucleated, linear and dispersed. You may be able to provide additional information, for example:

- nucleated settlements are clustered around key points such as road junctions
- linear settlements follow routeways, valleys or coastlines (name these where possible).

Maps show many different kinds of human activity. If the examiner asks you to identify and/or to describe these, you must start by studying the key to discover what the symbols on the map represent – and then include a range of the activities set out in diagram **C**. Try to identify any patterns that the activities make across the map's area – and don't forget to give grid references (and place names) in your answer!

Now Investigate !

1 List the three main stages of writing a good description of a settlement pattern.

2 Refer to these stages and write a brief description of the settlement pattern on the map on page 259.

B ▲ *Although water is important, some villages avoid the river's flood plain*

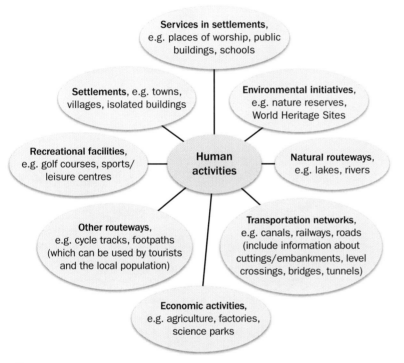

C ◀ *Human activities represented on maps*

Examinations often include questions on the type of topographical map that are found in an atlas. These are used to test your ability to identify and then describe distribution patterns. Most maps of this type are **choropleth maps**, which use different shadings and colours to show the physical or human features of an area (map **A**). They may be global maps, displaying patterns for the whole world, or larger-scale maps of continents or regions within them.

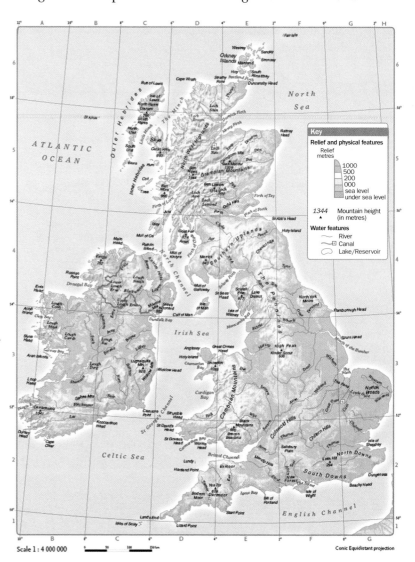

Relief (physical) map of Britain **A** ▶

Describing continental or regional maps

Your main aim when describing maps like map **A** is to keep your answer relevant to the question. Avoid including any extra information about an area or theme which you happen to know, but which is not required by the question. Such information won't gain you any extra marks, and could weaken your whole answer. To help you stay focused, try to write a 'word picture'. Include compass directions and named locations when appropriate.

Describing global maps

Compass directions can also be used when describing locations in continents and regions. Another way of locating places on global maps is to refer to the North and South Hemispheres, and to named lines of latitude and longitude. These are imaginary lines drawn across the globe to aid the location of places (map **B**).

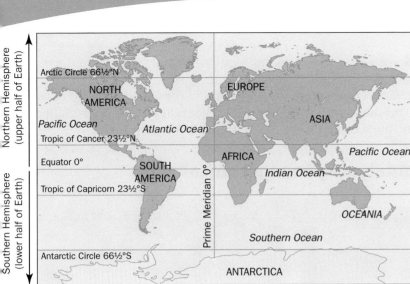

 B *The named lines of latitude and longitude*

Maps **A** and **C** are both types of choropleth map. Other common types of choropleth map are listed in table **D**.

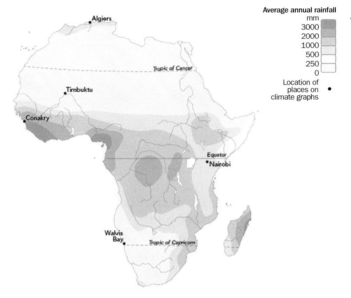

Average annual rainfall
mm
3000
2000
1000
500
250
0

Location of
places on   •
climate graphs

 C *Total annual rainfall*

| Temperature maps |
| Often separate maps for January and July, to show seasonal temperature differences due to the Sun's changing overhead position |
| Climate region maps |
| Show large areas that are tropical, arid, etc. |
| Natural vegetation maps |
| Show areas of desert, forest, etc. |
| Population density maps |
| Highlight areas having particularly high or low population densities; may also include major urban areas |

D *Types of choropleth maps often found in an atlas*

Some other types of choropleth map you may come across include:

- **energy and mineral production maps**, locating economic assets such as coalfields
- **environmental hazard maps**, highlighting areas where water and air pollution levels are especially high
- **natural hazard maps**, locating major tropical revolving storms and other natural hazard events – these may include plate boundaries and names, because the position of plates is a significant factor in the location of earthquakes and volcanic activity
- **political maps**, showing country boundaries and names – these often include capital cities and other major urban settlements.
- **urbanisation maps**, showing the percentage of people living in urban (as opposed to rural) areas
- **wealth distribution maps**, showing each country's average GDP per person per year.

Now Investigate ❗

1 Look through this book and find three choropleth maps. Explain what type of distribution each map shows. Hint: Look carefully at the map title and key.

2 Suggest why the three lines of latitude are included on map **C**.

Some examination questions are based on thematic maps which include additional information in the form of bar graphs and pie charts. Other questions invite you to compare two maps of the same area, which might present different types of information, or show similar information taken at different times.

Analysing topographical maps

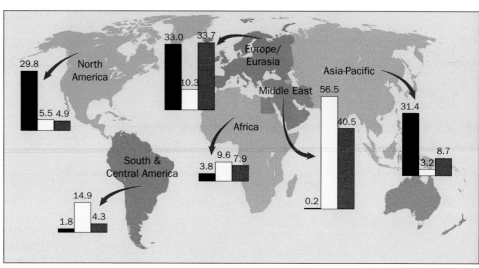

Global fossil fuel reserves in 2010

0 – 100%

■ Coal ☐ Oil ■ Natural gas

Map **A** is a thematic map with the extra information displayed as bar graphs. In response to the question 'Compare the fossil fuel reserves in the six regions' you would be expected to write statements like these, based on the six bar graphs:

- Every region has some reserves of all three types of fossil fuel.
- Reserves are significant in all regions except for coal in the Middle East, which is only 0.2 per cent of the world's total, and coal reserves in South and Central America which are much smaller than those in other regions.
- North America and Europe-Eurasia still have very large reserves of coal, even though much has already been used here since the industrial revolution, which made these the world's first major industrial regions.
- Europe-Eurasia still has one-third of the world's natural gas reserves, which are available for use as coal stocks begin to run out.
- Asia-Pacific's reserves of coal include those in China, which is currently undergoing its own coal-based industrial revolution.
- The Middle East is very rich in oil and natural gas – it is the region with the largest reserves of both of these fossil fuels.

Comparing topographical maps

If you are presented with two maps, their data will be linked in some way. You will be asked to identify the main links between them, and possibly suggest reasons for these links. Maps **B** and **C** both present information about Australia. Diagram **D** shows you how you can write an effective comparison of these

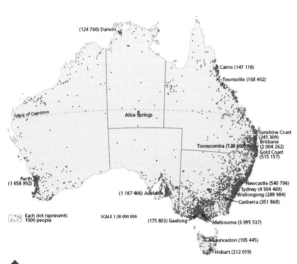

B Total annual rainfall in Australia

C Population distribution and major settlements in Australia

Now Investigate !

Using an atlas, find two maps of the same continent or region, one showing temperature and the other population. Write a comparison of the two maps.

Stage 1 Read the question *very* carefully and underline (or highlight in colour) any important words in it.

Stage 2 'Read' both maps – their titles and their keys.

Stage 3 Write brief statements describing what the 'independent' map shows – this is the one providing information that *might* influence the distribution on the second map. In this case, the independent map is map **B**, showing Australia's annual rainfall pattern. Examples:

- *Australia's general rainfall distribution follows a very basic pattern: the centre has much less rainfall in a typical year than most of its coastal regions.*
- *The north, north-east and the far south receive much more rainfall than any other coastal regions.*

Stage 4 Write a similar, brief description of the second map, using 'comparison' words and phrases where possible. Explanations can be added if asked for. Examples:

- *Most Australians live on or near to the coast, and this is where the major settlements are located.*
- *The interior is very sparsely populated, but more people do live where there are major rivers.*
- *The overall population distribution follows a similar pattern to that for rainfall, because large numbers of people live where rainfall is more plentiful. One likely reason is that there is enough rain for arable farming and for grazing animals.*
- *However, very few people live in the far north (except in Darwin) – a region where there is a larger than average amount of rainfall.*
- *Another significant difference is that people do live in areas of very low rainfall – if there is a major river nearby. This is probably because irrigation water from the rivers can compensate for a lack of rainfall.*

Stage 5 Make a final, summative statement. Example:
Overall, it appears that there is link between total annual rainfall and population distribution in Australia. However, there are several significant exceptions which means that this link is not particularly strong for the continent as a whole.

D How to compare two maps of the same region

Learning objectives:

Learning objectives:

- construct a range of graphs to illustrate numerical data

- present numerical data and locational data on a map

- describe and explain the patterns that such graphs and maps show

- suggest and use appropriate methods of representing numerical data.

One of the easiest and most common ways of presenting data is to draw graphs. There are several different types of graph and it is important for you to know which is the correct one to use.

Simple graphs

Line graphs show data that changes continuously as time passes. Time is always plotted along the horizontal (*x*) axis, and the variable data (such as temperature or number of vehicles) is plotted using the vertical (*y*) axis. Line graphs can also be used to predict how the variable may change in the future. Diagram **A** shows you how to draw a line graph.

Bar graphs are also simple to draw, but are often used wrongly, or not drawn correctly. Many students confuse them with histograms (see below). Bar graphs are only used to show data that fits into categories, for example types of vegetation or road vehicles, but *not* data that changes over time (diagram **B**). Bar graphs are always drawn with a space between each category (bar) on the *x* axis. More complex graphs can be used to display several data sets, and can also be used to compare data year by year.

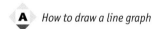

A How to draw a line graph

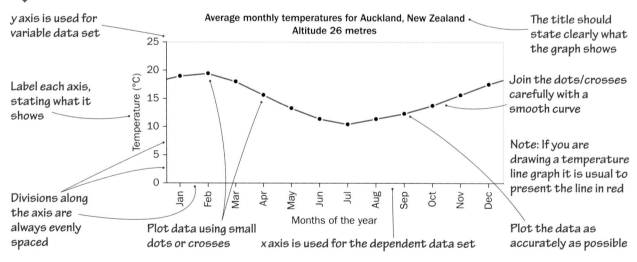

y axis is used for variable data set

Label each axis, stating what it shows

Divisions along the axis are always evenly spaced

Plot data using small dots or crosses

x axis is used for the dependent data set

The title should state clearly what the graph shows

Join the dots/crosses carefully with a smooth curve

Note: If you are drawing a temperature line graph it is usual to present the line in red

Plot the data as accurately as possible

Average monthly temperatures for Auckland, New Zealand
Altitude 26 metres

Histograms look like bar graphs drawn without spaces between the bars – and there is a more important difference too. They are used to show data that is continuous in some way. This may be data that changes as time passes (like monthly rainfall totals for a year) or values that vary across the data set (for example particle size in a soil sample). Remembering this crucial difference between bar graphs and histograms is the key to knowing which type of graph to draw. Diagram **C** shows two types of histogram which you may see in examinations – and which you need to be able to draw and interpret for Papers 3 and 4.

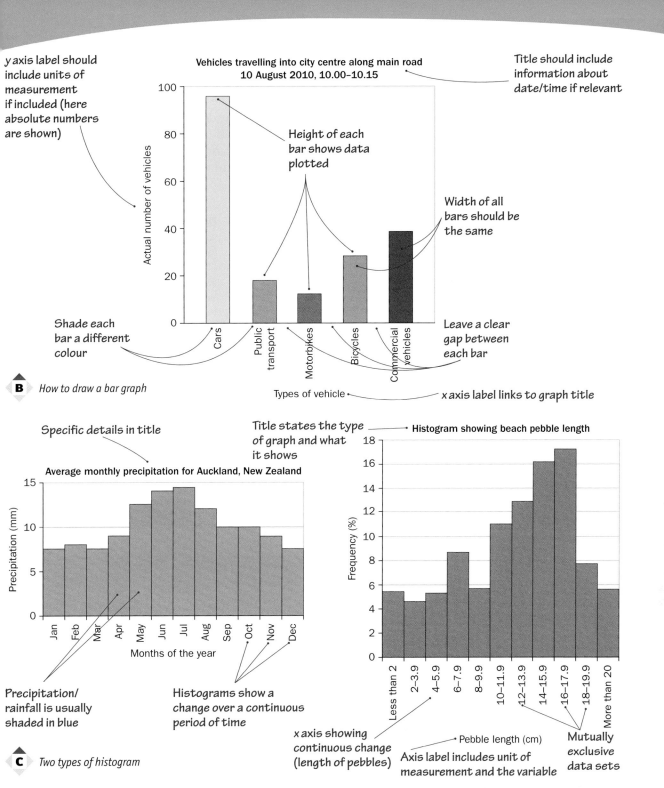

Vehicles travelling into city centre along main road 10 August 2010, 10.00–10.15

Title should include information about date/time if relevant

y axis label should include units of measurement if included (here absolute numbers are shown)

Height of each bar shows data plotted

Width of all bars should be the same

Shade each bar a different colour

Leave a clear gap between each bar

Actual number of vehicles

Cars | Public transport | Motorbikes | Bicycles | Commercial vehicles

Types of vehicle — *x axis label links to graph title*

B *How to draw a bar graph*

Specific details in title

Title states the type of graph and what it shows

Histogram showing beach pebble length

Average monthly precipitation for Auckland, New Zealand

Precipitation (mm)

Jan Feb Mar Apr May Jun Jul Aug Sep Oct Nov Dec

Months of the year

Precipitation/rainfall is usually shaded in blue

Histograms show a change over a continuous period of time

Frequency (%)

Less than 2 | 2–3.9 | 4–5.9 | 6–7.9 | 8–9.9 | 10–11.9 | 12–13.9 | 14–15.9 | 16–17.9 | 18–19.9 | More than 20

x axis showing continuous change (length of pebbles)

Pebble length (cm)

Axis label includes unit of measurement and the variable

Mutually exclusive data sets

C *Two types of histogram*

Now Investigate

Which type of graph would you draw to represent each of the following sets of data?

a   Six types of vegetation recorded in one area

b   Population growth over a number of years

c   Three different exports from a single country between 1990 and 2010

d   Three different exports from six different countries (data is presented as percentages of total of those three exports)

More complex graphs

Scatter graphs are plotted in a similar way to line graphs, but show two sets of changing data instead of one. This type of graph is used if it seems likely that one set of data is likely to be the cause of changes to a second set. For example, in diagram **A**, a country's GDP is thought to be the significant factor affecting the number of people in that country who own a cell phone. The data set that 'causes' the change is called the independent variable while the set that is affected by it is the dependent variable. Diagram **B** shows you how to use a scatter graph to identify and then analyse links between data sets.

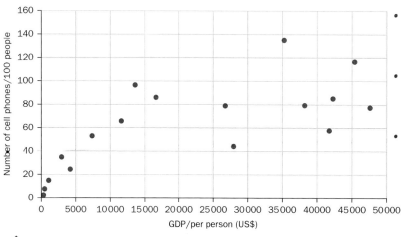

A *How to construct a scatter graph*

- Decide which is your independent variable (in this example, GDP) and which is likely to be the dependent variable (cell phone ownership).
- Plot your axes and decide on a suitable scale for each one. Note that the spaces between values must be the same along each axis.
- Plot the data as you would for a line graph, but do not join the dots:

	GDP/person (US$)	Cell phones per 100 people
USA	47 580	77.4
UK	45 390	116.6
France	42 250	85.1
etc. ↓		

- Identify the mid-point on your graph.
- Place a ruler through this point. (Hint: A clear plastic ruler makes this task easier.)
- Now rotate the ruler around this mid-point until it divides the dots on the graph so that half of them are above it and half below it.
- Draw a pencil line along the ruler's edge: this is your best-fit line.
- There are two key points to remember:
  - the line does not have to pass through the origin of the graph
  - while your aim is to split the dots 50:50, it isn't critical if you can't quite do this.

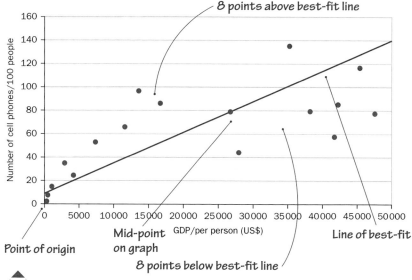

B *How to add a best-fit line to a scatter graph*

Population pyramids show population structure according to age and gender (diagram **C**). They are drawn using two back-to-back, horizontal histograms. Age is plotted on a central *y* axis, and the number of people in each age group is plotted along the *x* axis (number of people is sometimes presented as a percentage of the whole population).

A triangular graph is a way of showing three variables on one diagram. The triangular shape allows three axes to be shown. Diagram **D** explains how to read a triangular graph.

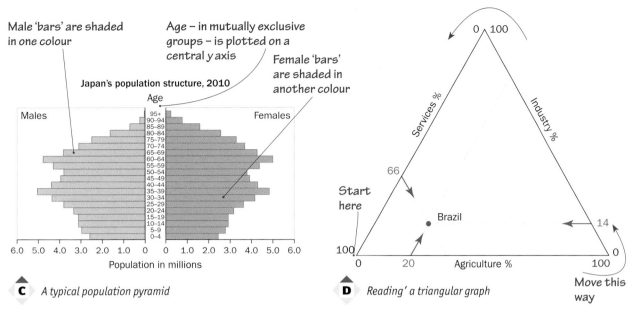

Male 'bars' are shaded in one colour

Age – in mutually exclusive groups – is plotted on a central y axis

Female 'bars' are shaded in another colour

Japan's population structure, 2010

Age

Males

Females

Population in millions

C A typical population pyramid

0 100

Services %

Industry %

66

Start here

Brazil

14

100

0

0 20 Agriculture % 100

Move this way

D 'Reading' a triangular graph

Pie graphs are sometimes called pie charts or circle graphs (diagram **E**). They are divided into sectors to illustrate proportions. When describing these graphs, you should comment on the size of each sector in relation to the whole graph, and compare the size of each sector with other sectors.

Wind rose graphs are often simply called rose diagrams. These are the most frequently used type of radial graph. They show the orientation of the data being recorded and are most often used to plot wind direction – hence their name (diagram **F**). The graph is made up of eight separate bar graphs, drawn outwards from a central octagon (to show the main compass directions); the length of each bar represents the number of days the wind blows from each direction.

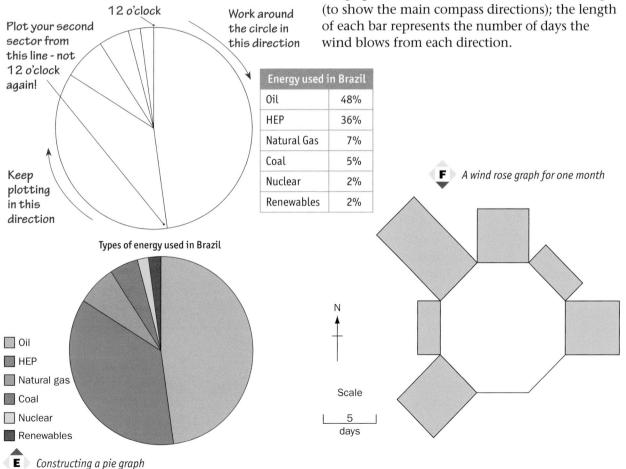

12 o'clock

Plot your second sector from this line - not 12 o'clock again!

Work around the circle in this direction

Keep plotting in this direction

Energy used in Brazil	
Oil	48%
HEP	36%
Natural Gas	7%
Coal	5%
Nuclear	2%
Renewables	2%

F A wind rose graph for one month

Types of energy used in Brazil

- Oil
- HEP
- Natural gas
- Coal
- Nuclear
- Renewables

E Constructing a pie graph

N

Scale

5
days

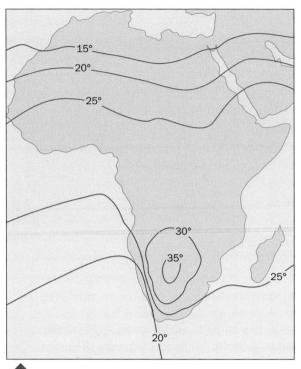

A *Isotherm map: average January temperatures across Africa (degrees Celsius)*

Not all the data we collect is presented as graphs. Some information is better shown as a map, because we need to include details of the area it covers.

Isolines are lines on maps that join points of equal value. You already know about contour lines, which are a type of isoline showing information about the altitude (height) of the land. Other examples of isolines are isotherms, which show temperature (map **A**), isohyets (rainfall, map **B**), isobars (atmospheric pressure), isotachs (wind speed) and isogons (wind direction).

A **choropleth** map is a type of thematic map. It provides information about a place, such as population distribution or energy consumption (see the map on page 176). The map is coloured or shaded to show changing distribution patterns within an area. Such maps can be drawn by plotting isolines, then shading the spaces between them (map **C**).

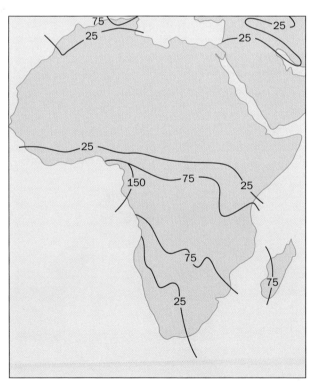

*Rainfall figures in centimetres

B *Isohyet (rainfall) map for Africa, November–April*

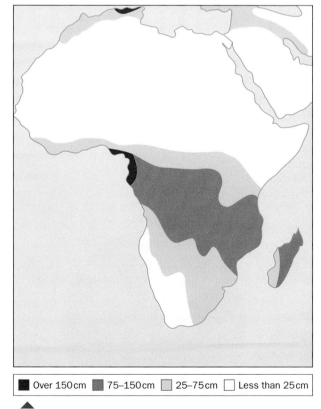

■ Over 150 cm ▩ 75–150 cm ▨ 25–75 cm ☐ Less than 25 cm

C *Choropleth map of rainfall across Africa, November–April*

Flow diagrams are usually used to show movement – of people, goods or even ideas – and so need to include a base map of the area where the movements are taking place. The simplest form of flow diagram is called a desire line map. Such maps or diagrams are a very effective way of showing the directions of movements (diagram **D**). This type of map is sometimes called a rose or ray diagram.

Desire line maps become flow line maps when they are drawn to show information about the commodity being moved, such as the volume of traffic or goods in each direction. This is done by varying the width of each line to show the volume of flow along it (diagram **E**).

Pedestrian traffic in Summertown, 10.00–10.15 on 11 November 2011

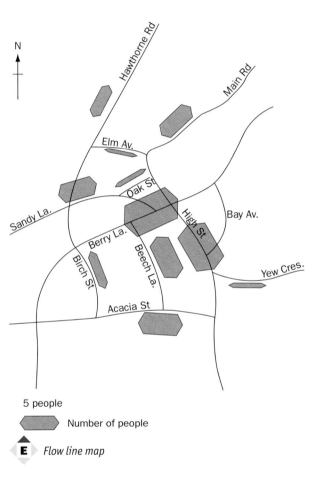

5 people

Number of people

E Flow line map

Direction and distance travelled to Main High School by pupils in Class 9

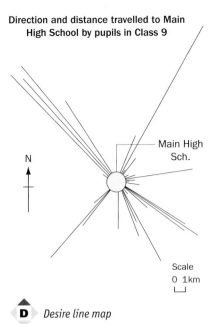

Main High Sch.

N

Scale
0 1km

D Desire line map

Now Investigate

Suggest an appropriate graphic presentation for each of the following sets of data:

a number of students moving along corridors in a school over a specified period of time

b pressure readings taken at many points over the continent of Europe

c frequency of wind experienced in one place from various directions over a 24-hour period.

Mapping land use

When geographers talk about *land use*, what we really mean is 'the human uses of land', for example fields, factories and housing. However, we manage and modify the natural environment too, even in wilderness areas, so these areas can also be mapped on land use maps. Such maps can be used to identify almost every natural resource, settlement type and economic activity on Earth.

Today, commercially produced land use maps are based on satellite imagery and aerial photography (photo **A** and map **B**). However, even with modern technology, map-makers often have to visit an area to check details and record the data, in just the same way that you can record land use in your work for your Papers 3 and 4.

A Satellite image of New York City

B Land use map of New York City

As you can see in map **B**, finished land use maps are usually presented as colour patches with a key. However, data collection is often done simply by writing onto a base map what each field, building or plot of land is used for, or using a coding system like those shown in tables **C**. Both of these methods are designed for urban or suburban surveying, but a similar coding system can easily be devised for farm surveys or other rural land uses.

Urban land use can be recorded across an entire built-up area. However, unless you are surveying a relatively small village, it is more likely that you will investigate land use in an urban zone (such as the CBD) or along a transect through a settlement. A transect is simply a route along which we walk, recording and counting

S	Shop
O	Office
E	Entertainment
D	Residence/dwelling
H	Hotel/guest house/motel
P	Public building
OS	Open space
R	Resort function
DEM	Building has been demolished
DER	Building is out-of-use and decaying

S1	Hypermarket/supermarket
S2	Grocery store
S3	Butcher
S4	Fishmonger
S5	Greengrocer
etc.	
O1	Solicitor
O2	Estate agent/realtor
O3	Accountant
O4	Surveyor
etc.	

C A simple land use coding system

A detailed land use coding system

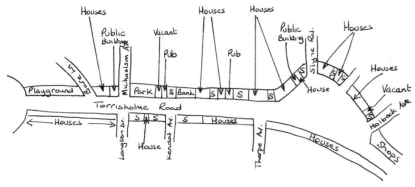

Key: S – Shops

D Fieldwork recording sheet showing land use along Torrisholme Road, Morecambe

occurrences of the topic of study, for example plants or building use. In towns and cities this is usually along a street or a road. Figure **D** shows a typical student's data recording sheet for a land use survey along a main road. Figure **E** shows the same information translated into a land use map.

Rural land use can also be recorded on a base map showing buildings and fields – especially if you are undertaking a farm study. However, if the relief of the land varies, a different type of transect based on a relief cross-section may be more useful. This will allow you to link land use to relief, geology and soil (diagram **F**). A transect such as this might also be useful in a built-up area if you wish to investigate how use is affected by relief – perhaps to see if land on a flood plain is different from that on higher land on either side.

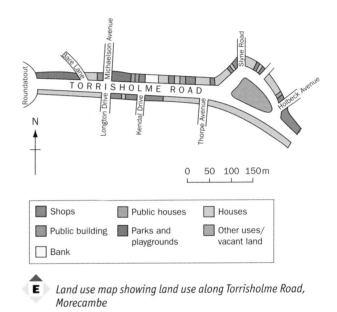

Shops	Public houses	Houses
Public building	Parks and playgrounds	Other uses/ vacant land
Bank		

E Land use map showing land use along Torrisholme Road, Morecambe

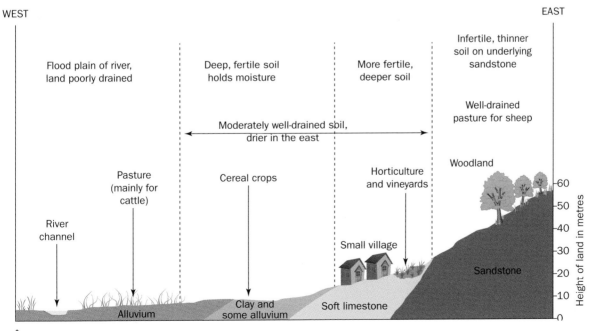

F Relief profile linking land use change to physical features

Interpreting graphs

Some questions in your examinations not only ask you to plot graphs and map data, they also require you to interpret (explain) such information.

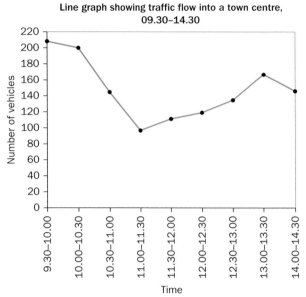

Line graph showing traffic flow into a town centre, 09.30–14.30

A *A line graph*

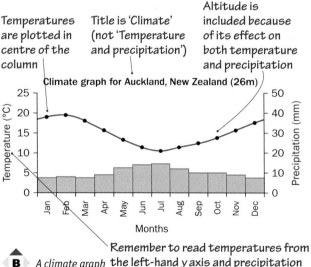

Temperatures are plotted in centre of the column

Title is 'Climate' (not 'Temperature and precipitation')

Altitude is included because of its effect on both temperature and precipitation

Climate graph for Auckland, New Zealand (26m)

B *A climate graph*

Remember to read temperatures from the left-hand y axis and precipitation from the right-hand axis

Line graphs, bar graphs and histograms

● Identify what is plotted along each axis, and the units of measurement used.
● Describe any trends (changes) in the data – do they show increase or decrease?
● Is any change steady or fluctuating (variable)? Is it rapid or gradual?
● Note any variations from the overall trend/s.
● Quote data from the graph to support every observation.
● If asked to, justify each observation, using your geographical knowledge and understanding.

Compound line graphs

When examiners include compound graphs, they expect answers that highlight any links between different sets of data.

Start by following the guidelines above for each data set. Then:
● State the relative importance of each component (variable).
● Identify any patterns or links between the different components.
● Justify any statements you make by quoting data from the graph.
● If asked to, use your geographical knowledge to suggest reasons for the patterns, trends and links that you have identified.

Climate graphs

● Describe the temperature pattern.
● Describe the rainfall/precipitation regime.
● Comment on humidity levels (dry/arid/damp/humid).
● Refer to the weather station's altitude (if provided). If appropriate to the question, comment on how altitude has influenced rainfall and temperature patterns.
● If the question asks you to give reasons for the climate data, do so using your geographical knowledge of climatic factors, for example latitude, movement of the overhead Sun, prevailing wind, continentality, relief.

Pie graphs

- Note and then use the correct units of measurement – not all pie graphs show percentages!
- Describe the relative size of each sector and identify the largest and smallest ones. Instead of writing brief statements such as 'Oil is the largest sector', provide detailed ones, for example 'Oil was the largest supplier of energy in Brazil in 2006'.
- If there are a number of pie graphs, compare and contrast the data within them. Always quote which graph you are referring to, and provide data from it to support your observations.

Population pyramids

- Identify the units used – they may be percentages or actual numbers of people.
- Comment on the width of the pyramid's base, then its height.
- Describe the overall shape of the pyramid.
- Identify and comment on the dependent and independent populations. What is the dependency ratio?
- Link every point you make to the country's population structure/policies/issues and quality of life.
- Are there any anomalies, for example bars that are much longer or shorter than the overall trend? Do these suggest the effects of migration/war/famine/'baby booms'?
- Note the likely level of development of the country (LEDC/MEDC), giving reasons for your decision.

Now Investigate

1   Look through this book and find examples of each of the graph types described above.

2   Choose one of the graphs you located in (1), and write a clear interpretation of that graph.

Learning objectives:

→ know how to describe a photograph or other image

→ create labelled/annotated sketches from photographs, maps or the landscape

→ explain and give reasons for information seen on a map or photograph.

Your examination papers are likely to include a photograph or some other type of illustration. For Paper 3 (fieldwork) you will be expected to use photographs and/or sketches as a record of the landscape you visited.

Photographs

The photographs you take and use may have been taken at ground level, but in Papers 1, 2 and 4 they are more likely to be aerial photographs or satellite images (photo **A**).

All photographs include information that does not appear on maps, for example land use in rural areas (see photo **A**) and traffic in urban zones. Examination questions may invite you to use a variety of skills, for example:

- simple descriptive writing about features in a picture
- more in-depth writing asking you to give reasons based on evidence in a photograph
- photograph interpretation – describing and explaining what you can see
- completion of a labelled or annotated sketch based on a photograph (see pages 224–25).

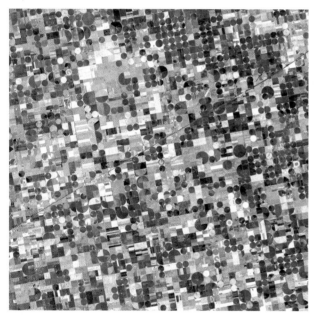

A   *Satellite image of land use in rural Kansas, USA*

Photo **B** shows part of the centre of Shanghai. Possible questions on this image might include:

- 'Describe what photo **B** shows you.'

  Your answer might include observations such as:
  - There are tall/high-rise buildings made of steel and glass.
  - These look like office buildings.
  - They are built very close together.
  - The roads are [insert info based on photo].

- 'Give evidence which suggests that this zone is part of the CBD.'

  Here, answers need to be more specific, for example:
  - The high-rise buildings are obviously very modern and this suggests that they are office blocks. They are typical of a CBD.
  - There is a dense network of straight, narrow streets [insert info based on photo].

B   *Aerial view of central Shanghai, China*

- 'What evidence is there in photo **B** that this city is in an LEDC?'
- This question tests your knowledge of urban land use models and your ability to use photographs. Your answer should focus on street patterns and building densities, because in LEDCs, city centre streets usually form a grid-iron pattern.

Interpreting an aerial photograph

'Interpretation' includes both description *and* explanation. You need to write clearly and use key terms to support your answer. Include information about both the physical and the human environments. You will find the following guidelines helpful.

Physical features

- Describe the relief and gradient of the land.
- Note the presence (or absence) of streams/rivers. Comment on their width and course. Do they meander or flood? Can you see a flood plain?
- Describe the coastline (if appropriate). Is it a lowland coast or are there cliffs? Is there a river mouth? What shape is the coastline? Are there headlands and bays? Is it a coastline of erosion or deposition? What evidence do you have?
- In rural areas, comment on the likely soil depth/fertility, supporting your observations with evidence such as vegetation cover and/or agricultural activity.
- Consider settlement sites/sizes/distribution patterns.

Human features

- In urban areas, comment on:
  - street patterns and building densities
  - building materials, height and possible age
  - possible building functions
  - any open space, and what it is used for
  - the urban zone shown (how can you tell?)
  - whether this place is in an MEDC or an LEDC (what evidence suggests this?)
- In rural areas, comment on:
  - field size and shape
  - types of field boundary and land use (is it arable or pastoral land, are there different crops? Tip: field colours may indicate different crops)
  - access for farm machinery (can it operate easily, how can you tell?)
  - evidence of manual labour/irrigation/ greenhouses.

Topic link

- See Topics 1.7 and 1.8 for more information on features of settlement.
- Look back at Topic 1.9 for information on urban land use models.

Now Investigate

1. a Describe the landscape in photo **C**.
   b Give two pieces of evidence in photo **C** which suggest that this area is an important tourist destination.
2. Write a brief interpretation of photo **A**, suggesting reasons why this area is important for agriculture.

Other illustrations

Sketching from maps

Sketching is a very useful geographical technique which you need to learn! This can involve drawing a sketch from a map or a photograph, or even sketching a landscape as part of fieldwork. Many students fear that their artistic skills are inadequate – but geographical sketches are not detailed, accurate representations of a landscape. They are summaries of important features, so drawing them is a skill that can easily be learned.

By following the guidelines below, you can learn how to draw sketches from 1:25 000 and 1:50 000 scale maps. The same guidelines can easily be adapted to help you sketch other types of map, for example those in an atlas. See map **E** on page 43 which is a sketch map showing the situation of Paris.

- Using a pencil and ruler, draw a frame for your sketch.
- Lightly add the grid lines, numbering them along the bottom and side edges.
- Draw in the main features required by the question (or your fieldwork task). Sketch lightly at first, adding the detail to each grid square in turn to help you locate features accurately. Firm up your outline sketching when you are happy with what you have drawn. Add colour as necessary, using pencil crayons.

- Try to avoid adding too much detail. Only include information that is relevant to the question. For example, on a sketch map showing the shape and land use zones of a town, it would be relevant to include some information about the surrounding area's relief and drainage, because these will have influenced the growth and shape of the settlement.
- Add a title, a north point, a scale line, a key, and labels or annotations as appropriate.

Sketching a landscape

Sketching from a photograph or outdoors during a field trip can seem difficult – but again, follow the tips below and you will soon master this important skill.

- Begin with a pencil-drawn frame.
- Divide this into quarters, drawing the lines very lightly as you will erase them later. If you can, add similar lines to the photograph, or make an overlay. The lines act as guides when positioning features on the sketch.
- Draw the major linear features first, for example the coastline, rivers and major contour lines. Add any transport networks.

Original site of settlement (now CBD) on higher land to reduce the risk of flooding

Hard engineering to reduce flood risk

Farmland on fertile, alluvial soils

Bridges provide access to town – but were easily defended in the past

More modern development outside river loop

River provided a natural routeway to other settlements

Open park land (and recreation uses) occupies land most liable to flood

River provided a reliable source of water (and fish) for the original settlement

 Annotated sketch to show the site of Shrewsbury, in the west of England

 B *Aerial view showing the site of Shrewsbury*

- Add the outline shapes of 'block' features such as settlements, woodland and open spaces. Then complete your drawing by marking on any key features, such as farms or civic buildings.
- Erase your guidelines and add colour if appropriate, using pencil crayons.
- Give your completed sketch a title, a north point (if known) and a key. Label or annotate your sketch as appropriate.

Photo **B** is an oblique aerial photograph of Shrewsbury. Diagram **A** is an annotated sketch of its main features.

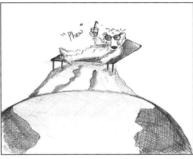

 C

Using cartoons

One distinctive type of illustration that is occasionally used in examinations is the cartoon. These are usually simple drawings which highlight a set of important ideas in a humorous way. Cartoon **C**, for example, shows some possible effects of global climate change.

If you have to answer a question based on a cartoon, study it carefully to identify its key message. Then:

- Write one or two brief statements suggesting the key point(s) the cartoon is making.
- Support your statements by explaining how the artist gets the ideas across.
- State how these ideas are relevant to the key message.

Now Investigate

1 Study the topographical map on page 259. Draw a labelled sketch map to show the main settlement features within the area defined by grid lines ww, xx, yy and zz.

2 Draw an annotated sketch to show the main landscape features visible from your school's recreation area (or a local viewpoint).

3 Which possible effects of climate change are illustrated by Cartoon **C**?

- design and plan fieldwork investigations for both physical and human geography studies

- carry out a wide range of techniques, including questionnaires, surveys and ground measurements

- understand why sampling is important and when to use different types of sampling

- know the limitations of the fieldwork investigations you are carrying out.

Questionnaires and interviews

When carrying out investigations for human geography we often want to ask members of the public for their views and opinions. This can be the best way to gather information on people's habits and the reasons why, for instance, they visit certain areas or use certain facilities. Examples of investigations where questionnaires and interviews are used include:

- studies on shopping habits at a local shopping centre
- investigations into the impacts of tourism in the local area
- when looking at how people feel about levels of immigration where they live
- studies on the use of different types of transport.

Planning is very important when carrying out this type of investigation. You need to make sure the questions relate to the topic you are looking into and that they are easily understood by the people answering your questions.

Questionnaires

Questionnaires are usually best asked face to face so that you can be sure you will get some replies. They can also be sent out by post or completed online – but then you run the risk that nobody will answer. The most important thing when asking face-to-face questionnaires is to be safe – always carry out such surveys with a friend (photo **A**). There are other things to take care of to ensure you get good results:

- Always be polite, introduce yourself and say why you want to ask questions.
- Keep the questions simple and easy to answer.
- Keep the questionnaire short with no more than 10 questions so that it can be completed quickly – most people will not want to spend a lot of time talking to you.
- Keep a note of when and where you carried out the questionnaire.
- Ask for some personal information, for example age-range, where the person being questioned lives – but keep it general.
- Say thank you when you've finished.

An example questionnaire for an investigation into National Parks is shown in diagram **B**.

Creating a decent questionnaire takes time and some practice. It is a good idea to try them out at school or with your friends before asking the public, to make sure the questions make sense. This is called a pilot study. It can also be tried out on a smaller number of people who are the same type as those you eventually want to survey.

A *Carrying out a questionnaire*

National Parks questionnaire

Name:	Location:
Date:	Time:

1 How often do you visit the National Park?

First time   Once a month   Once a year   Less than once a year

2 What are the main reasons for your visit?

Sightseeing   Walking   Wildlife   Bird watching
Watersports   Cycling   Fishing

Other (please write below):

_____

_____

.....

6 In what ways could your visit be improved?

Information boards   More facilities   Guided tours   Better public transport

Other (please feel free to give any more information):

_____

_____

7 Gender: Male   Female

8 What is your age range?

Under 16   16–25   26–40   41–65   Over 65

9 What town do you live in?

_____

......

Thank you for taking the time to answer my questions.

Interviews

Sometimes you may want a little more information than the basic details you can get from a questionnaire. Interviews are a way to ask more in-depth questions. For instance, once you have carried out the survey of visitor views using the questionnaire in **B**, you may want to find out what the National Park manager thinks of any suggestions or comments that have been given.

Although you should prepare some questions in advance, interviews can be more open, with fewer answers being picked from a list. You may change some of the questions or ask new ones depending on how the person you are interviewing responds.

Interviews can be carried out over the phone or in person, or even via email or through an internet conversation. However they are done, it is important to keep a record of what is said. You may want to use some kind of recording device, but always make sure you tell whoever is being interviewed that you plan to do this.

Now Investigate

1 What are the main differences between a questionnaire and an interview?

2 Design a questionnaire that could be used to find out about shopping habits in your local area. You should aim to ask between five and ten questions.

3 What ways could you use to display the information you get from asking your questionnaire?

4 Based on your questionnaire, think of five interview questions you could ask about shopping habits when talking to the managers or owners of local shops.

Sampling

Often, when carrying out fieldwork, we want to study groups with similar characteristics (for instance, couples with children living in a nearby town). However, these groups, called populations, can be very large and we don't usually have the time available to study every single member. Instead of trying to find out about them all we can save time by using sampling to look at a small percentage of the total population. Sampling is seen as being a fair and unbiased way of determining the characteristics of the whole group. There are three main types: random, systematic and stratified.

A *Random sampling*

Random sampling

In this type of sampling each member of a population has an equal chance of being chosen. You will need a list of random numbers, to work out which members are going to be sampled. There are applications on the internet that will generate random numbers but many calculators also have a random number key.

Using either of these methods you could end up with a list such as this:

6, 1, 5, 7, 9, 2, 5, 5, 6, 8, 3, 3, 3, 8, 2

This list can then be used to identify which members of a population you will be sampling. If, for instance, you are interviewing visitors to a National Park, you could stand at the gate and direct questions to the sixth person to walk past, followed by the first, followed by the fifth, and so on (photo **A**).

Systematic sampling

Systematic sampling is easier to work out than random sampling because it uses regular numbers. For instance, when interviewing members of the public, you could decide to talk to every fifth person you meet. This technique is also easy to use in physical geography fieldwork. For example, when looking at aspects of weather in a certain area, you could take measurements of wind speed and wind direction every three days.

The main disadvantage of systematic sampling is that you may miss out certain important groups because not everyone or everything has an equal chance of being chosen.

Stratified sampling

Sometimes we only want to sample certain groups within a population. If we were trying to find out the characteristics of different groups of workers in a town, for instance, we would need to concentrate our questionnaires on those groups. We could choose to look at twenty members of three different groups, for example the unemployed, factory workers and professionals. Breaking the population down into groups like this is known as stratifying.

Within our stratified sample we can then use random or systematic sampling methods to work out the particular people we are going to study.

> ### Now Investigate
>
> 1 Briefly describe how to carry out the three different types of sampling: random, systematic and stratified.
>
> 2 Give examples of fieldwork studies where you would use each of the three types of sampling.

Environmental quality surveys

The environment includes everything from natural features (mountains, lakes, rivers) to the factories and houses that people build. The environment can easily be spoilt or destroyed by our actions. We can use environmental quality surveys to try and identify problems or damage in the environment, and then set about trying to make it better.

Environmental quality survey sheets often look like the one in diagram **A**. Ticks are marked in the correct boxes depending on how the surveyor feels about the area they are looking at. Each box is worth a number of points. The higher the total number of points, the better the environment. This lets us compare different areas quickly and easily.

In some cases, not all the categories will be relevant. For example, there may be no housing in a pristine wilderness area. That category should then be left blank. You can still make comparisons between areas by calculating the average number of points for each survey, dividing the total number by the number of categories filled in.

B

Environmental Quality Survey Sheet						
Place:			Date:			Time:
High quality	5	4	3	2	1	Low quality
High-quality housing						Poor-quality housing
Peaceful						Noisy
Little traffic						Large amount of traffic
No litter						Lots of litter
No vandalism or graffiti						Large amounts of vandalism and/or graffiti
Clean						Dirty
Attractive surroundings						Ugly surroundings
Clean air (or water)						Air (or water) pollution
Safe						Unsafe
Interesting						Boring
	Total:					

 A An environmental quality survey sheet

Measuring the quality of the environment is a difficult fieldwork exercise. This is because it depends on what we feel about a certain place. The results of an environmental quality survey can be completely different from one surveyor to another. It is important that we try to be as unbiased as possible when we carry out this type of survey.

C

Now Investigate

1 Study the photos **B** and **C**. Complete an environmental quality survey sheet for each picture. Compare your results with somebody else in your class.

2 Complete an environmental quality survey sheet for at least five different sites around your school. Try to think of ways in which the information you have gathered could be used to improve your school environment.

Getting out and studying rivers is great fun but it can also be quite dangerous. Much of the fieldwork means getting wet, and you must find a safe place to carry it out – somewhere reasonably shallow and easy to access with no rapids or fast-flowing water.

River investigations often involve taking measurements at a number of different sampling points and then comparing the characteristics of the river at each point.

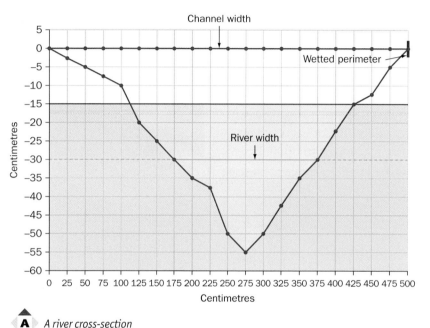

A *A river cross-section*

Width, depth and cross-sections

Width and depth are measured in centimetres. Measurements are taken with a tape measure and a metre ruler:

- The channel width is measured from the top of one bank to the top of the other. The tape measure needs to be stretched right across the channel at right-angles to the bank.
- The depth of the river needs to be measured at a number of points across the channel all the way from bank to bank – these should be around 20 to 25 cm apart.

> ### Topic link 🔗
>
> Remember: you can refer back to Topic 2.3 pages 80–87 if there are any river terms you do not understand.

- Finally, a note needs to be made of the height of the bank above the top of the river and of the width of the river within its channel.

The measurements taken can then be used to draw a cross-section. This is best done on graph paper (diagram **A**) but it can also be completed using a computer spreadsheet program.

First decide on the scale you are going to use and then draw in the channel width. Add the measurements for river height and depth. Join up the dots for river depth to form the cross-section. You should now be able to calculate the channel or river cross-sectional area (the depth × the width) by counting up the grid squares that are covered by the channel or river on the graph paper. You can also calculate the wetted perimeter by measuring the contact that the river has with the bank and bed. Rivers with a large wetted perimeter have greater friction.

Measuring velocity

The velocity (or speed) of a river is measured most easily using a flow meter (photo **B**). This is a device with a propeller which turns in the water and gives a reading for the speed in metres per second.

B *A flow meter*

Flow meters are expensive and there are other ways of measuring velocity that are more fun! All you need is an object (or some dye) that floats – for example an orange or a cork – and a tape measure and a stopwatch. Measure a distance of 10 metres along the river bank, throw the object in at one end and time how long it takes to travel 10 metres. Repeat the exercise at least five times to get an average time (photo **C**). This avoids errors if, for instance, the object gets stuck as it travels down the river.

The velocity can then be worked out in metres per second using the equation:

velocity = distance divided by time

If possible, measure velocity at various points across the river so that you can compare velocity with river depth using your cross-sections.

C *Measuring the velocity of a river*

Measuring a river's load

It is often useful to measure how big the load of a river is. This can be done in order to look at changes from the source to the mouth, or across different river features such as meanders. Wherever your sample point is you should take several measurements across the river's width.

1 At each point, reach into the river, pointing your index finger directly downwards.
2 Pick up the first pebble or particle that your finger touches.
3 If possible, measure the length of the pebble and note it down (photo **D**).
4 Repeat the process at several points across the river.

D *Measuring the size of a river's load*

If the river bed consists only of fine sediment, this can be collected in plastic bottles and left to settle. A visual comparison will then be needed to determine which is the smallest particle size.

Load carried in suspension can also be analysed using a similar collection in plastic bottles.

Changes in gradient

If you are studying a river's long profile you may also want to measure changes in gradient as it flows downhill. This can be done using a similar technique to measuring beach profiles – see page 232.

Coastal measurements

Topic link 🔗

Remember to refer back to Topic 2.4 pages 88–95 if there are any coastal terms you do not understand.

As with rivers, taking measurements along coasts is potentially dangerous. It is important (and more fun) to attempt such fieldwork in pairs or groups, and to take care when working on steep cliffs or near violent seas.

Destructive and constructive waves

There are many clues on a beach to help you identify whether it is affected more by destructive or constructive waves:

- Destructive waves have a stronger backwash than swash so they remove material, leaving a steep and narrow beach.
- Constructive waves have a stronger swash than backwash, depositing material on a more gently shelving beach.

Measuring wave frequency will help you identify wave type. Use a stopwatch and count the number of waves breaking on the beach in a five-minute interval. Then work out the number of waves per minute. While counting, remember also to make a note of the general wave height.

Destructive waves are more frequent and break between 10 and 15 times per minute. They are also taller than the less frequent constructive waves which break between 6 and 9 times each minute.

Taking a beach profile

For a complete profile you will need a number of different sampling points along the width of your chosen beach. These sampling points can be determined using one of the techniques outlined on pages 88–95. At each sampling point set up ranging poles (or standard 1 metre poles) from the top of the beach to the low water mark. Then take measurements using the following steps:

A *Using a clinometer for beach profiles*

1 Walk between the two poles and make a general note of the main changes in the profile (the less and more steep spots).

2 For the points where the slope changes, take gradient measurements using ranging poles and a clinometer (photo **A**). If a clinometer is not available, a protractor can be used to get a general idea of slope angles.

3 Measure the distance along the ground between each set of measurements you take.

4 Use the information you collect on angles and distances to construct a cross-section profile (using graph paper), as shown in diagram **B**.

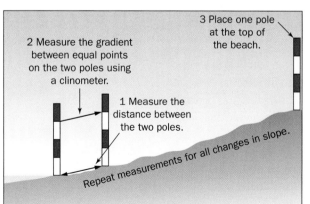

2 Measure the gradient between equal points on the two poles using a clinometer.

3 Place one pole at the top of the beach.

1 Measure the distance between the two poles.

Repeat measurements for all changes in slope.

B *Constructing a beach profile*

You can use the beach profiles to compare different transects along a single beach or to compare different beaches.

Beach material analysis

To gain a more complete picture of the differences between beach profile transects, measurements of beach material can be made.

You will need to decide which type of sampling system you are going to use and then select a number of points along each transect. At each point a quadrat can be used (with random number tables) to choose which pebbles or particles to measure. Alternatively, simply choose the ten pebbles that are touching your foot. Pebble or sediment size can then be measured using the methods outlined on page 231.

When analysing the distribution of beach material, you need to take account of recent or longer-term events. For instance, has the beach recently been affected by a storm? Or is it so well used that erosion through human activities is taking place on a daily basis?

Measuring longshore drift

Analysing the swash, backwash and how material is transported along a beach can give us an excellent idea of how longshore drift is operating in a certain area. Measuring this is quite simple:

1 Plot a distance of 10 metres along a section of beach and mark the start and end points.
2 Place a float (such as a cork or an orange) in the water at the point where the waves are breaking.
3 Watch the float and time how long it takes to travel the 10 metres along the beach.

As an alternative, you could measure how far the float travels in a specified period of time, for example five minutes.

Taking measurements at different sample points along a beach will show where longshore drift is at its most and least active.

Other indications of longshore drift

Material carried by longshore drift will pile up against natural rock outcrops and built features such as the artificial groynes that are used to stop beach erosion. Take pictures of the sediment piled up against these features (photo **C**) and make a note of the direction in which the sediment lies – this will tell you which way longshore drift is operating along a beach.

Measuring human impact

One final study we can complete along the coast is to look at the effects of erosion as a consequence of people walking on footpaths. Measuring infiltration rates shows how quickly water soaks into the soil and is a good indication of how people's footsteps are compacting the soil.

The basic technique is to put a bottomless cylinder into the ground, pour a measured amount of water into the cylinder and time how long it takes to soak into the soil (diagram **D**). Measurements from a number of different sampling points can then be compared.

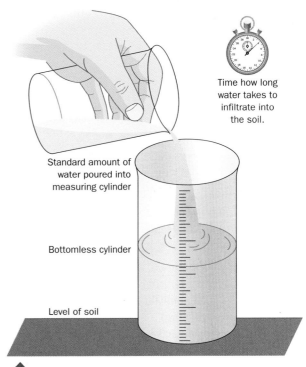

Time how long water takes to infiltrate into the soil.

Standard amount of water poured into measuring cylinder

Bottomless cylinder

Level of soil

C ▸ *Beach material accumulating against groynes*

D ▸ *How to measure infiltration rates*

What is Paper 1?

Paper 1 is your first theory examination. In this examination there are **six** questions on the paper from which you must choose **three** to answer. Two questions are set on each of the three themes:

- **Population and settlement** (population change, population structure, population distribution, urban and rural settlement, urban land use, impact of urbanisation)
- **The natural environment** (earthquakes and volcanoes, weathering, river and marine processes and landforms, coral reefs, weather, climate and ecosystems of the tropical rainforest and tropical desert)
- **Economic development and the use of resources** (agriculture, industry, tourism, energy and water resources, conservation and management of resources).

The aims of Paper 1 are:

- to encourage you to learn about geographical events happening in different areas of the world
- to give you an understanding of geographical processes
- to give you the opportunity to explore how people and the natural environment affect each other.

What is Paper 1 testing?

The examination tests three objectives:

1. your understanding of geographical concepts (ideas)
2. your knowledge of case study examples
3. your analysis of information and data.

You will not be told which objective each question is testing but you will recognise the objectives by the wording of the question.

How to use your time effectively

The Paper 1 examination is 1 hour 45 minutes long. In this time you must answer three questions; each question is worth 25 marks and is broken down into several parts. This means that there are 75 marks to get in 105 minutes, so you have 1½ minutes per mark. You may allow yourself about 35 minutes for each question, but remember: you also need to allow time to:

- read all the questions carefully
- choose which three questions you want to answer and in which order
- check your answers at the end of the examination to correct any simple mistakes you may have made.

Tip

- If you are to be successful in Paper 1, it is important to choose the correct questions to answer.
- You do not have to answer the questions in the order in which they appear on the question paper. Answer your best topic first and your weakest topic last.

To have the time to do all this it may be better to allow yourself 30 minutes to answer each question and use the extra 15 minutes on the other tasks. Look carefully at the number of marks available for each part of a question (shown in brackets at the end of each question). This is a good guide to how much time to spend on each part. Do not spend too much time on one part if it is only worth 1 or 2 marks, or write only a short answer if a question is worth 4 or 5 marks. The number of lines provided for your answer is another guide as to how much detail you need to include.

Choosing the correct questions to answer

Paper 1 is your only geography examination that gives you the opportunity to choose which questions you want to answer. You may choose any three questions, so read them all carefully before you make your choice. To help you to do this think about the following:

- Read all the separate parts of each question, especially the case study, which is worth most marks.
- Make sure you have studied the question topic! Some questions might look easier than others but you may not have enough knowledge about the topic.
- Think about which topics you have revised most thoroughly.
- Do not choose a question just because it has an interesting photograph, map or diagram.
- If you think you have chosen the wrong question you can change your mind once you have begun your answer. It is better to do this than carry on answering a question badly.

> **Tip**
>
> - Do not try to answer more than three questions. You will not have time to answer them properly.
>
> - If you change your mind and stop answering a question part way through, make sure you cross out what you have written.

Understanding the question

The six questions in Paper 1 test different parts of the syllabus. The questions have a common structure, as shown in the following example taken from a past examination paper.

(a) Study Fig. 8, a map showing pollution of a river in an MEDC.

   (i)   Describe how the water quality changes along the river between points A and B.   [1]

  (ii)   Using information from Fig. 8, give **two** reasons for the change which you have described in (a) (i).   [2]

  (iii)   Explain why, in many countries, waste is released into rivers.   [3]

  (iv)   River pollution is a threat to the environment. Explain what could be done to reduce this threat and improve the quality of water in rivers.   [4]

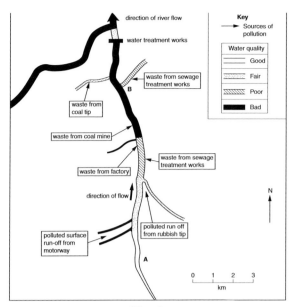

direction of river flow

water treatment works

waste from sewage treatment works

B

waste from coal tip

waste from coal mine

waste from sewage treatment works

waste from factory

direction of flow

polluted surface run-off from motorway

polluted run off from rubbish tip

A

N

Key

Sources of pollution

Water quality

Good

Fair

Poor

Bad

0 1 2 3
km

Fig. 8

(b) Study Fig. 9 which shows newspaper extracts about three proposed new developments on an island in the Atlantic Ocean.

Extract 1

NEW NORTH-SOUTH MOTORWAY PLANNED

Plans have been submitted to build a motorway across the mountains, through the valley of the White River ....

Extract 2

PLANS ANNOUNCED TO BUILD NEW FISH PROCESSING FACTORY

A multi-national company plans to clear woodland and scrub to build a factory to process and can locally caught sardines ....

Extract 3

LUXURY RESORT AND GOLF COURSE PROPOSED FOR SUMMER BAY

Plans have been submitted to build a resort and golf course on the sand dunes ....

Fig. 9

(i) Choose one of the proposed new developments and write down the number of the extract which you have chosen.

Explain **three** different ways in which the development could damage the local natural environment. [3]

(ii) Suggest what should be done to ensure that your chosen development is sustainable. [5]

(c) People can benefit when economic activities take place. Such activities include:

– transport

– tourism

– manufacturing industry.

Name an area which you have studied and describe an economic activity which takes place.

Explain how the activity benefits local people. [7]   [Total: 25 marks]

(Cambridge IGCSE Geography 0460 Paper 13 Q6 June 2010)

Part of question	Mark allocation	Type of question
(a) (i)	1	Interpretation of the first resource which shows river quality
(a) (ii)	2	Explanation of change based on the first resource
(a) (iii)	3	Understanding of an idea, waste in rivers, linked to the first resource
(a) (iv)	4	General understanding about river pollution and management
(b) (i)	3	Detailed interpretation and explanation of the second resource
(b) (ii)	5	Explanation linked to the second resource
(c)	7	Case study

The case study

Each question includes a case study which aims to test your knowledge about places. Here are two examples of case study questions:

> 1 Name an urban area which you have studied where there are not enough houses for people to live in. Explain why there is this problem and what has been done to solve it.

> 2 For a country or area which you have studied, describe the problems for people and the **local** environment caused by using wood and charcoal as sources of energy.
> (Cambridge IGCSE Geography 0460 Paper 13 Q5c June 2010)

Both questions have a *topic*, a *focus* and a *location*.

In **example 1** the *topic* is housing shortage, the *focus* is reasons for the housing shortage and what has been done to reduce the shortage, and the *location* is an appropriate named urban area.

In **example 2** the *topic* is using wood and charcoal for fuel, the *focus* is problems this causes for the local environment, and the *location* is an appropriate country or area.

What is the topic, focus and location in the following case study question?

> 3 For an area you have studied, describe the benefits and problems of living near the coast.
> (Cambridge IGCSE Geography 0460 Paper 13 Q3c June 2010)

In **example 3** the *topic* is living near the coast, the *focus* is benefits and problems, and the *location* is any appropriate area.

Answering case study questions

Read the following case study question and the two answers below it.

> In many parts of the world tropical storms present hazards to people. For a named area, describe the causes and effects of a tropical storm.

Answer from candidate 1

In 2005 Hurricane Katrina caused death and destruction in the USA. Hurricanes have strong winds and a lot of rain which cause flooding.

Tip

- Learn your case study examples thoroughly as there are 7 marks available for each answer.

- When you are revising your work, make a list of all the case studies you are learning. Highlight the topic, focus and location.

- You can use a case study that is local to your school as an alternative to the case studies in this textbook.

A hurricane is formed when warm air rises rapidly over water. When the temperature is high the air rises quickly and water evaporates. This causes high wind speeds. The wind blows across the sea and causes storm surges.

The city is built on low-lying land and this made the impact of Hurricane Katrina worse. Engineers had built barriers around the city to protect it from flooding. The storm was too strong and the levees broke causing a lot of flooding.

If the hurricane had hit poor countries in the Caribbean the effects could have been even worse because they have no protection against tropical storms and they are mainly farming countries.

Answer from candidate 2

In August 2005 Hurricane Katrina caused death and destruction in New Orleans in the USA. Hurricanes have very strong winds and a lot of rain which causes floods and damages property.

Hurricane Katrina began as a low pressure weather system which strengthened to become a tropical storm and eventually a hurricane. The storm started in the Atlantic Ocean within the tropics. Warm air rose rapidly over areas of deep water. Because the sea temperature was high the air rose quickly and absorbed water from the ocean. The rapidly rising air created an area of very low pressure called the 'eye' of the storm. The winds rotated around the eye sucking in more moist air.

The tropical storm moved west across the Atlantic Ocean and into the Gulf of Mexico. It hit the coast near New Orleans and caused a storm surge which created a wall of water which crashed down on the coastal area.

New Orleans is built on low-lying land and this made the impact of the flooding worse. The storm was so strong that the levees, built to protect the city, broke and much of the city was flooded. In places the floodwater was up to three metres deep. Over 1,200 people drowned and 10,000 were made homeless, especially in the poor inner city areas. Survivors were short of food and there was no access to clean water, which caused problems of disease from contaminated water.

Here is a list of eight characteristics of case study answers. Decide which four apply to the answers given by candidates 1 and 2. On a copy of the table tick the correct box and identify where each characteristic is found in the candidates' answers.

Characteristic	Candidate 1	Candidate 2
Uses geographical terminology.		
Makes simple statements.		
Includes information that is not relevant.		
Develops (expands on) points that are made.		
Does little to explain the causes of the floods.		

Characteristic	Candidate 1	Candidate 2
Includes relevant facts and figures.		
Gives a place specific answer (writes about actual places).		
Makes inaccurate, sweeping statements.		

How the case study is marked

If you learn how examiners mark case studies it should help you to write good answers. They mark them in 'levels' and your answer must increase in quality to reach a higher level. The question below shows how examiners mark your case study answers.

> Choose an example of rural to urban migration in an LEDC which you have studied. Name the areas between which people moved and explain why many people migrated. You should refer both to pull and to push factors.
>
> (Cambridge IGCSE Geography 0460 Paper 13 Q2c June 2010)

Level 1 (1, 2 or 3 marks)

Your answer includes limited details (simple statements) which explain why people migrated from rural to urban areas.

Level 1 answers would include reasons such as:
- There are more jobs in cities.
- There are better services in urban areas.
- There is not enough food in the rural area.

Level 2 (4, 5 or 6 marks)

Your answer includes more developed (detailed) statements which explain why people migrated from rural to urban areas.

Level 2 answers would include reasons such as:
- There are more jobs in cities where people can work as cleaners or shoe shiners.
- There is better access for the family to schools, hospitals and clinics in the city.
- People can buy food from markets rather than having to grow food for themselves on unproductive farmland.

Level 3 (7 marks)

Your answer includes three or more Level 2 developed statements and an appropriate named example with some detail about the named example.

Level 3 answers would include details such as:
- People come from the surrounding countryside to work and make money by offering shoe-shines to tourists in Placa de Republica, a main square in the city centre of São Paulo.
- People move to São Paulo to live in the Cinqua Pora area where basic concrete houses are being built, with piped water and sewage pipes. Even in the favelas which have developed on the steep hillsides the people have better access to healthcare and education than in the countryside.

- People living in the valley of the São Francisco River lost their farmland when dams and reservoirs were built along it for HEP generation, so they were forced to move to the city to look for work.

Now that you know how case studies are marked you should practise writing answers for all your case studies. Remember: to achieve top marks (Level 3) your answer must:
- include several developed ideas
- use the correct geographical terminology, where appropriate
- include details about the place you have chosen.

These are included in the answer to the case study question below. Read it carefully and pick out where Level 3 ideas are included.

> Name an area where small-scale subsistence farming takes place. Describe the farming system and explain why it is taking place in the area.

Rice farming is important in the Lower Ganges valley in India. (named area) One third of the world's population eat rice but it can only be grown in areas with very wet conditions and hot temperatures and sun. This area of India has a tropical monsoon climate, temperatures are around 27°C and rainfall is over 1,000mm per year, most of which comes in 4 or 5 months which suits rice farming. (place details)

This area has a high population density which suits labour-intensive farming (geographical terminology) like growing rice. The farms are very small, often about 1 hectare divided into many plots, so machinery cannot be used and most of the work is done by the farmer and his family. (developed idea) Water buffalo are used to pull a plough to prepare the padi fields for planting. (developed idea)

The farmer has to construct bunds (place detail), which are embankments, around the padi field to keep the water in the field. The farmer also has to build irrigation canals to get water to the fields in the drier season, and plant crops and harvest them. (developed idea)

Some farmers in the area grow high yield varieties of rice like IR8 (geographical terminology), but the seeds are expensive to buy and not all farmers can afford them. These farmers can sell some of their rice crop but most farmers only grow enough rice to feed their families. (developed idea)

Command words

Many candidates lose marks in the examination because they do not read carefully or understand the command words in the question. Command words tell you how to answer the question. You need to know what each command word means and follow its instructions. If you do not know the meaning of the command word you will answer the question incorrectly.

The groups of command words on the opposite page are commonly used in Paper 1.

Tip

Read the command words carefully. Do not explain when the question says 'describe'.

Command words used in Paper 1

Recall information, example or fact

Identify (pick out something from information you are given)

State   Name   Give (short answers using your own knowledge)

What (another way to ask you to recall information you have learned)

Identify three coastal landforms shown in photograph B. (photograph shows an area of coastline)

State two differences between the percentage use of water in Europe and Asia. (you need to use a bar graph from the examination paper)

Name two settlements where over 20 000 people were killed by the Sichuan earthquake. (you need to use a map from the examination paper)

Give three different reasons why rainforests are being cleared.

What is the difference between weather and climate?

Give a definition

Define   What is meant by   Give the meaning of (what the word or phrase means)

Define 'sphere of influence'

What is meant by high technology industry?

Which of the following definitions is the correct **meaning of** 'relative humidity'?

Description

Describe (give the main points about something)

Describe the sphere of influence of the shopping centre. 2 marks (you need to use a map from the examination paper)

Describe three likely impacts of flooding in the area shown in the photograph. 3 marks (photograph shows part of a river and its floodplain)

Describe the likely problems for an MEDC, such as Ireland, of having so many old dependants. 5 marks

Explanation

Give/Suggest reasons   Explain   Why   What (why something happens, or reasons)

Suggest three reasons why many thousands of people were killed by this earthquake.

Explain how the process of hydraulic action may erode the bed and banks of a river. 3 marks

Explain why there are high birth rates in LEDCs such as Nigeria. 4 marks

Explain why many people live in areas such as Sichuan, even though they are at risk from earthquakes. 5 marks

Why is erosion more likely at point S than point P? (you need to use a diagram from the examination paper)

What factors attract high technology industries to an area?

Case study commands

Refer to an area you have studied   For a named area/country

Name an area where   Choose a named example

The name of the place or area helps to make your case study 'place specific'.

Tip

- Notice the different mark allocations which mean that the descriptions will need different amounts of detail.

Tip

- Using a named example does not by itself make a case study 'place specific'. You must include more detail about the place in your answer.

- Command words are often linked together, as shown in the following question:

  Name and **explain** two processes by which a river transports its load. 4 marks

Resources

Before you answer each question, check that you are looking at and using the correct resources from the examination paper and Insert. The Insert may include a number of photographs, so it is particularly important that you study the correct one.

Examples of types of resources used in Paper 1

Map	World map to show distribution of the tropical rainforest or tectonic plate margins
	Map of a country or continent to show contrasts or information such as the distribution of nuclear power stations
	Local map of an area such as a river basin
Graph	Line graph to show population change over time
	Bar graph to show employment figures in different countries
	Climate graph to show temperature and rainfall in a tropical desert
	Pie chart to show types of employment in a country
	Scatter graph to show the relationship between the strength of earthquakes and the number of deaths
	Population pyramid to show population structure
Photograph	These can show many things, for example type of vegetation, industrial sites, types of farm, areas of a city, natural landscapes
Diagram	Geographical idea or theory such as settlement hierarchy
	Sketch of a feature such as a cliff
Information	Newspaper article
	Factfile
	Website image
	These can show many things, for example a volcanic eruption, government announcement about population policy, growth of tourism in a country

In Paper 1 you will have to read and interpret information from the resource. This is shown in the following examples.

> Study the map which shows information about internal migration in the USA. Describe the distribution of states where there are high rates of migration into the state.

> Study the three photographs which show different parts of Amman, the capital city of Jordan. Describe the main urban land use in each of the areas in the photographs.
>
> (Adapted from Cambridge IGCSE Geography 0460 Paper 11 Q1b (i) and (ii) June 2009)

Preparation for Paper 1

To do well in this paper it is important that you:

- Learn your work and revise it before the examination. There are different ways to learn your notes and your teacher will give you advice about them. Try out a few different ways to find out which suits you best.
- Ask your teacher for questions from previous examinations which you can use for practice. Sometimes it is useful to do this under test conditions.

- Ask your teacher how the questions are marked. You are given advice on pages 239–40 on how Paper 1 case studies are marked. Using mark schemes helps you to understand how to earn more marks by giving detailed answers and answering a question carefully.

Examples of two candidates' answers

You have now found out more about what Paper 1 is about and how to answer the questions well. Next you have the opportunity to look in detail at examination questions from a past paper. For each question there are answers from two candidates – one who is aiming for an A grade and the other for a C grade. These are followed by an explanation of why these marks were awarded.

Read the questions and look at the resources, then study the answers given by the two candidates. Can you understand how the marks are awarded? Finally read the commentary which explains the awarding of the marks and, where appropriate, gives advice about how the answer could be improved.

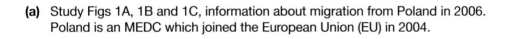

(a) Study Figs 1A, 1B and 1C, information about migration from Poland in 2006. Poland is an MEDC which joined the European Union (EU) in 2004.

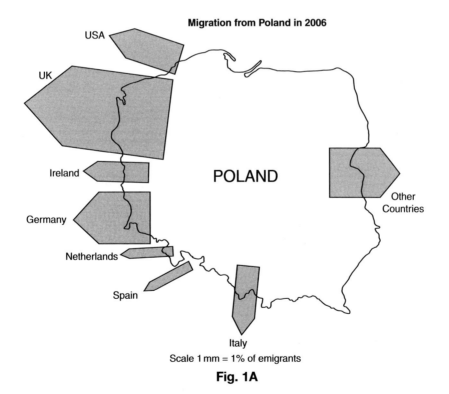

Migration from Poland in 2006

USA
UK
Ireland
Germany
Netherlands
Spain
Italy
POLAND
Other Countries

Scale 1 mm = 1% of emigrants

Fig. 1A

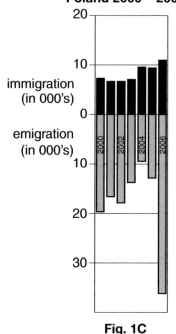

Emigration from, and immigration to, Poland 2000 – 2006

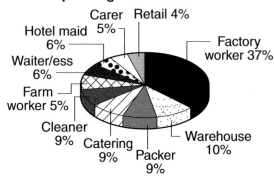

Top 10 Migrant Jobs in the UK

Carer 5%
Retail 4%
Hotel maid 6%
Waiter/ess 6%
Farm worker 5%
Cleaner 9%
Catering 9%
Packer 9%
Warehouse 10%
Factory worker 37%

Fig. 1B

Fig. 1C

(a) (i) Name the country which was the destination of the largest percentage of migrants from Poland in 2006.

(Cambridge IGCSE Geography 0460 Paper 12 Q1a(i) November 2010)

Candidate 1 answer   1/1 mark

UK (✓)

Commentary

The correct country was identified from the map.

Candidate 2 answer   1/1 mark

UK (✓)

Commentary

The correct country was identified from the map.

(a) (ii) For each of the following, suggest **one** reason why a greater percentage of migrants from Poland to the UK:

A were employed in factories rather than on farms

B were employed as cleaners rather than teachers.

(Cambridge IGCSE Geography 0460 Paper 12 Q1a(ii) November 2010)

Candidate 1 answer   2/2 marks

A: The factory (secondary) sector has a larger number of jobs available compared to the declining farming (primary) sector. (✓)

B: Teaching requires people to be qualified and most immigrants lack the qualifications and experience, but they don't have to be qualified to be cleaners. (✓)

Commentary

Both reasons are correct. In A the focus is on the different number of jobs, in B the focus is on the different need for qualifications. Notice that the candidate makes a comparison in both answers. This was needed to gain credit.

Candidate 2 answer   1/2 marks

> A: There were more factory jobs available for the migrants. (✓)
>
> B: There were more jobs available as cleaners.

Commentary

The first reason is correct. Although reason A is brief it does make a comparison between the number of jobs in factories and on farms. Reason B is not credited because it repeats the same idea. The significant difference between jobs as cleaner and teacher is the level of qualifications required. You should always use comparative words like 'more' or 'larger' when the question requires a comparison to be made.

(a) (iii)   Using Fig. 1C, briefly compare the amount of emigration from, and immigration to, Poland between 2000 and 2006.

(Cambridge IGCSE Geography 0460 Paper 12 Q1a(iii) November 2010)

Candidate 1 answer   3/3 marks

> Between 2000 and 2006 the number of emigrants was almost double the number of immigrants (✓). In 2004 the number of emigrants was almost the same as the number of immigrants (✓). In 2006 the number of emigrants was nearly three times more than the number of immigrants (✓).

Commentary

The candidate identifies three differences from the graph to score 3 marks. The first mark is for recognising the general imbalance between emigration and immigration. The second and third marks are for comparison in particular years. You will be given credit if you use information from the graph. This candidate does that by using words such as 'almost double', 'almost the same' and 'nearly three times more'.

Candidate 2 answer   2/3 marks

> In 2000 about 7,000 people immigrated to Poland and almost 20,000 emigrated from Poland. Between 2001 and 2005 immigration stayed low, emigration, on the other hand, fluctuated with some years having a high emigration rate and some years not (✓). In 2006 the immigration rate was at its highest at about 11,000 people and the emigration rate was also at its highest at about 36,000 people (✓).

Commentary

The candidate makes two comparisons between rates of immigration and emigration. The statement which describes the situation in 2000 is not awarded a mark because no comparison is made. The candidate needed to emphasise that emigration was more than immigration. There is no credit given for just reading data from the graph. A comparison is made between immigration and emigration rates between 2001 and 2005. The final idea is credited because it makes a comparison in a particular year, 2006.

(a) (iv) What difficulties might be faced by migrants from Poland when living in countries such as the UK?

(Cambridge IGCSE Geography 0460 Paper 12 Q1a(iv) November 2010)

Candidate 1 answer   4/4 marks

> Migrants may face discrimination because they are foreigners (✓). It will be difficult for them to mix with people from a different culture (✓). They will only be able to get low-paid jobs and will be the first to lose their jobs if the company is not doing well (✓). Because of low wages they will only be able to afford low quality housing (✓). Also may have to work very long hours for little pay.

Commentary

There are many possible answers to this question; the candidate correctly identifies four different difficulties. The candidate also suggests another difficulty of working long hours and this idea takes the answer above the maximum mark. Remember that the mark allocation (in this example it is 4 marks) gives you guidance about how many ideas to include. This candidate suggests five difficulties. It is a good idea to give more ideas than the number of marks in case they are not all worth 1 mark.

Candidate 2 answer   2/4 marks

> The migrants do not have enough money for decent housing so end up living in poor quality housing (✓). They cannot afford to live in nice areas. Many people from Poland might not be able to speak English so it will be difficult for them (✓). The children will not be able to understand lessons at school. Overall it will be very difficult for them.

Commentary

The candidate explains two difficulties: having to live in poor houses and being unable to speak English. The candidate could gain another mark by suggesting why the migrants have little money. The final sentence does not improve the answer because it just repeats the question. You will never get a mark for doing this. The answer will not be able to score maximum marks because it does not include enough ideas.

(b) Study Fig. 2, an article about migration from Poland to the UK.

'Nearly 600,000' new EU migrants

Almost 600,000 people from Poland and the seven other countries which joined the EU in 2004 have applied to work in the UK, where full work rights have been given to all citizens of EU countries. Each morning in Hammersmith, west London, many Poles gather to look in a shop window at adverts for work. Here you will find graduates scribbling down details of work in catering and cleaning, delivering pizza takeaway leaflets and ironing.

"I am not here to claim benefits," says Radek, 25. "I am here to earn money, as much as I can make and then go home. At home in Poland unemployment is 20 to 25% and the wages are very low." He notes down the number of a builder from an advert looking for plasterers, kitchen fitters and electricians. "I can do all of those, I studied at Poznan technical college as an electrician. I have a qualification." Newly arrived Poles, like many immigrants to Britain before them, are often doing the work that Britons seemingly no longer want to do. For example, when Tesco needed 140 new lorry drivers recently, it hired Poles because of the lack of British applicants.

Fig. 2

(b) (i) Use your own words to give **three** reasons why many people from Poland have migrated to the UK since 2004.

(Cambridge IGCSE Geography 0460 Paper 12 Q1b(i) November 2010)

Candidate 1 answer   3/3 marks

Polish people have migrated to the UK to get better paid jobs (✓) as wages in Poland are low. They hope to earn more money in the UK. They have also migrated to the UK because of the EU policy which protects people's rights to have a job in different countries (✓). Another reason is that there is a high unemployment rate in Poland so it hard for them to get jobs (✓). Another reason is that Britain has a lot of vacancies where manual labour is required.

Commentary

The answer makes three valid points about jobs, employment rights and higher pay. The question instruction is to 'use your own words' so no credit is given for copying from the article. The final idea about job vacancies is the opposite of the previous statement that there is a lack of jobs in Poland. A mark has already been awarded for the idea of jobs. It would be acceptable in a question that asks for 'three reasons' to number your ideas 1, 2 and 3 and write each answer on a different line.

Candidate 2 answer   2/3 marks

People have migrated from Poland to the UK because there are more job opportunities (✓). The jobs are better paid than the jobs in Poland (✓). Full working rights have been given to all citizens of EU countries.

Commentary

The answer makes two simple valid points: that there are more job opportunities, and wages are higher in the UK. The final reason is copied from the article and is not credited because the question instruction is 'use your own words'. This is an example of where a candidate is not following the command words.

(b) (ii) Explain the problems which may be caused in Poland by this migration.

(Cambridge IGCSE Geography 0460 Paper 12 Q1b(ii) November 2010)

Candidate 1 answer   5/5 marks

The migrants are usually men which means that families are separated. (✓) There are also less qualified, unskilled and semi-skilled people available to do the jobs in Poland. (✓) This can harm the economy and slow down development. (✓dev) It is usually the young who move away and leave the elderly which increase the dependent population for the government. (✓) If too many men move away this can cause a sex imbalance as there are more women left who will have to go to work (✓) and leave their family which can be against tradition (✓), especially in farming areas of the country.

Commentary

This is an excellent answer which includes well-developed ideas. The answer focuses on the problems of splitting up the family and loss of the economically active workforce. More than one point is made about both problems. These extra marks are called 'development' marks and are credited when the answer includes more detail. In this answer the loss of qualified workers could slow down economic development, and men migrating means women have to go to work, which is against tradition. In a question worth 5 marks you can score development marks, so try to make your ideas as detailed as possible.

Candidate 2 answer   3/5 marks

Most of the people who migrate from Poland are men so the sex structure of the country will be uneven. (✓) Most of the people who leave are the people who are economically active so there are less people working in Poland (✓) which means that it will affect the economy. The men leave so women have to look after the family as there is no father at home. (✓)

Commentary

The answer identifies three problems, but does not develop them to gain further credit. The candidate could explain a possible impact of gender imbalance in the country and could suggest what would be an impact of the migration on the economy of Poland, rather than just saying it will 'affect the economy'. All the answers could easily be developed to score more marks. You should always try to give more detail to your answer when the mark allocation is 5 marks.

(c) Name an example of a city or country to which large numbers of people have migrated from other countries. Describe the effects of international migration on your chosen city or country.

(Cambridge IGCSE Geography 0460 Paper 12 Q1c November 2010)

Candidate 1 answer   7/7 marks

Many Mexicans have migrated to the USA, particularly to cities like Los Angeles in California which is near the border between Mexico and the USA. They have moved to get better paid jobs and because their living conditions in Mexico were poor.

Most migrants are young adults who get jobs in the USA, working on farms or in services like cleaning or in shops. Often this work is for low wages and they work long hours. They do the jobs which Americans don't want to do. The Mexicans pay taxes to the government which helps to pay for services and supports the country.

Many of the migrants cannot afford good houses so they live in poor conditions in communities with other Mexican people. Many Californians do not like the immigrants because they say that they take some of the jobs which could be done by Americans. Also some of the immigrants have large families which need education and healthcare.

Many Mexicans try to cross the border into the USA illegally. Along some parts of the border fences have been put up with searchlights. Although there are many border police many of the illegal migrants are not caught. They end up living in the poorest slum conditions and cannot get jobs because they don't have work permits. This causes problems for the American government as sometimes there are riots and fights between the Mexicans and some American gangs who feel threatened by them.

Commentary

This is a good Level 3 answer.

In paragraph 1 the candidate names a city and country to which Mexicans have moved. The candidate then gives some brief reasons why the migrants moved but does not gain any credit because this is not what the question asks.

The focus of paragraph 2 is jobs. The effect is explained that Mexicans do low-paid jobs which Americans will not do. The idea is then developed as the Mexican workers pay taxes.

Paragraph 3 concentrates on a negative effect of immigration, that there is often conflict between Mexicans and Americans because of the competition for jobs and the needs of the large Mexican families.

Paragraph 4 focuses on illegal immigrants who cause social unrest because of their poor living conditions and conflict with American gangs.

All of the ideas are developed with extra detail and so are marked as Level 2 ideas. The answer contains four developed ideas and is 'place specific' so it is awarded 7 marks. Go back to the case study mark scheme on page 239 to check how this answer meets the requirements of Level 3.

Candidate 2 answer   3/7 marks

Turkish people moving to Germany

In Germany separate communities have formed such as different shopping areas for the Turkish and the Germans. The country has different cultures, food, dress and way of life. Often the Germans feel that the Turks are taking away their jobs. The Turks have poor living conditions.

In Turkey men leave and women and children stay. A great part of the working population migrates and elderly and young are left to be looked after by the government. The population becomes an ageing population.

Commentary

This is a weak Level 1 answer. The chosen example is appropriate to the question but paragraph 1 contains no developed ideas. Three effects are included: segregated shopping areas, different cultures, and competition for jobs. The poor living conditions of the migrants could also be credited. However, none of these ideas is developed into a Level 2 answer. Go back to the case study mark scheme on page 239 to check how this answer only meets the requirements of Level 1. The candidate could have given examples of different shopping centres or described how the culture is different between the two nationalities or how the Germans react to the competition for jobs. All of these would develop Level 1 answers into Level 2 answers. You should always try to develop your ideas, because even if you only develop one answer to Level 2 you will be awarded 4 marks.

Paragraph 2 is irrelevant to the question. It focuses on the effects of migration in Turkey rather than the country that is receiving the migrants. Try to avoid going away from the question when you are answering. You will not gain any marks for an answer that does not fit the question.

Tip

• Paper 2 tests much more than geographical skills. It also tests understanding and decision-making.

• The questions will test topics from any part of the syllabus. Unlike Paper 1, you do not require knowledge of specific places. The resources will give you the information you need to answer each question.

What is Paper 2?

Paper 2 is your second theory examination. In this examination there are six questions on the paper and you must answer them all. Question 1 is always based on an OS (Ordnance Survey) map extract and tests map reading and interpretation skills. You will learn how to 'read' and understand OS maps in Unit 4.1 on pages 200–07. Question 1 is worth 20 marks out of the total of 60.

The other five questions are each worth 8 marks. They test a variety of different skills but also your understanding of geographical concepts and your decision-making ability about different issues.

The aims of Paper 2 are:
• to give you the opportunity to use geographical skills
• to give you the opportunity to interpret an OS map
• to encourage you to make geographical judgements and decisions.

What is Paper 2 testing?

The examination tests three objectives:

1 your use of geographical skills

2 your interpretation and analysis of geographical data

3 your decision making.

You will not be told which objective each question is testing but you will recognise the objectives by the wording of the question.

How to use your time effectively

The Paper 2 examination is 1 hour 30 minutes long. In total the paper is worth 60 marks so you have 1½ minutes per mark. This means that Question 1 might take you 30 minutes and the other five questions about 12 minutes each. Remember you also need to allow time to:
• read all the questions carefully
• study the OS map extract and Insert
• check your answers at the end of the examination to correct any mistakes you may have made.

To have the time to do all of this it may be better to allow yourself 30 minutes to answer Question 1 and 10 minutes to answer each of the other five questions. You can then use the remaining 10 minutes on the other tasks. You will need more time to answer Question 1 because it is worth more marks, and to give you enough time to work accurately. Look carefully at the number of marks available for each part of a question (shown in brackets at the end of each question). The higher the mark allocation the more detail is required. The number of lines provided for your answer is another guide as to how much detail you need to include. Not all questions on Paper 2 require extended writing. Some questions may only need one word or a short sentence answer. You may be told to complete a table, put a tick in a tick list, or draw or sketch an answer.

Tip

Make sure that you attempt all questions. It is very easy to miss out a question if there are no answer lines.

Understanding the question

Question 1 always includes an OS map extract of an area in the tropics. An example of such a map is shown on page 259. Typical tasks in Question 1 are:

- Use the map symbols in the key to identify features on the map.
- Give four-figure and six-figure grid references.
- Find places on the map using four-figure and six-figure grid references.
- Work out the direction of one place from another.
- Work out the bearing of one place from another.
- Use the scale to measure distance between places on the map.
- Use contour lines and spot heights to work out the height of places.
- Calculate the gradient between points on the map.
- Describe natural or physical features, such as relief of the land, river and river valley, coastal area.
- Describe human features, such as types of settlement, road network.
- Describe distribution of features, such as types of farming, settlement pattern.
- Suggest or give reasons for features, such as distribution of settlement, location of farming types, direction of river flow.
- Use map evidence to identify features, such as functions in a town, different types of transport or services, comparison between two river valleys.

How to do well on Question 1

- Be accurate in measuring on the map.
- Give the correct units of measurement.
- Use the edge of a piece of paper to measure distance (see page 201).
- Use the information provided with the map, such as scale, key to map symbols, compass point.
- Practise basic map skills, such as grid reference, compass bearing (see page 200), cross-section.
- Learn how to calculate gradient (see page 203).
- Practise how to identify and describe features shown on the map.
- Follow the command words (see page 241 if you do not know what these are).

Common command words in Question 1 are:

Identify/Name	**Identify** the features shown on the map extract.
	Name five services found at the settlement.
Mark	**Mark** the position on the cross-section of ...
Measure	**Measure** the distance along the road.
	Measure the bearing.
State / Give / Circle	**State** the compass direction.
	Give the four-figure grid reference.
	Circle the six-figure grid reference (when a choice of answers is given).
Calculate	**Calculate** the gradient.
Describe	**Describe** the physical features of the river.
Suggest	**Suggest** why there are few settlements inland.

Other questions on Paper 2

These questions focus on different topics and include a variety of
resources (see page 257). The following questions are taken from a
past examination paper and show the different ways you could be
tested. Make a copy of the table on page 256 and complete the table
for Questions 4 and 5.

2 Study Fig. 5, which shows the structure of the total New Zealand population, and Fig. 6,
which shows the structure of the Maori population in 2006. The Maori people form part of the
population of New Zealand.

Total New Zealand population, 2006

Maori population, 2006

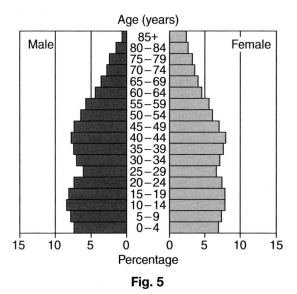

Fig. 5

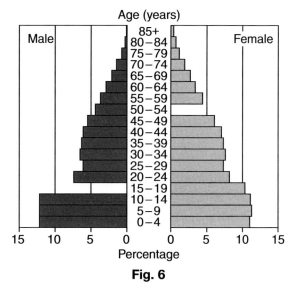

Fig. 6

(a) In 2006, 10% of the male Maori population were aged 15–19 and 5% of the female
Maori population were aged 50–54. Complete Fig. 6 by adding this data. [2]

(b) Complete the following sentences by adding the words **greater** or **less**.

(i) The percentage of 0–14 year olds in the Maori population is .... than
the percentage of 0–14 year olds in the total New Zealand population. [1]

     (ii) The percentage of over 55 year olds in the Maori population is .... than the percentage of over 55 year olds in the total New Zealand population. [1]

     (iii) The percentage of over 35–49 year olds in the Maori population is .... than the percentage of over 35–39 year olds in the total New Zealand population. [1]

(c) In 2006, the Maori population formed 14% of the total New Zealand population.

     (i) Using evidence from Figs 5 and 6 only, suggest how this may change over the next 50 years. [1]

     (ii) Explain your answer to **(c) (i)**. [2] [Total: 8 marks]

(Cambridge IGCSE Geography 0460 Paper 2 Q2 June 2009)

3 Photograph A (below) shows an area of small-scale subsistence agriculture in Asia.

(a) Describe the relief of the area shown in Photograph A. [4]

(b) The natural vegetation of the area is tropical rainforest but the forest has been affected by human activity. Which of the following statements describe the distribution of forest shown in Photograph A? Circle **two** correct statements.
- covering the whole area
- on the highest land
- on the steepest slopes
- in valleys
- completely removed [2]

(c) Soil erosion is a problem in the area shown in Photograph A. What features shown in the photograph may encourage soil erosion? [2] [Total: 8 marks]

(Cambridge IGCSE Geography 0460 Paper 2 Q3 June 2009)

4 The United Kingdom plans to increase the percentage of electricity it produces from renewable energy sources. Fig. 7 shows the percentage produced from renewable sources in 2005 and the targets for 2010, 2015 and 2020.

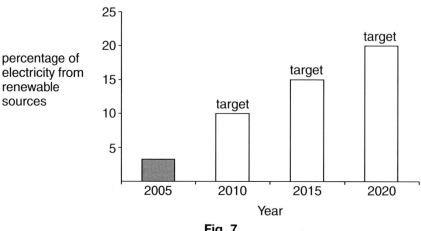

Fig. 7

(a) State the target for the percentage of electricity to be produced from renewable sources in 2015. [1]

(b) The target for electricity from renewable sources in 2020 is 20%. Plot this information as a pie chart on Fig 8. Use the key provided. [3]

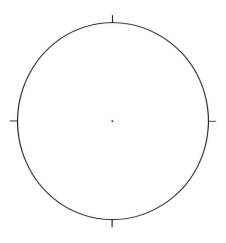

Key

 non-renewable sources   renewable sources

Fig. 8

(c) Wind power is one renewable energy source. Fig. 9 shows a wind farm and some of the advantages and disadvantages of wind power.

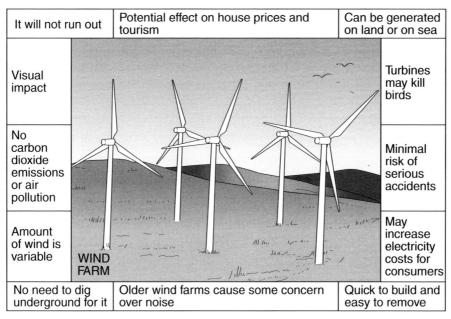

It will not run out	Potential effect on house prices and tourism	Can be generated on land or on sea
Visual impact		Turbines may kill birds
No carbon dioxide emissions or air pollution	WIND FARM	Minimal risk of serious accidents
Amount of wind is variable		May increase electricity costs for consumers
No need to dig underground for it	Older wind farms cause some concern over noise	Quick to build and easy to remove

Fig. 9

A new wind farm is to be built. Using Fig. 9 only, suggest how this may affect:

(i) energy supplies [2]

(ii) the natural environment. [2] [Total: 8 marks]

(Cambridge IGCSE Geography 0460 Paper 2 Q4 June 2009)

5 Fig. 10 is a map showing the islands of Japan and the surrounding region. Plate boundaries, plate movements and selected earthquakes are shown.

The depth of the focus of each earthquake is shown. The focus of an earthquake is the place in the Earth's crust where an earthquake originates.

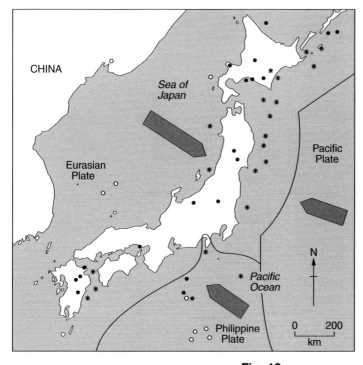

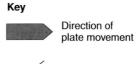

Key

➤ Direction of plate movement

⟋ Plate boundary

✳ Earthquake focus shallower than 100m below the Earth's surface

● Earthquake focus between 100m and 400m below the Earth's surface

○ Earthquake focus deeper than 400m below the Earth's surface

Fig. 10

(a) Which of the following statements describe the plate movements shown on Fig. 10? Tick **two** correct statements. [2]

Statement	Tick
plates sliding past each other	
plates moving towards each other	
plates moving away from each other	
plates moving north west and south east	
plates moving north east and south west	
plates moving north and south	

(b) Describe **one** feature of the distribution of the following earthquakes shown on Fig. 10:

    (i)   earthquakes with their focus shallower than 100 m below the Earth's surface [1]

    (ii) earthquakes with their focus between 100 m and 400 m below the Earth's surface [1]

    (iii) earthquakes with their focus deeper than 400 m below the Earth's surface. [1]

(c) Explain why and how earthquakes occur in the area shown on Fig. 10. [3]

(Cambridge IGCSE Geography 0460 Paper 2 Q5 June 2009)

Make a copy of the table below and complete it for Questions 4 and 5.

> **Tip**
> Use all the information provided for you. Only relevant information is included in the maps, diagrams, data tables etc.

Part of question	What you must do to answer the question
2 (a)	Complete the horizontal bar on the population pyramid.
2 (b) (i) (ii) (iii)	Interpret the data shown in the population pyramids.
2 (c) (i)	Suggest a possible change using evidence from the population pyramids.
2 (c) (ii)	Explain why the change you suggested might happen.
3 (a)	Describe the relief of the area shown in the photograph.
3 (b)	Describe the distribution of forest shown in the photograph.
3 (c)	Use evidence from the photograph to explain why soil erosion occurs.
4 (a)	
4 (b)	
4 (c) (i) (ii)	
5 (a)	
5 (b)	
5 (c)	

Command words

Command words tell you how to answer the question. You need to know what each command word means and follow its instructions. If you do not know the meaning of the command word you will answer the question incorrectly.

> **Tip**
> • Underline or highlight the command word to make sure you read it carefully.

Identify the common command words used on Paper 2 in the questions below.

- How many primary schools are there in Chatteris?
  (Cambridge IGCSE Geography 0460 Paper 2 Q2a November 2009)
- Using the information in Table 1 only, suggest the minimum population needed for a settlement to have a doctor's surgery.
  (Cambridge IGCSE Geography 0460 Paper 2 Q2c November 2009)
- Which one of the following statements about Fig. 3 is correct? Tick the correct statement.
  (Cambridge IGCSE Geography 0460 Paper 2 Q2e (ii) November 2009)
- Describe the physical features of the area shown in the photograph.
  (Cambridge IGCSE Geography 0460 Paper 2 Q3a November 2009)
- It is planned to build a dam in the area in order to provide a water supply for an urban area. Using evidence from the photograph, suggest **two** advantages and **two** disadvantages of the area for this purpose.
  (Cambridge IGCSE Geography 0460 Paper 2 Q3b November 2009)
- Name feature **X** shown on Fig. 5.
  (Cambridge IGCSE Geography 0460 Paper 2 Q5b (i) November 2009)
- Explain how feature **X** may have formed. You may add labels to Fig. 5.
  (Cambridge IGCSE Geography 0460 Paper 2 Q5b (ii) November 2009)
- Using the information from Fig. 6 and Table 3 only, give **four** advantages of the Western Cape for outdoor tourism.
  (Cambridge IGCSE Geography 0460 Paper 2 Q6c November 2009)

Resources

The question paper contains a lot of different resources which you will use to answer the questions. Check that you are looking at the right resource. The Insert will include photographs, so it is particularly important that you study the correct one.

Examples of types of resources used in Paper 2

Map	World map to show distribution of areas where there are food shortages
	Map of an island to show tourist developments
	Local map of an area around a city
Graph	Line graph to show change in birth rate and death rate over time
	Bar graph to show number of tourists to countries
	Climate graph to show temperature and rainfall in a tropical rainforest
	Pie chart to show types of energy source
	Scatter graph to show the relationship between the population of villages and the number of shops
	Population pyramid to show population structure
Data table	Change in employment figures over time
	Climate data for contrasting areas in world
Photograph	These can show many things, for example areas of a city, types of farming, natural landscapes and features
Diagram	Geographical idea or theory such as Demographic Transition Model
	Sketch of natural features such as a lowland river valley
	Weather instruments
Information	Newspaper article
	Factfile
	Annotated (labelled) map
	These can show many things, for example a disaster such as famine, types of weathering in different natural areas, climate contrasts in a country

In Paper 2 you may have to plot or draw information on a resource or read and interpret information from the resource. This is shown in the following examples.

Table 2 shows weather information for Pretoria, South Africa, for five days in 2006.

(i) Use the information in Table 2 to complete Fig. 9.

(ii) Which date has the greatest range of temperature? [2 marks]

(Adapted from Cambridge IGCSE Geography 0460 Paper 2 Q5a (i) and (ii) June 2008)

Read Fig. 4, which is an account of volcanic activity at Montserrat. Using information from Fig. 4 only, name **two** volcanic hazards affecting Montserrat. [2 marks]

(Adapted from Cambridge IGCSE Geography 0460 Paper 2 Q2b (i) November 2008)

Preparation for Paper 2

You might think that you cannot revise for Paper 2. There are no case studies to learn as in Paper 1, and you do not know which topics the questions will focus on. However, you can revise very effectively for this paper by:

- practising answering OS map questions from previous examinations
- revising the techniques you will use in the examination
- re-reading your work which you revised for Paper 1, except for the case studies – there are questions in Paper 2 which test your understanding of different geographical ideas and your ability to make decisions.

Tip

Be accurate in plotting and interpreting maps and graphs.

Examples of two candidates' answers

You have now found out more about what Paper 2 is about and how to answer the questions well. Next you have the opportunity to look in detail at examination questions from a past paper. For each question there are answers from two candidates – one who is aiming for an A grade and the other for a C grade. These are followed by an explanation of why these marks were awarded.

Read the questions and look at the resources, then study the answers given by the two candidates. In the exam, the map extract will be provided with a full key. The map shown on the opposite page is not reproduced with a key and is not to scale, but is provided as an example only.

Can you understand how the marks are awarded? Finally read the Commentary which explains the awarding of the marks and, where appropriate, gives advice about how the answer could be improved.

Study the map extract, which is for Port Louis, Mauritius. The scale is 1:25 000.

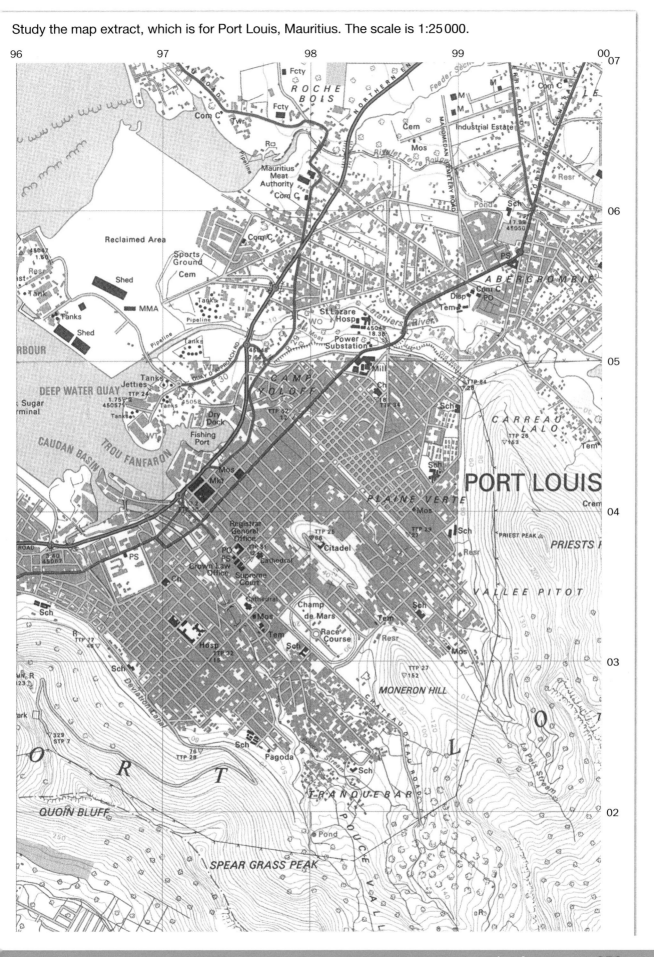

(a) Fig. 1 shows part of the coastal area of the map. Study Fig. 1 and the map extract and answer the questions below.

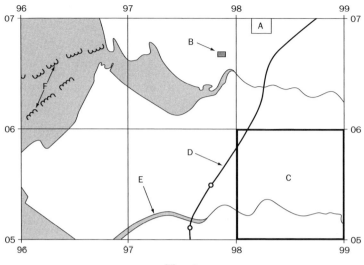

Fig. 1

Identify the following features shown on Fig. 1.

(i) the vegetation in area A

(ii) the named or public building at B

(iii) **two** services or functions in grid square C

(iv) the type of road at D

(v) the name of river E

(vi) feature F in the ocean.

(Cambridge IGCSE Geography 0460 Paper 21 Q1a November 2010)

Candidate 1 answer 6/6 marks

(i)   Tea (✓)

(ii) Factory (✓)

(iii) Hospital and power substation (✓)

(iv) Motorway (✓)

(v) Lataniers River (✓)

(vi) Coral (✓)

Commentary

All features were correctly identified.

Candidate 2 answer 4/6 marks

(i)   Tea (✓)

(ii) Fcty

(iii) Hospital and power substation (✓)

(iv) Northern Entrance Road

(v) Lataniers River (✓)

(vi) Coral (✓)

Commentary

Four of the six features are correctly identified. Answer (ii) is not accepted because although the candidate copies the correct label from the map this is not a building. The candidate must use the key (which will be provided in the exam but is not shown in this example) to answer the question correctly. Answer (iv) is also not credited because the candidate does not read the question carefully. The instruction is to identify the type of road not the name of the road. Do not lose marks carelessly by not reading and obeying the command word.

(b) Fig. 2 is a cross-section drawn from 975038 to 000038 through Priest Peak.

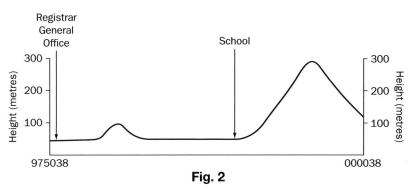

Fig. 2

Using labelled arrows, mark the following features on Fig. 2:

(i) the Citadel

(ii) Priest Peak

(iii) a power line.

(Cambridge IGCSE Geography 0460 Paper 21 Q1b November 2010)

Candidate 1 answer   3/3 marks

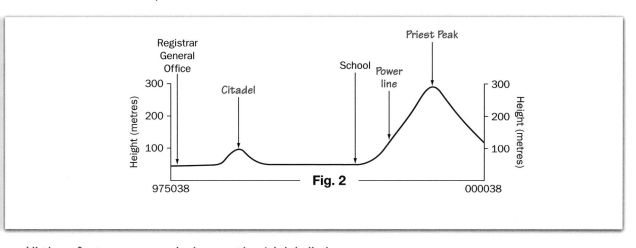

All three features are marked correctly with labelled arrows.

Commentary

All three features are marked accurately with correctly labelled arrows.

Candidate 2 answer 2/3 marks

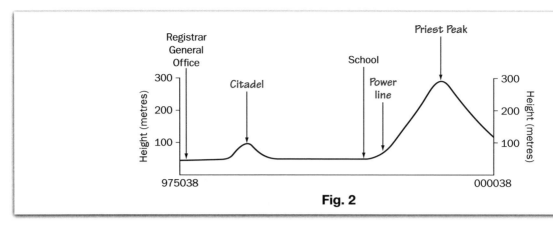

Fig. 2

Citadel and Priest's Peak correct. Power line in wrong position.

Commentary

The candidate correctly locates the citadel and Priest's Peak. The position of the power line is inaccurate and gains no mark. Remember that when marking features on a cross-section you must use an arrow and label it. Do not just write the name above the cross-section. Many candidates lost 1 mark in the examination because they wrote 'Priest's Peak' above the hill but did not identify the hilltop with an arrow. Another mistake made by some candidates was to point the labelled arrows at the base line of the cross-section not the cross-section line itself.

(c) The Port Louis area is an important commercial port in Mauritius.

  (i) State **two** features shown on the map which suggest that the area is a port.

  (Cambridge IGCSE Geography 0460 Paper 21 Q1c(i) November 2010)

Candidate 1 answer 2/2 marks

  1. Harbour (✓)
  2. Dry dock (✓)

Commentary

Both features were credited. The candidate correctly takes both labels from the map as instructed in the command words.

Candidate 2 answer 2/2 marks

  1. Harbour (✓)
  2. Deep water quay (✓)

Commentary

Both features are identified from labels on the map. No further description is needed.

(c) (ii) Using evidence from the map extract, describe **three** natural advantages of the area for the development of a port.

  (Cambridge IGCSE Geography 0460 Paper 21 Q1c(ii) November 2010)

Candidate 1 answer 2/3 marks

1. The bay makes a natural harbour for the city (✓).

2. The headlands protect the harbour (✓) and the ships going into and out of the docks.

3. Lataniers River provides transport for goods that are produced further inland so that they can be exported from the river.

Commentary

The candidate correctly identifies the bay and surrounding headlands and describes how they will protect the harbour. Although the answer about the river may be correct it is not really an advantage for the port and so is not credited.

Candidate 2 answer 1/3 marks

1. Flat land in most areas of the map.

2. Close to the sea, it's on the coast of the Indian Ocean.

3. Clear of coral at the port (✓) so that ships will not damage it.

Commentary

The first idea is too vague. The candidate needed to state that there is flat land next to the coast to gain the mark. Similarly, the second idea is far too general. Many areas are on the coast of the ocean. It does not describe why a port has developed at this particular place. The lack of coral was accepted. It appears from the map that there is a natural break in the coral reef at this location.

> **(d) (i)** Find the CBD (Central Business District) of Port Louis. State the **four-figure** grid reference of the square containing the CBD
>
> (Cambridge IGCSE Geography 0460 Paper 21 Q1d(i) November 2010)

Candidate 1 answer 1/1 mark

9703 (✓).

Commentary

The grid reference is correct.

Candidate 2 answer 0/1 mark

9702

Commentary

The candidate identifies the fishing port rather than the CBD. Look carefully at the map to find evidence. There are a number of buildings shown on the map which indicate the CBD of Port Louis including two cathedrals, a mosque, the law office and the Supreme Court.

> **(d) (ii)** State the meaning of the map symbol shown at 986029.
>
> (Cambridge IGCSE Geography 0460 Paper 21 Q1d(ii) November 2010)

Candidate 1 answer 1/1 mark

Minor trigonometrical station (✓)

Commentary

This is an excellent answer for 1 mark. The candidate has located the point correctly using the grid reference and then used the key to distinguish between the symbols for the major and minor trigonometrical points.

Candidate 2 answer   0/1 mark

Peak of Moneron Hill

Commentary

The candidate uses the six-figure grid reference correctly to identify the area of Moneron Hill. Unfortunately the candidate does not read the question carefully and does not realise the need to use the key to interpret the map symbol.

Skills link 🔗

You will find out more about how to interpret a six-figure grid reference on page 201 of Section 4 Geographical Skills.

(e)   Fig. 3 shows the area around Quoin Bluff. The area shaded is over 100 metres above sea level.

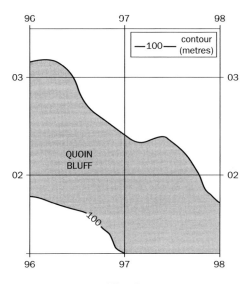

Fig. 3

Describe the relief of the area shaded on Fig. 3.

(Cambridge IGCSE Geography 0460 Paper 21 Q1e November 2010)

Candidate 1 answer   4/4 marks

The relief is very steep (✓). The area has a pass high in the mountains (✓) between the top of Quoin Bluff and Spear Grass Peak. The area has some cliffs (✓). The western side of the location is more gently sloping than the north or south. The area reaches a height of over 500 metres (✓).

Commentary

This is a good answer where the candidate shows understanding of the key word 'relief'. Four simple descriptive ideas are credited, these are steepness, the pass – a feature of upland areas, cliffs which are indicated in the key, and the highest point.

Candidate 2 answer   2/4 marks

The contours are very steep sloped (✓). It has the shape of a smooth ridge (✓). The Quoin Bluff gets higher towards the centre. Near the 100 m contour we can see a lot of scrub and

Skills link 🔗

You will find out more about how to describe relief of the land on page 202 of Section 4 Geographical Skills.

scattered trees all around Quoin Bluff. In square 9601 there is a small tea plantation. There is also a district boundary passing exactly through the middle of Quoin Bluff.

Commentary

The candidate does gain 2 marks and begins the answer well by show understanding of the term 'relief'. Marks are scored for recognising that the land is steep and that there is an upland feature called a ridge. However, the candidate then fails to maintain the focus on 'relief' and describes irrelevant features of the area. Try to avoid going away from the question when you are answering. You will not gain any marks for an answer which does fit the question.

2   The city of Cambridge in the UK lies close to important transport routes. People commute to work in the CBD from the suburbs and surrounding villages. The city suffers from traffic congestion. Fig. 4 below shows features of the transport routes in and around Cambridge.

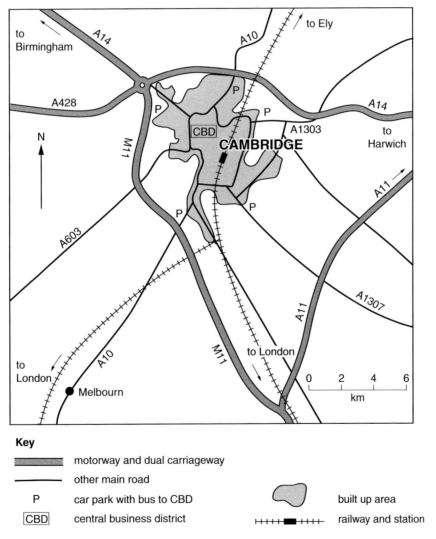

Key

▬▬▬▬	motorway and dual carriageway
————	other main road
P	car park with bus to CBD
CBD	central business district
⌁	built up area
┼┼┼━┼┼┼	railway and station

Fig. 4

(a) What features, shown on Fig. 4, help reduce traffic congestion for long distance travellers who do **not** wish to visit Cambridge?

(Cambridge IGCSE Geography 0460 Paper 21 Q2a November 2010)

Candidate 1 answer   2/2 marks

The M11 motorway (✓) helps to reduce traffic congestion as well as the railway (✓).

Commentary

Both features are credited.

Candidate 2 answer   1/2 marks

The motorway and dual carriageway do not go through Cambridge. This means that they are able to avoid traffic congestion that occurs by going around Cambridge (✓).

Commentary

The motorway and dual carriageway are only credited as one feature; even though the idea is developed the answer only scores 1 mark. A better answer is to name the features, such as the M11 motorway and the A11 main road. If the candidate had done this the answer would have scored 2 marks.

(b) (i) Find the village of Melbourn on Fig. 4. A commuter travels from Melbourn to Cambridge CBD.

Estimate the distance, to the nearest kilometre, that the commuter travels ....kilometres.

State the compass direction in which the commuter travels.

(Cambridge IGCSE Geography 0460 Paper 21 Q2b(i) November 2010)

Candidate 1 answer   2/2 marks

18 (kilometres) (✓)

Northeast (✓)

Skills link

You will find out more about how to measure distance on maps on page 201 of Section 4 Geographical Skills.

Commentary

Both answers are correct

Candidate 2 answer   1/2 marks

14 (kilometres)

Northeast (✓)

Commentary

The measurement is incorrect. The correct compass direction is given.

(b) (ii) Describe and give a reason for the location of the car parks shown on Fig. 4.

(Cambridge IGCSE Geography 0460 Paper 21 Q2b(ii) November 2010)

Candidate 1 answer   3/3 marks

People are able to park their cars outside the city and travel to the CBD (✓) by bus (✓). This reduces the amount of vehicles in the CBD (✓) because more people fit in a bus than in a car.

Commentary

The candidate describes the location of the car parks as 'outside the city' and explains the location by stating that people can travel to the CBD by bus which reduces congestion.

Candidate 2 answer   2/3 marks

The car parks have been strategically located around the CBD, most of them outside the built-up area (✓). They could have

located them around Cambridge so it is easier for the people
to park near where they live and get a bus to the CBD (✓).

Commentary

The candidate describes the location well as 'outside the built-up area'.
The explanation is not credited for the idea of proximity to where people
live, as this may not be true, but the bus link to the CBD is credited.

(c) Suggest **one** way of reducing traffic congestion caused by commuters from the suburbs
of Cambridge.

(Cambridge IGCSE Geography 0460 Paper 21 Q2c November 2010)

Candidate 1 answer   1/1 mark

The commuters could travel there by metro, they would get
an underground train into the CBD (✓). They could also cycle
there if there were routeways.

Commentary

There are many possible answers to this question; the candidate correctly
suggests a type of public transport – underground train. The candidate
also makes a correct second suggestion which is not needed.

Candidate 2 answer   1/1 mark

They could take a bus or train to the city centre (✓).

Commentary

The suggestion to use public transport is correct.

---

3   Study Fig. 5, which shows the Earth's tectonic plates and plate margins and Fig. 6, which shows
the world distribution of active volcanoes.

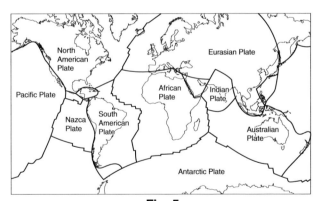

Fig. 5

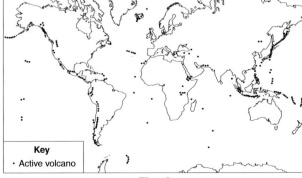

Fig. 6

(a) Using arrows, as shown below, label on Fig. 5 a plate margin where:

(i) plates are moving away from each other (◄——— ———►)

(ii) plates are moving towards each other (———► ◄———)

(Cambridge IGCSE Geography 0460 Paper 21 Q3a November 2010)

Candidate 1 answer   2/2 marks

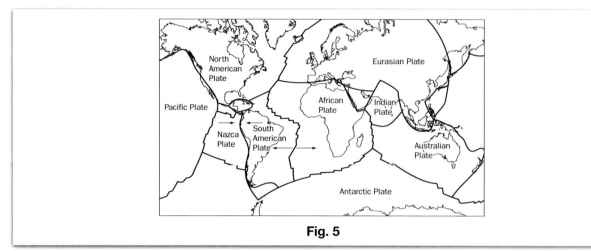

Fig. 5

(i) Arrows positioned on the boundary between the South American and African plates (✓)

(ii) Arrows positioned on the boundary between the South American and Nazca plates (✓)

Commentary

Both sets of arrows are drawn in correct locations.

Candidate 2 answer   1/2 marks

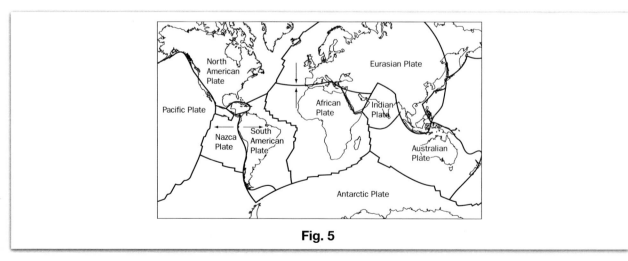

Fig. 5

(i) Arrows positioned on the boundary between the South American and Nazca plates

(ii) Arrows positioned on the boundary between the Eurasian and African plates (✓)

Commentary

The arrows to show the plates moving away from each other are on the wrong boundary. The arrows showing plates moving towards each other are in a correct location.

(b) Which **two** of the following statements about active volcanoes are correct? Tick only **two** statements.

(Cambridge IGCSE Geography 0460 Paper 21 Q3b November 2010)

Statement	Tick
They are mostly found in the centres of plates	
They are mostly found at plate margins	
They are found at every plate margin	
They may be found in the centres of plates	
They are only found at plate margins	

Candidate 1 answer   2/2 marks

They are mostly found at plate margins (✓)

They may be found in the centres of plates (✓)

Commentary

Both statements are correct.

Candidate 2 answer   1/2 marks

They are mostly found at plate margins (✓)

They are found at every plate margin

Commentary

One correct statement is identified. Although it is correct that active volcanoes are found at plate margins they are not found at every plate margin.

(c) Fig. 7 is a map showing some of the effects of the eruption of Mount St Helens, USA, in May 1980.

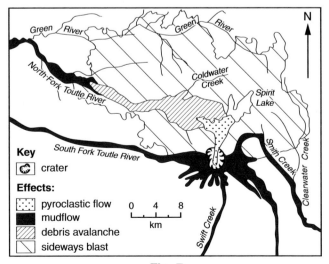

Fig. 7

(c) (i) Which effect of the eruption:

covered over 600 km² north of the crater

occurred in a single, 22 km long band west of Spirit Lake

covered an area from the crater to 8 km further north?

(Cambridge IGCSE Geography 0460 Paper 21 Q3c(i) November 2010)

Candidate 1 answer   3/3 marks

Sideways blast (✓)

Debris avalanche (✓)

Pyroclastic flow (✓)

Commentary

All three effects were correctly identified from the map.

Candidate 2 answer   2/3 marks

Sideways blast (✓)

Mudflow

Pyroclastic flow (✓)

Commentary

Two effects were correctly identified. The mudflow is not correct, even though it is west of the eruption. It is the debris avalanche that is located west of Spirit Lake.

(c) (ii) Suggest a reason for the distribution of mudflows shown on Fig. 7.

(Cambridge IGCSE Geography 0460 Paper 21 Q3c(ii) November 2010)

Candidate 1 answer   1/1 mark

The pyroclastic flow and sideways blast did not allow the mudflows to flow north so they flowed east, south and west following the same paths as rivers and creeks. (✓)

Commentary

The answer is over-elaborate but does include the correct idea that the mudflows followed the valleys.

Candidate 2 answer   1/1 mark

The distribution is mainly caused by the rivers, the South Fork Toutle River and the North Fork Toutle River. (✓)

Commentary

The idea that the mudflows followed the river valleys is credited.

4 Figs 8 and 9 show features seen at a weather station.

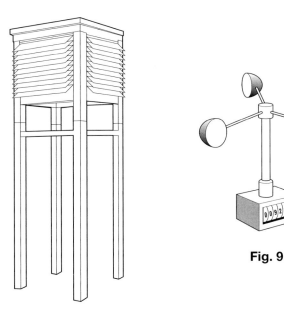

Fig. 9

Fig. 8

(a) (i) Why is the box shown on Fig. 8 raised above the ground?

(Cambridge IGCSE Geography 0460 Paper 21 Q4a(i) November 2010)

Candidate 1 answer 1/1 mark

So that the thermometers do not measure the heat radiated from the ground. (✓)

Commentary

This is a good accurate answer.

Candidate 2 answer 0/1 mark

So that insects or the material on the floor that could get into the box cannot be reached and does not ruin it.

Commentary

The candidate does not appear to have studied how a Stevenson screen operates. The answer is incorrect.

(a) (ii) Why are the sides of the box shown on Fig. 8 louvred (slatted)?

(Cambridge IGCSE Geography 0460 Paper 21 Q4a(ii) November 2010)

Candidate 1 answer 1/1 mark

To allow ventilation of the air (✓) so that the thermometers give an accurate reading of shaded areas.

Commentary

This is another excellent answer which gives two correct reasons: for ventilation and shade.

Candidate 2 answer 0/1 mark

The sides of the box are slatted so that when it rains water will not get inside and ruin it.

Topic link

You will find out more about how to interpret and understand weather instruments on pages 102–05.

Commentary

As in the previous answer, the candidate is not familiar with how a Stevenson screen works.

> **(b) (i)** What feature of the weather does the instrument shown on Fig. 9 measure?
>
> (Cambridge IGCSE Geography 0460 Paper 21 Q4b(i) November 2010)

Candidate 1 answer   1/1 mark

Wind speed (✓)

Commentary

The answer is accurate.

Candidate 2 answer   0/1 mark

Wind

Commentary

The answer is not accurate because different aspects of the wind can be measured (speed and direction).

> **(b) (ii)** What units are used to record this weather feature?
>
> (Cambridge IGCSE Geography 0460 Paper 21 Q4b(ii) November 2010)

Candidate 1 answer   1/1 mark

Metres per second (✓)

Commentary

There are a number of different units which are used to measure wind speed. The candidate correctly chose one of them.

Candidate 2 answer   0/1 mark

How much it spins.

Commentary

The candidate understands how the anemometer works but this is not a unit of measurement.

> **(c)** Clouds are recorded without using any equipment. Fig. 10 shows three types of cloud.

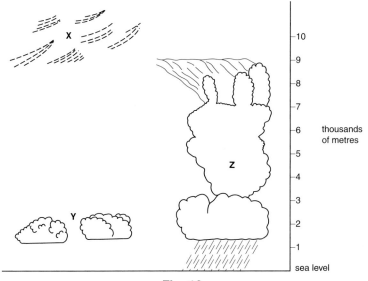

Fig. 10

(c) (i)   Name the **types** of cloud shown on Fig. 10.

(Cambridge IGCSE Geography 0460 Paper 21 Q4c(i) November 2010)

X

Y

Z

Candidate 1 answer   2/3 marks

X Stratus

Y Cumulus (✓)

Z Cumulo-nimbus (✓)

Commentary

Two of the cloud types are identified correctly. The candidate has mixed up stratus cloud with cirrus cloud in answer X.

Candidate 2 answer   1/3 marks

X Wind-blown cloud

Y Cumulus (✓)

Z Storm cloud

Commentary

The candidate correctly identifies one cloud. The description of a cumulo-nimbus cloud as a storm cloud is accurate but it is not the name of the cloud.

(c) (ii)   State the units used to estimate the **amount** of cloud cover.

(Cambridge IGCSE Geography 0460 Paper 21 Q4c(ii) November 2010)

Candidate 1 answer   1/1 mark

Oktas (✓)

Commentary

This is the correct unit.

Candidate 2 answer   1/1 mark

Eighths (✓)

Commentary

This alternative answer is also acceptable.

What is Paper 3?

Paper 3 is your coursework examination. You do not sit an examination paper but complete **one** fieldwork assignment which is set by your teachers and approved by the examination board.

Paper 3 is worth 60 marks but instead of having a time limit like Papers 1 and 2, Paper 3 has a maximum word limit which is 2000 words. The examination board suggest to your teachers that the coursework assignment should take between four and five weeks to complete in classwork and homework time. Your teacher will decide when you do your assignment and how long you will have to complete it.

Your teacher can also decide on the topic to investigate. The topic that is chosen will be:

- interesting to investigate
- relevant to the course and topic which you are studying
- investigated in an area that is local to your school or within easy travelling distance, so you can easily visit the place and possibly return to do further work if necessary
- broken down into different hypotheses or ideas to be tested.

The aims of Paper 3 are:

- to encourage you to think for yourself and test a hypothesis
- to give you the opportunity to use your geographical skills away from the classroom
- to give you an understanding of geographical concepts and theories by testing them.

What is Paper 3 testing?

Doing a coursework assignment tests three objectives:

1 your understanding of the geographical concepts (ideas) which you are testing through fieldwork

2 your data collection and presentation techniques and your analysis of the data

3 your conclusions about the ideas you are investigating and your suggestions for how to improve the investigation.

Why do fieldwork?

Fieldwork is an important part of geography. It gives you the opportunity to go out of the classroom and find out geographical ideas for yourself. You do this by testing these ideas in real places and with real people. This may take place in the grounds of the school, in a local village or town, in a river or coastal area near to school, or further away if you go on a field trip for one or more days.

Fieldwork gives you the chance to learn the methods that geographers use to test ideas and concepts. It gives you the opportunity to work with other students in measuring and collecting data. You will probably discuss in class suitable hypotheses (ideas) to test during your fieldwork, but you should also have the chance to think of and test some hypotheses of your own.

Follow the 'route to geographical enquiry'

Whatever fieldwork investigation you undertake you should follow the 'route to geographical enquiry'. It will help you to plan, undertake, and write about your fieldwork investigation.

1 Identify a topic to investigate and think of some hypotheses to test

Although your teacher may decide the topic, you will have the opportunity to discuss it in class and agree some hypotheses to test. You may also think of some extra hypotheses to test yourself. To think of a suitable hypothesis you need to make a sensible guess of a possible outcome of your investigation. A suitable hypothesis is 'The river will flow faster as it goes downstream', or you could write this hypothesis as a question: 'Does the river flow faster as it goes downstream?'

2 Collect relevant data to test your hypothesis

You can either collect data by yourself or in a group. Often you will do this with other students. You will need to think about safety whilst collecting data, what equipment you will need to take, and how you can make sure that the data which you collect is reliable and accurate. As well as collecting 'primary' data – that is, the information you collect yourself – you can also get data from 'secondary' sources such as the internet, books, maps and newspapers.

3 Record and present your results

You must include maps at different scales to show the location of your study area. Put statistics that you have collected during the fieldwork into tables so that they are clear to read. Draw a variety of graphs, not just one type, but make sure they are appropriate for the data you are displaying. If appropriate, plot some data on a map. Also use field sketches and photographs to illustrate your work.

Skills link

You will find out more about how to record and present your results on pages 212–21.

4 Analyse your results

You must explain what your maps, tables, graphs and diagrams show. Identify the general patterns or trends which your results show. Look for any individual results that do not fit the pattern – these are called anomalies.

5 Make a conclusion about your hypothesis and evaluate your investigation

Look back at your hypothesis. Then refer to your results and analysis to make a conclusion about whether the hypothesis is true and supported by evidence, or not true because there is no evidence to support it. Maybe the evidence of your fieldwork does not clearly prove or disprove your hypothesis. This is also an acceptable conclusion. Your conclusion may lead you to suggest how you might improve the investigation if you were to repeat it, or what extra work you could do with more time.

Practical hints to make your fieldwork successful

Safety

Make safety your first priority. Be sensible to stay safe. Rivers, beaches and town centres are just some fieldwork locations that can be dangerous places. What hazards and dangers do you think a student would need to be aware of at each of these locations?

Answers
- Rivers: deep water, fast-flowing current, wet and slippery rocks, polluted water, animals in the river
- Beaches: large waves, strong current, wet and slippery rocks and groynes, being cut off by rising tide
- Town centres: traffic along busy roads

Precautions

Take the following precautions. They can save a lot of worry.
- Work in pairs or small groups.
- Tell an adult where you are going and what time you will return.
- Take a mobile (cell) phone, making sure it is fully charged.
- Don't do fieldwork in bad weather or when it is dark.
- Wear sensible clothing and footwear.

Equipment

Make sure that you take the correct equipment with you and that you know how to use it. Test the equipment before you set off to make sure that it is working properly.

Planning

Plan your investigation before you set off. If more than one person or group is collecting data, make sure that everyone knows what to do. Each person or group should use the same method of measurement, use the same questionnaire, and do the tally count for the same length of time.

In their evaluation many students say that errors such as inaccurate measuring or different groups not doing the task in the same way have made their results unreliable. Good planning removes this problem.

Practice investigation

It is a good idea to do a practice or 'pilot' investigation before you do the 'real' fieldwork. This gives you the chance to check equipment and your methods, and it might give you an idea of what results you might expect to get in the actual investigation. A practice investigation can be done near school, for example in a local stream or road. You do not need to use your actual investigation site.

Collecting data

Collect as much data and information as you can in the time available. It is better to have more data than you need than not have enough. You can always discard some when you begin to analyse it back at school.

Recording data

Prepare a form for recording your results before you begin your fieldwork. It is much easier to fill in a prepared form than having to write you results out in full. If you are doing fieldwork in wet conditions, keep your recording sheet in a plastic bag or envelope. Many fieldwork investigations are spoiled by having illegible results because the recording sheet has soaked up water!

Politeness

Be polite when speaking to people and asking them questions. Remember that you want them to help you. Explain the purpose of the interview or questionnaire. People will be more willing to give you answers if they know why you want them. Don't ask questions that are intrusive or personal.

The questionnaire on the right was produced by two students. They were investigating the 'catchment area' of their local football club and opinions about whether the club should move its ground to a new location.

Explain why their teacher did not approve the questionnaire.

Hi, my name is Jo and I need to ask you some questions.

1. What is your name?
2. Where do you live?
3. How did you get to the ground?
4. Why have you come?
5. Do you think the club should move the ground or stay here?
6. Where would you like the new ground?
7. Would you go to the new ground?

OK that's it.

Answers

The introduction does not give any background information about the fieldwork.

Jo does not explain why she needs to ask the questions.

Question 1 is irrelevant and personal.

Question 2 is too vague and may not get a precise answer and it is too personal.

Question 3 is badly worded and it would be better if possible alternative answers were given.

Question 4 is probably going to get only one answer – to watch the match.

Question 5 is a closed question and needs to be followed up by asking why the person has given their answer.

Question 6 is too vague and will get too many different locations to be useful.

Question 7 is a closed question and needs to be followed by asking the reason for the answer.

The final comment is abrupt and impolite.

Skills link

You will find out more about how to produce a questionnaire on pages 226–27 of Section 4 Geographical Skills.

How your coursework is marked

If you understand how your coursework is marked it will help you to get higher marks. Your assignment will be marked in 'levels' with Level 1 being the lowest mark for simple work, and Level 3 being the highest mark for detailed work that links together well. Your work is marked in levels under five headings. Your work must improve in quality to reach a higher level. The five headings that are used to mark your coursework are:

- Knowledge with understanding
- Observation and collection of data
- Organisation and presentation of data
- Analysis
- Conclusion and evaluation

How to achieve Level 3 in your coursework assignment

Knowledge with understanding

You need to show good knowledge of the topic which you are investigating in your coursework, for example why land values vary in a city. The best place to do this is probably in the introduction, but you will also be able to show your knowledge in the analysis and conclusion. Do not have too many hypotheses to test (between two and four is best). Make your hypotheses clear to understand and not too complicated. You will then be able to explain what you are trying to find out and why. Candidates who reach Level 3 often add their own extra hypothesis to the ones being tested by the class. This helps the candidate to show more clearly their understanding of the topic.

Observation and collection of data

Describe clearly how you carried out your fieldwork and the methods or techniques you used. There are many different fieldwork techniques which you can use. Some of the more common ones are listed in the table below. These techniques are described in Section 4 Geographical Skills. Level 3 answers also explain why the candidate uses these methods (not just because their teacher told them to!).

Common fieldwork techniques

Questionnaire
Interview
Sampling
Perception study, e.g. as part of an environmental survey
Land use mapping, e.g. the CBD, farm
Field sketching
Counting, e.g. pedestrians or traffic
Measuring: River, e.g. depth, width, velocity, cross-section, wetted perimeter, load, gradient Coast, e.g. longshore drift, beach material, waves, beach profile, cliff profile Weather, e.g. temperature, rainfall, wind speed and direction, pressure, relative humidity, cloud cover and type

Organisation and presentation of data

To achieve Level 3 you should put your work in a logical order. This order will probably be:

1 Explain what you are investigating and state your hypotheses.

2 Describe your methods of investigation.

3 Display your results.

4 Analyse your results.

5 Make a conclusion to your investigation, evaluate your fieldwork and suggest improvements.

If your work is not in this order you will not be awarded Level 3 for this section. For example, do not describe your investigation methods before explaining why you are investigating the topic.

It is also important to use a range of methods for presenting the data which you have collected. Some methods are more complex than others and so gain you more credit. If you only display your results in bar graphs or pie charts, even if they are computer-generated, you will only be awarded Level 2 for this section. You need to use more challenging presentation techniques to achieve Level 3, for example a map with proportional symbols or flow lines.

Skills link

You will find out more about how to draw proportional symbols and flow lines on page 217 of Section 4 Geographical Skills.

Analysis

The best way to achieve Level 3 for this section is to include a high-level method of presentation, such as a scatter graph with a trend line drawn on it, and use this as part of your analysis by including a written commentary next to the graph which identifies the important information shown on it. You may also link the graph to your original hypothesis and make a comment about whether the evidence supports it or not. By linking the data and analysis you can show a high level of understanding. This is a much better approach than drawing lots of graphs and having a separate section for analysis.

Conclusion and evaluation

To achieve Level 3 you must refer back to your hypotheses and summarise the information which you have found to support each one. You should also refer to the information that was inconclusive or suggested the opposite of what you expected to find. From this you can make your own conclusion about the hypotheses.

A Level 3 evaluation will identify how reliable the information which you collected might be and what factors affected its reliability. Do not focus your evaluation on what went wrong during the fieldwork, such as 'there was not enough time to collect data' or 'people would not answer my questions'. These may have affected your results but they are really weaknesses which should have been avoided.

You may include in your evaluation your thoughts about how useful the results might be and which groups of people might benefit from the conclusions you reached. For example, you might suggest how an area may be improved based on your results of a perception survey. You might also include in your evaluation new hypotheses which could be tested in future fieldwork.

Preparation for Paper 3

To do well in your coursework assignment it is important that you:
- think of clear hypotheses to test
- prepare your investigation before you go to do the fieldwork
- collect relevant data
- link your analysis to the different maps and graphs that you draw
- think carefully about what your investigation shows about your hypotheses and write about this in your conclusion.

Examples of two coursework investigations which achieved Level 3 marks

You have now found out more about what Paper 3 is about and how to produce good coursework. Next you have the opportunity to look in detail at two examples of coursework which were produced by two candidates who are aiming to achieve Level 3 in each section of marking (see page 278 for a reminder of these headings). These are followed by comments and advice that you might get from your teacher.

Study the coursework produced by the two candidates. Can you understand how Level 3 is achieved? Finally read the commentary, which explains the awarding of the level and, where appropriate, gives advice about how the work could be improved.

Example 1 A river study

Knowledge with understanding

The candidate writes a general introduction about the river and the area which it flows through, describing the relief of the area and the location of the source and mouth of the river. This is supported by two maps: a small-scale map showing the position of the river in the country, and a large-scale map showing the river drainage basin.

The candidate identifies five survey sites and locates them on the map of the drainage basin. She also describes the landscape at each site and explains why these sites were chosen.

Next the candidate states the aim of the investigation: 'To find out if this river has typical characteristics of a river'. She follows this with five hypotheses which she will be testing to investigate the overall aim. These hypotheses are:

1 River velocity increases with distance from the source.

2 River depth increases with distance from the source.

3 The length of the river cross-section increases with distance from the source.

4 The wetted perimeter of the river increases with distance from the source.

5 Bedload size and roughness decrease with distance from the source.

The candidate supports her hypotheses with a brief explanation of why she expects these changes to occur downstream. For hypothesis 5 she writes:

> I believe that this would be an appropriate hypothesis because a typical river's bedload size decreases with distance from the source due to the increase in velocity in the water. This increase in velocity increases the river's ability to transport rocks and to erode them, making them smaller and more rounded. I believe that as you get closer to the river's mouth, the bedload would gradually change from larger, more angular boulders to small, round pebbles.

Commentary

This is a high Level 3 piece of work. The introduction contains relevant background information about the river. The maps help to put the river 'in context' so that it is clear where the investigation has been carried out. The large-scale map is useful to show the locations of the investigation sites. The aim of the study and the hypotheses are straightforward and stated clearly. The explanation of each hypothesis shows understanding of the processes that are being investigated. Five hypotheses are more than usual but the results will provide a comprehensive conclusion to the study's aim.

Weaker fieldwork studies:

- do not include maps so they do not locate the investigation
- do not explain why the hypotheses are being tested
- contain a lot of theory often copied from a textbook – a little theoretical background is useful but the main focus must be on the practical tasks.

Observation and collection of data

The candidate works with three other students to collect data. Having identified five investigation sites the group go to each of the sites in turn to do their fieldwork. For each hypothesis the candidate includes a list of the equipment which the group used, with photographs and drawings where needed. She describes in detail their method of data collection for each hypothesis. This is supported by field sketches of each site and labelled photographs of the students making their measurements. The candidate's description of the method used to test hypothesis 1 (River velocity increases with distance from the source) is as follows:

> To find the average velocity at each point in the river we measured out a length of 10 metres along the river using the tape measure. One member of the group stood at each end of the 10 metre distance. The person upstream had the float and the other person had the stopwatch. The person placed the float in the river when the person downstream started the stopwatch. When the float reached the person downstream she stopped the stopwatch, called out the time taken and it was recorded. This was repeated five times to make sure that the result was reliable, and then an average time was calculated.
>
> To limit air resistance the group used a thin piece of wood (painted red so it could be seen easily). This floats on the surface. However, this technique only measures the surface velocity of the river, which is not the greatest velocity due to friction slowing it down. A more accurate way to measure velocity is to use a flowmeter but we did not have this equipment. In the test, sometimes the float got stuck behind rock or reeds in the river or got washed into the side of the river and did not move. So we had to repeat that test.

Photographs show the students laying out the tape along the bank to measure 10 metres downstream, and the float in the river.

Commentary

The measuring method is described and explained in detail and meets the requirements of Level 3. The method is justified and the candidate comments on the weaknesses of the test and the problems encountered whilst collecting the data.

Weaker fieldwork studies:

- do not describe the method in detail
- do not explain the method used
- focus on problems that are due to 'operator error', such as not timing the test accurately; these are not weaknesses in the methodology of the fieldwork but are examples of poor fieldwork technique.

Organisation and presentation of data

The fieldwork report is organised so that there is a different section for each hypothesis. In each section the candidate follows the same order:

1 Description of the method (as shown above)
2 Record of data collected in a data table

3 Presentation of the data in an appropriate graph

4 Analysis of the data

The data collected at one site to test hypothesis 2 (River depth increases with distance from the source) is shown below. This data was also collected and plotted on graphs for the other four sites.

Distance across river (m)	Depth of river (cm)
0	0
0.5	13
1	21
1.5	16
2	17
2.5	21
3	20
3.5	18
4	21
4.5	19
5	15
5.5	14
6	6
6.5	0

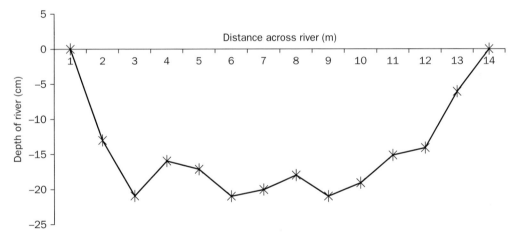

A different type of graph or diagram is used to illustrate each hypothesis, including a sketch of the river with flow lines to show velocity in hypothesis 1, and a multiple bar graph to show bedload size and roughness in hypothesis 5.

Commentary

This is acceptable for Level 3. The coursework has a clear structure which makes it easy to follow and understand. The method, results, data presentation and analysis are linked for each hypothesis. The diagrams and graphs can be easily compared to see any changes downstream.

The candidate uses a computer program to produce the graphs. Whilst this is acceptable, the candidate needs to make sure that the graph is accurate. In the graph above the distances across the river are points 1–14, not the actual distance across the river as shown in the data table. The river should also be shaded to show the channel clearly.

Weaker fieldwork studies:

- do not show organisation in the written work
- put all the results together, all the graphs and diagrams together, all the analyses together – there is no integration of the different parts, which makes it difficult to relate the results, presentation and analysis for each separate hypothesis
- do not contain a variety of appropriate presentation methods – they are often restricted to one type of graph.

Analysis

The candidate makes an analysis of the results for each hypothesis. She begins her analysis by describing what the results showed, including the identification of a pattern which supports the hypothesis and picking out anomalies that do not fit with the hypothesis. The results of hypothesis 4 ('The wetted perimeter of the river increases with distance from the source) are shown below, with the candidate's analysis of these results.

Investigation site	Length of wetted perimeter
1	2.0
2	6.4
3	11.8
4	7.8
5	8.1

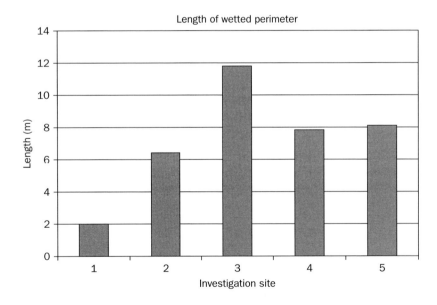

Length of wetted perimeter

You can see from the graph that site 1 has the shortest wetted perimeter. However, site 3 has the longest measurement, which does not fit the overall pattern that the wetted perimeter gets longer away from the source. The wetted perimeter at site 3 is more than three metres wider than site 5, which should be the largest according to the hypothesis. The graph also shows that sites 1, 2, 4 and 5 fit the pattern as the wetted perimeter gradually increases in length.

Overall these measurements prove the hypothesis is correct. The river is typical in terms of its wetted perimeter, as it increases from 2 metres at site 1 to 8.1 metres at site 5. Site 3 is much wider than would be expected. This might be because the river is joined by a tributary at this site and so the river channel is wider.

Skills link

You will find out more about how to interpret maps and graphs on pages 200–21 of Section 4 Geographical Skills.

Commentary

There is a clear analysis of the results for each hypothesis. The candidate describes how the results change downstream and suggests why the results may vary, including an explanation of any anomaly, as shown above. The explanation may not clearly explain the anomaly but the student is showing understanding of a possible reason. This is supported by a photograph of site 3 which does not fit the overall pattern. The candidate refers back to the hypothesis in each individual analysis. This is clearly a Level 3 analysis.

Weaker fieldwork studies:

- include a simple level of analysis which is usually a description of the graph or results
- do not attempt to explain the results
- do not identify anomalies
- include the analysis at the end of the investigation report but it is not linked back to individual hypotheses.

Conclusion and evaluation

The candidate goes back to the original aim of the study which was stated in the introduction. She makes the conclusion that the river has typical characteristics which change downstream. She follows this with a conclusion to each individual hypothesis, as shown below for hypothesis 1.

My first hypothesis 'River velocity increases with distance from the source' was proved to be correct. I discovered that site 1 did have the slowest velocity and that site 5, furthest from the source, did have the fastest velocity. This shows that the river is a typical river in terms of river velocity. However, site 3 was irregular and had a greater velocity than sites 4 and 5, meaning that this point in the river was not typical.

Later in the conclusion the candidate writes:

Site 3 did not fit the pattern of any of the hypotheses, so it must be an anomaly. I think that the main reason for this is that the river is joined by a tributary before that site and therefore there is suddenly a lot of extra water in the river. This might explain why the results are different for site 3.

Finally the candidate makes an evaluation of her investigation. She picks out some weaknesses in methodology and suggests how it could be improved in the future, for example as in the following comment about measuring velocity:

The equipment which was available to us was not very accurate which meant that our measurements could have been inaccurate. When measuring the velocity of the river the float would only show the surface velocity of the river and would get slowed down by obstacles such as large rocks.

The candidate also suggests strengths of the investigation which she believes makes the conclusion acceptable. She writes:

> As we were in groups of four there were many helping hands when collecting the information. We could have one person recording the results, whilst the other members of the group took the measurements. Also the investigations and measurements were repeated a few times so that we got enough data to calculate an average for all the measurements.

Commentary

The conclusions are well thought out and worth Level 3. They are relevant to the data which has been collected and fit the analysis of these results. The candidate also makes an overall evaluation of the investigation which draws together the conclusions about the separate hypotheses. The candidate also recognises weaknesses in her methodology and suggests how they can be improved. The suggestions are sensible and practical and will increase the reliability of the results.

Weaker fieldwork studies:

- do not link the conclusion back to the original aim or hypotheses
- often just repeat the analysis in the conclusion
- have a negative evaluation which blames the other members of the group for inaccurate results
- suggest improvements such as 'repeat the experiment', 'take more care in measuring', 'check our results carefully' but there is no explanation how these will be done.

Example 2 A study of tourism

Knowledge with understanding

The candidate begins the investigation report with a question:

> Why has my local area grown as a centre for tourism and what impact has the growth of tourism had on the area?

In his introduction the candidate briefly describes the physical and human attractions of the area and locates the area on a map of the country. He then states that the aim of the study will be 'To find out what attracts tourists to this area and what impact tourism has had on the area'. To do this he puts forward three hypotheses:

1 Tourists will be attracted by both physical and human factors.

2 The impact of tourism on local people will be more positive than negative.

3 Areas near the coast will have most visitors compared to areas which are inland.

The candidate supports his hypotheses with a brief explanation of why he expects these outcomes. For hypothesis 3 he writes:

In tourist areas there will be more traffic and pedestrians than areas where locals live. The areas near the coast will be busiest because this is where many tourist attractions, such as the beaches and entertainment parks, are located. Areas which are not near the coast will not be as busy because people in these areas are working and shopping and doing their daily tasks.

Commentary

This is a Level 3 piece of work. The introduction makes it clear what is the main focus of the investigation and where the investigation is taking place. It is clear that there are two parts to the investigation:

1 Why do tourists visit the local area?

2 What impact does tourism have on the area?

The aim is reflected in the hypotheses. These hypotheses are quite complex and each one contains two elements to consider: physical and human factors in hypothesis 1; positive and negative impacts in hypothesis 2; coastal and inland in hypothesis 3. The explanation of the hypotheses, like the one shown above for hypothesis 3, shows clear understanding of what the candidate predicts that the outcomes of the investigation will be.

Weaker fieldwork studies:
- do not locate the study area
- use simple hypotheses
- do not suggest what the outcome of the investigation will be.

Observation and collection of data

The candidate works as part of a group to collect data. Each hypothesis requires a different method of investigation. Hypotheses 1 and 2 were researched by different questionnaires, and hypothesis 3 was investigated through a traffic survey and a pedestrian count done in different parts of the area. These different fieldwork techniques give the candidate opportunities to plan and organise them. This is shown in the candidate's description of the method used to test hypothesis 1 (Tourists will be attracted by both physical and human factors) as follows:

> We conducted interviews with tourists. Our first task was to devise a questionnaire which we could use with visitors. We produced the questionnaire shown below. First we had to ask if the person we wished to interview was a visitor. If they were not we thanked them and moved to the next person. We divided the attractions into physical and human groups. We asked for the overall attraction last to see which group people thought was more important. We went to the main tourist area where there are lots of hotels to use our questionnaire.

Commentary

The collection of data meets the requirements of Level 3 because a range of investigation techniques are used. These different methods also provide opportunities for the students to work in pairs and in a group. The questionnaire shown on the right, which is used to investigate hypothesis 1, is easy to understand and can be completed quickly. The candidate shows that he has considered in advance likely

---

Tourist questionnaire

We are doing a tourism survey as part of our Geography coursework. If you are a visitor please will you answer the following questions?

1. What are the main physical attractions which you are visiting?

   Waterfalls ☐
   Mountains ☐
   Hot springs ☐
   Botanical gardens ☐
   Wildlife reserve ☐
   Butterfly farms ☐
   Gorge ☐

2. What are the main human attractions which you are visiting?

   Hill villages ☐
   National museum ☐
   Flower market ☐
   Temples ☐
   Royal palace ☐
   Prehistoric sites ☐
   Royal pagoda ☐

3. Overall which attracted you most to this area?

   Physical attractions ☐
   Human attractions ☐

Thank you for your time.

responses to the questionnaire and has made the task of recording the answers easier by providing a number of alternatives to choose from. This technique will also make the calculation of results easier. The questionnaire contains a brief introduction to explain why the students are doing this survey. It is also polite and contains simple instructions. The candidate does not explain if any sampling technique was used to select people to interview in order to get an unbiased sample.

Weaker fieldwork studies:

- include only one technique such as a questionnaire
- do not organise the methodology to make results easy to calculate
- do not explain why different techniques are being used.

Organisation and presentation of data

The fieldwork report is organised so that for each hypothesis the tasks are put in the same order: description of the method, recording and presentation of data, analysis. The different fieldwork techniques produce varied pieces of data which are recorded in tables under the appropriate hypotheses.

For hypothesis 1 the results rank the physical and human attractions which are plotted on two bar graphs. For hypothesis 2 the results show positive and negative impacts which are plotted on pie charts. For hypothesis 3 the results show traffic data which is drawn as flow lines on a local map, and pedestrian flows which are used to plot an isoline map of the area.

Commentary

The structure of the coursework is logical and easy to follow and understand. The different methods of displaying the data which has been collected are clearly Level 3. These methods include simple techniques such as a bar graph or pie chart, and more complex techniques such as flow lines and isoline construction. These presentation methods are appropriate for the data which they are being used to display. The presentation of pedestrian and traffic data makes it possible to see the contrasts needed for high-level analysis.

Weaker fieldwork studies:

- use simple map or graph techniques, and often only one presentation method is used
- do not use maps to display fieldwork data – everything is shown on graphs whether or not it is appropriate to do so
- only use results for one area.

Analysis

The candidate analyses each set of results in turn. He does this by summarising what the results show and then explaining why these results were found. His analysis for hypothesis 1 (Tourists will be attracted by both physical and human factors) is shown with the results of the questionnaire survey below.

Skills link

You will find out more about how to produce a questionnaire on pages 226–27 of Section 4 Geographical Skills.

You will find out more about sampling techniques on page 228 of Section 4 Geographical Skills.

Skills link

You will find out more about how to draw flow lines and plot an isoline map on pages 216–17 of Section 4 Geographical Skills.

Q1 Physical attractions	Number of visits made
Mountains	42
Waterfalls	35
Wildlife reserve	34
Gorge	20
Hot springs	19
Botanical gardens	13
Butterfly farms	7
Total	170

Q2 Human attractions	Number of visits made
Outdoor market	45
Hill villages	33
Temples	27
Prehistoric sites	11
National museum	10
Royal pagodas	8
Royal palace	6
Total	140

Q3 Overall opinion	Number of tourists
Physical attractions	38
Human attractions	32

You can see from the results that the mountains and waterfalls attracted many people. This is because of the beautiful natural scenery and also because there are human attractions in the area such as whitewater rafting, trekking trails and the hill villages. This will also explain why these villages are a main attraction because they are only found in this area. The wildlife reserve is also a popular attraction as it is world-famous and many visitors want to go to it.

The most popular human attraction was the outdoor market which is in a main tourist area of the city. It is easy to get to and many people will go there to buy the craft products and local foods. The temples are also popular with visitors who are interested in the history of the country.

Overall the physical attractions are more popular than the human attractions, but there is not much difference between them. The overall opinion of visitors is that they are attracted by both types of attractions. Most visitors go to both physical and human attractions which are in the same area, such as the mountains and the villages.

Commentary

There is a clear analysis of the results for each hypothesis, as shown in the analysis of hypothesis 1 above. The candidate describes the main pattern of results and highlights the main attractions. He realises that physical and human attractions may be found together, which will help to explain the pattern of results. He also suggests why these attractions are most popular. His final point of analysis is excellent. He does not simply state that physical attractions are more popular but shows his understanding that there is little difference between the results.

For the other hypotheses the candidate describes the patterns shown by the maps and graphs and any results which do not fit the overall pattern. A good analysis of a flow-line diagram and an isoline map are both Level 3 responses. His analysis of how the tourist and local areas are different also meets Level 3 criteria.

Weaker fieldwork studies:

- describe the results of a survey but do not explain the results
- do not describe spatial variations on a map
- do not explain variations between areas.

Conclusion and evaluation

The candidate makes a conclusion to each hypothesis in turn. Most candidates agree that their hypothesis is correct. However, a Level 3 conclusion will also refer to results that do not agree with the hypothesis. The candidate's conclusion to hypothesis 1 is as follows:

> I conclude that it is both the physical landscape and its culture which attract tourists to the local area. From the results of the questionnaire you can see that they mostly come for the mountains, shopping, waterfalls and the hill villages. More people say that they are attracted by physical than by human attractions but I think many visitors will come to see both. The most popular attraction is shopping at the outdoor market which attracts many visitors because it is easily accessible.

The candidate makes an excellent evaluation of his investigation. He identifies four factors that could have affected his results. These include factors affecting the questionnaire and pedestrian and traffic counts shown below.

> We asked 70 people to complete the questionnaire which is a good sample size. We would have asked more people but some tourists did not speak English as their first language and so did not understand what we were asking.
>
> The problem with the traffic survey and pedestrian count is that they were not all taken at the same time of the day. This meant that the results could be affected by factors like people going to and from work. If we repeat these surveys we would have to make sure that different groups do the counts at the same time.

Commentary

The conclusion tends to repeat some of the ideas from the analysis section. Also the conclusion neither agrees with nor rejects the hypothesis. The candidate does make a decision about hypothesis 1 but does not say exactly what this decision is.

The candidate's evaluation is well thought out and includes practical difficulties such as trying to use a questionnaire with people for whom English was not their first language. This is a common problem with questionnaires. One way to overcome the difficulty is to have one member of the group who can speak the local language. Carrying out the pedestrian count and traffic survey at different times is a common error and this should be considered when planning an investigation. Overall this section is worth a lower Level 3 mark.

Weaker fieldwork studies:

- use the conclusion to describe again the methodology and how the results are presented
- state that the hypothesis is correct or incorrect but give no explanation to support this conclusion
- suggest that a way to improve the investigation is to 'gather more information'
- suggest improvements such as 'repeat the experiment', 'take more care in measuring', 'check our results carefully' but there is no explanation how these will be done.

Learning objectives:

> confidently prepare for the Paper 4 examination

> fully understand the examination questions

> make the best use of resources in the examination paper.

What is Paper 4?

Paper 4 is an alternative examination paper if you do not do a coursework assignment. You may still do fieldwork assignments in class and in your school grounds and local area but they will not be assessed by the examination board. The aims of Paper 4 are:

- to encourage you to think for yourself and apply your understanding to different geographical questions
- to give you the opportunity to use geographical investigation skills in an examination.

What is Paper 4 testing?

The examination tests three objectives:

1 your understanding of the ideas being investigated

2 collection and presentation of data and your analysis of this data

3 your conclusions about the ideas being investigated and suggestions to improve the investigation.

You will not be told which objective each question is testing but you will recognise the objectives by the wording of the question.

How to use your time effectively

The Paper 4 examination is 1 hour 30 minutes long. In this time you must answer two questions; each question is worth 30 marks and is broken down into several parts. If you divide the duration of the examination by the number of marks to be earned – that is, 90/60 – it means that you have 1½ minutes per mark, so a question worth 4 marks should take about six minutes to answer. You should not think too much about this in the examination itself, so allow yourself about 45 minutes for each question – but remember: you also need to allow time to:

- read the question all the way through to make sure you understand the investigation topic
- study the insert and check which question each resource is used with
- check your answers at the end of the examination and make sure you complete any answers which you may have missed out.

To have the time to do all this it may be better to allow yourself 40 minutes to answer each question and use the extra 10 minutes on the other tasks. The mark allocation (shown in brackets at the end of each question) is a good guide about the length of answer or amount of detail required. The higher the mark allocation the more detail is required. The number of lines provided for your answer is another simple guide as to how long your answer needs

Tip

Keep a check on time during the examination and use all your time.

to be. Remember that in Paper 4 in particular, answers may also involve doing tasks such as:

- plotting data onto maps and graphs
- doing calculations
- reading information from maps and graphs.

These tasks do not require any extended writing but the mark allocation can still be used as a guide as to how much time you should spend on answering the question.

Tip

Follow the mark allocation.

Understanding the question

The two questions in Paper 4 will test different themes from the syllabus. One question may test a 'human' theme and the other question may test a 'physical' theme. There are three components of each question: the introduction, the hypotheses, and the individual parts of each question.

The introduction

The focus of each question is explained in the introduction which 'sets the scene'.

What is the focus of the following question?

Question 1

> A group of students studied how a river changes downstream. They wanted to see if the river was typical of most rivers.
> (Adapted from Cambridge IGCSE Geography 0460 Paper 4 Q2a June 2009)

The focus is a river investigation.

The hypothesis

Each question includes two hypotheses. These describe what the students are testing in order to reach a conclusion which they can explain. The hypothesis is a statement which you may find evidence to support or to disagree with, or you may not make a definite decision.

Tip

Make a decision about the hypothesis where needed and state this decision.

The following hypotheses follow the introduction above.

> The students decided to test the following hypotheses:
>
> **Hypothesis 1:** Velocity increases downstream.
>
> **Hypothesis 2:** The size and shape of the bedload changes downstream.
> (Adapted from Cambridge IGCSE Geography 0460 Paper 4 Q2a June 2009)

The questions

One question is shown below.

> The students selected six sampling sites along the course of the river. Suggest **three** factors the students should have considered in choosing the sample sites.
> (Adapted from Cambridge IGCSE Geography 0460 Paper 4 Q2a June 2009)

Important words

Many candidates lose marks in the examination because they do not read carefully or understand important words in the question. Before you answer a question you should read it carefully. Use a pen to underline the important words or use a highlighter. The important words are:

- 'command' words which tell you what to do in the question
- 'context' words which tell you what the question is about.

Command words are particularly important as they tell you how to answer the question. You need to know what each command word means and follow its instructions. If you do not know the meaning of the command word you will answer the question incorrectly.

The important words in the following questions are highlighted:

Tip

Read the command words carefully. Do not explain when the question says 'describe'.

Tip

Support your decision with evidence from resources where required.

> **What is meant by** (command words) the term **'sampling'** (context words)?
>
> **To what extent** (command words) is the hypothesis: **'The number of visitors to the safari park varies during the year'** (context words) accurate? **Use evidence** (command words) from the Table and Fig. to support your view.

What are the important words in the following questions?

- To measure atmospheric pressure the students used a barometer. Describe how the students would do this investigation.
- Whilst doing the investigation one student suggested that tourism may increase the amount of litter in the area. Suggest a suitable hypothesis to test this idea and describe how the students could investigate your hypothesis.
- Describe two possible problems in measuring river velocity.
- What is a pilot study and why is it important in an investigation?
  (Adapted from Cambridge IGCSE Geography 0460 Paper 41 Q1c (i) November 2010)
- What decisions would the students have to make on organising and carrying out the survey on the impact of tourism?
  (Adapted from Cambridge IGCSE Geography 0460 Paper 41 Q1c (ii) November 2010)
- Identify one similarity and one difference between the results for the two sites.
  (Adapted from Cambridge IGCSE Geography 0460 Paper 41 Q1d (ii) November 2010)
- State two human activities which could cause air pollution.
  (Adapted from Cambridge IGCSE Geography 0460 Paper 41 Q2a (i) November 2010)
- Use information from Figs 1 and 2 to explain why the level of acidity in rainfall varies with the wind direction.
  (Adapted from Cambridge IGCSE Geography 0460 Paper 41 Q2c (v) November 2010)

Command words used in Paper 4

Recall information, example or fact

Identify (pick out something from information you are given)

State   Name   Give (short answers using your own knowledge)

What (another way to ask you to recall information you have learned)

Identify one similarity and one difference between the results at the two sites.

State two safety precautions that students should take when doing fieldwork in a river.

Name two pieces of information shown by a wind vane.

Give three characteristics which may indicate the position of the centre of the town.

What is a pilot study?

Give a definition

Define   What is meant by   Give the meaning of (what the word or phrase means)

Define 'sphere of influence'

What is meant by 'systematic sampling'?

Which of the following definitions is the correct **meaning of** 'relative humidity'?

Description

Describe (give the main points about something)

Describe two differences between the rainfall patterns at the school and the airport. [2 marks] (you need to use a graph from the examination paper)

Describe one appropriate sampling method used to obtain a sample of people to be interviewed. [3 marks] (you must answer by using your own knowledge of what you have revised)

Describe how students could carry out an investigation into one other aspect of life in a squatter settlement. [4 marks] (you must answer by using your understanding of how to do a fieldwork investigation)

Tip

Notice the different mark allocations which mean that the descriptions will need different amounts of detail.

Explanation

Give/Suggest reasons   Explain   Why   What (why something happens or reasons)

Give two **reasons** why the students did the pedestrian count at five different times during the day. (only two reasons are required)

Suggest reasons why the velocity of the river varied between the two sections of river. (look at the mark allocation for a guide of the number of reasons required)

Explain the process of longshore drift.

Why is a pilot study important?

What did the students learn from the investigation about the impact of longshore drift on the movement of pebbles?

Tip

Command words are often linked together, such as 'describe and explain'.

Identify similarities and differences

Compare (you need to give similarities and differences)

Contrast/Identify the differences between (you only need to give differences)

Compare the buildings shown in the two photographs.

Contrast the land use in the two areas shown on the map.

Identify two **differences between** the beach profiles.

Tip

Your answer needs comparison or contrast in a sentence. Do not give two separate descriptions and leave it to the examiner to make the comparison or contrast.

Make a judgment or reach a conclusion

To what extent (you need to work out how much support the results give to your conclusion)

Do you agree (answer 'yes, I agree' or 'no, I do not agree' and be prepared to explain your decision)

What conclusion (decide if the hypothesis is true or false and be prepared to explain your conclusion)

Do the results (answer 'yes' or 'no' and be prepared to explain your answer)

To what extent do the results shown in the table support the hypothesis?

The students concluded that the hypothesis was correct. **Do you agree** with them?

Using the data which they collected, **what conclusion** could the students make about the hypothesis?

Do the results of the investigation agree with the hypothesis?

Data

Estimate (you may not be able to measure accurately so give an approximate result)

Calculate (you may use a calculator to work out the answer)

Use data/evidence (refer to figures from a table or graph or information from another resource)

Support your answer/conclusion (use data or other information)

Estimate the average measurement from the top of the groyne to the beach.

Calculate the average rainfall per day at the airport.

Use data from Table 1 to complete the bar graph.

Use data from Fig. 4 to **support your conclusion**.

Practical

Complete (fill in the missing information)

Draw (this refers to lines or graphs not pictures)

Shade in (make your shading clear and accurate)

Complete the recording sheet by inserting the correct total

On Fig. 4 **draw** the isoline to show 100 pedestrians.

Shade in the part of the river where the current is greater than 40 cm per second.

Resources

Finally, before you answer each question check that you are looking at and using the correct resources from the examination paper and insert. This is particularly important in Paper 4 as you are instructed to look at and use many different resources and you will waste time by looking at the wrong one.

Many different types of resources are used in a geography examination, particularly Paper 4. The following table summarises the main types of resource used in Paper 4.

Tip

If you use a calculator to do a calculation, you will still need to show your working.

Tip

Be careful not to miss out these practical questions. There will not be any answer lines so answer on the resource indicated. This may be a map, graph, table or diagram.

Tip

Maps, graphs and diagrams contain valuable information. Do not ignore them.

Examples of types of resources used in Paper 4

Map	Large-scale map such as a town plan or map to show river fieldwork sites Isoline map to show pedestrian flow Land use map of an industrial area
Graph	Line graph to show river velocity at different sites Bar graph to show height of vegetation Wind rose Dispersion graph to show the results of an environmental quality survey Pie chart to show types of shops and services in a village Scatter graph to show the relationship between wind direction and rainfall
Photograph	Fieldwork equipment such as a flowmeter Feature such as a coastal groyne Aerial view of an industrial area
Table	Data such as results from a traffic survey Results of river measurements Information such as results of a questionnaire
Diagram	Fieldwork equipment such as a flowmeter Recording sheet of fieldwork measurements Field sketch such as sand dunes
Information	Questionnaire used in a tourist survey Factfile of information about a topic such as acid rain

Remember that these resources may be included in the examination paper itself or in the separate insert. In Paper 4 you may be required to put information onto a resource or read and interpret information from the resource. This is shown in the following examples.

Tip

Use data accurately, both for plotting and interpreting.

Include the correct units of measurement where required.

Example 1

The students recorded their results in a summary table. Use these results to complete the scatter graph and draw in a best-fit line.

The students accepted the hypothesis: Rainfall is more acidic after a period of dry weather. Do you agree with them? Support your answer with evidence from the completed scatter graph.

Example 2

Use the data from the results table to draw in the flow lines on the map to show the number of vehicles travelling along Station Road at 17.00.

Use the information on the two maps to describe the variation in traffic at the two survey times of 08.00 and 17.00 along Independence Way.

It is important that you take care when plotting data because marks are only awarded for accurate answers. Look at the two answers (A and B) to each task below and decide which answer is correct.

Task 1: Use the results in the table below to complete Fig. 4, to show the average height of vegetation at points 8, 9, 10 and 11 across the transect at Site A.

sample point	1	2	3	4	5	6	7	8	9	10	11
average height of vegetation (cm)	14	11	7	4	2	0	3	4	5	12	17

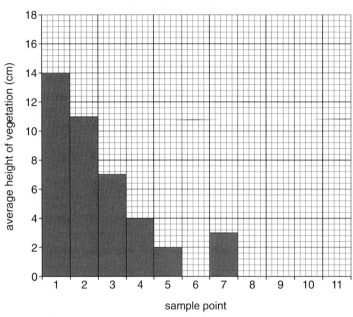

Fig. 4

(Adapted from Cambridge IGCSE Geography 0460 Paper 4 Q1a (iii) November 2009)

Answer A

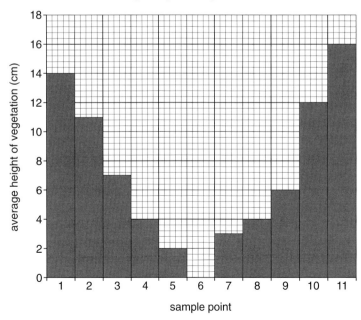

Fig. 4

Answer B

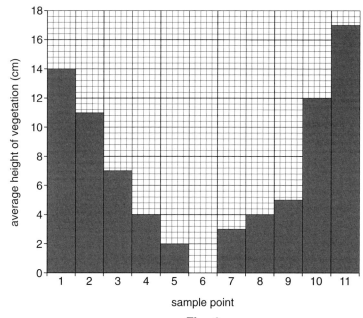

Average height of vegetation at Site A

Fig. 4

Task 2: On Fig. 3 shade in the land valued above 60 thousand US$/m².

(Adapted from Cambridge IGCSE Geography 0460 Paper 4 Q1f (ii) June 2007)

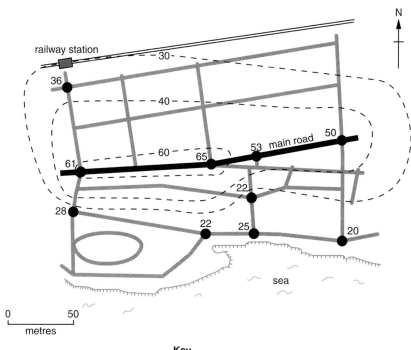

Key

– -60- – isoline of land value (thousand US$/m²)

━━━ minor road

Fig. 3

Answer A

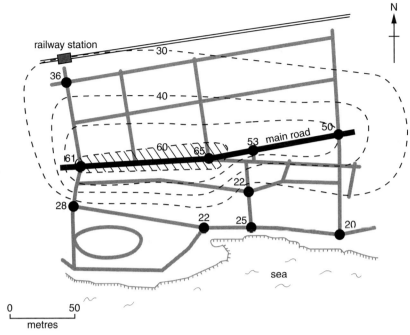

railway station

30

36

40

50

60 65 53 main road 50

61

22

28

22 25 20

sea

0 50
metres

Key

– -60- – isoline of land value (thousand US\$/m²)

minor road

Fig. 3

Answer B

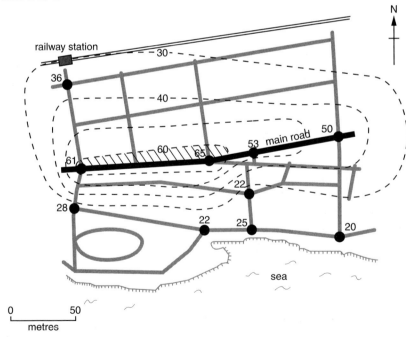

railway station

30

36

40

60 65 53 main road 50

61

22

28

22 25 20

sea

0 50
metres

Key

– -60- – isoline of land value (thousand US\$/m²)

minor road

Fig. 3

Preparation for Paper 4

To do well in this paper it is important to have experience of carrying out real fieldwork assignments. The best way to prepare for Paper 4 is to do simple geographical investigations where appropriate during your geography course. The fieldwork can be carried out:

- around the school site, for example conducting a questionnaire survey with other students to investigate the catchment area of the school
- in the local area, for example measuring river velocity or drawing a simple land use transect through the town.

In your fieldwork investigation you should follow the 'route to geographical enquiry' which has five steps:

1 Create a hypothesis.

2 Collect relevant data.

3 Present the data in maps and graphs.

4 Analyse the data which you have collected.

5 Make a conclusion about the hypothesis and evaluate the investigation.

You might think that you cannot revise for Paper 4. There are no case studies to learn as in Paper 1 and you don't know which themes the two questions will focus on. However, you can still revise very effectively for this paper by:

- looking through any fieldwork investigations you have done during the course
- practising the map and graph skills which are used in the examination paper
- understanding the principle of hypothesis testing
- learning details of fieldwork methodology such as sampling
- knowing how you could evaluate an investigation and suggest improvements.

Skills link

You can find out more about the route to geographical enquiry in Section 5.3 on pages 275–76.

Tip

Make realistic suggestions for improvement to an investigation.

Examples of two candidates' answers

You have now found out more about what Paper 4 is about and how to answer the questions well. Next you have the opportunity to look in detail at examination questions from a past paper. In this section you will find the questions and resources from one examination question. For each question there are answers from two candidates – one who is aiming for an A grade and the other for a C grade. These are followed by an explanation of why these marks were awarded.

Read the questions and look at the resources, then study the answers given by the two candidates. Can you understand how the marks are awarded? Finally read the commentary which explains the awarding of the marks and, where appropriate, gives advice about how the answer could be improved.

Fig. 1 for Question 1

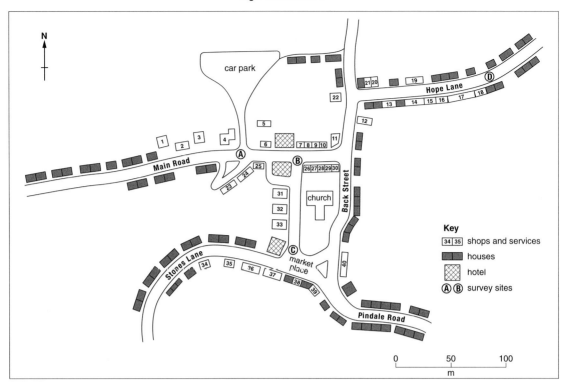

Key to shops and services

Number on map	Type of shop or service	Number on map	Type of shop or service
1	Gift shop	21	Chemist
2	Food Take Away	22	Restaurant
3	Gift shop	23	Gift shop
4	Tourist Information	24	Café
5	Sweet shop	25	Book shop
6	Public House	26	Gift shop
7	Restaurant	27	Book shop
8	Gift shop	28	Gift shop
9	Book shop	29	Gift shop
10	Café	30	Café
11	Bank	31	Public House
12	Post Office	32	Museum shop
13	Butcher	33	Restaurant
14	Food store	34	Food Take Away
15	Baker	35	Flower shop
16	Sweet shop	36	Restaurant
17	Public House	37	Food store
18	Hairdresser	38	Gift shop
19	Food store	39	Café
20	Flower shop	40	Art Gallery

Fig. 3 for Question 1

Scoring sheet for the survey of the impacts of tourism

Site:

	-2	-1	0	1	2	
Lots of litter						No litter
Noisy						Quiet
Crowded						Few people
Many tourist signs and adverts						No tourist signs and adverts
Lots of tourist buildings						No tourist buildings

Table 2 for Question 1

Classification of shops and services

Customers

Used mainly by tourists	Number	Used mainly by local residents	Number	Used by both tourists & local residents	Number
Art Gallery	1	Baker	1	Flower shop	2
Book shop	3	Bank	1	Food Take Away	2
Café	4	Butcher	1	Public House	3
Gift shop	8	Chemist	1	Sweet shop	2
Museum shop	1	Food store	3		
Restaurant		Hairdresser	1		
Tourist Information	1	Post Office	1		
Total	**22**	**Total**	**9**	**Total**	**9**

Table 3 for Question 1

Results of the survey of the impacts of tourism

	Site A	Site B	Site C	Site D
Litter	-1	-2	-1	0
Noise	-1	-2	-1	2
Crowding	-2	-2	0	2
Tourist signs and adverts	-1	-2	-1	2
Tourist buildings	-1	-2	0	1
Total score	**-6**	**-10**	**-3**	**7**

Table 1

Details of shops and services

Type of shop or service	Tally	Total	Percentage of total number of shops
Art Gallery	/	1	2.5
Baker	/	1	2.5
Bank	/	1	2.5
Book shop	///	3	7.5
Butcher	/	1	2.5
Café	////	4	10.0
Chemist	/	1	2.5
Flower shop	//	2	5.0
Food store	///	3	7.5
Gift shop	### ///	**8**	
Hairdresser	/	1	2.5
Museum shop	/	1	2.5
Post Office	/	1	2.5
Public House	///	3	7.5
Restaurant			10.0
Sweet shop	//	2	5.0
Food Take Away	//	2	5.0
Tourist Information	/	1	2.5
Total		**40**	**100**

Students wanted to investigate the possible impacts of tourism on a village visited by many people. They wanted to find out if there were both positive and negative effects. To do this they decided to test the following hypotheses:

Hypothesis 1: Tourism has a major impact on the shops and services in the village

Hypothesis 2: The impact of tourism decreases away from the main car park

To investigate the importance of tourism, the students mapped different types of shops and services, as shown on Fig. 1, to see if they were mainly used by tourists or local people.

Question (a) (i)
How many hotels are shown on Fig. 1?
(Adapted from Cambridge IGCSE Geography 0460 Paper 41 Q1a(i) November 2010)

Candidate 1 answer   1/1 mark

3 (✓)

Commentary

The hotels are counted accurately.

Candidate 2 answer   1/1 mark

3 (✓)

Commentary

The hotels are counted accurately.

Question (a) (ii)
Look at Fig. 1 and complete the tally and total number of restaurants on Table 1.

(Adapted from Cambridge IGCSE Geography 0460 Paper 41 Q1a(ii) November 2010)

Candidate 1 answer   1/1 mark

4 (✓)

Commentary

Tally and total are completed accurately.

Candidate 2 answer   0/1 mark

5

Commentary

Tally and total are completed inaccurately, due to miscounting. You should always check tasks like this to make sure that you have not made a simple error.

Question (a) (iii)
Calculate and write in the missing percentage for gift shops on Table 1.

(Adapted from Cambridge IGCSE Geography 0460 Paper 41 Q1a(iii) November 2010)

Candidate 1 answer   1/1 mark

20% (✓)

Commentary

The candidate correctly calculates 8/40 to be 20%.

Candidate 2 answer   0/1 mark

No response

Commentary

The candidate misses out the question. This may be because the question does not have any answer lines and the answer had to be written in a table. Always read through the question paper again before the end of the examination to make sure you have not missed out any questions.

To test Hypothesis 1, the students classified the shops and services into three groups just by looking at them:

- Used mainly by tourists;
- Used mainly by local residents;
- Used by both tourists and local residents.

The results of the decisions the students made about this classification are shown on Table 2.

Question (b) (i)
Why would the students have found it difficult to classify some shops and services?

(Adapted from Cambridge IGCSE Geography 0460 Paper 41 Q1b(i) November 2010)

Candidate 1 answer 2/2 marks

Because some shops might fall into two categories (✓) and it is difficult to decide which type a shop is. Also because just looking at them you do not know if it is certain that only one type of customer visits them (✓).

Commentary

The answer makes two valid points: that some shops are difficult to classify because categories overlap, and the student cannot distinguish between residents and tourists just by looking at them.

Candidate 2 answer 1/2 marks

Because they don't really know exactly what services would tourists and local people use, they didn't know who were tourists and who were local people (✓).

Commentary

The answer makes one valid point: that it is not possible to distinguish between residents and tourists just by looking at them.

Question (b) (ii)

How could the students be more certain that the customers of each shop were tourists or local residents?

(Adapted from Cambridge IGCSE Geography 0460 Paper 41 Q1b(ii) November 2010)

Candidate 1 answer 2/2 marks

By interviewing customers and asking where they came from (✓). Also by asking the shop owner if the customers were local people or tourists (✓).

Commentary

Credit is given for the suggestions of interviewing customers and the shop owners.

Candidate 2 answer 1/2 marks

By asking them through a survey if they are tourists or local people (✓).

Commentary

The answer is credited for the suggestion of interviewing customers. The answer needs a second idea such as asking the shop owner about the different types of customer. Remember that if there are 2 marks to be scored in a question you will need to suggest two ideas.

Question (b) (iii)

Use the results in Table 2 to complete the pie graph shown in Fig. 2.

(Adapted from Cambridge IGCSE Geography 0460 Paper 41 Q1b(iii) November 2010)

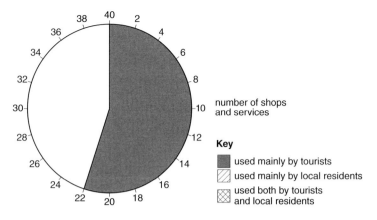
Pie graph of classification of shops and services

Fig. 2

Skills link

You will find out more about how to complete a pie chart on page 215 of Section 4 Geographical Skills.

Candidate 1 answer   2/2 marks

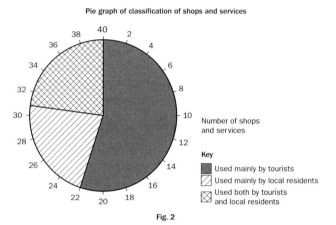
Pie graph of classification of shops and services

Fig. 2

Commentary

Both marks are gained through accurate plotting of the line at 31 and both segments are shaded.

Candidate 2 answer   1/2 marks

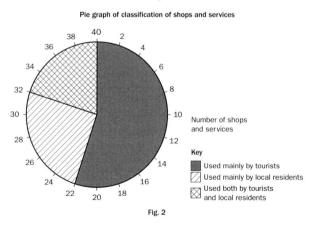
Pie graph of classification of shops and services

Fig. 2

Commentary

The line is inaccurately plotted at 32. Credit is awarded for shading both segments correctly.

The students accepted **Hypothesis 1** that tourism has a major impact on the shops and services in the village.

Do you agree with them? Support your answer with evidence from Table 1 and Fig. 2.

(Adapted from Cambridge IGCSE Geography 0460 Paper 41 Q1b(iv) November 2010)

Candidate 1 answer   2/2 marks

> The hypothesis was correct (✓) because 55% of the total number of shops was used mainly by tourists (✓). This shows that tourism has a major impact on shops and services.

Commentary

The answer scores 2 marks. The first mark is for a correct decision about the hypothesis (that it is correct). The second mark is awarded for appropriate supporting evidence (55% of shops used mainly by tourists).

Candidate 2 answer   2/2 marks

> I agree with them (✓) because the number of shops and services used mainly by tourists are much more than that used by local people (✓).

Commentary

The answer scores 2 marks. The first mark is for an appropriate decision (to agree with the hypothesis). The second mark is awarded for appropriate supporting evidence (number of tourist shops is greater than those used mainly by local people). The evidence does not have to include percentage figures.

Next the students tested Hypothesis 2: The impact of tourism decreases away from the main car park. They devised a scoring system to measure the impacts of tourism at four survey sites in the village. These survey sites are labelled **A** to **D** on Fig. 1. Fig. 3 shows the final scoring sheet after the students completed a pilot study.

Question (c) (i)

What is a pilot study and why is it important in an investigation?

(Adapted from Cambridge IGCSE Geography 0460 Paper 41 Q1c(i) November 2010)

Candidate 1 answer   2/2 marks

> A pilot study is an investigation done before an actual test (✓) to see if the survey sites are good for the study. It is important in the investigation because it helps the people to be sure of the information they collect (✓).

Commentary

This is an excellent answer which shows good knowledge and understanding of the term 'pilot study'.

Candidate 2 answer   1/2 marks

> A pilot study is a practice study (✓). It is where the students write the results of the survey before putting it on the final scoring sheet.

Commentary

The candidate does know the basic idea of a 'pilot study', but the second idea is irrelevant.

Question (c) (ii)
What decisions would the students have to make in organising and carrying out the main survey?

(Adapted from Cambridge IGCSE Geography 0460 Paper 41 Q1c(ii) November 2010)

Candidate 1 answer   3/3 marks

The students would need to decide where would be the survey sites (✓) and how many there would be (✓). Also they would have to decide what impacts they wanted to investigate (✓).

Commentary

There are many possible answers to this question. This answer identifies three possible decisions: where to locate the survey sites and how many sites to choose. A third decision is what impacts to measure in the survey.

Candidate 2 answer   2/3 marks

What they will test in the survey (✓) and at what points in the village they will do the survey (✓).

Commentary

This answer identifies two possible decisions. The first suggestion ('What they will test in the survey') is rather weak but just credited. The answer would have been better if 'characteristic', 'feature' or 'criteria' was used rather than just 'what'. The second idea of where to locate survey points is correct. A third suggestion is needed to score full marks.

The results of the main survey of the impacts of tourism are shown on Table 3.

Question (d) (i)
Complete Fig. 4 by plotting the results for tourist buildings for sites **B** and **D** from information given in Table 3.

(Adapted from Cambridge IGCSE Geography 0460 Paper 41 Q1d(i) November 2010)

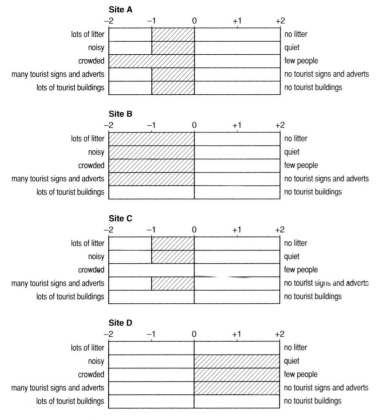

Fig. 4

Candidate 1 answer   2/2 marks

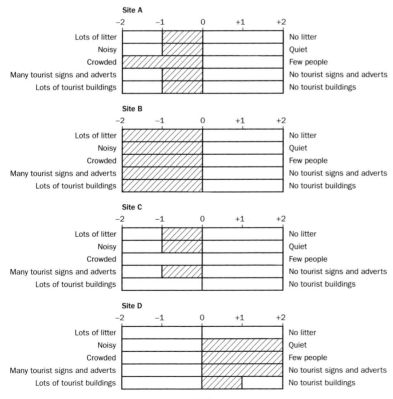

Fig. 4

Commentary

Both bars are plotted accurately and shading is done correctly.

Candidate 2 answer   1/2 marks

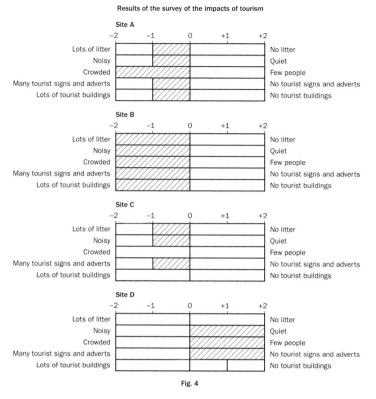

Fig. 4

Skills link

You will find out more about how to draw a bar graph on page 213 of Section 4 Geographical Skills.

Commentary

Site B is completely accurate, but no mark is awarded for site D because the bar is not shaded.

> ### Question (d) (ii)
> Identify **one** similarity and **one** difference between the results for sites A and C.
>
> (Adapted from Cambridge IGCSE Geography 0460 Paper 41 Q1d(ii) November 2010)

Candidate 1 answer   2/2 marks

Similarity: Litter scored −1 at both sites A and C. (✓)

Difference: Crowding is −2 at site A and 0 at site C. (✓)

Commentary

Both similarity and difference are interpreted from the graph accurately. Although the difference is not comparative, using a phrase like 'more crowded at site A', the mark is awarded because the candidate includes figures from the graph.

Candidate 2 answer   1/2 marks

Similarity: Both sites are noisy.

Difference: Site A is more crowded than site C. (✓)

Commentary

The similarity is too vague to be credited. The answer needs to state that the score for noise is the same at both sites. The difference is credited because the answer is comparative, even though measurements are not included.

Question (d) (iii)
To what extent do these results support **Hypothesis 2** that the impact of tourism decreases away from the main car park?

(Adapted from Cambridge IGCSE Geography 0460 Paper 41 Q1d(iii) November 2010)

Candidate 1 answer   2/2 marks

The hypothesis is correct (✓) because the sites that are further away are the ones with less signs of the impact of tourism. However, site A (the one which is closer to the car park) presents less impacts than site B which is further away (✓).

Commentary

The answer scores 2 marks. The first mark is for a correct decision about the hypothesis (that it is correct). The second mark takes account of the question asking 'to what extent' by identifying an anomaly in the results (site A has less evidence of impact even though it its closer to the car park than site B).

Candidate 2 answer   2/2 marks

I support the hypothesis (✓) because if you *do* a survey near the main car park you will get a lot of litter, noise, crowded by cars, but far away from the car park less litter and noise will be found (✓).

Commentary

The answer scores 2 marks. The first mark is for a correct decision about the hypothesis. The second mark is for evidence which supports the hypothesis (this is an alternative to identifying an anomaly).

Tip

If a question asks for your opinion about a hypothesis you will always score 1 mark for giving a correct opinion, such as 'I agree with the hypothesis' or 'The hypothesis is correct'.

Question (d) (iv)
Suggest reasons for the results of the survey of the impacts of tourism. Refer back to Fig. 1.

(Adapted from Cambridge IGCSE Geography 0460 Paper 41 Q1d(iv) November 2010)

Candidate 1 answer   3/4 marks

Site B has most impacts because it is closer to the hotels (✓), the majority of the shops and the car park (✓). Site D has least impacts because it is located near a residential area (✓) and is far away from the car park. So the places where tourist attractions are clustered are the places with the most impacts of tourism.

Commentary

Three reasons for the varying impacts are credited. These reasons relate to evidence from the map, as required. The answer could have scored a fourth mark if the shops had been identified as 'tourist shops' because the investigation is about tourism.

Candidate 2 answer   1/4 marks

Site A is more crowded, some litter, a bit noisy and some buildings. Site B has a lot of litter, is very noisy, very crowded, has many signs and lots of buildings. Site D has some litter, very quiet, few people, no tourist signs and very few buildings. This is because sites A and B are nearer to the car park (✓).

Commentary

The answer does not answer the question until the last sentence. The question asks for possible reasons for differing impacts of tourism at the survey sites, but the answer focuses on the varying levels of impact. This is an example of how a candidate has misinterpreted a question. You should always think carefully, 'Am I answering the question which has been set?'

> ### Question (e)
> Suggest **one** other issue the students could have investigated in the village. Briefly describe how they could have done their investigation.
> (Cambridge IGCSE Geography 0460 Paper 41 Q1e November 2010)

Candidate 1 answer   4/4 marks

> They could have investigated how traffic varies between different sites (✓). They could have done this by counting how many cars, lorries. motor bikes etc. pass in a certain time (✓), for example five minutes (✓). They could count by filling in a tally chart (✓) and then putting all their results into a table to compare them (✓).

Commentary

This is another excellent answer which could be awarded more than 4 marks. An investigation issue is clearly stated – how traffic amounts vary in the village. The answer gives details of methodology to be used in an investigation. Note that this question does not require a specific hypothesis to be identified.

Candidate 2 answer   2/4 marks

> They could have investigated the number of pedestrians in a certain amount of time at specific places. They could visit different sites and with a stopwatch record the time. As pedestrians pass by they make a line on the tally results (✓), and when the time is finished they count and get a total (✓).

Commentary

The answer suggests a possible issue for investigation – variation in pedestrian flow – but this is not stated clearly enough for credit. A better issue would be to investigate if pedestrian flow varies between different places in the village, or if pedestrian flow varies at different times in the village. However, the methodology of a pedestrian survey is described in sufficient detail to gain 2 marks.

Preparing for Paper 5

Paper 5 is a computer-based alternative examination to Paper 4. Paper 5 is still at the pilot stage and so it is not included in the syllabus for 2012 and 2013. Students at the examination centres involved in the pilot also take Paper 4. Paper 5 is not available at all centres. The examination also is 1½ hours long. It is an online test which you will do under examination conditions. However, instead of writing your answers on paper you use your computer keyboard. Paper 5 tests the same objectives as Paper 4 and is quite similar to the written examination in its style and content. During the examination you will test hypotheses, describe methodology, collect and display data, make conclusions and evaluate the investigation. A screen view of one page of the computer-based test (Paper 5) is shown below.

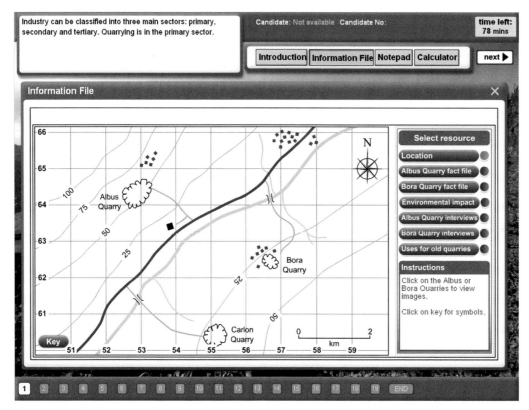

Note the following features:

- The individual questions are listed at the bottom of the page. To 'turn over' click on 'next', or to go to a particular question click on the number. As you do this the question appears in the centre of the page.

- The timer tells you how much time you have left in the test. Keep a check on this as you work your way through the questions, to help you to plan your time.

- The 'Introduction' includes the focus of the investigation and 'sets the scene' for the future tasks. It also contains the hypotheses which will be tested. This screen appears first when you start the test.

- The 'Information File' contains the resources needed to answer the questions. It is similar to the 'Insert' for Paper 4. In the Information File you will find a variety of resources under different headings, as shown in the screen view. You will be informed which specific resource you need to look at to answer each question. The resources include maps, photographs and computer simulation exercises such as measuring, animated diagrams, video clips and audio clips.

- The 'Notepad' can be used for any rough notes or calculations you do in the examination.

- The calculator can be used to do calculations.

All the tabs are available throughout the examination and you can access them at any time. You can also go back to previous answers or change your answers at any time during the test.

There are two main ways to answer the questions, by:

- making a choice from multiple choice questions
- extended writing in a textbox – this expands as you write your answer.

On each question page there is an introduction to the specific question at the top of the screen. The question instructions and resource appear below it in the main screen. As in all questions the mark allocation guides you about how much detail is needed in your answer.

The following screen from a computer-based test shows a question page where you must type your answer into the text boxes.

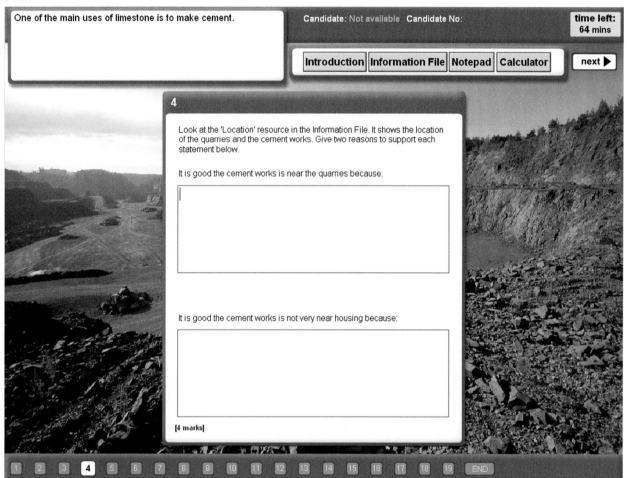

The best way to prepare for Paper 5 is to do simple fieldwork where appropriate during your geography course. The fieldwork can be carried out:

- around the school site, for example conducting a questionnaire survey with other students to investigate the catchment area of the school
- in the local area, for example measuring river velocity or drawing a simple land use transect through the town.

Glossary

Acid rain rainfall that damages the environment because it has been made acidic by pollution in the atmosphere

Adaptation the way in which plants and animals change to survive the environmental conditions where they live

Age dependency the link between the number of adult people who create wealth and the young and elderly population which depends on them for support

Agent of erosion water (ice, sea, rivers) and wind

Agribusiness large companies involved in agriculture, often with many different farms

Algae simple, plant-like organisms

Alluvium the material deposited by a river

Altitude the height above sea level

Anemometer an instrument used to measure wind speed

Anti-natalist policies strategies designed to limit a country's population growth

Aquifer a layer of porous rock which stores underground water

Arch rocky opening through a headland

Aspect the direction that land faces

Atmospheric pressure the pressure at a point on the Earth's surface due to the weight of the air above that place

Attrition when boulders and large stones carried by the river bash into each other and break up into smaller pieces

Avalanche a sudden downhill movement of snow that occurs as a result of a natural trigger, for example an earthquake, or human activity

Backwash the movement of water back down a beach towards the sea

Bar ridge of sand or shingle across the entrance to a bay or river estuary

Barometer an instrument used to measure atmospheric (air) pressure

Bed the bottom of a large expanse of water such as a river or the sea

Bedload the load found on the bottom of the river

Biodiversity the range of species within an ecosystem

Biofuel fuel made from plants

Biogas power from rotting plants and animal matter

Biological weathering the breakdown of rocks due to the actions of plants and animals

Birth rate the average number of live births in a year (for every 1000 people)

Blue Revolution the increase in growing fish as a source of food

Calories the unit used to measure the energy we get from food

Capital money used to invest in industry or business

Carbonation chemical weathering of limestone by acidic rain or water

Cash crop a crop grown to sell for profit

Catchment area/sphere of influence the area served by the shops and other facilities in an urban settlement

Cave area at the base of a cliff that has been hollowed-out by wave action

Census a count of a country or region's population

Central Business District (CBD) the central and most accessible zone within a large settlement, which has many offices, large shops and public buildings

Chemical weathering the breakdown of rocks by chemical reactions

Choropleth map a map that uses colour shading to show a distribution pattern

Cliff steep rock outcrop

Climate average weather conditions over a period of at least 30 years

Climate change changes to global climate and weather patterns caused by the increase in greenhouse gases (global warming)

Collision margins where two pieces of continental crust move towards each other

Comparison goods items such as cars which are expensive and bought only very occasionally

Condensation the change of state of a gas (water vapour) to a liquid (water droplets) as a result of cooling

Congestion charges a charge imposed on vehicles entering a central urban zone to reduce its traffic congestion and level of air pollution

Conservation the protection of the Earth and its natural resources

Conservative margins an area where two plates slide past each other

Constructive margins where two plates move away from each other

Constructive waves low-frequency waves of low height, with a strong swash but weak backwash; the waves therefore build up material on a beach

Contamination when pollutants are added to the natural environment

Contour line an line on a map joining points of equal height above sea level

Conurbation a very large built-up area formed by urban sprawl

Convectional rainfall precipitation formed by rising currents of warm, moist air

Converging plate boundary an area where tectonic plates move towards each other

Coral bleaching the whitening of coral due to expulsion or death of their symbiotic algae, usually as a result of changing environmental conditions

Coral reef underwater structures made from calcium carbonate secreted by polyps

Core the extremely hot centre of the Earth

Corrasion/abrasion when sand and stones carried by the river rub against the bank and bed and knock off other particles

Corrosion/solution when acids in the river dissolve the rocks that make up the bank and bed

Counter-urbanisation the movement of people from cities to the countryside

Crust the top layer of the Earth; it can be either continental (with land on top) or oceanic

Currency money used in a specific country

Death rate the average number of deaths in a year (for every 1000 people)

Decomposition when rocks are broken down into their individual minerals and elements

Deforestation the removal of tree cover in an area for farming or other activities

Delta the area where silt is deposited as a river enters the sea (or a lake)

Demographic Transition Model (DTM) a line graph showing how birth and death rates usually change as a country or region becomes more economically developed

Densely populated describes an area where a lot of people live (often a number of people per 1 km^2)

Deposition the laying down of material that has been transported (by water, ice, sea, rivers, wind)

Desertification the process in which semi-arid environments change to become more desert-like

Desire line map a map which uses straight lines to show movements between places

Destructive waves high-frequency, steep waves which have little swash and so move little material up a beach; however, they have strong backwash and so drag material down the beach into the sea

Dipterocarp a family of 500 species of tropical lowland rainforest plants, most of which are tall tree species that are important for essential oils, balsam, resins and as a source of plywood

Disintegration when rocks are worn away and fall into pieces

Dispersed describes the way that isolated farms or houses are scattered over an area, far apart from each other

Diurnal temperature range the difference between the highest and the lowest temperature in a 24-hour period

Eastings grid lines running vertically over a large-scale map

Economic activity the ways in which people make money for themselves and for their country

Economic migrants people who migrate to find work

Ecosystem a community of plants and animals that live within a physical area

Ecotourist a tourist who particularly wants to experience the natural environment

Emigrants people leaving a country

Energy security when a country has enough sources of power to cover most, if not all, of its energy needs

Erosion the wearing away of the land by an agent of erosion

Estuary the tidal mouth of a river

Evaporation the change of state from water droplets (liquid) to water vapour (gas) caused by heating

Evapotranspiration loss of water into the atmosphere from plants (*transpiration*) and water surfaces (*evaporation*)

Exclusion zone an area where people are not allowed to go

Exfoliation (onion-skin weathering) physical weathering where outer layers of rock are affected by heat

Exploit to use, usually to try to make money

Exports the goods that a country sells overseas

Factor anything which influences where a place is, what it is like or what function(s) it fulfils

Fault a fracture in rock caused by earth movements

Fertility rate the average number of children people in a country or region have in their life time

Fetch the distance across open sea or ocean over which the wind blows to create waves; the longer the fetch, the greater the possibility of large waves

Flash floods dangerous flow of surface water following unusually heavy rainfall

Flood plain the area to the sides of a river channel which floods when the river overflows its banks

Flow line map a map which uses straight lines whose thickness is proportional to the volume of traffic along routes between places

Fold mountains the types of mountains that are formed by the squeezing of rock at converging plate boundaries

Footloose an industry that is not tied to specific location factors

Forced migration when people are made to leave a country, for example because of war or natural disaster

Formal sector regular employment providing people with taxable earnings

Fossil fuels energy resources such as oil, gas and coal

Freeze–thaw (frost-shattering) physical weathering involving the freezing of water in gaps in the rock

Fuelwood wood (twigs, branches etc.) used as an energy source for cooking and heating

Function the way that a place provides employment and services for the people who live in or visit it

Geothermal power power from magma, hot rocks and hot water within the Earth

Gradient how steep a slope is

Green belt a rural area in which new residential and industrial developments are strictly limited; green belts control urban sprawl and maintain the historical character of villages

Greenhouse gases gases in the atmosphere that act like a blanket and reflect heat

Grey water water which has already been used but not been 'treated'(cleaned)

Grid lines numbered parallel lines drawn over a map to make it possible to locate features and places accurately

Grid references a system for locating places and features accurately using numbered grid lines

Grid square the space bounded by two adjacent northings and eastings

Gross domestic product (GDP) the total annual value of the goods manufactured and services provided by a country

Groundwater underground water supplies

Groyne barrier of wood or stone built down a beach to stop beach materials from being washed away

Gullies channels in the soil caused by water erosion

Habitat the 'home' of a plant or animal

Halophyte plant that has adapted to live in salty conditions

Headland point along a coast where harder rock juts out into the sea

HIV/AIDS viral infection (Human Immunodeficiency Virus) which leads to AIDS

Human Development Index (HDI) a system of ranking countries based on their **GDP (gross domestic product)** per capita and rates of adult literacy and life expectancy

Humus soil material rich in nutrients due to the decomposition of animal and vegetable material

Hydraulic action when the force of the water knocks particles off the sides (banks) and the bed of the river

Hygrometer an instrument used to measure relative humidity

Illegal immigrants people entering a new country without the permission of the authorities

Immigrants people arriving in a new country

Impervious does not let water through

Imports the goods that a country buys from overseas

Industrial location where a factory or business is found

Infant mortality rate the proportion of children dying at birth or before their first birthday

Infiltration the downward movement of water into the soil

Informal sector employment which has no set hours or employment benefits; its low, irregular earnings are not taxed

Infrastructure the network of services needed for industry and services to run efficiently – transport, communications, energy supplies, water and sanitation systems

Insolation solar energy which reaches the Earth's surface

In situ in the same place

Irrigation artificially diverting water to fields to grow crops

Isoline any line on a map which joins places having the same value

Labour workers

Lagoon area of salt water separated from the sea by a bar or reef

Lahar highly dangerous, fast-flowing mixture of rainwater and ejected volcanic materials

Land use zones urban areas which have different functions and characteristics to other nearby areas

Landslide a sudden downward movement of a section of hillside or cliff face

Leaching the removal of nutrients and other minerals from the soil as rainwater washes the minerals downwards through the soil

Leaf litter dead plant material that falls to the ground, releasing nutrients as it decomposes

Less economically developed country (LEDC) one of the poorer countries in the world

Levels of consumption the amount of energy used

Linear describes long, narrow-shaped settlements, often built along a road

Load all the material carried by a river

Long profile the appearance of a river from beginning to end

Longshore drift the transportation of material along a coastline

Low pressure the result of air rising; the weight of the air pressing down on the Earth's surface is reduced and so is lower than average

Magma liquid rock found beneath the Earth's crust

Magnitude the strength of an earthquake

Malnutrition the condition that results when the body does not get enough vitamins, minerals or other nutrients

Mantle the part of the Earth between the core and the crust

Marram grass species of grass able to survive on the dry habitat of shifting sand

Maximum-minimum thermometer an instrument used to measure both the highest and lowest temperatures within a 24-hour period

Meander winding bends found along a river's course

Megacity a city with more than 10 million inhabitants

Meteorologist a person who is able to forecast (predict) future weather by referring to previous, similar atmospheric conditions

Migration the movement of people from one place to another

Monoculture growing only one type of crop, usually in large amounts

Monsoon season of very heavy rainfall resulting from the seasonal shift of pressure belts

More economically developed country (MEDC) one of the wealthier, more industrialised countries in the world

Mouth where a river enters the sea

Multiplier effect the additional economic effects experienced when money is spread throughout a community

New town a planned, self-contained settlement usually built to re-house people from a large urban area

Newly industrialised countries (NICs) countries that are developing their economies through rapid expansion of secondary industries

Nomadic a lifestyle that involves moving around with no permanent home

Non-renewable energy which is used once and cannot be used again

Northings grid lines running horizontally over a large-scale map

Nucleated describes a 'compact' settlement, about the same width in most directions, built around a central point such as a road junction or river crossing

Okta the unit used to measure and record cloud cover; describes the proportion of the sky which is covered by cloud

Optimum population the number of people needed to make the best possible economic use of a country's natural resources

Over-population when a country does not have the resources to give all its people an adequate standard of living

Oxidation chemical weathering when minerals in a rock react with oxygen

Pandemic an outbreak of an infectious disease on such a large scale that it results in millions of deaths across large parts of the world

Permaculture people growing their own food in local garden areas

Photosynthesis the process where plants convert carbon dioxide into oxygen

Physical weathering the breakdown of rocks with no change in their chemical composition

Pie graph a circular diagram with sectors which show the different size of parts of a data set

Plate boundaries (margins) the edges of tectonic plates

Pollutants substances that have harmful or hazardous effects

Pollution what happens when the environment is harmed; its four types are air, noise, visual and water pollution

Population density the number of people living in a 1 km² area

Population distribution the way in which a population is spread out over an area

Population explosion the dramatic rise in world population which took place during the last two centuries

Population pyramid a diagram which uses horizontal bar graphs to show the age-gender characteristics of a population

Population structure the way a population is composed of different age-gender groups

Poverty line the minimum income needed to provide an adequate standard of living

Primary industry industries that take something from the ground or sea

Pro-natalist policies strategies designed to stimulate a country's population growth by increasing its fertility rate

Pyroclastic flow flow of materials such as ash ejected during a volcanic eruption

Quality of Life Index an indicator of how people assess their lifestyle based on criteria which include GDP per capita and life expectancy

Quaternary industry high-technology or research-based industries

Radial graph (also called a rose diagram) a circular diagram which uses different sized sectors to show how often a particular type of data occurs

Rain gauge an instrument used to measure the amount of rain that falls

Rainshadow the sheltered side of a range of mountains which receives little rain, also known as the leeward side; air is descending and warming, therefore moisture evaporates and rainfall is unlikely

Rapid transit systems a transport network, such an underground railway, designed to carry large numbers of people within a urban area

Rapids areas of turbulent water found along a river

Raw materials the things that are used to make something else

Reactor the machine that produces electricity in a nuclear power station

Recycle to turn waste into something that can be used again

Redevelopment raising housing standards by demolishing and then replacing existing accommodation

Refugees people who are forced to move, often by war or natural disaster

Relative humidity the ratio between the actual amount of water vapour in the air and the total amount of water the air could hold if it was saturated at a particular temperature

Renewable energy sources of power that can be used over and over again

Renovation raising housing standards by improving peoples' accommodation, not demolishing and replacing it

Revenue the money earned (by a country, for example)

Richter Scale the scale used to measure the magnitude of an earthquake

Salinity the amount of salt that something (for example soil) contains

Salt marsh wet, low-lying area near to the coast that is regularly flooded by the sea

Sand dune ridge of sand created by the wind; found in deserts, near lakes and the sea

Scale the relationship between the actual size of an area on the ground, and the representation of the same area on a map

Scatter graph a diagram used to show the strength of a relationship between two sets of data

Sea-floor spreading the bottom of the ocean growing wider at a constructive margin

Secondary industry industries that make products from raw materials

Sedentary settled and permanent

Sediment any material, regardless of size, which has been transported by an agent of erosion

Seismograph (seismometer) a machine used to measure the strength of an earthquake

Self-help scheme a way of raising housing conditions for squatters by providing them with some land and the basic materials needed to build and improve their own homes

Settlement any place, ranging in size from a hamlet to a mega-city, where people live and work

Settlement hierarchy arranging settlements according to their population size

Shifting cultivation a type of rainforest agriculture which involves moving on from one plot of cultivated land to another

Site a small area of land on which the first part of a settlement was built

Site and service Scheme a way of raising housing conditions for squatters by providing them with basic accommodation and facilities such as water supply and sewage disposal

Situation the location of a settlement in relation to the wider area around it

Slumping weathered material moves down-slope due to lubrication by rainwater

Smog air pollution due to a combination of smoke and fog

Soil degradation the process of soil becoming less fertile

Soil exhaustion when soils can no longer support plants and crops

Solar power power from the sun

Source the start of a river

Sparsely populated describes an area (usually 1 km²) where few people live

Spit ridge of sand or shingle attached to the land at only one end

Spot height a point on a map measured to its exact height (in metres or feet) above sea level; spot heights are marked with a small dot on a map at the exact location, with the height alongside

Squatter settlement/shanty town an area of poorly built, low-cost housing on land not owned or rented by its inhabitants

Stack pillar of rock surrounded by sea and separated from the mainland

Stevenson Screen a wooden box on legs used to house weather recording equipment

Storm surge a significant increase in sea level due to sudden, very low air pressure

Stump the remains of a stack that has been eroded almost to sea level

Subduction zone where oceanic crust is forced under continental crust

Subsidies payments given to farmers, usually by governments

Subsistence crop a crop grown to feed a farmer and his family

Surface runoff the movement of water over the ground surface following precipitation – also known as overland flow

Sustainable something that can be used on a long-term basis with very little effect on the environment

Swash the body of water rushing up a beach after a wave has broken

Tectonic plates the Earth's crust, divided into large pieces called plates

Temperate a region characterised by mild temperatures

Tertiary industry industries that provide a service

Textile industry industries concerned with making clothes and fabric

Thematic map a map which displays information on a particular theme

Threshold population the minimum number of people needed to support a facility or service

Tombolo ridge of sand linking an offshore island to the mainland

Topographical map a map that shows accurate, large-scale representation of relief, usually by using contour lines, and other features in the landscape

Tornado narrow column of air that rotates rapidly around an area of very low air pressure, causing widespread devastation in its path

Tourism the industry associated with people going on holiday; can be either national or international

Toxic poisonous

Traffic congestion occurs when roads cannot cope with their volume of traffic

Transect a section which shows how features change across an area

Transnational company a very large business operating in many countries

Transpiration loss of water from vegetation into the atmosphere

Transportation the removal of weathered material

Triangular graph a type of diagram which allows three sets of data to be plotted against each other

Tributary a small river that joins a larger one

Tropical depression area of low atmospheric pressure that forms in tropical regions

Tropical revolving storm intense spinning storm with high winds and torrential rain around a calm centre (the eye) at a certain point of intensity it becomes a cyclone or hurricane

Tsunami huge sea wave created as a result of a major earthquake or volcanic eruption

Under-populated describes an area where the population is well below that which can be supported by its natural resources

Uninhabited describes an area where very few, if any, people live

Urban sprawl the outward growth of a built-up area into nearby rural areas

Urbanisation an increase in the percentage of people living in urban areas

Velocity the speed at which the river flows

Water deficit a situation where available water supplies do not meet all the needs of local people

Water table the upper edge of the saturated zone in porous rocks

Water transfer the movement of water from an area of surplus to one having a shortage

Water vapour water held in the atmosphere in the form of a gas

Wave-cut notch indentation along the base of a cliff where wave action is strongest

Wave-cut platform gently sloping surface of rock that is the result of cliff retreat and is exposed at low tide

Weather short-term, changeable, atmospheric conditions which include air temperature, cloud cover, precipitation and wind direction and speed

Weathering the wearing away of the land *in situ*

Wilderness an uncultivated, uninhabited and inhospitable region

Wildfire forest fire that rages out of control

Wind rose graph a diagram showing the proportion of winds that blow from each compass direction at a given place

Wind vane an instrument used to indicate the direction of the wind

Index

Acknowledgements

The publishers wish to thank the following for permission to reproduce photographs. Every effort has been made to trace copyright holders and to obtain their permission for the use of copyright materials. The publishers will gladly receive any information enabling them to rectify any error or omission at the first opportunity.

Key: t = top, c = centre, b = bottom, r = right, l = left.

Cover & p i Yanhongbin1023/Dreamstime, p 2l Monkey Business Images/Shutterstock, p 2r VikramRaghuvanshi/iStockphoto, p 4l Tomasz Otap/Shutterstock, p 4r Dmitry Kalinovsky/Shutterstock, p 8l faberfoto/Shutterstock, p 8r tamapapat/Shutterstock, p 10 guentermanaus/Shutterstock, p 11 Alan Gordine/Shutterstock, p 13 gary yim/Shutterstock, p 15t Cameron Laird/Rex Features, p 15b Friedrich Stark/Alamy, p 17 Stephen Ford/Alamy, p 18 jeremy sutton-hibbert/Alamy, p 25t wavebreakmedia ltd/Shutterstock, p 26t Komar/Shutterstock, p 26b Giancarlo Liguori/Shutterstock, p 27tl oksana.perkins/Shutterstock, p 27tr Andre Nantel/Shutterstock, p 27bl Hung Chung Chih/Shutterstock, p 27br Vitalii Nesterchuk/Shutterstock, p 28l Pakmor/Shutterstock, p 28r Maria Gioberti/Shutterstock, p 29 Graham Norris/iStockphoto, p 32l Thomas Cockrem/Alamy, p 32r Mike Gonzalez, p 33 alanf/Shutterstock, p 34 homeros/Shutterstock, p 36l Evgeny Murtola/Shutterstock, p 36r ziggysofi/Shutterstock, p 38 Sam Strickler/Shutterstock, p 39 map sourced from Exam Extract No 717/St Lucia © Government of Saint Lucia, p 40 N Vasuki Rao/iStockphoto, p 41 Jon Arnold Images Ltd/Alamy, p 42l David R. Frazier Photolibrary, Inc./Alamy, p 42r imagebroker/Alamy, p 43 Samot/Shutterstock, p 44 Justin Kase z04z/Alamy, p 47 Jack and Meg Gillett, p 48 Aman Khan/iStockphoto, p 50t Hung Chung Chih/Shutterstock, p 50b Baloncici/Shutterstock, p 51t Nickolay Vinokurov/Shutterstock, p 51c iofoto/Shutterstock, p 51b David Bagnall/Alamy, p 52l Greg Balfour Evans/Alamy, p 52r s duffett/Shutterstock, p 53 r.nagy/Shutterstock, p 55 Petronilo G. Dangoy Jr./Shutterstock, p 57t Holger Mette/iStockphoto, p 57b Holger Mette/iStockphoto, p 58t Peter Treanor/Alamy, p 58b Caroline Penn/Impact Photos/Imagestate, p 59t Terraxplorer/iStockphoto, p 59b toonman/Shutterstock, p 60 Ellas Design/Shutterstock, p 61 Rodrigo Riestra/Shutterstock, p 62t Andrew Holt/Alamy, p 62b stocker1970/Shutterstock, p 63 xtrekx/Shutterstock, p 64 Marcelo Rudini/Alamy, p 65t Wesley Jenkins/iStockphoto, p 65b Hervé Collart/Sygma/Corbis, p 66l Robert Harding World Imagery/Alamy, p 66r Stocktrek Images, Inc./Alamy, p 67 bbbar/Shutterstock, p 70 Justin Kase z10z/Alamy, p 71t Andrew Woodley/Alamy, p 71b Robert Harding World Imagery/Alamy, p 72 Aflo/Rex Features, p 73l NOAA, p 73r Propaganda/Alamy, p 74 B Christopher/Alamy, p 75tl Michael Steden/Shutterstock, p 75tr Jim Lopes/Shutterstock, p 75bl Joe Gough/Shutterstock, p 75br Wil Tilroe-Otte/Shutterstock, p 75cr B.G. Smith/Shutterstock, p 76l Max Topchii/Shutterstock, p 76r Pablo H Caridad/Shutterstock, p 77t Catalin Petolea/Shutterstock, p 77c Jason Patrick Ross/Shutterstock, p 77b nickichen/Shutterstock, p 78t Pozzo di Borgo Thomas/Shutterstock, p 78b Jan Rihak/iStockphoto, p 79 Natalia Siverina/Shutterstock, p 81 Leslie Garland Picture Library/Alamy, p 82l melodija/Shutterstock, p 82c The Photolibrary Wales/Alamy, p 82r Karel Gallas/Shutterstock, p 85t NASA, p 85l beboy/Shutterstock, p 85r Kees Metselaar/Alamy, p 87l Robert N. Dennis collection, p 87r Angela/Wikimedia Commons, p 87c NASA Goddard Space Flight Center, p 88tl MartiniDry/Shutterstock, p 88tr Piotr Wawrzyniuk/Shutterstock, p 88bl Iakov Kalinin/Shutterstock, p 88br Thierry Maffeis/Shutterstock, p 89l Philiphist/Wikimedia Commons, p 89r Kaspars Grinvalds/Shutterstock, p 92 simon gurney/Shutterstock, p 93l Adam Gregor/Shutterstock, p 93r David Wall/Alamy, p 93b Sarah Pettegree/Shutterstock, p 94 David Wall/Alamy, p 95 map sourced from NZTopo50-BA35 Whitianga. Crown Copyright Reserved, p 96t Specta/Shutterstock, p 96b Zeamonkey Images/Shutterstock, p 97l Wolfgang Steiner/iStockphoto, p 97c mary416/Shutterstock, p 97r Simon Parker/iStockphoto, p 99t Images & Stories/Alamy, p 99b Khoroshunova Olga/Shutterstock, p 100tl B747/Shutterstock, p 100tr Gregory Gerber/Shutterstock, p 100bl Asianet-Pakistan/Shutterstock, p 100br Brykaylo Yuriy/Shutterstock, p 102c Pablo Paul/Alamy, p 102tl Caroline Green, p 102tc Caroline Green, p 102tr donvictorio@o2.pl/Shutterstock, p 102bl Artur Synenko/Shutterstock, p 102bc ID1974/Shutterstock, p 102br VVO/Shutterstock, p 105 Malinovskyy Kostyantyn/Shutterstock, p 107l iofoto/Shutterstock, p 107c Serg64/Shutterstock, p 107r paul prescott/Shutterstock, p 111 Vitaly Titov & Maria Sidelnikova/Shutterstock, p 113 Eric Gevaert/Shutterstock, p 114 Alexander Yu. Zotov/Shutterstock, p 116 Patrick Poendl/Shutterstock, p 117t Pichugin Dmitry/Shutterstock, p 117l mauritius images GmbH/Alamy, p 117r Jens Peermann/Shutterstock, p 118 NASA, p 119 Katherine James, p 120tr Tony Magdaraog/Shutterstock, p 120t Asianet-Pakistan/Shutterstock, p 120c Martin Haas/Shutterstock, p 120b Darrenp/Shutterstock, p 123 Jeff Schmaltz/NASA, p 125t Mike Goldwater/Alamy, p 125b Koustav2007/Wikimedia Commons, p 126 LiTn/Shutterstock, p 127 hipproductions/Shutterstock, p 129 NASA, p 131t PHOTOCREO Michal Bednarek/Shutterstock, p 131b corepics/Shutterstock, p 132 kataleewan intarachote/Shutterstock, p 134l Marko5/Shutterstock, p 134r Ryan Rodrick Beiler/Shutterstock, p 135 Daniele Silva/Shutterstock, p 137 Eky Studio/Shutterstock, p 139 gallimaufry/Shutterstock, p 140 David Mercado/Reuters, p 141 Photoshot Holdings Ltd/Alamy, p 142 AFP/Getty Images, p 143 Bob Sacha/Corbis, p 145 David Mercado/Reuters, p 146tl Catalin Petolea/Shutterstock, p 146tr wavebreakmedia ltd/Shutterstock, p 146bl Zurijeta/Shutterstock, p 146br Nomad_Soul/Shutterstock, p 147t Image Source/Alamy, p 147c Werner Buchel/Shutterstock, p 147b JJM Stock Photography/Alamy, p 147r Supri Suharjoto/Shutterstock, p 148t Jason Duggan/Shutterstock, p 148b SDBCHINA/Alamy, p 149 wavebreakmedia ltd/Shutterstock, p 150 Hans Martens/iStockphoto, p 153 David R. Frazier Photolibrary, Inc./Alamy, p 154t Sapsiwai/Shutterstock, p 154b Shamleen/Shutterstock, p 155 nostal6ie/Shutterstock, p 158 Chris Schmidt/iStockphoto, p 159 Jiri Rezac/Alamy, p 160l 3d brained/Shutterstock, p 160r Nicholas Monu/iStockphoto, p 160b vovan/Shutterstock, p 161t Henry Leong Him Who, p 161b Peellden/Wikimedia Commons, p 162l Dianne Maire/Shutterstock, p 162tr Pincasso/Shutterstock, p 162br l i g h t p o e t/Shutterstock, p 165tl Julia Zakharova/Shutterstock, p 165tc StockLite/Shutterstock, p 165tr ndrpggr/Shutterstock, p 165bl iofoto/Shutterstock, p 165bc iofoto/Shutterstock, p 165br doglikehorse/Shutterstock, p 167l Eric Isselée/Shutterstock, p 167r Irene Abdou/Alamy, p 168tl Image Source/Alamy, p 168tr Yun Yulia/Shutterstock, p 168bl Phil Date/Shutterstock, p 168br RamonaS/Shutterstock, p 171r Aurora Photos/Alamy, p 171l loong/Shutterstock, p 172t Geralda van der Es/iStockphoto, p 172b Patrik Dietrich/Shutterstock, p 173 Kailash K Soni/Shutterstock, p 175t Eugene Suslo/Shutterstock, p 175c lafoto/Shutterstock, p 175b Darren Baker/Shutterstock, p 175l Joerg Boethling/Alamy, p 177t VLADJ55/Shutterstock, p 177c Clynt Garnham Energy/Alamy, p 177b Yury Zakharov/Shutterstock, p 179t Vlade Shestakov/Shutterstock, p 179b Kletr/Shutterstock, p 180 Belinda Pretorius/Shutterstock, p 181t iofoto/Shutterstock, p 181b wesley bakker/Shutterstock, p 182t PT Images/Shutterstock, p 182b Olivier Asselin/Alamy, p 183l Ken Brown/iStockphoto, p 183c haveseen/Shutterstock, p 183tr newphotoservice/Shutterstock, p 183br Ilya Andriyanov/Shutterstock, p 185 gopixgo/Shutterstock, p 186 Randy Plett/iStockphoto, p 187 ostill/Shutterstock, p 188 grynold/Shutterstock, p 189l Worldwide Picture Library/Alamy , p 189r Sue Cunningham/Worldwide Picture Library/Alamy, p 191 jeremy sutton-hibbert/Alamy, p 193t Yurikr/Shutterstock, p 193b NASA image courtesy MODIS Rapid Response Team, Goddard Space Flight Center, p 194l Andresr/Shutterstock, p 194c Mario Savoia/Shutterstock, p 194r photoflorenzo/Shutterstock, p 195 Photononstop/Alamy, p 196 Pete Niesen/Shutterstock, p 197 Robin Jeffries, p 199t Richard Bowden/Shutterstock, p 199c Stephen Meese/Shutterstock, p 199b chris2766/Shutterstock, p 204t Sky Light Pictures/Shutterstock, p 204l Studio 37/Shutterstock, p 204c Kinlem/Shutterstock, p 204r Peter Wey/Shutterstock, p 204b Valuykin Sergey/Shutterstock, p 206 Martin Lehmann/Shutterstock, p 207 Jorg Hackemann/Shutterstock, p 218l NASA, p 222t NASA/GSFC/METI/ERSDAC/JAROS and U.S./Japan ASTER Science Team, p 222b allensima/Shutterstock, p 223 Pakmor/Shutterstock, p 224 Brian Granger/Van Rhijn Aerial Photography, p 226 Bubbles Photolibrary/Alamy, p 228 William Silver/Shutterstock, p 229t Chee-Onn Leong/Shutterstock, p 229b Roman Mahmutoff/Shutterstock, p 230 Graham Bool Photography/Geopacks, p 231t Ashley Cooper pics/Alamy, p 231b Martin Shields/Alamy, p 232 Royal Geographical Society (with IBG), p 233 Sue Robinson/Shutterstock, p 259 map sourced from Extract No 1544/Port Louis © Government of Mauritius.